SATHER CLASSICAL LECTURES
VOLUME NINETEEN

PINDAR

PINDAR

BY

GILBERT NORWOOD

Ἀγλαΐην ἐφίλησα καὶ ἀγλαΐη με διώκει

UNIVERSITY OF CALIFORNIA PRESS
BERKELEY, LOS ANGELES, LONDON

UNIVERSITY OF CALIFORNIA PRESS
BERKELEY AND LOS ANGELES
CALIFORNIA

UNIVERSITY OF CALIFORNIA PRESS, LTD.
LONDON, ENGLAND

THIRD PRINTING, 1974
ISBN: 0-520-01952-0

MANUFACTURED IN THE UNITED STATES OF AMERICA

TO MY WIFE

PREFACE

THESE LECTURES, with substantial omissions, were delivered at Berkeley last spring under the terms of my appointment as Sather Professor of Classical Literature in the University of California for the year 1943–4.

To that University I express my gratitude not only for the signal honour thus conferred, but also for the happiness enjoyed during my sojourn in a State which, already blessed by Nature, has received enrichment from the liberal zeal wherewith her citizens foster education and scholarship. To my colleagues and students there I offer warm thanks for a hundred acts of charming friendliness; above all, to Professor W. H. Alexander and other members of the classical staff, whose unwearied aid and kindness have meant a heartening experience which shall not be forgotten. The learning, precision, and considerateness of the University Press editor, Mr. Harold A. Small, have laid me under a most pleasant obligation.

For able and varied help I am much indebted to my wife.

GILBERT NORWOOD.

TORONTO, CANADA.
APRIL 26TH, 1945.

CONTENTS

ILLUSTRATIONS

THE APPROACH TO PINDAR

Two REASONS impelled me to choose Pindar for my theme: reasons simple and, if you will, commonplace; but no weightier can be conceived.

First, he is a great poet. The aim of art is, finally, to create and satisfy in us a deeper relish for existence: not merely a gusto for life, which is the aim of education; but a relish for mere existence itself. That is why art has no concern with morality; and why the artist, in the profound language of the Book of Job, feels himself in league with the stones of the field. If I were asked to account for my love of Pindar's work, no doubt I could, and indeed I shall, describe various specific merits; but ultimately the truth is that, by whatever means, he fills me with triumphant illumination. That is what earns a man the title, "a great poet": triumphant illumination, which he experiences and which he has power to impart. But, magnificently as Pindar deserves that title, this addition must unflinchingly be made, that he is nothing more. You may read most other wonderful writers, and with profit, for reasons utterly severed from their special excellence: Cicero as an historical authority, Milton for his theology, Villon for his old French, Dickens or Mark Twain to learn the moods and habits of the lowly. But Pindar, more than any other consummate author known to me, is practically valueless save for one superb merit.

My other reason is that he has been studied less deeply, less sympathetically, less often than his eminence deserves: the really fine books about him number, perhaps, not more than half a dozen. I conceive that much remains to be said, and that concerning the very marrow of his art.

Such were my reasons, so powerful that I submitted, despite the difficulties that plainly threatened. Most of these will make themselves felt in due course; one, however, should be faced at the outset: language. The value of translations in the study of literature is by no means so novel a question as some believe, and I cannot contribute anything new to the main discussion, especially as the highest possible authorities have spoken on opposing sides. Dante refused to expound his poetry to Germans and Englishmen because (he writes) "nothing harmonized by the bonds of music can be transformed from its own diction into another without losing all its sweetness and harmony."[1] Goethe said that in Greek and Latin "you get on very far with a good translation."[2] (Note, however, that he cited Frederick the Great, who read Cicero —not Pindar—in French). Nor need I labour the familiar truth that poetry by its nature defies translation: poetry, not verse, for one can imagine a translation of Horace's *Satires* fully as good as the original. In poetry, we all know, many effects depend on the very sounds: Charles Kingsley[3] remarked that the Greek phrase βοὸς μεγάλοιο βοείην is not really translated by "great ox's hide." But one point does remain to be stated: the difficulty thus attached to all poetry is more formidable in Pindar than in any other first-rate poet. Let me offer but one instance. Concerning *Nem.* IX 16 Bury writes a charming comment which depends entirely on this, that in the Greek text ἀνήρ, "man," is the last word of one stanza, and the next stanza opens with ἀνδροδάμαντα, "man-quelling." This juxtaposition, according to Bury, is vital. But in Myers' translation no less than thirty-three words separate them. That is mere accident: Myers owned a magnificent sense of poetry, as his great essay on Virgil proves. But the point is that one who based himself only on Myers *could* not appreciate the passage as Bury did. You derive a quite respectable idea of Homer and Hesiod from a translation, if wisely and adroitly written. Of Pindar a good deal more vanishes; and it is significant that here prose versions are actually better, or less bad, than verse. On the whole, Abraham Cowley was not far from the truth when he declared that, if a man translated Pindar literally, readers would think one madman had translated another.[4]

These lectures have for their sole object the elucidation of

Pindar's poetry: that is, to show its virtues with whatever force and precision may prove attainable; and, negatively, to remove those obstacles to enjoyment and illumination that are inherent in his language, in his topics, and in other differences that separate a modern reader from a Greek of the fifth century before Christ.

An exacting enterprise, this, no less than delightful; but it permits us to ignore much that some might expect from us. Too often, after determining to appreciate a poem in itself, we drift off upon themes which, though they have nothing to do with poetry, yet give us a piteous illusion like Ixion's that we embrace the goddess though in truth we lavish caresses upon a phantom of cloud. Our libraries swarm with the unnatural offspring:[5] those disquisitions upon the poet's "attitude" to this or that; those lists of his prepositions and spondees; investigations of the books he may have read and the women he may have loved. The radiance, the potent vitality, of great writings dazzle our weak sight and fatigue our puny strength: we stumble away from the shrine to gossip with the sacristan about dates and measurements. This childish, though not ignoble, desire to create some relation, however trivial, between a poet and ourselves has produced numberless "studies" and "aspects" which enlighten us no more, on the only subject about which enlightenment is worth having, than the purchase of Aeschylus' writing-tablet inspired the prince of Syracuse.[6] "What have these details to do with his poetry?"—that is the test, which, while it condemns much pretentious research, yet approves much humdrum study. Hearing that Ovid's *Metamorphoses* contain a narrative parallel to the scene played by Bottom and his mates, the true student of poetry reads it eagerly—not because he wishes to discover what books Shakespeare read, not because he means to write a thesis on "The Teaching of Latin under the Tudors," but only in case he may light upon something that increases his relish of the passage in *A Midsummer Night's Dream*.[7] If a man chooses to read Wordsworth's correspondence, let him; just as he may, if he chooses, play chess or prune his roses after he has read the *Ode on Intimations of Immortality*. Either he has seen the vision, or he has not. The roses matter nothing, the rook or the bishop nothing—and "the man Wordsworth" nothing, even after the discovery of Annette. She can, perhaps, enable us to see why he wrote thus or thus; and the reason mattered vastly to him. For us it has no value, our concern being not why he wrote so, but that he wrote so; there stand the noble lines: upon them and them only must we fling our souls.

Such concentration upon the words themselves in their full power is by no means the simple exercise it might seem. There are poets whom it is hard to follow, as we call it, because the loveliness of their verse casts a spell over our intelligence, just as a man listening to the woman whom he loves may find when she ceases that he does not know what she has said, because he has been hearing her voice, not her words. Such is often the effect of Pindar's poetry, and a failure to recall the details of some glorious picture or opulent narrative finds a plain excuse. Yet, if a man does address himself to prosaic discussion of Pindar's statements, he must be on his guard against enchantment, or he will fail in his apparently simple task. Many have shown themselves incapable at times of seeing what lies upon the page. Editor after editor, essayist after essayist, has reported that in the Eighth Pythian Pindar saw Alcmaeon in a dream, though the assertion is plain that Alcmaeon actually met him on the road to Delphi.[8] Two readers, one a laborious scholar, Hermann Gundert, the other a learned poet, Abraham Cowley, flatly give Pindar the lie about the reason for Achilles' translation to the Islands of the Blest. Gundert[9] offers a no doubt admirable cause, that Achilles' excellence as a man of action secured this honour; Cowley writes: "*Cadmus* was chosen to be named here for one of the *Heroes*, by an apparent reason, *Theron* being descended from him; as for *Peleus* and *Achilles*, there is no particular cause."[10] But Pindar himself plainly tells us concerning Achilles' translation that it was the influence of his mother Thetis upon Zeus.[11] Fraccaroli,[12] who has written of poetry and of Pindar

with charming wisdom, yet discusses the opening of the First
Olympian as if it sang "il corso del sole," and this *course* of
the sun is important to his discussion; but Pindar says only
"the sun." Perrotta,[13] whose sturdy acumen it would be hard
to overpraise, writes, when dealing with the words (*Ol.* VI 61)
νυκτὸς ὑπαίθριος, "upon the head of Iamus as he prays the stars
look down," an idea curiously foreign to Pindar, and not
hinted in those words, which mean only "under the open sky
at night." Even the greatest of all who have combined poetical
genius with wide learning, Goethe himself, has misdescribed
Pindar's feeling about the Great Games:[14]

> Wenn die Räder rasselten,
> Rad an Rad rasch ums Ziel weg,
> Hoch flog
> Siegdurchglühter
> Jünglinge Peitschenknall,
> Und sich Staub wälzt',
> Wie vom Gebirg herab
> Kieselwetter ins Tal,
> Glühte deine Seel' Gefahren, Pindar,
> Mut.

"When the wheels were rattling, wheel on wheel away to the
goal, high flew the cracking whip of youths all aglow for victory, and dust whirled as down from the mountain pebbles
rolled into the valley—then, Pindar, thy soul glowed with
courage at the dangers." Undoubtedly we should have expected such vivid descriptions; but Pindar omits these excite-
ments.

The books, pamphlets, essays, notes that have been published concerning the Pindaric poems number, I imagine, at
least one thousand; of very few can it be said that they are,
and have always been, nothing but waste paper. Still, we
should cultivate the historical sense. Boeckh's edition, for
example, long possessed enormous importance; today it has
far less, because what was sound, illuminating, and permanent in it has been absorbed into later books. We must not fail
to keep this perspective in mind; otherwise, impressed by the

immense learning, the noble industry and patience, shown by
our predecessors, we may glide into the wasteful opinion that
we in our day should be content to creep about the fields
which they harvested, sift over and over the chaff left by
their muscular threshing: that is nothing but *chercher midi à
quatorze heures.*

It cannot (of course) be denied that, just as one who even
in this later age explores cellars and apple-lofts for the first
edition of Omar Khayyám may, despite the efforts of a thousand predecessors, in the twilight of his dusty days embrace
that treasure at the last, so may some belated researcher even
now light upon a really satisfying emendation of Pindar's
text, as when Mair's study of the *Etymologicum Magnum*
resulted in the admirable εἷραν for ἀγοράν in *Nem.* III 14. But
the law of diminishing returns operates here strongly. In his
day Erasmus Schmid[15] could emend right and left with cer-
tainty; in ours, all the obviously bad readings have been cor-
rected, and what mostly happens is attempts to foist upon
the text forms of that invaluable word ἑτός, which can generally be contrived where some part of ὁ ἁ τό stands in the vulgate; or, by altering punctuation, cases, and vocabulary, to
mould lines noble and debonair till they conform with a Xeno-
phontean frame of mind.

Classical scholarship, then, so far as concerns the great
ancient poets, has finished its task of removing the textual
difficulties that prevented us from envisaging them as we
envisage the modern. At any rate, we can do no more: we are
dissatisfied with our text of Aeschylus, true; but progress has
stopped. It is now far more fruitful to study Propertius in the
light of Donne or Keats than in the light of Callimachus. In
this field a vast amount of attractive study awaits us—attractive, but genuine and strenuous, for this is no affair of dilet-
tantism, of superficial phrase-mongering. A. C. Bradley has
said: "Research, though toilsome, is easy; imaginative vision,
though delightful, is difficult; and we may be tempted to
prefer the first."[16] Tempted, because the old highway of research is so richly provided with maps, filling-stations and a

highly trained constabulary. The investigator need fear nothing if he never allows his left hand to quit a *Jahrbuch* before his right clutches the comforting bulk of an *Archiv*. Such activity was needed so long as corruptions swarmed in our texts. It is still justified in archaeology, and in other departments of classical learning partly or quite scientific. But in the study of Greek and Latin poetry it is utterly out of date and would not be crawling over those now radiant blooms and gleaming marbles but for the belief that even this study must become a squalid imitation of the applied sciences.[17] We now need classical scholars who are at least as well versed in great modern literature as in *Beiträge*, who will no longer believe that a first-rate edition of Catullus can be produced by a man whose acquaintance with Burns is limited to the chorus of *Auld Lang Syne*, if only he scans galliambics undismayed and remembers who proposed *num* for *tum* in 1862. We should hope, moreover, for a seemly elegance in our editions and resent it as an outrage if we open a copy of Theocritus only to find a horrible *apparatus criticus* lurking at the bottom of the page like some open sewer at the end of a gracious promenade, with repellent outcast conjectures wallowing in hideous decay under the sunlight. Let an editor make the best text he can, and then present his Sophocles in tranquil stateliness. If his conscience demands an apparatus, let him banish it to the end of the book: our enjoyment of Greek and Roman poets should no longer be marred by such intruders, wailing from below like Old Hamlet's ghost in the cellarage. Textual criticism exists in order to give us a text; when that has been made, the bye-products should be destroyed or hidden. No one would be more surprised than the old-fashioned scholar if at a college feast he found the high table festooned with kitchen-refuse.

From some errors in our handling of Pindaric poetry we are already shaking ourselves free. The complaint about "mere digressions" grows less frequent as students realize that it is far more likely that they, rather than Pindar, do not remember or do not know what he is talking about. But Alexandrian scholars were much perplexed by these so-called digressions, of which I shall have a good deal to say; and many centuries later the stalwart Eustathius[18] called some odes "pot-bellied" for the same reason. But in our time very few scholars expect poets to be as rational as themselves, and rational in the same way as themselves. The German savant who emended a passage in *As You Like It* so as to run

> Stones in the running brooks,
> Sermons in books

lived (if at all) in days long past, as did Voltaire, who apostrophized Pindar as writing verses that no one understands but everyone must admire.[19]

To sweep aside all such hasty petulant stuff, to insist on patience and suspension of judgment, to wonder not that we understand so little but that we understand so much—this preparation and temper are now fortunately common, though (alas!) not universal. But they cannot free us completely from the prepossessions of more self-complacent readers. Blame Voltaire as we will for expecting Pindar to be Voltairean, we too expect him to be a little like ourselves—a demand entirely justified: for, were he not, he would be no man at all, nor could we appreciate a single line. The most careful and modest student sooner or later has to face passages which he feels compelled to think irrational or irrelevant. In the end he may have to resign himself, not blaming Pindar but murmuring Pliny's comfortable phrase, "omniscience is bad taste": *oportet nos aliqua nescire*. Yet before this surrender he will take pains to reduce the number of such passages, and the area of darkness. But how? After the traditional kind of study has failed, and purely intellectual effort which would serve equally well for Thucydides, another method of solution remains. Can we find a relevance not logical at all, which will not so much refute the charge that Pindar is careless or scatter-brained as show that such charges are not in point, since he permits fancy, imagination, emotion to override, even to banish, thought? Shall we not, while expecting him (as was said) to be a little like ourselves, consent to believe that he may resemble us not as Masters of Arts, but as grown-up children, while he plays beautifully with emotion or fancy and with the musical delicacies of language?

That is a mode of criticism more subtle, more penetrating, and (some will say) more dangerously whimsical than discussion cautiously based on allusions to Salamis or the *Works and Days*, but no less vital to fruitful study of most poets, of Pindar perhaps beyond all. With patience and caution we must tread the maze, hoping to emulate those "acute persons" of whom Eustathius writes that "they make their way unerringly through that labyrinth of [Pindar's] utterance which baffles most people; and, after passing along the convolutions right to the centre, trace their winding course back again and are restored to their homes with intelligence unimpaired."[20] For this quest few precise rules can be formulated. But one thing is vital. We must try always to feel the words themselves and relish the flavour of the idiom, so as to be alert for assonances—chimes foolish (it may be) to the intellect, but distinct enough to catch a poet's ear—and sensitive to curious turns of phrase whereby we may win a glimpse of some picture that has arisen in the poet's imagination.

The next topic in this approach to Pindar must be an account of his life. It shall be a mere outline, helping us to appreciate the odes—nothing more ambitious, partly because (as you have heard) I dislike biography dressed up as literary criticism,[21] partly because Pindar's life has been so often set forth. Farnell's account, though I cannot accept it all, seems to me admirable. Wilamowitz' *Pindaros* is, as far as possible, biographical throughout: a grave error which lessens the value of a masterly book.[22]

He was born in 518 or (less probably) in 522 B.C., at the time of a Pythian festival, as he himself reports: "The quadrennial feast, where oxen are led forth, when first I was laid in swaddling-clothes, a beloved child."[23] His birthplace was a hamlet called Cynoscephalae near Thebes, the capital

of Boeotia, a state in Central Greece. His father was named
Diophantus or (according to some) Pagondas: in any case he
belonged to a noble family, "the Aegeidae, my ancestors."[24]
A pretty tale relates that when he was a child bees laid honey
upon his mouth while he slept. His uncle Scopelinus taught
him the flute, an instrument in favour at Thebes, and the boy
must have shown high promise: he was sent for a thorough
musical training to Athens, even in that early day a centre of
Greek culture and art. He studied under Agathocles and
Apollodorus, who was a master of dithyrambic choirs; the
latter entrusted the training of a chorus to his pupil who,
though but a lad, gained repute for his performance of this
task. The famous Lasus of Hermione taught him the lyre.
Aeschylus, destined to be the greatest of all ancient play-
wrights, was his slightly elder contemporary: Eustathius[25]
says that Pindar "met him, became his companion and derived some benefit from Aeschylus' grandiloquence." That is
a mere assumption,[26] natural and attractive, but in its full
implications incredible. It is very likely that the two met, but
the suggestion of something like a Wordsworth-Coleridge
association must be rejected. Aeschylus did not begin to
exhibit tragedies till 500 B.C., by which date Pindar had
almost certainly quitted Athens.

Returning to Thebes, he commenced as a professional
composer of lyrics. The Boeotian poetess Corinna interested
herself in him. His first poem she censured for containing no
myth, that is, legendary narrative; accordingly, the youth's
next effort was crammed with myths: we still have its opening lines:[27] "Shall we sing Ismenus, or Melia of the golden
distaff, or Cadmus, or the holy race of the Sown Men, or blue-
snooded Theba, or the all-daring might of Heracles, or the
hilarious glory of Dionysus, or the white-armed damsel on her
marriage-day, even Harmonia?" All we who are teachers
have known pupils like that! Corinna's comment on this rig-
marole passed into a proverb: "You must sow with the hand,
not with the whole sack."[28] At another time she rebuked him
for using an Attic word.[29] During this period Pindar defeated

Myrtis, another local poetess: of her Corinna said: "I blame the clear-voiced Myrtis because, though a woman, she entered into strife with Pindar."[30] But she had herself defeated him in other competitions: Gildersleeve remarks on "the sweet inconsistency of her sex." Pindar's comment was less charming: Aelian alleges that in his chagrin he called Corinna a pig.[31]

At the age of twenty he received his first commission. The ode is what we call the Tenth Pythian (by "Pythian" is meant "connected with the Pythian Games," which were celebrated at Delphi), the traditional numbers having no reference to chronology. (For instance, the First Olympian was written as late as 476 B.C., when Pindar was forty-two: Thomas Magister says that it was placed first in the collection because it contains a panegyric on the Olympian festival and relates the story of Pelops, "the first man to compete in Elis.") This Tenth Pythian celebrated a Thessalian boy-athlete, and the commission was given by Thorax, a powerful noble of Larissa in Thessaly. The next three odes also commemorated Pythian victories: it is fairly clear that Pindar's vogue at first depended in some degree upon his close connexion with Delphi, the greatest centre of Apolline religion: "not only is the Tenth Pythian markedly Apolline in its colour, but the Hyperborean myth, its leading theme, was rooted in Delphi as in Thessaly."[32] Pindar of course relied on personal effort as well as on Apollo. His first contact with the great Sicilian despots was his own doing. In 490 B.C., Xenocrates, brother of Thero, tyrant of Acragas, won the chariot-race at Delphi, and the official ode was entrusted to Simonides, then at his zenith; but Pindar wrote the Sixth Pythian as a private compliment to Xenocrates' son Thrasybulus. He found it harder to get a start as poet for Olympian successes: his earliest Olympian ode, the Fourteenth, honours a victor from Orchomenus, close to his home. Probably it belongs to 488 B.C., when he was thirty.

The years 480 and 479 B.C. were momentous for him as for all Greeks, and indeed for all succeeding Western civilization.

The overthrow of the Persian invaders, glorious beyond panegyric, complete without any vestige of doubt or disappointment, stands among the most heroic and most permanently
valuable achievements of mankind. But not only did certain
states hold aloof from the Greek confederacy: some earned
deathless infamy by siding with the barbarian—Thessaly and
Pindar's own Thebes. The blame does not fall upon those
communities, but only upon the oligarchies which governed
them and which looked for an extension of their power in
Greece under a Persian suzerain. At Plataea the Theban
cavalry performed a brave but disgraceful exploit, routing a
Greek contingent with heavy loss. Their leader was one Asopodorus,[33] who has been plausibly identified[34] with the Asopodorus complimented by Pindar in the First Isthmian. Thorax
of Larissa, who (as I said) gave the poet his first commission,
helped Xerxes to escape after Salamis and lent the Persian
Mardonius open assistance in his march upon Central Greece.[35]
Vigorous efforts have been put forth to rebut the view expressed just now in the phrase "deathless infamy." Gildersleeve writes: "It was no treason to medize before there was a
Greece, and the Greece that came out of the Persian war was
a very different thing from the cantons that ranged themselves on this side and on that of a quarrel which, we may be
sure, bore another aspect to those who stood aloof from it
than it wears in the eyes of moderns, who have all learned to
be Hellenic patriots."[36] To this it seems obvious to reply: first,
that Greece continued as a multitude of cantons not only
after the Persian menace had been destroyed, but throughout
her history until her absorption into the Roman Empire;
secondly, that the meaning of the struggle was fully realized
at the time—as fully as any modern realizes it today—by in-
numerable Greeks in the very hour of crisis, by the Athenians who left their city to be ravaged that they might strive
to the death on the waters of Salamis, by the Spartans whose
heroism at Thermopylae lit for all lovers of freedom a beacon
that has never been quenched. As for writers, not to mention
Herodotus who wrote somewhat later, Aeschylus, who fought

at both Marathon and Salamis, produced his *Persae* only eight years later—a drama showing the fullest appreciation of all the issues, human and divine, involved in that tremendous quarrel.

What stand did Pindar himself take? Polybius the historian is often quoted on this:

Nor do we praise the Thebans in the Persian war, because they stood aloof from the perils that were faced in the cause of Greece and chose the Persian side through fear, nor Pindar who encouraged them to stay inactive, writing these lines: "Let us bring the commonwealth into tranquillity, searching for effulgent Peace that maketh great men, and casting spiteful Faction from our hearts, for the gift of her hands is poverty and the babes that she nurseth die."[37]

Despite Polybius' normal excellence as an historian, we must reject his rebuke of Pindar, whose words he has misapplied. That the poet urged his countrymen to keep out of the Persian war is not proved by the quotation, which says nothing whatever about it, but condemns only internal dissension, the invariable meaning of his word *stasis*. In the Eighth Isthmian (vv. 5–16), however, we find unmistakable, though not unambiguous, allusion: we cannot be sure whether the deliverance of Greece was uppermost in his mind, or the troubles of Thebes, which after the battle of Plataea had been humiliated by Pausanias' execution of the leading traitors.

Though my heart is heavy, they beg me to summon the golden Muse. Freed from great sorrows let us not fall into bereavement of garlands; nurse not thy griefs; ceasing from desperate ills, let us raise a sweet song for the people, even after pain. For the stone of Tantalus above our heads, a toil intolerable for Hellas, some god hath turned aside from us. As for me, the terror hath passed and freed me from sore anxiety—and it is best to look on whatever business the moment brings to hand. The life that overhangs mankind is full of wiles, marking an intricate course wherein their days shall move. Yet, if mortals have but freedom, even that is not past cure. Man's duty is to cherish good hope.

In those lines of the First Pythian where he proclaims the doughty exploit of Gelo and his brothers at Himera against

Carthage, Pindar briefly compares it (vv. 75 ff.) with Salamis and Plataea. A fragment[38] from a dithyramb declares that "sons of Athenians laid the shining foundation-stone of freedom"; and we know from Plutarch that he refers to the seafight off Artemisium. The Fifth Isthmian alludes finely to Salamis where "the Lord sent forth slaughter like much rain; and, even as the hail there fell blood from men beyond number." But the next line shows that he speaks with some reluctance or embarrassment: "Nevertheless, quench vaunting with silence."[39] From all this one gains the impression that might have been expected: Pindar is distracted between joy over the deliverance of Greece and loyalty to his own class, the nobles who had favoured the national enemy.

Some few years later, most likely in 476 B.C., Hiero, the despot of Syracuse, induced Pindar to visit him. This meant much. In the Greek world, so tiny by our scale, Sicily was a name to fire both imagination and ambition—the powerful, wealthy, and exciting land of the west. Such a journey then was like removing from Denmark to New York in modern days. Moreover, Hiero was a puissant and illustrious prince, than whom the whole Hellenic world could show no more impressive figure. Being also notably astute, he enhanced his prestige and the splendour of his reign by two devices, both perfectly designed to catch the imagination of Greeks: he sent his racehorses and charioteers to win prizes in the Great Games at Olympia and Delphi; he attracted to his court the leading poets, some of whom commemorated these victories, while some practised other poetical forms in what shone for a while as the most dazzling focus of Greek culture; just as Italian artists, philosophers, and poets joined the brilliant court of Lorenzo de' Medici. Thither came Simonides, the greatest of all Ionian poets since the epic period, whose Danae-fragment is among the loveliest remains of Greek art, and whose epitaphs on those who fell in the Persian wars remain unrivalled; Bacchylides, his nephew, so often foolishly decried because outshone by Pindar, but at his best an exquisite writer who in his choral poem for Delos reached the level of Tennyson;[40] Epicharmus, the sophisticated and vigorous founder of comedy; and the mighty Aeschylus himself, who wrote one of his tragedies in Sicily, honouring Aetna, the city re-founded by Hiero. Thither came Pindar also, for a sojourn lasting nearly two years. He was now in his forties, and at the height of achievement.

The date of Pindar's death is variously reported. Some say he died at sixty-five: that would be in 453 B.C.; others give him eighty years: that would fix his death at 438 B.C. Sundry tales were related which attest his repute both as a poet and as a man of God. It was while Thebes and Athens stood at daggers drawn that he wrote his famous dithyramb on Athens, describing her as the bulwark of Hellas; the Thebans fined him a thousand drachmae, and the Athenians paid the fine for him. When Alexander the Great burst into Greece and destroyed Thebes, he spared, among private houses, that of Pindar alone.[41] Milton quotes this incident in his sonnet, *When an Assault was intended upon the City:*

> The great Emathian conqueror bid spare
> The house of Pindarus, when temple and tower
> Went to the ground.

The god Pan was observed in the mountains, singing a poem written by Pindar. Demeter appeared to him in a dream, complaining that for her alone he had made no hymn, whereupon he remedied this omission. The prophet at Delphi each day, when about to close the temple, used to cry: "Let Pindar the poet enter to dine with the god." Pausanias records that the Pythian priestess bade the Delphians give Pindar a share of all the first-fruits offered to Apollo; that his iron chair was to be seen at Delphi; and that Persephone—this, no doubt, is only another version of the story given above—told him in a dream that she alone of all deities had not been sung by him, but that he should do so, when he came to her: before the day had passed, death took him. Later, Pindar in his turn appeared to an aged kinswoman and recited his poem on Persephone, which she wrote out on awaking.[42] It has not survived.

We must next discuss Pindar's relations with his numerous and highly varied clients. One of his earliest poems was an *encomion* for Alexander, king of Macedonia.[43] For Sicilian princes, as we have seen, he produced gorgeous odes, meant by them and by him to preserve their grandeur from oblivion—a hope magnificently fulfilled. Other Sicilians were thus honoured: the Sixth Olympian, one of his very finest, commemorates Hagesias of Syracuse; part of it has been found stamped on a brick in that city.[44] The Seventh celebrates a man dwelling at the other end of the Greek world, Diagoras of Rhodes—the poem which the Rhodians admired so vastly that they had it written up in golden letters on the wall of Athena's temple at Lindus, one of their cities.[45] Three noble poems, the Fourth and Fifth and Ninth Pythians, were despatched to the far south where Arcesilas reigned over Cyrene; in Libya, the temple of Zeus Ammon contained a pillar inscribed with a hymn sent by Pindar.[46] Far to the north, the colony of Abdera in Thrace received a poem, fragments from which have been unearthed in our day from the sands of Oxyrhynchus in Egypt. His native Thebes naturally inspired several poems, and we possess one exquisite ode for a boy-athlete from the little city of Orchomenus close by. Distant Locri in Italy received an Olympian. The Aegean islands provided him with matter, above all that which he so deeply admired and loved, Aegina: no less than a fourth of the triumphal odes are devoted to Aeginetan athletes. It is remarkable that he wrote little for the most famous cities of the mainland: among the extant odes, two (both very brief) are for Athenians, one for an Argive, one for a Corinthian, for Spartans none[47] at all.

With nearly all these renowned islands, great cities, princes and nobles, citizens and boys living under tyrannies, oligarchies, or democracies, his relations were admirable. Though he received fees for his poems, he maintained absolute independence of manner, combined with a lively understanding of each client's peculiar interests and history. If we set certain odes side by side this must strike us at once. The Ninth Olympian celebrates a wrestler from Opus, a quiet little town in Central Greece: its style is slightly stiff and archaic; the myths, set out with stark power but no elaboration, are primitive, one telling of the Deluge itself. The First Pythian blazes with a glory of language and sovereign imagination that (as we shall see later) brings before our eyes the soul of Greek civilization and the processes of the Universe. The Tenth Nemean, in honour of an Argive citizen, resounds with ancient names from the Peloponnese and contains the noblest Dorian work in literature, the last fight of Castor and Pollux. Everywhere, or almost everywhere, Pindar knows how to identify his outlook with that of the victor while never surrendering his own spiritual and artistic independence. This latter is shown in two very different ways.

First, he gives advice without fear or favour, whether it is likely to be palatable or not. The Fourth Pythian, addressed to King Arcesilas of Cyrene, was not commissioned by him, but by one Damophilus, a banished noble who hoped by this unique present to secure his own recall. At the close, Pindar with splendid urbanity but perfect directness reads the king a lecture on forbearance towards citizens. The odes to Hiero contain not only condolences on the despot's ill-health, but also vigorous advice on government and the need of freedom for Greeek citizens: he wishes Hiero to show himself a constitutional monarch.

So much detachment in a commissioned poet did not always, we may suppose, leave the client's good humour unruffled. Hiero in 476 B.C. won at Olympia with a single racehorse. Pindar composed for this the First Olympian, and expressed a hope that he would later have to celebrate a success in the chariot-race. Hiero in fact did attain this a few years later, but gave the commission for an ode to Bacchylides,[48] not to Pindar. No doubt he felt that the earlier poem contained too little about himself, far too much about Tantalus and Pelops.[49] Admonitions to lowlier friends concerning the good life—use of wealth, the give and take of city politics, grandeur chastened by taste and caution,—these are beyond number. Let us be quite clear about this attitude. The courtliness and compliment—though without the faintest sycophancy—are just as marked as the admonition. Pindar does not set himself up as a reformer: he is far less severe and unceremonious than Aristophanes, speaks with scarcely a hint of Aeschylus' *ex cathedra* tone, and has altogether too much humanity, as well as common sense, to indulge in the venomous cynicism of Theognis.[50] He was a great gentleman and a consummate man of the world.

That he should accept the standpoint of his client, identifying himself with his ideas and hopes, was natural and artistically desirable, if not inevitable. But scholars have too often—nay, well-nigh always—ignored what seems an obvious corollary. We must not assume that all the doctrines, every political view, enunciated in these odes were Pindar's own. In a later lecture it will be shown that he cannot have held all the beliefs that he sets forth. Whether we call this hypocrisy, or art, or transient sincerity, matters little. That he used this . . . broadmindedness (there is another label!) is beyond question.

The second mark of independence is utterly different and to modern readers vastly more surprising. Though almost every ode forms part of a public celebration, Pindar does not hesitate to introduce his personal concerns—not merely a brief phrase or so about his love for Aegina or friendship with the victor, but quite elaborate defence or explanation. We cannot but feel something like embarrassment, twenty-four centuries too late, when we imagine a public chorus dancing and singing in the presence of a great assembly such remarks as the close of the Seventh Nemean: "Never will I own that my heart maltreated Neoptolemus with unseemly language; but to repeat the same thing three or four times is hopeless." A good deal will be said later on this curious theme: at present let us examine but one example of this independence, because it is the most thorough-going of all.

The Thirteenth Olympian celebrates the signal achievement of Xenophon, a Corinthian who in 464 B.C. won two

successes, the quarter-mile and the *pentathlon*, a combination
of five contests. The Oligaethidae, to which family Xenophon
belonged, had gained an astounding number of victories—including sixty at the Isthmus and Nemea,[51]—and it appears
that Pindar was instructed to commemorate everything,
down to the last bay-leaf. He does provide an enormous list,
so faithfully that in the last stanza he hints that he is on the
point of drowning in his material (v. 114)—ἄγε κούφοισιν
ἐκνεύσω ποσίν. But for everyone's sake he divides this chronicle
into two parts, between which is placed (with briefer passages) the story of Bellerophon. Closing the first catalogue, he
reveals his own opinion, though the fact that his comment
opens a new stanza seems to have hidden the fact from some
editors. "Concerning the number of your victories I am at
odds with many, since in truth I could not tell precisely the
number of the sea-pebbles. Measure is a seemly element in
all things, and naught is it better to observe than proportion."[52] The last sentence, immediately following a cataract
of place-names and a comparison of their number with the
pebbles on a beach, betrays Pindar's feeling that the Oligaethidae have had altogether too much of a good thing—that
they are what English colloquialism would call a family of
pot-hunters. First-rate Corinthian athletes, after local victories, might well seek glory at Olympia or other such Games;
but to chase petty successes in Arcadia, Thebes, across the
sea to Euboea and so far afield as Sicily, was grossly bad
taste.

This hinted criticism is nothing compared with what comes
later. After beginning his second list he glances at the formidable *dossier* supplied him, consults his half-completed manu-
script, and murmurs (vv. 101 f.): "The Olympian items have
been worked off in the early part, I fancy."[53] And we are to
imagine a troupe of Corinthians chanting this "with appropriate gestures and dance"! Observe especially that (if we
except the mere naming of his victories) Xenophon receives
not a word of praise from one end of the ode to the other. His
family stand in hardly better case: at the opening they are

given two brief phrases: "a house gentle to fellow-citizens and
at the service of strangers." Not even the length at which
Pindar was forced (it appears) to unfurl his catalogues can
excuse this significant omission. He did not love Xenophon.

Nor, to all seeming, was he lovable. Whatever offences the
silence of this ode may be thought to imply are aggravated by
the constraint which Xenophon imposed on Pindar to prepare
an *encomion*[54] for the dedication of a hundred[55] courtesans
whom our versatile Corinthian had vowed to Aphrodite if he
gained success in this same Olympic festival. For once we
have no need to hum and haw about modern prudery and the
simple directness of the ancient Greeks. Pindar himself rue-
fully asks what "the lords of the Isthmus" will say of him for
"devising such a prelude to a honey-hearted drinking-song
associated with"—then he comes roundly out with it—"common women." The best that the lords of the Isthmus or anyone else could say for him is what he writes himself: σὺν δ'
ἀνάγκᾳ πᾶν καλόν, "necessity annuls dishonour."[56] Those words
are applied to the courtesans, but Pindar may well have
his own embarrassment also in mind: the reflexion that he
writes for pay comes upon him at other times[57] too, but not
(we may believe) with such pungency. The ode, as well as this
encomion, shows him in revolt, we remember; and those words
in his last prayer, "Heaven make us decent," as we are
tempted to render Ζεῦ τέλει', αἰδῶ δίδοι (v. 115), have more
applications than one.

Other matters, though less important, combine to deepen
our impression that Pindar is at best lukewarm. In v. 7 Peace
is among the city's divine inhabitants; in vv. 23 f. the war-
god also "blooms" there: the passages are not side by side,
but one suspects that he is not feeling what he says. His frequent mention of gold and the like need not suggest vulgar
display; nevertheless one of these passages (vv. 76 ff.) arouses
misgiving: "The daughter of Zeus, whose spear is the thunderbolt, herself bestowed on him that spirit-quelling gold."
The last words describe the bridle wherewith Bellerophon
tamed the winged steed Pegasus; but they suggest the power

of wealth to corrupt a man's honesty. Other Corinthian glories (save one) show here but poorly. The dithyramb[58] and the temple-pediment[59] are not so described as to fire our blood. Moreover Pindar has forgotten the trireme, Corinthian vases, Adeimantus who commanded the city's squadron at Salamis, and—to crown all—her commercial greatness![60] Nevertheless, the story that Corinth saw the invention of the bridle gives occasion for a splendid passage, his narrative of Bellerophon and Pegasus, the climax of which has superb graphic power (vv. 86 ff.): "Sheathed in bronze he mounted forthwith and went through the sword-play. Aye, and with that steed once he slew the female host of Amazons, smiting them, despite their arrows, from the cold bosom of the empty sky."[61] Thus does Pindar rise on his own Pegasus above "the female throng" of Corinth, concerning whom he has just written or is soon to write. The phrase αἰθέρος ψυχρῶν ἀπὸ κόλπων ἐρήμου, magnificent in its direct meaning, grows lovelier still as our mind turns to the cold bosoms of those women-warriors who hated men. This whole story has an air somewhat chilly and aloof: the reminder at its close, that Bellerophon's end was bitter, cannot have pleased the listeners whose pride in the legend is shown by the Pegasus upon their coins (see Plate I, 1, facing p. 130).

HIS SUBJECTS; HIS VISION OF THE WORLD

PINDAR'S WRITINGS were collected, arranged, and edited[1] in the great Library at Alexandria by distinguished scholars and writers, the chief part being taken probably by Aristophanes of Byzantium, perhaps best remembered for his work on the written Greek accents. This collection, made in the third century before Christ, comprised seventeen books, of which but four survive. Of the others we possess fragments, which have come down to us in three ways. First, some are due to the scholiasts, whose marginal notes on our manuscripts of the surviving odes often cite passages from the complete edition.[2] Secondly, later Greek authors quote Pindar precisely as Burke and Macaulay quote Milton, and thus fossil bits of his poems are found up and down the subsequent Greek literature. For instance,[3] an exquisite passage about Delos is preserved by a geographer, an arresting comment on justice by a rhetorician, a brief yet august description of Paradise by an essayist. Thirdly, during the last half-century the excavations at Oxyrhynchus in Egypt have produced a flood of papyri; and among these precious, variegated, and copious discoveries are remnants of Pindar. The original complete edition of seventeen books arranged the poems according to nine types:

Hymns (one book). This was a very wide class. Though it included work much like our modern hymns, there was a great deal besides; and probably we cannot expand Gildersleeve's terse sentence: "῞Υμνοι, the fundamental notion of which is praise (κλέος)."

πρῶτον μὲν εὔβουλον Θέμιν οὐρανίαν
χρυσέαισιν ἵπποις Ὠκεανοῦ παρὰ παγᾶν
Μοῖραι ποτὶ κλίμακα σεμνὰν
ἆγον Οὐλύμπου λιπαρὰν καθ᾽ ὁδὸν
σωτῆρος ἀρχαίαν ἄλοχον Διὸς ἔμμεν·
ἁ δὲ τὰς χρυσάμπυκας ἀγλαοκάρπους
τίκτεν ἀλαθέας ῞Ωρας.

"In the beginning the Fates led celestial Justice, that good counsellor, in a golden chariot from the springs of Ocean up the solemn ascent along Heaven's shining highway, to be the primeval consort of God the Saviour; and she bore the truthful Seasons, golden-snooded, bestowers of radiant fruit." (Fr. 10 = 30.)

Paeans (one book). The main note of this type is triumphant thanksgiving and praise. Our paean-fragments have greater bulk than those of any other class; nearly all come from the rubbish-dump at Oxyrhynchus. They include valuable work: for instance, parts of the Sixth Paean, on which a good deal will be said later. Here are the lines which, beyond all others of Pindar, seem to prophesy of Shelley.

τότε χρύσεαι ἀ-
έρος ἔκρυψαν κόμαι
ἐπιχώριον κατά-
σκιον νῶτον ὑμέτερον.

"Then tresses of golden mist concealed the spine of your native mountains, wrapped in shadow."[5] (Fr. 40, 137 ff.; Schroeder, p. 539.)

Dithyrambs (two books). Of all lyric types, this was the most popular, dealing with a divine or heroic theme in a series of incidents. Associated originally with Dionysus, the god of ecstasy, this form was noted for excitement, sometimes frenzy, in language, music, and dance. But naturally it was handled differently by different poets; Pindar's dithyrambs were more reserved and stately than the ravings of Timotheus,[6] for example.

κλῦθ' Ἀλαλά, Πολέμου θύγατερ,
ἐγχέων προοίμιον, ᾇ θύεται
ἄνδρες ὑπὲρ πόλιος τὸν
ἱρόθυτον θάνατον.

"Hearken, O War-Cry, thou daughter of Battle, prelude to the spears, in whose name men are sacrificed as a holy offering of death for their country." (Fr. 66 = 78.)

Prosodia (two books). These were processional chants, sung by worshippers approaching a temple.

χαῖρ' ὦ θεοδμάτα, λιπαροπλοκάμου παί-
δεσσι Λατοῦς ἱμεροέστατον ἔρνος,
πόντου θύγατερ, χθονὸς εὐρείας ἀκί-
νητον τέρας, ἄν τε βροτοὶ
Δᾶλον κικλήσκοισιν, μάκαρες δ' ἐν Ὀλύμπῳ
τηλέφαντον κυανέας χθονὸς ἄστρον.

"Hail, god-built Island, blossom whereon shining-tressèd Leto's children set their deepest love, daughter of the Sea, broad Earth's marvel unremoved, that mortals name Delos, but the Blessèd in Heaven name thee a far-gleaming star upon the dark-blue Earth!" (Fr. 78 = 87.)

Partheneia (three books). These were songs for choruses of girls, and known in Dorian states only. Though, like certain other types, they eulogized gods or mortals, religious auster-ity and official tone were tempered by a personal note which gave a charming naturalness to these maiden chants. Dio-nysius of Halicarnassus reports[7] that Pindar's partheneia were different from all his other works.

ἀλλὰ ζωσαμένα τε πέπλον ὠκέως
χερσίν τ' ἐν μαλακαῖσιν ὄρπακ' ἀγλαὸν
δάφνας ὀχέοισα πάνδοξον Αἰολάδα σταθμὸν
υἱοῦ τε Παγώνδα

ὑμνήσω στεφάνοισι θάλλοισα παρθένιον κάρα,
σειρῆνα δὲ κόμπον
αὐλίσκων ὑπὸ λωτίνων μιμήσομ' ἀοιδαῖς . . .

"Come, let me quickly girdle my gown and, bearing in my tender hands a sheeny branch of bay, sing the famous abode of Aeoladas and his son Pagondas, my virgin head gay with garlands, and to the music of reed-pipes I shall mimic in song the Water-Spirit's loud acclaim." (Fr. 84, 5 ff.; Schroeder, pp. 550 ff.)

Hyporchemes (two books). In these the dance, which was pantomimic, predominated markedly over the music and the

words. They dealt with both religious and secular themes. In
diction they often resembled paeans: a famous song that Pindar wrote for the Thebans on the occasion of a solar eclipse
(478 or 463 B.C.) is by many taken for a paean.

> ἀκτὶς ἀελίου, τί πολύσκοπ' ἐμήσαο,
> ὦ μᾶτερ ὀμμάτων, ἄστρον ὑπέρτατον
> ἐν ἀμέρᾳ κλεπτόμενον ; τί δ' ἔθηκας ἀμάχανον
> ἰσχύν τ' ἀνδράσι καὶ σοφίας ὁδὸν
> ἐπίσκοτον ἀτραπὸν ἐσσυμένα ;
> ἐλαύνεις τι νεώτερον ἢ πάρος ;
> ἀλλά σε πρὸς Διός, ἱπποσόα θοάς,
> ἱκετεύω, ἀπήμονα
> εἰς ὄλβον τινὰ τράποιο Θήβαις,
> ὦ πότνια, πάγκοινον τέρας.

"O far-seeing Sunbeam, thou mother of vision, what hast thou
devisèd, stealing from us in daytime the lord of stars? Why
hast thou baffled human power and the ways of wisdom,
rushing thus along a darkened path? Drivest thou upon us
some change unknown aforetime? Nay, I beseech thee in
God's name, speedy charioteer, turn this universal portent,
O Queen, to some ungrievous blessing for Thebes!" (Fr.
44 = 107.)

Encomia (one book). These were songs in praise of human
beings alone. They thus resembled *epinicia* (to which we shall
come in a moment), though less public and formal. Here is a
scrap from a poem addressed to Hiero, despot of Syracuse.
Sympathy underlies the exhortation, for Hiero was long af-
flicted by a painful disease.

> μήδ' ἀμαύρου τέρψιν ἐν βίῳ· πολύ τοι
> φέριστον ἀνδρὶ τερπνὸς αἰών.

"While thou livest, suffer no waning of delight: man, be sure,
hath naught better than delightful days." (Fr. 110 b = 126.)

Dirges (one book). This is a more definite class—lamentations for the dead, and consolations therewith. Of those who
have been initiated into the mysteries, as they were named,
he writes: "Blessèd is he who hath seen them before depart-

ing beneath the earth! He knoweth the end of life; he knoweth its god-sent beginning." (Fr. 121 = 137 a.)

ὄλβιος ὅστις ἰδὼν κεῖν' εἶσ' ὑπὸ χθόν'·
οἶδε μὲν βίου τελευτάν,
οἶδεν δὲ διόσδοτον ἀρχάν.

Triumphal or epinician odes (four books). These, which survive almost completely, altogether eclipse for us the rest of Pindar's work. The reason for this preservation is best given by quoting two distinguished Pindaric scholars. Eustathius writes: "They are the most widely disseminated because they have more human interest, fewer legends, and less obscurity, compared with the other works."[8] Smyth comments: "The other forms of choral song were either too narrow in their range and too local in their cults to awaken the sympathy of the Greeks of the Alexandrian age, who had ceased to cling to the traditional faith; or, as in the case of the dithyramb and the nome, whose success depended on the virtue of their music, neglect was the result of the loss of the melodies."[9]

This enumeration gives the seventeen books that formed the Alexandrian collection. Certain ancient accounts add other types of work on which we need not dwell. Some are wrongly attributed to our poet; others fall under the categories just named: for instance, the vivid erotic poem in Theoxenus' honour, which is occasionally called a *scolion* or drinking-song, most scholars put among the *encomia*.

The epinician odes celebrate successes in athletic games. A very small number are not true epinicians: for example, the Eleventh Nemean congratulates a man who is taking up office as chief magistrate of his native island, Tenedos; but even this commemorates his athletic record. Throughout the Greek world many athletic contests were held at regular intervals; four festivals, often called the "Great Games" and "Holy Games," were immensely prominent and attracted competitors from the whole Greek world; foreigners were not allowed to enter. These four festivals were held: at Olympia, in the northwest of the Peloponnese; at Delphi, in Central Greece, where the festival was called "Pythian"; at Nemea, in the north of the Peloponnese; and at Corinth, where the festival was called "Isthmian." The odes, accordingly, are arranged as Olympian, comprising fourteen odes; twelve Pythian; eleven Nemean; eight Isthmian. The whole mass comprises between thirty-four and thirty-five hundred lines.

Far the greatest celebration was the Olympian, which served as a model for all. Dedicated to Zeus, the king of the gods, it was founded in 776 B.C., and recurred at intervals of four years; that is, the second festival was held in 772 B.C. This period, called an Olympiad, formed the basis of Greek chronology; for instance, whereas we say that Marathon was fought in 490 B.C., Greeks placed it in the third year of the seventy-second Olympiad.[10] When the time approached, the state of Elis, in which Olympia lay, sent heralds throughout Greece to proclaim a sacred truce; and anyone entering Elis under arms during the festival was held as a prisoner of war. The games took place in August and (after 472 B.C.) lasted five days. The prize was a wreath of wild olive, and in Pindar's time the contests numbered fourteen, thus:

a) Equestrian: four-horse chariot, mule-car, single riding-horse.
b) Running: *stadion* (200 yards) for men.
   stadion for boys.
   diaulos (400 yards).
   dolichos (2,400 yards).
   race in armour.
c) Wrestling: for men.
   for boys.
d) Boxing: for men.
   for boys.
e) *Pancration:* wrestling and boxing combined.
f) *Pentathlon:* jumping, running, discus, javelin, wrestling. (The prize was no doubt awarded to the best all-round man.)

A complete list survives of all victors in the *stadion* from the beginning down to 217 A.D.—almost a thousand years.[11]

The Pythian festival, in honour of Apollo, dates from 582 B.C., and was celebrated in August once every four years, in the third year of each Olympiad. The prize was a bay-wreath, and the contests much the same as at Olympia, save that there were also musical competitions, from which indeed the whole festival was developed.

The Nemean games, which, like the Olympian, were in honour of Zeus, took place in July of the second and fourth year in each Olympiad. They date from 573 B.C. The prize was a wreath of fresh celery. We have no exact information about the list of contests.

The Isthmian games, in honour of Poseidon, began in 581 B.C., and were held in April of the second and fourth year of each Olympiad. The wreath was woven of dry celery. Here too we are without exact information about the contests: both the Isthmian and the Nemean, however, resembled the Olympian.

All the Games were celebrated continuously until A.D. 393, when an edict of the Roman Emperor Theodosius forbade pagan festivals.

The glory encircling a victor, especially an Olympian victor, can scarcely be exaggerated. When he returned to his native town a breach was made in the walls to admit him.[12] In Athens, he and his descendants were given the signal honour of taking their meals in the Prytaneum, or town-hall. Pausanias[13] relates that the Athenians captured in a sea-fight one Dorieus of Rhodes, who had given vigorous aid to Sparta against them; but set him free in recognition of his sensational athletic successes. His father, Diagoras of Rhodes, for whom Pindar composed the Seventh Olympian, was the most illustrious of Greek boxers: he won at all the four Great Games, thus gaining the title περιοδονίκης, or "victor in the whole circuit." Moreover his three sons and two grandsons were victorious at Olympia. Cicero[14] tells of a Spartan who saw this overwhelming Rhodian carried on the shoulders of two garlanded sons, and exclaimed: "Die, O Diagoras, for you cannot ascend into Heaven!" Quite naturally, triumphant song swelled the rejoicings. Long before elaborate odes came the "Song of Archilochus," beginning τήνελλα καλλίνικε, "hail to thee, glorious winner," though τήνελλα is not exactly a word, but imitation of a twanging harp. Then came special songs written by friends, and finally the official odes by distinguished poets such as Simonides, his nephew Bacchylides, and Pindar. This work was of course professional; it demanded arduous and varied training in music, poetry, and the dance, all three being blent in the performance of epinician odes. In consequence, the poets received fees; sundry curmudgeons reviled both Pindar and Simonides for avarice.

As it was Pindar's business to extol men who had gained supreme honour by fleetness of foot, skill in driving, and the like, we should expect to find incessant allusions to the adroitnesses, the excitement, the technical details, to everything with which we are familiar in modern reports of athletic contests—raised (no doubt) to whatever poetical heights wrestling or boxing allow. Not so: the rarity of such technicalities and thrills is amazing: for a reason which will soon appear, it is worth while to give a full list of them.

a) *Ol.* IX 91 ff.: "Quelling each man by quick guileful shifts of balance, himself unthrown, amid what shouts he passed across the arena in the beauty of life's springtime and fair achievement!"

b) *Ol.* X 72 f.: "Niceus, with a whirl of the hand, flung the stone outdistancing all, and a mighty shout ran roaring along the line of his comrades."

c) *Pyth.* V 49 ff.: "Now art thou home again, after bringing thy chariot unharmed through the race with fearless heart, though forty drivers fell."

d) *Nem.* VII 72 f.: ". . . sendeth a man free from the wrestling, his neck and strength clear of sweat, before the burning sun falleth upon his limbs."

Those four passages make a complete list of athletic details about the contests which Pindar immortalizes! Why? There can be no thought that Greek feeling held these topics too low for high poetry. Homer gives plenty of such detail in the funeral games of Patroclus; Sophocles in *Electra*, where the messenger describes a chariot-race at Delphi; and Theocritus relates a boxing contest full of technical points.[15] The real cause is Pindar's conception of human greatness and of his own profession. Success in the Games is good because it proves quality, perseverance, and Heaven's favour; because it gives a man glory, because it therefore sheds glory upon his city, and because it reasserts and proves man's kinship with the gods. Pindar's own task was not so much to be the teacher[16] of Greece as to be the prophet of human greatness—of a tradition that was accepted, indeed, by the society whose culture he shared, but had never been so eloquently proclaimed. That is one of his reasons for dilating upon the sources of his inspiration and his brilliant powers as an executant of song. In this way the actual race or wrestling-bout becomes a mere starting-point; and though he gives on occasion a catalogue of successes won by his client or his client's family, they are never integral to the ode as a work of art: they have no likeness to Virgil's pageant of Roman heroes in the Sixth Book of the *Aeneid*. In this way, too, we understand the myths, or the narrated legends, found in nearly all the great odes. Unless quite brief, the myth is never a mere ornament added to a poem that could have dispensed with it, but a vital element in the presentation of what lies next to Pindar's heart: it stands like a magnificent mirror[17] wherein the athlete of yesterday finds his deeds and his temper reproduced on the grand scale by Achilles, Telamon, or Heracles. Pindar, as will be shown later, was no clear-headed moralist; but whatever we may think of his views, there can be no doubt of his spirit. He understood grandeur: nay, he lived grandeur. That is why he thinks of himself as an eagle that soars from earth into the empyrean: that is why he views the glory of success—however ephemeral, yet won by exertions of the whole body and spirit—as a significant part of the Universe: a Dorian universe, true, but at least it has engendered poetry that is immortal and has found no rival or successor.

Pindar worshipped splendour, beauty triumphant over darkness. That worship was his deepest instinct, and explains his manner of looking at the world and expressing his vision; for he was among those few to whom beauty has been more fundamental than virtue or happiness: Χάρις, ἅπερ ἅπαντα τεύχει τὰ μείλιχα θνατοῖς—"Beauty, which bestows on mortal men every joy they know" (*Ol.* I 30). To him it means what the Form means to Aristotle, creating true existence: he would have altered Spenser's great line[18] into "*Beauty* is form, and doth the body make." But Aristotle argues for a theory which teaches the mind, whereas Pindar sings in the fulness of an instinct which irradiates the imagination. Just as Aeschylus was a religious man not merely by belief and habit, but by instinct too, so that he explains all events, all institutions, all creatures human and non-human in terms of God's will and guidance, so Pindar adds to the normal Greek joy in "the pride of the eyes and the lust of life" an intuition that the ultimately real is beauty, giving to all persons and objects, every act, thought, and emotion, whatever value and significance are theirs.

But from this we are not to draw inferences that would be natural were it said of a modern man. His devotion to beauty does not mean that he consciously rejected other interests, other standards, other types of poetical activity. He lived before the age of ordered thinking, of self-analysis and most other kinds of analysis. Keats had the same instinct and passion, but also reasoned about it clearly, exclaiming in one of his letters: "O for a Life of Sensations rather than of Thoughts!"[19] Shelley's *Defence of Poetry*, in its whole spirit and method, lies outside the range of anything Pindar could have conceived: he made no scheme of art or life, separating for instance beauty from righteousness. He might, indeed, had the point been put to him, have accepted Arnold's dictum that "conduct is three-fourths of our life," and we shall note later his numerous statements on theology, conduct, and politics. But these (whatever their interest and value) are expressions of his beliefs as a man and a citizen, not poetry; and they affect his poetical excellence not a whit. Nor is he a hedonist, despite a superb song which conveys with relish and insight the easeful rapture of boon-companionship, and despite his exhortation to Hiero about the waning of delight.

No doubt he enjoyed what his friends enjoyed, "the lordly bloom of good living," "the vine's masterful child," and "love's joyous blossom," as those vigorous phrases[20] and many others suggest. His rapture in the presence of loveliness appears again and again, most poignantly perhaps in the Eighth Nemean where he sings of the abiding-places where beauty is enthroned, the subtle curve of brows and closed eyelids, the hands gentle yet strong as doom.[21] But all this does not make him a hedonist, for he was not obsessed by pleasure; like Aristophanes, like perhaps every Greek earlier than the fourth century, he quaffed life as a generous wine, for the Epicureans had not yet turned it into a liqueur, or the Stoics into a gruel. Nor, though his gaze was fixed so often with passionate intentness upon the Here and Now, do his eyes glitter with the febrile stare of Rufinus and other such piteous voluptuaries of the *Anthology*. Again, no man has seen more clearly, felt more poignantly, that things dear and lovely fleet fast away; but he has written nothing that resembles those wistful utterances, "Où sont les neiges d'antan?" "Verweile doch! Du bist so schön." "Joy, whose hand is ever at his lips, bidding adieu." He points serenely to that fairness which does not pass away, the radiance of Nature and the gods, himself moreover arraying in deathless verse τὰ ἐν Ἑλλάδι τερπνά (*Pyth.* X 19), "the delights that are in Hellas." His sense of the glorious present is equalled by his realization of the gorgeous past, and of the future renown, at moments of the future bliss, conferred on those who have wrought fair deeds.

What right, then, have we to say that his deepest instinct was for beauty, rather than any other aspect of life, or all aspects together? We may detect any man's dearest concern by watching his talk for phrases or allusions that are, on a normal view, irrelevant, because "out of the abundance of the heart the mouth speaketh." When Wordsworth says "I wandered lonely *as a cloud*," when Virgil likens a young warrior in death to a drooping *flower*, when Dante writes that in the flame of those four stars the heaven seemed to *rejoice*—

"goder pareva il ciel di lor fiammelle"; then, precisely because the verbal turn might (if we were so obtuse) be called
far-fetched, we suddenly peer deep into the poet's heart.[22] So
in Pindar. Consider the famous description[23] of Iamus' birth
in contrast with another powerful narrative—the birth of Ion
as told by Euripides. The tragedy relates with dreadful
poignancy Apollo's serene ruthlessness, the mother's anguish
and utter desolation. In Pindar there is small question of
morals, and all else is winsomeness, even to the word ὠδῖνος,
"birth-pang," itself the adjective "lovely," ἐρατᾶς, being
added. Similar effects may be found in profusion. Even the
smoke of a funeral-pyre takes on a momentary charm—not
λευκὸν καπνόν, "white smoke," but λευκανθέα, "like a white
flower." The Twelfth Pythian is unusually grim, yet amid the
ghastly details of the monster's death beams a touch of
loveliness: she was εὐπάραος, her cheeks were beautiful. The
giants leagued against Heaven are overthrown at Phlegra
and their tresses befouled with soil—the tresses radiant till
then. Some have found an adjective in the last line of the
Sixth Pythian needless and therefore weak. Pindar says that
his friend's social charm "surpasses the *crannied* work (τρητὸν
πόνον) of bees." The word is not otiose, but an insertion of the
same kind as the rest. He is charmed—and who is not?—by
the honeycomb's pattern; so he reminds us of it. Amid the
darkness and lamentation that surround the pretended funeral of the infant Jason gorgeous colour blazes for an instant:
"in purple swaddling-clothes." These and other such phrases
reinforce strongly, because to all appearance so casually, other
passages where beauty, grace, radiance—αἴγλα—are proclaimed the climax of our existence. The most explicit, as
well as the most solemn, of these is appropriately set in the
latest written of all Pindar's surviving stanzas, where he sets
forth with grave power his central thought concerning human
life (*Pyth.* VIII 95 ff.):

> ἐπάμεροι· τί δέ τις ; τί δ᾽ οὔ τις ; σκιᾶς ὄναρ
> ἄνθρωπος. ἀλλ᾽ ὅταν αἴγλα διόσδοτος ἔλθῃ,
> λαμπρὸν φέγγος ἔπεστιν ἀνδρῶν καὶ μείλιχος αἰών.

"Creatures of a day, what are we? What are we not? The
dream of a shadow, such is man. But when God bestoweth
radiance, then a glory is upon us, and days of pleasantness."

Beauty takes countless forms, and not all awake in Pindar
equal, or any, rapture. He dwells but rarely on charm that is
wistful, wan, or fragile; little care for things small and lovely:
what can we find to set beside that magical passage in the
Sixth Olympian where he depicts the sheen of colour thrown
by wild flowers in the copse upon a baby's limbs? Even the
stars mean little to him: rarely does he suggest that they are
beautiful. More than once (*Ol.* I 27 ff., *Ol.* VI 57 ff.) he describes a youth pouring out his soul in ardour of love or gallant enterprise beneath the midnight sky; but it is night that
he names, and not the stars. What a sublime picture of the
storied constellations might he have given us, a picture that
he left for the austerer Sophocles to hint at in an august lyric
of the *Trachiniae!* With what lordly opulence of phrase, what
glittering mosaic of legend, might he have set forth "the sweet
influences of Pleiades and the bands of Orion, Arcturus and
the chambers of the south"! The faint loveliness of the new
moon is not mentioned: she is ever at the full, like the sun her
brother. Strangest of all, he utters no praise of sculpture—he
who composed that noblest, most heart-piercing masterpiece
of Dorian poetry, the myth of the Tenth Nemean, which it
seems impossible to read without recalling the Aeginetan
marbles. His frequent use of ποικίλος and its cognates may
allude to painting, yet he clearly mentions that art but once.[24]
The effulgence of ruby, diamond, and carbuncle aroused in
him no more delight than in any other classical Greek writer.[25]
Of all the great poets, he who was as completely dominated
and inspired by loveliness as any, surrendered heart and senses
to the fewest of its manifestations. One critic[26] has said: "It is
indeed marvellous that Pindar, neglecting so many sources of
poetic effect, could have produced such poetry." How, then,
was it produced? We must return to this when we discuss his
technique. Here, where we are concerned with his vision of
the world, it must be enough to observe that he gains his un-

surpassed effects by envisaging a few splendid sights[27]—heroic action, the brilliant hue of sun, gold, and wine, the charm of flowers, the fair bodies of gods and goddesses or godlike men and women—against a background null, unsympathetic, even sinister.

To feel and see with Pindar is infinitely more important than to think with him. In reading these poems we should at every turn insist on visualizing whatever can be visualized: here at least we need fear no excess, since in comparison with Greeks, above all with him, most moderns are nearly blind. At each fresh perusal we take *Theba* as "Thebes"—a collection of walls and streets,—hurriedly readjusting our mental focus when we find on a sudden that this will not do, for she is a nymph: "My mother's mother is Stymphalian, even fair-flowering Metopa, who bore Theba, smiter of horses" (*Ol.* 84 f.). We shall read him but ill if we take such points only when they are forced upon us by a word like ἔτικτεν, "she bore." For him Theba and a hundred such names mean both nymph and city; and this, although "nonsense" indeed, should charm and enlighten anyone who knows that (as we are still prepared to phrase it) a place may have a soul, who has paced Cambridge courts, the Canongate in Edinburgh, the quiet early-lit streets of Grasse at Christmas time, or the Old Bridge of Florence. If Chipping Campden were a goddess, what a goddess she would be! But (alas!) there is no such person, and we do not really think, for all our researches, that Pindar would have believed in her any more than we. So, when on opening the Fourth Pythian we read that Battus founded his city ἐν ἀργινόεντι μαστῷ, we explain the words as "upon a gleaming hill: i.e., a hill of chalk." But the poet imagines Libya a nymph and so calls the place her gleaming *breast:* he knew the Greek word for "hill" as well as his editors, and would have used it had he thought with them. Towards the end he urges the king τᾶς εὐδαίμονος ἀμφὶ Κυράνας θέμεν σπουδὰν ἅπασαν, "to bestow all eagerness upon blest Cyrene." Mere bricks and mortar? Arcesilas should support all worthy causes in our progressive city? No doubt: but he should also—and that is what Pindar means—resemble the dashing Argonauts and throw his ardent soul without reserve into championship of that happy goddess who claims his devotion. We retain grace enough to laugh when told that "an average man consists" of so many pounds of nitrogen, water, and other such luggage. So would Pindar have laughed had he been informed that Rhodes or Aegina was a large mass of soil and stone. He has "naïveté dans la magnificence":[28] in the Sixth Olympian he justly refuses to be called a Boeotian hog, but a Boeotian he was; and to enjoy him aright we must indulge his artlessness if we have deplorably lost our own.

A moment ago I mentioned the Fourth Pythian, and it would be well to offer straightway some account of this ode, by far the longest and possibly the most impressive, illustrating, moreover, many of the ideas that have just been set forth.

Arcesilas, or Arcesilaus, the Fourth, hereditary king of Cyrene, won the chariot-race at Delphi in 462 B.C. The Fifth Pythian is the normal epinician for that victory; the Fourth, which barely mentions the race, was intended to be sung at a banquet celebrating it, perhaps by one singer—certainly it was not composed for the usual *comos* or procession, as στᾶμεν, "to stand," in v. 2 is sufficient to prove. The occasion of its composition was unusual. Damophilus, a Cyrenian noble, had been banished by Arcesilas for membership in a political party that opposed the king. Visiting Thebes, he became the poet's guest; and, relinquishing his political activities, he sought to make his peace with Arcesilas by the gift of an ode which he commissioned Pindar to write. The work thus took the shape of an elaborate panegyric upon Arcesilas and his ancestors, followed by a skilful recommendation of Damophilus. This panegyric rests almost wholly upon legend; which, however, Pindar and his public took for genuine history. Arcesilas was the eighth king of Cyrene, the first being Battus, who was sent by the Delphic oracle to found a realm in Libya. And why? To fulfil a compact made in a still remoter age. A distant ancestor both of Battus and of Arcesilas, named

Euphamus, had met upon the coast of Libya a divine stranger who gave him a clod of earth as a sign that he should possess the land. But why had Euphamus come to that far-off shore? He was one of the Argonauts, returning by a devious voyage from the quest of the Golden Fleece, sought by Jason and his comrades at the eastern limit of the known world. Thus does the poet find occasion for his superb myth, telling for the first time in extant literature with full power that most glorious and varied among tales of adventure, which has fired so many imaginations that the Golden Fleece became, as later the Holy Grail, a very symbol of romance. Vivid pictures show us Medea prophesying of the future Cyrene, Euphamus leaping down from Argo's prow to receive the clod of destiny, Jason descending from the uplands and entering his enemy Pelias' town to claim his kingdom, and the strange bitter clash between two kinsmen; Pelias consents to yield if Jason will seek Phasis to bring home the soul of Phrixus and the Fleece; the heroes gather for the voyage; Argo sails between the Justling Rocks; Jason wins Medea's love, yokes the fire-breathing bulls and ploughs the deadly furrow, thereafter slaying a guardian-dragon and taking the Fleece; on the homeward voyage they touch at Lemnos, and Euphamus becomes ancestor of Battus' line.

The story thus told has received countless praises, and rightly. Jason as he strides into the market-place or throws off his saffron mantle and, putting his trust in God, lays hand to the deadly plough, affects us like a canvas or fresco of Raphael, heroic and debonair; such also is the spirit of this Dorian rhythm, rolling in sonorous glory through thirty-nine unsurpassable stanzas. All have noted too the adroit distortion of chronological order in the episodes, whereby the relation of Cyrene and her king with the Quest of the Fleece is made plain at the opening and the close alike. The masterly employment of magic thrills us throughout. In Homer, sorcery is but a device to deepen interest and excitement, as when Athena casts a spell upon Odysseus so that coming to his own longed-for island at last he cannot recognize it. But here magic has a spiritual potency without which these high exploits could never have been achieved. When Triton disguises his deity under the likeness of a "noble man," the device is Homeric; but without the magic bird used as a love-charm by Aphrodite, Medea would not have become enamoured of Jason and taught him the way through his else fatal adventure. Magic, one element in romance, joins here with others, the beckoning of remote beauty—love and a high-hearted quest amid outlandish folk beside waters that lave the edge of the world—and the life-quickening things that are inanimate in our humdrum homes: a handful of soil is pregnant with destiny, a βῶλαξ δαιμονία; the ship must be bridled like a gallant horse and becomes through Hera's spell the object of heroic passion; even the oar-blade is insatiable as it devours the leagues of water that heave between Iolcus and the Inhospitable Sea; night is made accomplice of perilous doings; the Justling Rocks are twin living creatures,[29] until the escape of demigods brings death upon them; and, as so often, names that we take but as areas of land prove to mean goddesses, Europa being the mother of Euphamus and Libya giving her white-gleaming breast to Battus and his followers.

Yet another device heightens the charm and thrill—Pindar has used two time-schemes, or two planes of time. As a matter of "history," the Quest is made immensely remote: seventeen generations before the dynasty of Arcesilas was even founded, Medea prophesies concerning another prophecy that shall be uttered in a later age; the Euxine is furrowed by the earliest keel, dragons and fire-breathing bulls infest the earth, Love itself has but yesterday[30] descended among mortal men and women, and the vast migrations of Greeks lie still in a future discerned only by divine foreknowledge. But earlier, beyond this awful vista of slowly opening centuries, the poet sets an adventure vibrant with gallant speed and excitement, fresh and radiant under our eyes that gaze upon it over the sill of time. Pelias drives his team headlong into the crowded market-place; Euphamus leaps down upon the beach to clasp hands with a noble stranger; Jason and his kinsmen rush into

the palace; Aeetes, for all his consternation, instantly discloses the second adventure; oars swing greedily in rapid
hands; the heart of man is all too quick; Castalia's oracle bids
that a vessel be built with speed to bring back home the
ghost impatient for Hellas. Nothing could be more charged
with the uncanny yet delicious charm of fairyland than all
this eager brilliant vitality placed on the far side of a perspective wherein dim generations unfold themselves.[31]

These elements in the narrative are obvious enough; but
there remains one that has been rarely (if ever)[32] described,
not because it is unobtrusive but because, in a poet of Pindar's epoch, still more in a poet of his traditions and temper,
it is antecedently most improbable—nay, we should have
said, downright impossible. In this ode, for the first and last
time in classical literature, there appears in full expression
the idea of Chivalry.[33] Courage we find elsewhere in plenty,
even the high-hearted gallantry that seeks peril for adventure's sake alone; splendid courtesy under dreadful strain, in
the twenty-fourth book of the *Iliad*, where Priam and Achilles
meet; romantic love, though not often; again and again a
passion for music; still more often, religion, though religious
emotion is rare. Here by miracle they are all interfused in a
radiance that was not to return until the Middle Ages conceived the Arthurian Legend.

For chivalry was as complex as beautiful, blending courage,
high breeding, courtesy, a passion for adventure, joy in song,
a deep sense of knightly comradeship, pity and protection
bestowed on the weak and helpless, love of woman and utter
reliance upon God. Each of these qualities, ardours, and aspira-
tions can be found in the Fourth Pythian. As to courage, no
word is needed. The courtesy of Jason charms us all: Παῖ
Ποσειδᾶνος Πετραίου—was ever anything more perfectly said?
Consider the situation: what a consummate fusion of dignity,
tact, irony, and kindliness! In θεμισσαμένους ὀργάς we find to
our astonishment a Pindaric phrase for the spirit of the duel—
"let us quarrel like gentlemen." High breeding? Pelias the
villain can on occasion show a knightly manner: his ἔσομαι τοῖος

is flawless; Jason makes known his royal lineage and gentle
nurture; when the heroes gather for their perilous voyage, the
muster-roll proclaims each the son of a god. And how marvellously is the passion for adventure described! Has any
phrase of but two words expressed so much of the paladin-
spirit as αἰδεσθέντες ἀλκάν?[34] Martial achievement was the
Lady of their worship. The very word for "knightly" is used
by Jason: ἱππόταις, he says, ἱππόταις εὔθυνε λαοῖς δίκας. Most
stirring of all are those lines in which the full splendour of a
high and gallant enterprise shines forth (vv. 184 ff.):

> τὸν δὲ παμπειθῆ γλυκὺν ἡμιθέοι-
> σιν πόθον ἔνδαιεν "Ηρα
> ναὸς 'Αργοῦς, μή τινα λειπόμενον
> τὰν ἀκίνδυνον παρὰ ματρὶ μένειν αἰ-
> ῶνα πέσσοντ', ἀλλ' ἐπὶ καὶ θανάτῳ
> φάρμακον κάλλιστον ἑᾶς ἀρετᾶς ἄ-
> λιξιν εὑρέσθαι σὺν ἄλλοις.

παμπειθῆ γλυκύν—an overmastering delicious spell was laid
upon them; πόθον 'Αργοῦς—a passion as different from a sense
of duty as from a love of frolic: ἔνδαιεν "Ηρα—this passionate
enchantment was a flame from Heaven; ἐπὶ καὶ θανάτῳ—even
at the cost of life. φάρμακον ἑᾶς ἀρετᾶς is among the divine
achievements of literature—virtuosity of idiom, a lordly yet
subtle thought, the very core of noble prowess. φάρμακον
ἀρετᾶς alone would be fine—"a talisman to create valour."
But ἑᾶς adds much: the young hero seeks a beautiful exploit
that will bring his courage home to his own soul, and cannot
rest until he has proved himself. It is a golden phrase for
what the poet has already (83 ff.) worded more simply:

> τάχα δ' εὐθὺς ἰὼν σφετέρας
> ἐστάθη γνώμας ἀταρβάκτοιο πειρώμενος
> ἐν ἀγορᾷ πλήθοντος ὄχλου.

"Stepping quickly straight onward, he stood in the market-
place thronged with folk, and made trial of his unflinching
will." Small wonder that this peril "bound them with strong

nails of steel!" In the final words of our passage yet another thought appears, the inspiration of comradeship—ἄλιξιν σὺν ἄλλοις, which may recall the Homeric summons, ἀλλήλους αἰδεῖσθε κατὰ κρατερὰς ὑσμίνας,[35] "be loyal to each other amid the mighty affray": but here we perceive high-hearted worship of adventure as a kind of religion, whereas Homer's heroes remember not seldom prizes, plunder and ransom, their families and possessions.

For pity, for championship of the weak, this legend allowed small opportunity; but the homeless ghost of Phrixus does not appeal in vain, and Pindar, when urging Arcesilas to emulate his ancestor the Argonaut, reminds him (v. 291) that Zeus released his own enemies, the Titans. That love for music and song which exhilarated the medieval knight marks one passage only, yet perhaps the most haunting of all: "And from Apollo came that player on the lyre and father of songs, even Orpheus the well-praisèd." But with the enchantments of women or goddesses the whole narrative tingles. Medea dominates the adventure in Colchis and by her prophecy enters into the chronicle of Cyrene. Hera fires the demigods with worship for Argo. Aphrodite brings among mankind Love unknown before, bearing the speckled bird as a charm to make Medea dote on flight to Hellas. Jason has ever dealt in knightly manner with the ladies, as with the master, of Chiron's cave: "Unto them I used no unseemly deed or word." Read through the poem once more to note the number of goddesses, nymphs, women that shed beauty or danger, desire or inspiration, upon men and heroes, from the gleaming bosom of Libya in the first stanza to Theba in the last, where the banished man found a well of ambrosial verse: Lemnian brides, Tyro, Medea, and Iphimedeia, Aphrodite, the Fates, Hera and Artemis, the Pythian priestess, nameless women and the illustrious mates of immortal gods.

The last element that we noted in the full conception of chivalry was a sense of God. This blazes forth most gloriously at the climax: "Thus, then, spake the king. Thereat did Jason, throwing aside his saffron garment, put his trust in

God and set hand to the work." It is expressed majestically at the setting-forth when with a golden beaker in his grasp he stands upon the prow and calls to the Father of heavenly beings, Zeus whose spear is the thunderbolt.

Such, then, is the myth of the Golden Fleece as Pindar sings it, a story ruled by πόθος, the yearning that reaches forth to attain a bride, or glory, or the assurance of a youth's own heart that he is a man of valour, or (as in Phrixus) the return home even after death: that yearning of which the dappled Wryneck is a heaven-sent symbol. And if, finally, we ask whether the whole ode, as well as this great portion of it, has unity, whether the leading idea extends its power into the briefer yet momentous admonition to Arcesilas, we shall be able to discover a reply. For it is clear that Damophilus too cherishes his πόθος—"he prays that he may see his home," like Phrixus; clear, too, that he loves music and song, and that he shares Jason's gusto for vigorous life and joyous living, as one marvellous phrase reveals—a phrase that suggests a Provençal troubadour: θυμὸν ἐκδόσθαι πρὸς ἥβαν, "yield his heart to the joyance of youthfulness."[36] That is much, but not enough; and in other ways Pindar's guest was no demigod or paladin. More nobly sounds the call to Arcesilas himself, the call which we interpreted a few moments ago, that he should bestow his eager zeal upon Cyrene. The king is adjured to imitate in his day the knightly homage paid to goddesses and women by his heroic forebears. So alone (be it noted) has τλᾶθι,"dare," any real value; ἅπασαν,"all thy eagerness," too, is exigent—there must be no minor, distracting, loyalties. "Find courage to spend thy loyalty on blessèd Cyrene, and none other." Behind all this, we may conjecture, stands much more. This consummate picture of knightliness has been painted for a Greek ruler, but ruler of a realm on the very horizon of Pindar's world. That, perhaps, may account for its unique manner. When we remember the tone of his other Cyrenian odes, the tender story of Apollo's wooing in the Ninth Pythian and that exquisite phrase in the Fifth which calls the city "sweet garden of Aphrodite," when we reflect

that in a later age the philosophic school of Aristippus,[37] if
nothing else, bears witness to the social freedom and deep
respect enjoyed by the ladies of Cyrene, we shall think it
likely that Pindar has here written what would have been
understood by few in Thebes or Aegina or Syracuse, but was
understood to the last word and ardently acclaimed in that
remote outpost of Hellas.

VIEWS ON THE LIFE OF MAN

THE PRECEDING LECTURE was an attempt to describe what I called Pindar's vision of the world. Now let us consider his views on the life of man. The shape of that phrase has some importance. "Vision," and "views": both words derived from the same Latin word, yet how divergent in sense—for all of us, for poets more than any! The Wordsworth who wrote his vision near Tintern Abbey sat far from the Wordsworth who held views on the first Reform Bill. Again: "the life of man": is not that rather loose or amateurish? Why not announce, with crispness and a touch of academic pomp, "Pindar's Religion, Ethics, Sociology, and Politics?" For two reasons. First, those interests of humanity cannot be studied apart in any Greek who lived earlier than the fourth century before Christ. Secondly, Pindar baffles us, even more than any other among early writers, by his pronouncements on these topics. You will be disappointed to find the present lecture largely negative: for my task is, in the main, to exhibit a tangle of contradiction and prejudice; to show (as exactly as may prove to be within my power) the reasons for this tangle; and to adumbrate the shape of chaos. All who are fascinated by the history of human thought and civilization examine with natural eagerness the doctrines expounded or implied by Greek poets, philosophers, orators, and historians; but Pindar, though a mighty poet, has here little importance.[1] My aim is to prove this at least, in order to save others unneeded pains.

An adequate yet lucid abstract of Pindar's expressed views concerning the divine nature and government, human life, happiness, and death is not merely difficult to make, but impossible. The cause of this must be sought in the civilization, and in the particular phase of culture, wherein he grew and worked. The Athenian Age of Enlightenment had not yet dawned. Even the Ionian spirit of his own day was foreign to

him: his great rival Simonides,[2] for instance, showed much
greater intellectual power and clarity of ethical expression.
From the scientific thought of his own day he turned with
dislike and contempt. Stobaeus[3] reports that his phrase "they
pluck wisdom's fruit while yet unripe" was directed against
the students of nature. Pindar was as much behind the times
in science as in politics: one can hardly believe that he lived
and wrote a whole century later than both Solon and Thales.
Yet one editor could write: "In every department of intellectual and aesthetic culture, mighty waves of progress kept
rolling over Hellas in the first half of the fifth century B.C.,
communicating irresistible impulses to a man of Pindar's
genius and temperament."[4] That monstrously misleading sentence exemplifies our modern passion to "trace influences"
and arrange genealogical trees of poetry. The Ninth Paean
shows that Pindar knew no more than a savage about solar
eclipses, though Thales had explained them.[5] In another fragment he avers that the Nile-flood is caused by a statue six
hundred feet high, moving its feet.[6] He is so sure that the
Pillars of Heracles—what we call the Straits of Gibraltar—
mark the limit of western navigation that he uses them to
typify the bounds impassable to human enterprise;[7] yet his
younger contemporary Herodotus knew of many who had
sailed through them. We shall never appreciate Pindar if we
think of him as of Goethe, who in his study at Weimar read
everything, heard everything, that was passing in Europe
and corresponded with, or was visited by, countless significant and attractive people, from Napoleon the First down to
the latest budding poet or diplomatist. But even more momentous than ignorance about mere facts, or even about
scientific method, was the lack of mental training, of conscious and definite intellectual discipline, which hampered all
Greeks born before the Sophistic Age. He was unable to do
what became easy enough two generations later: namely, to
form concerning religion, sociology, ethics, and politics a body
of ideas which, however mistaken or insufficient, was yet coherent and defensible. His mental state was such that we can

hardly describe it, still less enter into it: we contemplate a man of poetic genius, glorious yet steadily controlled imagination, perfectly trained for his profession, who nevertheless did not know how to think, in the full sense of apprehending, marshalling, coördinating facts and beliefs about them.

To discuss Pindar's views in our own day is, then, to employ a language, ruled by logic and destined to the systematization of facts, concerning a man who was logical only by fits and starts; whose power to correlate truths or views was rudimentary and rarely applied; who, being destitute of the scientific temper, overlooked crude inconsistencies in the doctrines that he from time to time propounded. Homer, his predecessor, we never regard as a thinker at all; Euripides, forty years later than Pindar, was clearly a conscious and adroit philosopher; but here stands a poet in whose work constructive thought stirs indeed, yet only in embryo. Into the world of radiant myth a breath of intelligence has stolen: he feels dimly the eternal truth that man must understand life or perish, and seeks half instinctively to transform emotions into ideas. What are we to do with him, we who could not write[8] a line of these odes but whom twenty-four centuries of mental experience have endowed with a skill, which he would have looked on as superhuman, in the manipulation of facts, fancies, theories, and their conglomerations?

The usual method has been somewhat ludicrous, recalling those agile Lilliputians who swarmed over the bound and recumbent body of Gulliver. We advance upon Pindar with brains full of logic, ethics, anthropology, and Heaven knows what, saying: "Let us draw up a report on the system of doctrine inherent in the productions of this remarkable stranger!" We work over him until we evolve an intelligible and coherent conspectus, which, however, the poems as they stand, if read with an open mind, invariably refute in whole or in part. Here we have to face the authority of Professor Werner Jaeger, the most recent scholar to offer a systematization, who in *Paideia* deals with whatever alleged aspects of Pindar seem relevant to his own subject: namely, Pindar as an educator,[9] a description of him which I at least cannot accept. Jaeger discovers "a whole system of philosophy" in his remarks concerning ancestry and the changes of merit and fortune in the succeeding generations of noble families.[10] What system? Pindar's remarks (apart from his poetic magnificence, which, though beyond praise, is quite another affair) are the baldest truisms, such as that in the Sixth Nemean (vv. 8–11), where Alcidamas brings glory to his family after a generation without fame, "like the fruitful ploughlands, which by turns now grant men copious livelihood from the plains, now again rest from bearing and gather strength." Jaeger's eloquent and striking discussion of the myths is no more convincing. Here is one typical passage. "His heroes are contemporary living and struggling men. He sets them in the mythical world . . . a world of ideal patterns, whose lustre beams over them and whose renown will as they strive exalt them to similar heights and arouse their best powers. That is what gives the use of myth in Pindar its special purport and value."[11] Wilhelm Schmid[12] also affirms this view that the myth is often presented so as to give Pindar's friends a pattern of conduct— "You have heard what Heracles did: imitate him." That is mere assumption without evidence, easy for even such admirable scholars to make, because we moderns know how we should set to work if (for instance) we wrote a lyric eulogizing some young clergyman and saw fit to adorn our poem with the story of St. Paul and the snake at Malta. We should say "Imitate St. Paul"; certainly not "St. Paul reminds me of you." But this latter corresponds to Pindar's normal intention, though (to be sure) he expresses it less crudely. For we must remember not only his usual attitude towards success in the Games, but also the fact that, save in one passage[13] alone, he drops not a hint of this notion about patterns found in the heroic age; and—perhaps even more notably—the Sixth Pythian[14] says, in so many words, that the hero of myth, Antilochus, resembles the athlete whom Pindar is now extolling. In any case, ethical system there is none to see, nor indeed does Jaeger here claim to find any, only a reason for a

single element in Pindar's work. He is far more cautious and
balanced than a good number of earlier scholars whose
tortured arguments, wanton assumptions, and astounding
results compose a dismal museum of sterile and repellent
monsters. We are told that such absurdities as the following
are Pindar's views. "Man is to conquer his fate."[15] If he does, it
cannot be fate: in any case, Pindar says nothing even faintly
like this. "It is a god who bestows virtue, and a god *who takes
it away*."[16] This assertion of something more diabolical than
any diabolism otherwise known to me is made by its inventor
the basis of his doctrine that Pindar has kinship with—of all
people on earth—Plato! "Power is identical with justice."[17]
That Pindar held no such frantic view is proved by I know
not how many passages. "Apollo teaches the philosophy of
the One and the Many."[18] Pindar, of course, knew no more
about this doctrine than he knew about the binomial theo-
rem; and Apollo, I conceive, was in like case.

These conclusions, and others only less surprising, would of
themselves raise suspicion that Pindar's ideas defy systematization; and unprejudiced scrutiny of his writings will prove
its impossibility. No specific attack upon any one doctrine or
statement of Pindar's is here intended. Some, to be sure, will
be dismayed by his worship of success, still more by his gibes
at those who fail[19]—though here I must interpolate that,
whatever he writes concerning the Games, he bestows majestic and poignant eulogies upon men who went down to heroic
defeat in battle. The epinician odes, despite notable exceptions, undoubtedly leave us, on the whole, with a superficial
and selfish conception of the good life.[20] But, again, such a
tone may be partly excused by the very nature of an epinician
ode and by a wish to delight the patron. In any case, my intention is not to display the superiority of your principles or
mine to Pindar's, not to dwell on his omission to define elementary moral ideas such as justice, or the extreme paucity
of his specific rules;[21] but to show that he had no system at all.

Let us drive straight at the heart of this, and point to his
most fatal irrationality—an ambiguous use of the word *areta*.

There are, perhaps in all languages, words that sum up root-ideas of the race which uses them, and are accordingly the translator's despair;[22] *areta* is one of these. It can best be translated "excellence," if we insist on one word. In philosophers it usually means "virtue"; in non-philosophic writers it may be moral excellence or any other, normally with an implication of beneficent potency. But we may spare ourselves travail over this elusive word, which in Pindar has only by fits any moral content. The point is that he uses it both of excellence[23] and of the success won thereby. Here are two examples on each side. In *Pythian* I 94 "the kindly *areta* of Croesus meets not death"; in *Olympian* VI 9 ff., "*aretae* untried by peril receive honour neither among men nor in hollow ships"—there is the "excellence" meaning. In *Olympian* VII 89, "a man who has won *areta* by boxing"; in *Nemean* V 52: "to win a double *areta* by victory in boxing and in the *pancration*"—there is the "success" meaning. A writer who uses the same word for merit and for success puts himself hopelessly out of court as an exponent of ethics.

And how, according to Pindar, does a man succeed? Here we stand at the very centre of Pindar's . . . the only word I can find is "brooding"—not thought or emotion or faith, but consciousness that man lives amid forces greater than he. Nothing could be more familiar than that sense: Homer has it, centuries before Pindar, and so has everyone else who can be called human. But Pindar uses language suggesting that he holds some definite answer to our question, language that apparently deceives the poet himself and has certainly deceived many students. In truth, his brooding (as I called it) and his statements are sadly muddled; let me offer the clearest description of this tangle which I have been able to produce.

He often names[24] three factors as needed for success, though he never[25] mentions all three as combined. One is *phua*, literally "nature"; in Pindar it means "good innate quality," and embraces both what we call "virtue" and what we call "talent" or "natural aptitude," whether of mind or of body.

Another factor of success is personal effort. Another is Heaven's grace—God causes us to win. What relation exists between these three? The connexion between *phua* and effort seems plain enough: they are the material and the use thereof, like the stones and the mason's labour which together produce a wall. What of Heaven's favour? We never hear in so many words that if it is added to the other two factors we must succeed, only that if it is not added we cannot succeed. Nevertheless we are compelled to assume the former proposition; for, if a man having all three elements does not necessarily succeed, it is impossible to tell what agency can thwart Heaven and make him fail, impossible to understand how anyone ever succeeds. Now: suppose two men, both possessing *phua*, both using effort, wrestle for a prize. A wins; and this, by the rule just stated, proves that A has God's grace (otherwise he would have lost), and that B has not God's grace (otherwise he would have won). Thus we behold two men, equal in other respects, on one of whom grace is bestowed, to the other of whom grace is denied. For the grant or refusal of this blessing no reason is, on the premises, conceivable:[26] that is, we know nothing about the divine favour except that it shows itself in the result. Therefore "divine favour" is merely a lofty periphrasis for "success": the man does in fact win and we therefore assume that he must have God's grace. And what we have said about the wrestling-match is true of more important and lengthier enterprises—of what we call success in life. His frequent phrase τύχα θεῶν— significantly hard to translate: "divine fortune" seems best— is then merely a pious flourish resulting not from theology or any other species of thought. It says nothing whatever about either God or man, being an empty phrase, useless except to prevent boastfulness in those who do not see through it.

Next, what of *phua?* We can know nothing about its quality, its quantity, even its existence, until it reveals itself in action. For instance, we must not infer it from ancestry, for the poet reminds us more than once that a man with no particular *phua* may spring from heroic stock;[27] though, it is important

to remark, if on the other hand he does possess *phua*, he de-
rives it from noble ancestors. So we observe a person succeeding after effort and for that reason only we assume his
phua, which thus appears as the moral analogue of "divine
fortune," and is brought in because of Pindar's preoccupation
with ancestry, just as Heaven's grace was brought in by his
instinctive piety. Once more, the whole position crumbles to
this, that some succeed while others fail! Still at a loss to
understand whereon success according to Pindar is based, we
turn to the third factor, effort; and learn that one may put
forth vigorous effort all to no purpose, because *phua* or divine
grace, or both, are lacking. In the Third Nemean (40 ff.) he
thus delivers himself: "Through inborn glory a man hath
mighty weight; but whoso hath acquired only instruction,[28]
dim light is his: now to this, now to that, his spirit turneth,
never doth he come forth with decisive step, but to no purpose
his heart tasteth of enterprises without number." There is
effort, and there its outcome, if inherited excellence of spirit
does not aid.

In the fascinating and varied legends of Greece Pindar
found one example of failure which profoundly impressed his
heart and imagination. Ajax[29] was not only conspicuous among
the heroes who fought at Troy, but also a member of that
family which Pindar delighted to eulogize beyond all others.
Yet his end was dreadful: nay, ignominious. After the death of
Achilles, he and Odysseus both laid claim to the weapons of
their comrade, as being next to him in desert. The Greek
army adjudged them to Odysseus, and Ajax in bitter disappointment slew himself. Why this collapse of so great glory?
Ajax had *phua*, his efforts were long-continued and heroic.
Does Pindar, then, allege that he lacked the favour of
Heaven? No—if only because such an explanation would
have been resented by the poet's friends and patrons. In this
particular case, forgetting all the fancies which we have
sought in vain to organize, he suddenly remembers a solution
which would apply in endless other instances of failure: the
power wielded by a dishonest opponent; for Odysseus, he

writes, gained the award by his cajoling eloquence. So the
base after all do often prosper—only for a time,[30] it is true;
but it cannot be said that the good have any advantage over
them here, for he repeatedly asserts that no mortal enjoys
lasting good fortune.[31]

At the outset we noted that in studying Pindar, perhaps
even more than in studying any other Greek of the great
ages, it is misleading to mark off separate departments such
as religion or politics. True; but you and I are modern people,
for whom clearness of head is, if not an achievement, at least
an aim. Therefore I cannot avoid saying at this point: "Let
us next consider the gods—their nature, conduct, and place
in the Universe, their dealings with man now and hereafter."
In Pindar's mind these topics are interwoven; and I shall be
forced to repeat some matters already discussed. Moreover,
his statements on religion and the future of the soul, though
more intelligible than those on ethics, contradict one another
even more sharply.

Nevertheless, we may open with a fact simple as well as
interesting. However we judge Pindar's doctrinal pronouncements, we can all see that he was a man of strong and genuine
religious *mood*, of piety. It has been admirably said that
"What matters is the quality of his concern with religion and
behaviour. If his disapproval seems capricious or his reme-
dies inadequate, it is because he was scarcely concerned with
a system of life, whether in theory or in practice."[32] His devotion to Delphi and its god was one of the two profoundest
and most enduring passions of his life. Beside his own house
he built a chapel dedicated to the Mother of the Gods and to
Pan.[33] Croiset[34] has noted that many details told of the gods
by Homer are quite alien to Pindar in spirit: we cannot (for
example) imagine his writing of Hephaestus' limp. Aeschylus
himself, though endowed with immensely more spiritual
depth, was no readier to revise current myths in the name
of edification.[35] The difference between them here is that,
whereas Aeschylus was a moral and intellectual reformer of
theology, Pindar's imagination was fired by the divine or

heroic figures that blazed in the verse of Homer, Hesiod, and Stesichorus; and he alters legend for the sake of τὸ καλόν, the noble and lovely, to keep the adored radiance undimmed.[36] In the First Olympian he proclaims his rejection of a traditional story as a slander upon the gods, offering a new version; and that is only the most celebrated instance. Theoretically inconsistent with this, but in temper appropriate, is the rebuke: "What hopest thou of wisdom, wherein but little, surely, one man availeth beyond another? Thou shalt find no way to search out the purposes of Heaven by human mind, that was born of a mortal mother."[37] Nevertheless, gods and men are akin, as we learn in the opening lines of the Sixth Nemean. "One is the race of men, one the race of gods, and from one mother we both draw breath. Yet an utter diversity of power sundereth us, so that one race is naught, while for the other Heaven's bronze abode endureth unshaken everlastingly. But none the less we draw near in some measure to the immortals by greatness of mind or form, although we know not the course that fate hath ordained we should run, whether in the day or in the hours of night."[38] Not only has he much to say concerning piety and worship: he thrills also to the gaiety and excitement attending upon religious celebrations. Dionysius of Halicarnassus has preserved[39] for us the opening of a dithyramb which summons the gods to holy revels. Here is Rhys Roberts' translation of the first lines:

> Shed o'er our choir, Olympian Dominations,
>> The glory of your grace,
> O ye who hallow with your visitations
>> The curious-carven place,
> The heart of Athens, steaming with oblations,
>> Wide-thronged with many a face.
> Come, take your due of garlands violet-woven,
> Of songs that burst forth when the buds are cloven.

Possibly the most extraordinary of Pindar's works is another dithyramb, or rather, a tattered portion[40] thereof, which after a vigorous remark on an early and, as he says, "spurious" pronunciation of the letter S, leaps at once to a wild and (to tell the truth) incredible picture of a carnival in Heaven itself. Everyone seems to be there, even the Naiads and Artemis, all celebrating a Dionysiac festival! Another scene in Heaven we know, unfortunately, by report alone.[41] Aristides the rhetorician writes that, according to Pindar, when Zeus, at his own wedding, asked the gods if they had any boon to ask, they begged him to create certain gods who should glorify in word and music his mighty achievements and all the frame of his creation. That reads like a prophecy of the archangels' song wherewith Goethe opens his *Faust*.

What is the relation between these heavenly powers and the Universe? Let us first speak of the "present world," discussing later the soul's destiny. Pindar asserts that man's life depends on divine government; but this doctrine is so familiar to us that we must here be especially on our guard against hasty assumptions and note precisely what it is that he says.

Dominion lies in the hands of a personal authority, entitled "God" ($\theta\epsilon\delta s$), or "gods" ($\theta\epsilon o\iota$), or, by the traditional name, Zeus, King of Heaven. A passage (vv. 49 ff.) in the Second Pythian proclaims his majesty and unchallengeable power, in language that recalls the Old Testament. "The Lord accomplisheth every purpose according to his desire. He overtaketh even the eagle upon the wing and passeth by the dolphin amid the waters. He hath bowed down the man of high stomach and upon another he bestoweth glory that waxeth not old." But we seldom[42] read of the material Universe in this connexion, never[43] of any jurisdiction over individual deities. We hear, in fact, three things only about the divine rule of our present life. First, as we noted earlier, success and happiness depend upon God's favour; and this (we saw), as presented by Pindar, means nothing. Second, our life is a system, not a chaos; but the evidence[44] justifying attribution of this doctrine to Pindar is meagre and disputable. A passage (vv. 25 ff.) in the Eighth Olympian implies, perhaps, that Aegina's justice reflects Heaven's justice;[45] and the close of the Second Pythian points, in my view, to a *régime* that embraces man-

kind.[46] Third, one sole passage declares plainly that in this
life God rewards righteousness as such, purely as a matter of
principle and with no reference at all to the personal comfort
or interests of an individual deity. That memorable pro-
nouncement occurs in the Fifth Nemean (vv. 32 ff.), where
Peleus rejected Hippolyta because (we are told) he dreaded
the anger of Zeus if he violated the laws of hospitality, and
the god, "noting it well," granted him the divine Thetis as
his bride. Elsewhere, the reason given for kindnesses conferred by individual gods upon men—such reason, however,
being seldom offered—is never righteousness. The man or
woman has kinship with the god, or has granted him some
boon: hospitality is mentioned, and what may be termed
love.[47]

Pindar thus stands far below his Athenian contemporary
Aeschylus in theological profundity, power, and clearness.
Nevertheless, a passage in his latest-written ode shows him
groping towards the concept of a universe morally governed.
The first three stanzas of the Eighth Pythian set us in presence of a religious apprehension that begins to feel its way
past the traditional names and figures of the Greek pantheon.

Daughter of Justice, gracious Tranquillity, whereby cities come
to greatness, thou that holdest the master-keys of war, accept the
glory that Aristomenes hath won by victory at Pytho. For thou
knowest how, at the due moment, to perform or to receive acts of
gentleness. But whenever one thrusts merciless rancour upon his
heart, thou sternly confrontest the might of thine enemies, and their
insolence falleth into the deep. And he, even Porphyrion, knew not
that it was thou whom he unrighteously assailed; but that profit is
best which a man taketh from the house of one who consenteth
thereto. Even the proud their own violence throweth down at the
last. Typhos, the hundred-headed Cilician, escaped it not, nor
the king of Giants: they were quelled by the thunderbolt and by
the arrows of Apollo.

Pindar, here touched by the belief, vivid throughout Aeschylus' tragedies, that the Universe is governed, and governed by
a moral Power, conceives this Power as some kind of person,

as possessing (that is) emotions and will in addition to a rule
or standard of government: hence the personification of Tranquillity and the surprising description of her nature. The history of Greek religion offers few more exciting moments than
this, if we observe precisely how far Pindar moved towards
creating, like Aeschylus, a new theology. Zeus and Apollo
here, and here only, in his works, are subsidiary to this new
goddess Hesychia, or Tranquillity—to this extent, that,
whereas she is said to overthrow *hubris* or Insolence, in general, they overthrow its exponents, the giants Porphyrion and
Typhos. She is, quite exactly, a "spirit," whereof Zeus and
Apollo are representative. But the poet never says so much:
only if we study his language and state with modern precision
what he suggests, do we arrive at so striking a dogma; and we
are especially to mark that he refuses, almost in so many
words, to accept that dogma firmly, for though he mentions
Apollo by name, he will not mention Zeus, but only his
weapon—"they were quelled by the thunderbolt and by
Apollo's shafts." This passage, then, permits us an exact conception of the difference between Pindar and Aeschylus in
theological boldness and mental clarity.[48]

But all this, the momentous and engaging outcome of an
instinctive piety and a sense of righteousness irrational (however strong), meets repeated contradiction when the poet
deals with legends or popular doctrine which irrational instinct, again, induces him to accept. Gods as individuals perform, without censure from him, actions which he condemns
in men. Whereas murder is deplored even when committed by
his favourite Aeginetans,[49] Apollo causes the death of Coronis'
innocent neighbours without evoking a censorious word; but
the god suddenly becomes very tender of the guiltless when
his own unborn child is threatened in the course of the same
affair (*Pyth.* III 36 ff.). Zeus intervenes in the Tenth Nemean
with what we should call shameless injustice.[50] What does
Pindar call it? He first broadly hints[51] that Castor and Polydeuces (whom Zeus aided) were in the wrong, but after the
god has thrown omnipotence into the scale we find only this

comment: "whoso striveth with his betters will regret the meeting." In the First Nemean, Hera seeks to destroy the baby Heracles, and comment there is none. As for sexual morality, it cannot in fact be said that the standard set for mankind is higher than the standard applied to gods, because the latter does not exist. Hippolyta receives censure for her conduct toward Peleus (*Nem.* V 52 ff.), Coronis for her amour with Ischys (*Pyth.* III 11 ff.), Clytaemnestra for the murder of her husband which sprang from adultery (*Pyth.* XI 17 ff.); but gods indulge themselves without stint or blame,[52] the chief instance being Zeus' amour with Alcmena, a uniquely atrocious affair (as we should say) on which Pindar thrice[53] dwells fondly, in one place citing it among the glories of Theban history. Gods, as individuals, never right any wrongs that are not directed against themselves: they stand for nothing at all except their own comfort, rank, and privileges, exactly like the Dorian nobles eulogized by Pindar, who were not leaders in any spiritual or moral sense. Here I cannot refrain from pausing to remark once more how woefully scholars have been led astray by their insistence on reading into him moral or theological ideas familiar elsewhere. Coppola[54] describes Ixion, Coronis, Asclepius, and Tantalus as examples not only "of the truth" (whatever that may mean) but also "of God's awful justice," although not a syllable of this can be found in Pindar, who on the contrary tells us at each incident, save perhaps in the case of Asclepius, that the wrongdoer had annoyed the particular deity by encroaching on his privileges.

By one legend Pindar is confessedly disconcerted: for a moment he realizes the mental and moral chaos which we are studying. One of Heracles' labours was to steal the herd of Geryon, a giant dwelling in Spain, and drive it back, undiminished, to his taskmaster in Greece. Two fragments deal with this story. One is quoted in a passage of Plato's *Gorgias*, where Callicles uses it to prove the right of the strong over the weak: the first phrase was quoted more often in antiquity than any other that Pindar wrote. To this we should join

another fragment, which (as the metre shows) belongs to another poem; but that for our purpose matters nothing. The
whole compound,[55] then, goes something like this. "Custom,
the king of all mortals and immortals, leadeth on the extreme
of violence with a high hand, justifying it. This I gather from
the deeds of Heracles; for to the giant-built portal of Eurys-
theus he drove the kine of Geryon, taking them without
prayer or price. . . . Thee, O Geryon, I praise compared with
him; howbeit, let me keep utter silence concerning what Zeus
doth not prefer." Here theological and moral bankruptcy
finds plain avowal. Heracles being a son of Zeus, whatever he
does must be called just though we know it is unjust.

In that age there was a strong belief in the spite, the φθόνος,
of Heaven. This should be distinguished from the personal
annoyance felt, and revenge exacted, by a specific deity for a
specific offence, as when Athena, vexed by the sauciness of
Arachne, who claimed to spin better than the goddess, transformed the girl into a spider. No: the *phthonos* doctrine was
even more discouraging: divine power, "Heaven" as we say,
"the god" as Greeks often said, punishes and destroys notable
eminence or success among mankind, not because of any sin
or foolishness, but automatically. This view is trenchantly
set forth by the Persian Artabanus in Herodotus. "Do you
observe that God blasts exalted creatures and does not suffer
them to be shown forth, but what is petty does not gall him?
And that it is always upon the largest buildings and the
tallest trees that he hurls his thunderbolts? God is wont to
curtail all eminence . . . for he suffers no other save himself to
be proud."[56] Now, Pindar twice endorses this belief, once in
his earliest poem, the Tenth Pythian (vv. 20 f.), written when
he was twenty years old, the other in the Seventh Isthmian
(vv. 30 ff.), when he had passed sixty. But we must not over-
emphasize these two widely sundered utterances. Each is
merely a brief prayer: "These people have high fortune: may
Heaven's spite not pounce upon them." Pindar is but quoting, unwisely as we may think, a popular belief.

Concerning the forces that govern human life, only one

further remark seems needed. Again and again he says or implies that whatever happens to man is due to an impersonal State of Things named *moira* or *potmos* or *tyche*, regarded sometimes as a definite agency (whether identified or not with Heaven's will), sometimes as a brief rendering of the fact that the future is hidden. The first idea we may call Fate, the second the Inscrutable. Let us see examples. First, the definite agency identified with Heaven's will: "they came, not without the gods, but some *moira* led them" (*Pyth.* V 76). Second, the definite agency not identified with Heaven's will: "Whatever excellence Lord *potmos* has granted me, the course of time will bring to fruition" (*Nem.* IV 42). Third, the inscrutable: in the Eighth Isthmian (v. 36) destiny, τὸ πεπρωμένον, actually defeats the wishes of gods—Zeus and Poseidon; in the Sixth Paean we read that Troy was bound to fall, and that "Zeus dared not cancel fate."[57] Pindar, in fact, imbibed from popular superstition and talk the virus of that most dangerous and common error, to sum up a collection of facts under a proper name and then suppose that mention of the name accounts for the facts thus summarized. The most familiar example is Fortune, whose immense vogue stands high among the achievements of stupidity. Though nothing more than a convenient name for the fact that we do not know what is to happen, it has been elevated by countless writers into an authentic Person *with a power over human life*. Many, including Pindar, though they have not always definitely personified the unknown future, have yet accepted the error for which the personification stands, namely, that Fortune, Destiny, Doom, Chance are separate from events and have power over them. Again and again in the odes we come upon this night of the intelligence. The Second Olympian proclaims (vv. 35 ff.) that Moira *brings* joy blent with sorrow: the absurd distinction, between what befalls us and the quasi-deification of what befalls us, is complete and emphatic. Apart from certain virtues of language, the sentence has less than no value: it conveys nothing beyond the familiar tidings that prosperity is not permanent, that sooner or later things change; and its verbal elaboration sets up a pernicious semblance of knowledge. The First Isthmian, after telling us that Asopodorus was wrecked on the boundless main, proceeds: "but now again his natal star hath set his feet in the way of his old prosperity."[58] A moment's thought about this "natal star" will dissolve it like vapour. We are simply not told *how* Asopodorus regained his original prosperity: Pindar infers that the man was "born lucky." In *Pythian* XII 30, "the fateful is beyond shunning" must be thought inferior even to *che sarà sarà*, because the pretentious wording may persuade the unwary that something has been said.

Concerning the soul and its destiny Pindar has left us passages[59] that are among the most beautiful and impressive that he, or indeed any other pagan, ever wrote. A little while ago we heard verses from the Sixth Nemean where to men is attributed kinship with the gods. That idea receives more vigorous expression in this fragment of a dirge: "The body of all men is subject unto o'ermastering death; but the wraith of him that lived endureth yet alive, for that alone cometh from the gods. It sleepeth while the limbs are active; but while we sleep it showeth in many dreams the oncoming judgment of bliss and woe."[60] The soul's immortality had long been a familiar doctrine, but Pindar was the first to explain it by a divine origin.[61] Of the judgment after death which those last words foreshadow, an august picture is given by the Second Olympian,[62] where for the first time in European literature we hear the tremendous doctrine that reward and punishment for the deeds of earthly life are meted out in another, on a principle moral and moral only.

Wicked spirits of the dead forthwith pay here the penalty, and one below the earth judgeth sins done in this realm of Zeus, delivering the account with hostile rigour. But the righteous, alike in the night-watches and by day, possess the sun for ever, receiving a life that hath less trouble. They vex not earth with the strength of their hands, or the sea-waters, for an empty livelihood: nay, those who rejoiced in keeping their oath pass a tearless life beside honoured gods; the others bear a load of suffering whereon the eye dwelleth not. All who have endured, for three sojourns on either side, to keep their souls utterly from injustice, traverse the highway of Zeus to Cronos' tower. There ocean-breezes are wafted round the island of the blessèd; and golden flowers blaze, some on land from shining trees, and others the water nourisheth, with garlands whereof they entwine hands and brows amid the just counsels of Rhadamanthys, whom the mighty Father keepeth as a ready helper seated beside his throne.

Another fragment from the dirges also depicts the blessed.

Upon them below the earth shineth the sun's power, while with us is night. In meadows of scarlet roses lie their city's outskirts, shaded by frankincense, heavy with golden fruits. Some take their pleasure in horses and bodily feats, some in chess-play, some in the harp, and among them perfect bliss gloweth ever in flower. Fragrance is spread over that delightful region everlastingly as they mingle all kinds of incense upon the altars of the gods amid flame that shineth afar.[63]

Into the details of Pindar's eschatology this is not the place to enter, especially as in a later lecture we shall return to the Second Olympian and the cycle of lives.[64] These and other passages are based upon doctrines taught by the religion, or religions, of "mystery," as it was called—a revealed religion, a personal way of life, distinct from the state-cults which appear far more frequently in Greek literature. It is from a Father of the Church, Clement of Alexandria, that we know Pindar's words concerning the blessedness of initiation into the mysteries: "Happy is he who hath seen them before he goeth below the earth! He knoweth the end of life; he knoweth its god-sent beginning."[65]

But, whether the reason for these visions of eternity is or is not a momentary assumption of doctrines favoured by the patron for whom he writes,[66] we must recognize that elsewhere he strangely forgets this awful radiance which beams upon his page from the confines of the Universe. In another mood he proclaims that the only reward after death for righteousness is fame. The Tenth Olympian asserts that, if a man has wrought fair deeds but dies without the glory con-

ferred by song, his effort is empty and the joy that he has
gained lasts but a fleeting moment.[67] Our condition beyond
the grave is shadowy and negative: nothing happens to us
except that our "dim mind" receives news of honour won by
our descendants, as he says concerning Cyrene's buried
kings.[68] We remember those poignant words in the Eighth
Pythian: "Creatures of a day, what are we? What are we not?
The dream of a shadow, such is Man. But when God bestoweth radiance, then a glory resteth upon us, and days of
pleasantness." All we may hope is a splendid hour. The
Eleventh Nemean (13 ff.) gives yet gloomier warning: "If a
man hath prosperity and surpasseth another in beauty and
showeth forth his might by gaining the prize of contests, let
him remember that he arrayeth himself in mortal limbs and
shall at the end of all assume a garment of earth."

My ungrateful and invidious task, of exhibiting a great
poet's incoherence and irrationality in theological and moral
doctrine, can now be closed, by citation of two notable passages.[69] They show his thought just as it unfolds and allow us
to surprise him (as it were) in the act of failing to disentangle
ideas. We have already noted the story of Peleus in the Fifth
Nemean. There Pindar is beyond reproach: with no fumbling
he tells us that Peleus avoided adultery because he feared
God's anger, and that God because of this rewarded him. But
examine the story as told in the Eighth Isthmian. Peleus belongs to the Aeacids, splendid warriors who are also "chaste
and discreet of heart" (v. 28). "These things the blessèd gods
also remembered in their council" ... and so Thetis was given
to Peleus as "most pious" (v. 44). Thus far, the Isthmian
agrees with the Nemean; but here the whole matter springs
from personal desires of Zeus and Poseidon, each wishing to
marry Thetis. Had there been no domestic trouble in Heaven,
Peleus and his virtue would never have been thought of.
Here, then, is to be discerned a blend of the moral-govern-
ment idea with a conception of deities no less absorbed than
men in their personal concerns.

Another instance of such imperfect development can be

found in the Fourth Pythian (90 ff.), where, indeed, suspicion may arise that the language is purposely ambiguous. "The speedy arrow of Artemis hunted down Tityos, so that one should set his desire on embracing love which lieth within his power." That is hard to translate fairly, because it contains a rather pleasant but also rather baffling manipulation—shall we say juggling?—of idiom. It can be, and on the face of it surely is, one more report of divine action prompted only by personal reasons, not by a zeal for morals in general. Most of Pindar's audience would find nothing more than the sense: "Artemis slew him to thwart and punish his lustful attempt." Such use of a purpose-clause attached to mention of punishment can be paralleled easily:[70] they correspond to our colloquial threat: "I'll teach you to"—do something already done, which we threaten to punish. Nevertheless, Pindar does say "one," which, though in Greek often used with allusion only to the particular person concerned, admits the possibility of taking the clause in a non-rhetorical sense; that is, as a real purpose-clause, meaning that the goddess slew Tityos so as to provide a moral lesson for all mankind. We must not dogmatically assert that Pindar meant only one[71] of these two things: here again is confusion of two ideas, a deity's private revenge and a deity's championship of righteousness.

Quo semel est imbuta recens . . . The most alert and original thinker never frees himself from all the unreason, all the inconsistencies, cherished in early years: some dogmas remain unchallenged because unconscious; and Pindar combined with poetic genius a capacity to retain prepossessions, despite all shocks and all evidence, which would have made even Samuel Johnson shake his head. We are not to wish him otherwise, for such things add pungency to his work.

Of sociology and politics it is even truer than of religion and ethics that Pindar's views—vigorous though not profound—cannot be discussed under the two heads separately without a frigid and misleading schematization. The two subjects must, of course, merge in any case; for him, they so merge as to form practically one. You will recall the Fourth Pythian, an ode

written to persuade King Arcesilas of Cyrene that he should
permit an exiled noble to return home. In the final stanzas,
social and political ideas are inextricably mingled: a state
shaken by discord, good-fellowship, slander, last-ditch politi-
cians, opportunism, drinking-parties, music, political quiet-
ism. That is but the strongest evidence of a spirit which
appears repeatedly: we must, then, follow Pindar's cast of
mind. Fortunately we shall meet here rarely or never the
self-contradiction that baffles us in our study of his religion
and ethics.

He shared without misgiving the interests and standards of
those kings, despots, and land-owning nobles for whom almost exclusively his odes were composed, whereas the democratic city of Athens claims but two brief and undistinguished
items in this collection. Pindar's loyalty, both instinctive and
conscious, clung to an order that was losing ground in the life
of Greece: he loved the old pieties and traditions of quiet rural
folk, oligarchical in their government, who found in military
and athletic distinction enough to gratify ambition or pride.[72]
Here certain misunderstandings may easily arise, which it is
important to dissipate. First, it may be objected that, since
we possess little save his epinicians, we cannot expect to gain
a full view of his interests: taking in hand to celebrate a
boxer's or a wrestler's or a charioteer's success, he extols
prize-winning more loudly than he might in his paeans, dirges,
or dithyrambs; when his patron commands great wealth and
influence, it need mean little if he dilates on those advantages
with frequency and rapture. Second, it may with even greater
cogency be remarked that his other works, fragmentary as
they now are, present another picture. In addition to the religious fragments already noted, and the tender play of emotion, more frequent in these half-lost poems than in the
epinician odes, who can forget the noble praise of that democracy which led Greece in its battles for liberty? At Artemisium, he says, "the sons of the Athenians laid the glorious
foundation-stone of freedom";[73] and the most celebrated fragment of all salutes her thus: "O glistening city, violet-crowned,

dear to song, bulwark of Hellas, famous Athens, haunted by divine presences!"[74] The conclusion from all this lies near to hand, that he not only did his best (as was inevitable and proper) to sympathize with those for whom he wrote, but also deliberately feigned unquestioning enthusiasm for their prejudices. A good deal was said about this in the first lecture; and no sincere critic can fail to set beside the fragment about Geryon and convention the notably outspoken advice to a youth, that he must imitate—as we should put it—the chameleon: "My son, with whatever city thou consortest, let thy mind resemble the skin of the sea-beast on its rock: cheerfully accepting circumstance, let thy thought alter as occasion bids."[75] All this has truth and importance; nevertheless we shall find it easy to learn whereon Pindar's heart is really set if we read him with an open mind, allowing his spirit to work upon us, and above all if we note advice or comment which, being on the face of it irrelevant, must reveal his true mind, as in the great passage of the First Pythian where he urges Hiero to grant his newly founded city a Dorian constitution; and the enthusiasm of his earliest ode for "worthy governments wielded by the high-born, generation after generation."[76] It cannot be gainsaid that far the most pervasive and important of his social and political interests is devotion to the ideals and method of life followed by that old nobility to which he himself belonged.[77] He proclaims the divine right of aristocracy.

Pindar's beliefs are based, here as elsewhere, not upon coördinated principles, but upon what is in fact done, or traditionally stated to have been done, by people whom, because of his temperament, upbringing, and personal concerns, he happens to admire.[78] Though ever insistent that his friends' wealth and power be rightly used, he shows no inclination to discuss the methods by which they were acquired; though Herodotus reports that the great Aeginetan fortunes were made by swindling the helots who pilfered and sold what they could of the immense loot gained by the victory over Persia at Plataea.[79] He is prone to judge the fruit by the tree. Be-

tween the gods and the nobles of his own day he observes
differences great, indeed, but less than they have ever been in
the view of any other civilized man. That grave and stately
ode, the Sixth Nemean, where Achilles and Memnon move
closer to us than the sturdy athletes not long dead, begins
(you will remember) in austere grandeur with a proclamation
that gods and men are one race, drawing the breath of life
from the same mother. Despite the vast superiority of the
gods in power, despite their immortality, Pindar discerns an
unbroken, though steeply descending, line of existence and
glory that stretches from Zeus or Poseidon to the Aeginetan
victor of yesterday: "as if (says Pater) the actual roads on
which men walk, went up and on, into a visible wonderland."[80]
Why not, if his friends are literally god-descended? To grasp
this unfamiliar thought, we need but try to imagine Aeschylus
relating, as Pindar relates, that Heracles faced three con-
federate deities in combat.[81] Assuredly he thought a youth,
beautiful, well-born, and bathed in glory won at the Games,
comparable with Hector or Heracles and so (at however great
a distance) with Apollo. That may explain why he consist-
ently omits the, to us, obvious admonition that the youth
should take Heracles as his model: he belongs by right of
birth to that shining brotherhood. Had we all kept these
ideas in mind, less surprise would have been aroused by the
Sixth Pythian, where a lad who showed loyalty to his father
in some matter of charioteering is compared to Antilochus,
who before Troy laid down his life in defence of his father
Nestor.[82]

How wide a gulf yawns here between Pindar and Homer,
the men of whose day are utterly outshone by the heroes that
besieged windy Troy! When Hector advances to burst open
the gates of the Greek camp, he snatches up a boulder "which
not two men, the best in the village, could easily have heaved
up onto their waggon from the ground—such men as live
now: but he tossed it lightly single-handed."[83] Pindar por-
trays the unity of glorious present with glorious past—equally
glorious, he would fain believe, despite King Pausanias' ven-

geance upon the poet's native Thebes, despite the Athenian
subjugation of his beloved Aegina, because the salvation of
Greece at Salamis and the wrestling-prize at Pytho are alike
illumined by the one joy worth supreme effort: by αἴγλα (that
is his great word), "radiance"—almost what we mean by
"halo." An astounding failure in perspective, true; but shared
by many. An Olympian festival was celebrated during the
very days when Xerxes was marching into Central Greece
and the allied fleet falling back from Artemisium.[84] There are
phrases in the Fifth Isthmian[85] which can be understood only
if we believe that Pindar, at any rate for the moment, sets
athletic success on a level with the victory at Salamis; and
Marathon, which he mentions thrice,[86] was for him nothing
but a centre of athletic contests. Who shall discern limits to
the lethal stupidity of a long-dominant class whose education
has been moulded to suit, not to correct, their prejudices? In
the struggle against Persia, Thebes had covered herself with
infamy, siding with the invader and actually fighting against
Greece at Plataea. Small wonder that her poet speaks faintly
and ambiguously! But in the Eighth Isthmian (vv. 6 ff.), to
our relief, he utters nobler language, though still in sorrow
and doubt: "We are freed from mighty griefs . . . some god
hath averted from us the stone of Tantalus that hung over
our heads." Then he turns back to his never-failing joy, the
praise of gymnastic prowess.

In this devotion to his own class and their chosen forms of
achievement he is haughtily serene and free from misgiving.
Euripides sneered at athletes as "ornaments of the piazza,"[87]
and Pindar would have thought that excellent, if too curt.
Xenophanes complained that such pursuits "do not fatten
the public treasury."[88] "Why should they?" Pindar would
ask. These men exist beautifully: it is they who make the city
splendid; without them, whether the treasury was empty or
crammed, it would be a scene of brisk squalour. He feels no
temptation to conciliate the ordinary citizen by spurious
addenda like the English journalist's praise of a duke as
"democratic" because he resembles the artisan in his excite-

ment about pugilism or horse-racing. (It would be just as
sensible to call the artisan "aristocratic.") He loves the noble-
man for his lineage and his instincts, with no pretence that
he has once in his life done anything for his lowly fellow-
citizens save permit them to bask in the radiance of his
achievement.[89] It is a curious fact, proceeding from the poet's
own austere avoidance of material detail no less than the
spareness of Greek life as compared with the modern, that,
for all his admiration and loyalty, Pindar nowhere developes
a picturesque background for these beautiful triumphant
figures[90] corresponding to that painted by modern writers,
particularly the English. Here are no stately homes with
echoing corridors, panelled dining-rooms, gracious lawns and
sunken rose-gardens, no rich and powerful public-school tradition:[91] and nothing which, however different, could evoke
similar emotions.

Vast changes were coming in Pindar's day, and coming fast:
he was the prophet of ideals that vanished as he sang, and
lived to see the Athenian *demos* attain the height of glory,
wealth, dominion, and self-confidence. In Athens, "patriot-
ism" had taken on a meaning which he could barely understand, certainly not accept. He thought himself a patriot; and
some might hold that he was justified therein, since, no less
than Aristides himself, he was all for the *polis*, the city-state,
which had given him birth, education, ideals, and a religion.
But the vital difference lay here, that his affection for oligarchy enabled him to identify his country (as we should call
it) with his own class. As Coppola remarks: "for him a free
state is one where the power is in the hands of the nobles."[92]
That is why the multitude never comes to life in his poems as
an assemblage of real persons. Despite his unforgettable praise
of Athens as freedom's bulwark against Persia, he had no love
for democratic principles. Nor, despite his friendship with the
princes of Sicily, did he love monarchy. His most notable
comment on political life occurs in the Eleventh Pythian,
where (be it observed) sociology and ethics are as much in
view as politics. Let me for once offer a paraphrase in our

modern terms. "Of all classes in the state, I find that the
bourgeoisie enjoys the greatest prosperity. The life of monarchs
offends me. My heart is set on the communal virtues, which
keep envy at arm's length. If a man avoids arrogance by
quietly seeking eminence in those virtues, and those only, he
will end his life in happiness and leave his children the best
legacy, a good reputation."

So much, then, for Pindar's views, or prejudices, about God
and man. His maxims deserve serious attention only when
considered each for the moment in its special context: quite
apart from their truth or falsity, they cannot be organized
into a body of doctrine or even into coherence of prejudice,
save where they show his affection for land-owning aristocracy. But even if we appraise them in isolation, we must
not attribute to them remarkable potency. There is less than
nothing in the notion that they are "keys" to the myths
wherein they occur.[93] Occasionally, no doubt, we understand
a particular passage better if we observe the aphorism and if
we also possess the contemporary facts that caused the poet
to moralize. But to grasp a mass of writing intellectually
differs altogether from appreciating a poem; and in Pindar
the latter has a thousand times more value. Anyone who followed Dissen[94] would be prepared to use Canterbury Cathe-
dral as a storehouse of obsolete passports; for these maxims
are uniformly trite and obvious. But they were not trite to
Pindar's contemporaries, or to Pindar himself? That may be;
and granting for the sake of argument that the poet supposed
the value of his myth to lie in exposition of the aphorism
which introduces or closes it, that possibility affects nothing
except his status as a critic. Morality does not make great
poetry, or poetry at all. Greatness resides in his rendering of
glories won today or long ago, to which the aphorism is no
more a key than the stairway by which we enter a picture-
gallery is the key to Botticelli's "Birth of Venus" or Turner's
"Crossing the Brook." Greatness may reside too in the language, not the matter, of the aphorism itself: Perrotta writes
concerning that noble passage in the Second Pythian where

the might of God is said to outstrip the eagle and the dolphin: "So vigorous an assertion is no longer a maxim: it is a sentiment."[95] Precisely! Pindar's genius works by imagination and feeling.

That is to say, he is a poet. Does any poet think at all while actually making poetry, not discussion in verse? What intellectual quality inheres in his work results from his training and experience—his verse is grammatical, because he has been to school; it declares the Alps more majestic than the Laurentian Mountains, because he has travelled. But his poetry, the quality in which the work differs from prose, is not intellectual and cannot be intellectual, for it springs from emotion caused by spiritual insight and governed by imagination. His relation to the world within and without him resembles not the relation of an astronomer to the stars, but the relation of a saint to God. It is possible to prove the astronomer mistaken by the use of mathematics: it is impossible to prove the saint wrong by the use of theology. Pindar, in some ways unparalleled, is here at one with all the genuine poets that ever sang. Some things which he wrote are utterly obsolete and were never of great value. His poetry endures; because, like all poetry, it outsoars the region where obsolescence has its reasons and its meaning.

It is right, then, that we should at once remind ourselves of a poem where, passing far beyond Dorian political notions, he has produced the noblest example of Dorian poetry ever written, the myth of the Tenth Nemean. No doubt, as we remarked a few moments ago, the intervention of Zeus in the combat should be condemned as unrighteous. But we are now to contemplate the whole story in another mood, the emotion evoked by grave beauty of language and by the sublimity of Polydeuces' choice, which raised up his dying brother to share his immortality. Even Pindar has nowhere else attained this perfection of austere beauty, the counterpart in verse of those Aeginetan marbles which hold for ever the exquisite brief moment when rigour passes into plain yet heroic dignity. With the simplest language and a strong majestic

rhythm he creates an awful loveliness; the straightforward
tale by miracle takes on sublimity. Could human language be
more frugal than that which describes the epiphany of Zeus?

ὣς ἔννεπε· Ζεὺς δ'
ἄντιος ἤλυθέ οἱ,
καὶ τόδ' ἐξαύδασ' ἔπος· Ἐσσί μοι υἱός . . .

"Thus he spake; and Zeus came unto him face to face and
uttered this word: 'Thou art my son . . .' " When the smok-
ing thunderbolt crashes down, and Idas with his brother dies,
we find an unsurpassed example of that rare achievement,
grandeur evoked by the plainest phrase: ἅμα δ'ἐκαίοντ' ἐρῆμοι,
"together in the wilderness they were consumed by fire." *E
solo in parte vidi il Saladino.* Though their antagonists were
thus destroyed, one of the Twin Brethren fell mortally
wounded, and the climax of the story is Polydeuces' loyalty
to his dying brother—loyalty in a situation even stranger and
more distracting than some have realized. For Polydeuces
believes that he himself (like Castor) is mortal,[96] prays that in
this hour he may find the death which one day must overtake
him, and laments his plight as a mortal bereft of a faithful
friend. Then comes the revelation "thou art my son," and
the strange secret of his own and his brother's begetting,
which on a sudden reveal to Polydeuces that Heaven is his
for the asking, while Castor, gasping at his feet, will soon
depart for ever below the earth—unless the choice is taken of
one day's death and one day's life for both in everlasting
alternation. At this moment of confused heartbreak and dazzling wonder the hero takes his decision without a pause.

Greater love was not known in Greek legend, or greater
loyalty.

TECHNIQUE IN CONSTRUCTION AND NARRATIVE

Having dealt as faithfully and lucidly as we could with Pindar's remarks about what we call religion, politics, sociology, and ethics, so as to make sure that these spectres will not haunt us, as they have haunted so many of his admirers, and distract us when concerned with the only thing about him that matters—to wit, his art,—let us go on to the various facets or elements of his poetical technique: here too in no spirit of pseudo-science, but, by scrutiny and—so far as that is feasible—analysis, to deepen our enjoyment of his work. It was in order to secure this frame of mind that we glanced earlier at one of the simplest among his supreme achievements, the Fourth Pythian. In all these questions of technique we must have recourse to scholarly research alone; for the poets, who might have aided us much, give little help. Even Goethe, so immensely competent, does nothing for us here. Coleridge, fine poet, acute critic, admirable scholar as he was, has nevertheless made but one remark of value, and even that has been offered independently by a foreign *savant*.[1] Humboldt's German translations excite equal pleasure and admiration, but naturally throw light on no part of our topic except to some degree on Pindar's verbal manner.[2]

Let us begin with construction[3]—the arrangement of topics, the form built up by creative imagination.

Now, first, if one were content to seek a mere scheme without care for artistic development, one could at once make out a plan of the normal Pindaric ode—a composite photograph, as it were. He begins with gods and prayer, proceeds to details about the victor, his family and his native city, then narrates a brief legend more or less clearly relevant to the occasion, next goes back to the victor, and ends with prayer; moral reflections are scattered up and down the whole. That is true, but blankly obvious and correspondingly barren; so that our attention and sympathy leap out to anyone who attempts to find a scheme both definite and instructive, remembering that Pindar himself more than once mentions a τεθμός,[4] an "ordinance," to which his song conforms. The most specific and concrete scheme was produced by Westphal,[5] followed, with some modifications, by Mezger:[6] that nearly all Pindaric odes contain the seven parts of the *nomos* or melody devised by the illustrious musician Terpander, who flourished about two centuries before Pindar. The seven elements are: *prooimion* ("prelude"), *archa* ("beginning"), *catatropa* ("transition"), *omphalos* ("navel": that is, "centre"), *metacatatropa* ("after-transition"), *sphragis* ("seal": that is, "consummation"), *exodion* ("exit," or "finish").[7] This seems attractively full and precise; but on examining Mezger's application of it we discover much unnaturalness[8]—some of the elements are missing at times, and the parts vary greatly in length: we find it hard to believe that Pindar was in truth following this scheme; and (vastly more important) we see that, even if he was, the fact has no value. To prove such a fixed arrangement of items would be useful because (but only because) a breach of the rule would make us appreciate more crisply the bearing of the whole poem or of the irregular element. But no such benefit accrues. The Terpandrian theory, then, is pedantic and leads nowhere.

Far more attractive is the attempt to discover unity, to find some point of view from which an ode, at first perusal incoherent, will be seen to consist of elements that support and illumine one another. "But," it may be objected, "why should a poet not be incoherent? Does not complete coherence mean the absence of poetry? Again, why *discover* unity? It it exists, surely it needs no unearthing: do we need a microscope to find the colour of a daffodil?" Anyone to whom those questions seem relevant has mistaken the problem. Distinction must be made, as regards their incoherence, between gorgeous raving like *Kubla Khan*, the natural disjointedness of emotion at its sublimest as in Browning's "O Lyric Love . . .," and the perfectly controlled manner in which the Eleventh

Pythian relates four murders that have (so we are told) no
connexion with the rest of the poem.[9] It will not suffice to say,
"All poets write in a fine frenzy: why seek to find sanity in
them?" Whatever frenzy inspired the Eleventh Pythian is
not manifest in its verses: Pindar shows there a markedly ju-
dicial tone, and if his topics seem crazily disconnected, the
implication is that we should search for something that will
banish that appearance. And next, the objection that "discovering unity" approches a contradiction in terms is equally
erroneous. Waiving all that might be said about the difficulties which surround poetry in general, we must remember that
Pindar's date and the conditions in which he worked, without
parallel in our day, make it certain *ab initio* that we shall find
obscurities of which he could not be conscious. But of not a
few, again, he was beyond question fully aware; and in one
place (*Ol.* II 83 ff.) he warns his hearers that his speedy
arrows of song, though they have meaning for the wise, yet
need an interpreter to the multitude. Perrotta, therefore,
misses the whole point when he acidly remarks: "The modern
interpreter's sagacity succeeds in revealing to us what the
poet (it is not known why) has hidden with so much care."[10]
Wilamowitz, too, averred that it is folly to try to know the
poet's intention better than the poet himself.[11] Such judg-
ments raise doubt whether their promulgators know what
criticism is. The various attempts to find unity in an ode,
though their results may fail to convince, are yet in themselves quite justifiable, because neither Pindar nor any other
man in his senses—least of all, any fifth-century Greek in his
senses—would produce a jumble of beautiful but unrelated
items and present it to the world as a poem on a particular
man and a particular event. Unrelated they assuredly often
seem to us; even at the time they no doubt seemed so to
many hearers; they cannot have been unrelated in the view of
Pindar himself. It is the business of criticism here, and incom-
parably the most important, the most delightful, business, to
gaze and study—with caution, indeed, and humility, yet re-
fusing to follow side-issues—until it finds the vantage-ground

from which everything is at last seen in true perspective. Wilamowitz, of whom I wish to speak (and usually do speak) with the reverence due to the greatest Greek scholar of all time, was content to stride up to a glorious but complex masterpiece like the Sixth Olympian and announce that "the two heroines, who are present for no other purpose than bearing a child to a god and getting out of it as quickly as they can, are unsatisfactory inventions."[12] Yet he would have been as ready as anyone to laugh at a man who should plant himself six inches from Raphael's "Disputa" and grumble that it was out of focus.

Many attempts[13] to show unity in this or that ode, all the attempts to show it everywhere, have failed because the unity thus reported has been nebulous, trivial, or forced. Boeckh insisted that each poem was throughout concerned closely with the person and career of the victor: to prove this he excogitated entirely unproved "allegories": for example, Ixion's attempt upon Hera in the Second Pythian shadows forth the supposed advances made by Hiero, despot of Syracuse, to his brother's wife. Boeckh was a mighty scholar, but he should have left poetry alone. In his heavy-footed search for mares'-nests he had distinguished followers, Tycho Mommsen being the most ardent, Hermann perhaps the bravest, certainly the unluckiest, for one at least of his mares'-nests contained wasps. The Seventh Nemean has a curious passage about Neoptolemus, which we shall discuss later; an ancient commentator explained it by referring to a paean, subsequently lost. Hermann[14] rejected this note as random invention and accounted for the Neoptolemus-story by assuming that Pindar's client had once been defeated in the Pythian Games and is now being consoled by the story, dragged in for this amiable purpose. Since then the lost paean has been recovered from the sands of Oxyrhynchus: we learn that the ancient commentator was right and that the random invention was after all Hermann's own. Dissen hit on another way of forcing unity, and Hermann at times followed him too, but with his eyes wide open, for he remarks: "If Boeckh introduced what Pindar did not write, Dissen has invented what Pindar could not have written."[15] The new method consisted in finding and gleefully embracing a "unity" which was simply a motto or curt description of the poem. Dissen returns triumphantly from the chase brandishing such trophies as "prosperity should be combined with wisdom," or "how different are love and envy!"[16] The sublime and richly varied First Pythian is treated by Hermann with incredible childishness.[17] "If anything is certain," he writes, "it is that the mention of the gods and of Typhos serves for ornament only . . . the whole ode can be summed thus: 'Harp, sing the city of Aetna, illumined by Hiero's victory, and wish for him concord, peace, prosperity, a just and liberal government.' " Later scholars are less sweepingly dogmatic and far less inept. Croiset[18] describes, indeed, the nature and function of the "idée lyrique" with a true sense of poetry and does not profess to solve all enigmas of construction; but he gives us no real assistance. His conclusion runs thus: "While writing the words of his ode, the poet saw hovering before his gaze, above the diversity of details, a certain general colour, sometimes more luminous, sometimes darker, which was (so to speak) the summation of the particular shades appropriate to the various details." What use is that? Coppola discerns a unity based on what he calls "aesthetic feelings harmoniously governed by ethical feeling":[19] he anticipates Jaeger when he finds a "good formula for defining the unity" in the "ethical idea and ethical interpretation of the myth."[20] Again we note what we discussed earlier, the insistence that in the criticism of Pindar ethics must outweigh aesthetics—an error which more than any other single cause has spoiled appreciation of this poet. In any case, Coppola's results, for all his rhetoric and self-confidence, prove to be few and insignificant.[21]

That remorseless search for unity prosecuted in the first half of the nineteenth century produced at length an equally uncompromising refusal to see unity anywhere. Some accepted with gratitude Boileau's earlier dictum: "chez elle (l'ode) un beau désordre est un effet de l'art"[22] and insist on chaos, whether *beau* or not, everywhere. Dornseiff writes: "The loveliness is entirely that of a fragment. One sees suddenly a gleaming picture, or hears a note which haunts one. But to follow exactly the train of thought in a longer poem is almost impossible . . . not because it is too profound, but because everything is too unorganized."[23] Perrotta goes far along this road, even condemning those who take the proem of the First Pythian to symbolize "armonia morale,"[24] and maintaining that the invocation to Hora in *Nemean* VIII has nothing to do with Deinis, the victor.[25] He promises better when, avoiding Dornseiff's disastrous quest for a "train of thought," he warns us to distinguish between aesthetic and logical unity.[26] But (alas!) aesthetic unity (we read) exists only in certain very brief odes without myth, such as the Fourteenth Olympian.[27] This seems a mere fury of destruction. Nevertheless, he offers an effective general comment. "Those, then, who read Pindar in order genuinely to understand his poetry will not concern themselves with these laboratory demonstrations, and will easily see that elements so diverse do not fuse, do not fully become poetry, and will learn to distinguish the truly poetical parts, where the Pindaric eagle attains sublime heights, and the prosaic parts, where the poet eulogizes, discusses, or preaches without touching poetry."[28] He is to all seeming right when he denies both logical and aesthetic unity to *Nemean* I—the first part being mediocre, the second a fine triptych;[29] nor can it be denied that the myth of the Dioscuri in *Nemean* X stands (except for a mechanical link) completely severed from what precedes it.[30]

The next three lectures will describe a method of reading Pindar—new, so far as such things ever are new—which reveals essential unity in most of the longer odes, including those that, since Alexandrian days, have been given up as in this respect hopeless. But even where far more substantial structure is demonstrated than has heretofore been discerned, we shall agree with Perrotta that unassimilable masses exist: even in that most beautiful example, the Seventh Olympian, we must set the proem and the catalogue of victories outside the conception that binds all else together.[31] The whole topic is less mysterious than scholars have made it seem. Pindar, like everyone else, tends strongly to write one composition as one composition, not as a series of oddments; but he had not, and could not have, that complete control over the material which most lyrists are free to exercise. Mr. T. S. Eliot[32] has said that alloy is needed in all art, and that the alloy differs in each generation. For Pindar the alloy was often supplied by his client—at times lavishly, as by Xenophon of Corinth, whom you may remember from the first lecture; when his patron gave a free hand, as did the Sicilians, consummate unity is attained. In short, unity cannot with any success be studied as a matter of general principle: each ode must be examined by itself. But two details of Pindaric construction may conveniently be mentioned here.

The first is noted only by Fraccaroli,[33] whose masterly exposition has passed unmarked by his successors. To many the fact must have seemed woefully inartistic, that often the grammatical sentence does not close with the end of the stanza, but sweeps on into the next stanza, sometimes even into the next triad. In *Pythian* IV the first verse of Jason's rather long speech is the last verse of a triad. Now (says Fraccaroli), though the stanza-division in such cases does not coincide with the grammatical period, it does coincide with the *periodo plastico*, the grouping of imagery. He points, among other instances, to *Pythian* XI 22, where the words "that ruthless woman" end a long sentence but open a fresh stanza. Here, whatever the syntax, *plasticamente* these words belong to the group of images in the stanza thus opened, for therein the reasons are discussed which impelled Clytaemnestra to slay her husband.

The second characteristic is, for us moderns, sadly disconcerting: a good many odes "tail off" in a flat obvious way, some quite casually. The Fourth Olympian opens tremendously: "O God most High, who drivest the tireless-footed thunder!" and after but thirty-one lines closes with men "grey-haired before the fitting time of life," a descent suggesting the American bison, whose magnificent head and shoulders are followed by a puny dog-like structure in the rear. Most surprisingly of all, the massive Seventh Nemean dwindles down to a brisk conversational remark about poverty of thought and senseless babble. Dornseiff's description, though it exaggerates the random quality, is acute and important. "The beginning must be beautiful—Pindar prides himself on that: *Ol.* VI, *Pyth.* VII, *Nem.* IV—then the rest creeps plethorically along at random without a centre. The European method, work preparatory to a great poetical climax—any intensification, that is—cannot be found. Generally the beginning is superb, the close dull. That is the archaic art of composition, preceding the Attic centralized manner."[34] This peculiarity, though not so frequent as Dornseiff says, suggests a primitive genius who for all his power has not evolved a perfect form: we are reminded of the saying that the *Iliad* does not end, but leaves off. On the other hand, Pindar's more frequent device, of coming back near the close to some topic treated near the opening, offers the contrary suggestion. We conclude that he was like so many other writers; in some aspects of his art a consummate master of professional devices, in others less steadily assured—now magnificent, now feeble. Virgil's battles compared with his storms or his landscapes, Dickens' heroes compared with his comic figures, are only the strongest instances of what is perhaps universal.

A few moments ago I quoted Boileau's line about "beautiful disorder." Many earlier, as well as later, readers than he have thought Pindar's leading characteristic, next to gorgeous diction, to be incoherence: to judge by the *scholia*, or marginal notes in our manuscripts, few comments were more frequent among ancient scholars than lamentations over untimely and unwelcome digressions. That Pindar has in most ages received less applause and study than he deserves is due to these incoherences, outbursts, and digressions quite as much as to his unique point of view and the difficulty of his Greek. With regard to this last, let us note in passing: first,

that hard as he is, he is no harder than Aeschylus; second,
that by Heaven's grace (to quote his favourite phrase) it is
precisely his best writing that presents least difficulty.

We should mistake seriously if we drew into one category all
these obscurities, these real or apparent failures in construction. Obscurity, or strange curtness, or apparently irrelevant
detail is at times due to condensation, or rebuttal by restate-
ment, of some narrative in an earlier writer: we happen to
know, for example, that some of these passages thus refer to
the lost *Eoeae*, attributed to Hesiod.[35] Again, the sudden
jerks or twists are often nothing but sprightly flourishes designed to charm or arouse the hearer. Thus in the Eighth
Isthmian (v. 47) instead of "strife" he writes "leaves of strife,"
νεικέων πέταλα, to suggest that contention can sprout like a
tree. Others—very many others—result from our own failure
to get, as our phrase goes, the "hang" of the whole composition. A number of these we may hope to solve later, when we
develop a new method of reading Pindar.

Again, there are what I will call "hush-passages."[36] In the
Ninth Olympian (vv. 35 ff.), after describing shortly the
combat of Heracles with the three gods Poseidon, Phoebus,
and Hades, Pindar exclaims: "Fling away that story, tongue
of mine! To revile gods is hateful wisdom."[37] In the Fifth
Nemean (vv. 14 ff.) he hints broadly at the sin of Telamon and
Peleus, favourite heroes of his, who murdered their kinsman
Phocus, but suddenly pulls himself up: "I will halt: not every
truth is the more profitable for revealing all its lineaments."[38]
The other two examples, *Pythian* XI 38 ff. and *Nemean* III
26 ff., are less startling; but in both he stops short, declaring
that he has entered upon the wrong subject. At these four
places we ask why, if he objects to the topic, he does in fact
bring it forward; and why, if he does not object, he should say
that he does. If he has made a blunder, why not throw the
lines away and begin anew—or at the least refrain from jog-
ging the hearer's elbow and saying "Why do I talk like this?"
Here is a very real puzzle which demands far more attention
than editors and essayists have vouchsafed it.[39] The explana-

tion probably lies in his feeling about the change which he has wrought in lyric narrative—a change which shall be described in a subsequent lecture.[40] He takes pride in it and is sensitive to the criticism which it has undergone. At points where his novel method is strongly at work he grows self-conscious, more self-conscious than usual . . . the eyes of the world are upon him, and he stares back defiantly . . . the car of the Muses veers abruptly . . . proud of his new-found virtuosity, affecting and perhaps feeling some astonishment like a child half delighted, half scared, by a new toy that performs exciting prodigies, he underlines the novelty by a pretence that his inspiration has run away with him, precisely when it is feeling the rein most strongly. In the Phocus-passage he gives an extreme instance of the device in which he joys, for he actually introduces it with a deprecatory phrase. Beside these four "hush-passages" we may set others which more simply express the same thought: without feigning that the way has been lost, they direct the poet to quit his theme. In *Pythian* X 51 he thus stops the tale of Perseus: "Check the oar, and quickly dash anchor into the ground." The Fourth Nemean (vv. 69 ff.) suddenly leaves the celebrated Wedding of Peleus and Thetis. "Beyond Cadiz toward the dark no man may pass. Turn the ship's gear back again to the shore of Europe, since to relate the whole story of Aeacus' sons were for me a baffling journey."

Finally, among the alleged digressions for which Pindar has so often been censured, some are genuine. He obtrudes his personal interests with a freedom that astonishes us in official performances honouring a popular hero and the city that wins lustre from his achievement. His contemporaries felt less surprise or none, for though such public odes differed clearly and widely from the personal lyrics of Alcaeus and Sappho, the distinction was not yet so complete as that between Victor Hugo's *La Vendée*, let us say, and Ronsard's *Forêt de Gastine*. Even the lyrics of Euripides, though performed as an act of worship by the whole Athenian state, nevertheless contain notably personal features.[41]

Realizing this, we shall not balk at brief allusions to himself, such as his distress about the Persian Wars (*Isth.* VIII 13 f.), his dislike of Archilochus (*Pyth.* II 54 ff.), and the wish that he could find some marvellous physician whom he might bring, "cleaving the Ionian Sea," to heal his patron King Hiero (*Pyth.* III 63 ff.). More arresting are a few rather quaint allusions to his professional engagements. The Tenth Olympian begins: "Read the entry in my heart, where stands the name of Archestratus' son, victor at Olympia: I owe him a sweet ode, but I forgot the debt." In the First Isthmian he declares that he must first write an ode to Thebes, postponing Delos: "let not craggy Delos be angry with me, for I am devoted to her." The Eighth Pythian contains a notable outburst[42] concerning his own way of life: "My King, I pray that with willing heart under thy guidance I may see things in true perspective at every step I take"; it contains also the information that Pindar banked his money in the shrine of Alcmaeon! Nor are there lacking brilliant though acrid remarks on rivals or critics. Few Pindaric passages are better known than the two (*Ol.* II 86 ff., *Nem.* III 80 ff.) where he compares himself to an eagle, his competitors to crows and jackdaws. The Fifth Nemean opens gorgeously: "No maker of statues am I, to write slumberous images standing inert upon their pedestals. No: upon every merchant-vessel, every skiff, sweet Minstrelsy, speed for Aegina, to spread the tidings that Lampon's son, Pytheas of mighty thews, has won the garland in the *pancration* at Nemea, though not yet upon his cheek appears the tender bloom like the down of budding grapes." In that loveliest of poems, his Sixth Olympian, he does not scruple to bring himself forward, in some of the most sinewy, sonorous, and trenchant verses that he has left for us: "My mother's mother is Stymphalian too, fair-blossoming Metopa: she brought forth Theba, smiter of horses, whose delightful water I drink, weaving for warriors my embroidered song. Rouse now thy comrades, Aeneas, first to sing Hera, goddess of Maidenhood, and then to learn whether we are truly arraigned[43] by that ancient gibe, 'Boeotian swine.' For thou

art an accurate envoy, that bearest the fair-tressed Muses'
secret message, a sweet mixing-bowl of loud-pealing minstrelsy." Pindar's more technical remarks on his own art we
shall find it convenient to defer.[44]

Of all his digressions, the most surprising to us are those in
which he defends his own conduct. They are not, indeed, so
frequent as many readers have believed: for instance, the
Eleventh Pythian[45] and the Second Isthmian[46] have in this
regard (as in others) been misunderstood. But examples certainly occur, the most elaborate being that in the Seventh
Nemean. Commissioned to celebrate the victory of an
Aeginetan boy, Pindar inserts a detailed account of the hero
Neoptolemus' visit to Delphi, the quarrel in which he was
killed, and his honoured tomb in the holy precinct: a story
which has never been shown, even by the most determined
exponents, to have any connexion with young Sogenes. Not
content with this, at the very close, after sprightly matter
about the boy, Pindar abruptly returns to his Delphi-story
and winds all up thus: "Never will my heart confess that I
mangled Neoptolemus with untoward words: but to repeat
the same thing thrice or four times shows poverty of mind,
like one who babbles to children 'Corinth, son of Zeus.' " Can
we explain a digression so irrelevant, so long, and apparently
so important to the poet himself?[47] When extensive fragments
of the Sixth Paean were discovered in Egypt, everything became clear, and would be recognized as such were not many
of us obsessed by the delusion that a great poet is the just
man made perfect.

First of all, Pindar composed a paean for the Delphians,
wherein he told the story of Achilles' son Neoptolemus, who
never returned from Troy to his mother and his kingdom, but
came to Molossia, for Phoebus Apollo swore that the man
who slew Priam at the altar should not see home or reach
old age; and the god in his own precinct killed Neoptolemus
when fighting with the attendants about certain . . . honours
(the papyrus is faulty here). Pindar, that is, wrote in his
paean what would please the Delphians—a narrative highly

creditable to Phoebus, but portraying Neoptolemus as a mur-
derous ruffian. Now, Neoptolemus belonged to the Aeacidae,
the god-descended Aeginetan family: no matter—Aegina was
not near Delphi. But to the poet's chagrin, the Aeginetans,
great patrons of his, after all heard of the paean and clearly
resented this treatment of their heroic fellow-countryman.
How was Pindar to extricate himself? What followed was a
masterly blend of serene audacity, perfect diction, and impec-
cable manner. He calmly takes the opportunity afforded him
by the first ode (after the paean) which he is asked to compose
for an Aeginetan, and makes of it a use so thorough-going
that Alexandrian scholars[48] went to ridiculous lengths in
hopes to palliate the digression. Aristarchus had the face to
assert that the victor was not Sogenes after all, but some
altruistic athlete from Epirus named—here is the clever
point!—Neoptolemus, who allowed Sogenes to be proclaimed
as victor, "so as to give him pleasure." Aristodemus suggested that the trainer's name was Neoptolemus. Callistratus
less wildly but even more ineptly pointed out that, whereas
Sogenes was a neighbour of Heracles, the hero Neoptolemus
was, in death, a neighbour of the Delphic god, Apollo. When
a ruthless scholar takes the bit between his teeth, there is no
holding him. The simple fact is that Pindar for his own
utterly irrelevant purpose foists the original "hero" Neoptolemus upon poor Sogenes and his ode, proceeding to explain away the offensive paean by a cool insistence that he
had not said what he had said therein. But *littera scripta
manet*—what a man has written, he has written? Not always;
and the best way of erasing it is to write admirably on the
same subject but in other terms. And, in fact, Pindar nearly
succeeded. He succeeded perfectly till A.D. 1908, in which
year the papyrus was discovered. Even the Royal Library at
Alexandria had no copy of the paean, as appears from the
bungling explanations which emanated thence.

   In such a predicament it was no use to mince matters. He
cuts the knot by asserting (as we saw) "never will I agree
that I slandered Neoptolemus." To make this good he offers a

second and complete version far more creditable to the hero and in consequence vastly more pleasant to Aeginetan ears. But he is shrewd enough to realize that he must follow the outline of his offensive version, though with mitigations at each point. The result is a fascinating exhibition of urbane disingenuousness as he obeys his own maxim: "Cheerfully accepting circumstance, let thy thought change as occasion bids."[49] For the savage murder of Priam at the very altar he substitutes "when he sacked Priam's city."[50] He adds perhaps the most dextrous touch of all . . . how shall we translate it ambiguously enough—τᾷ καὶ Δαναοὶ πόνησαν? "About which," that is, Troy, "the Greeks also suffered"? The interpretation "where the Greeks also toiled," however flat, cannot be excluded; and Pindar does not wish it excluded: it thickens the mist which he so sedulously raises between his two versions. But the main intention is "through which the other Greeks also suffered"—an allusion to the famous calamities that so many Greek heroes faced on their return from Troy, hinting that Neoptolemus was no worse than Agamemnon or Odysseus. That leads on gently and beautifully to the description of his departure: "He, sailing off, failed of Scyros" (Neoptolemus' island home). "They wandered and came to Ephyra." This, for all its lack of emphasis, nevertheless corresponds to the paean's dire language about Phoebus' oath that Priam's murderer should never see again his ancestral fields. The same skill can be observed in the next line: "Over Molossia he reigned a brief time." Few and evil were his days: but that is suggested by only one word, "brief," and the consolation instantly follows: "Howbeit, his race for all time bears this honour." Next, the slayer of Neoptolemus is no longer Phoebus, as in the paean, but some anonymous "man with a knife." The occasion, too, is now commonplace: "in a fight about meat," remarks Pindar, with a baldness of diction almost laughably in contrast with the frightful reason for the hero's death which he had promulgated at Delphi. It is admirably conceived. Most people are prone to mistake crudity for candour, and these frigid words seem proudly to avoid that "soaring power" and "glamour" whereby Homer (as Pindar complains in this very ode)[51] passed off fiction for history. At the end of this superb piece of juggling he blandly affirms (v. 44) that all this was the doing of Fate—for it had to be that one of the Aeacid family should throughout the future abide at Delphi as overseer of the heroic processions—whatever they were.[52]

So far concerning structure or the failure of structure: let us advance now to a fresh theme—a side of his poetical quality which is for many of us the most delightful thing in Pindar. When relating a myth, he offers us, not a narrative in the normal manner, but a series of pictures. Homer's method is simple: he tells us everything, and practically always in chronological order; Pindar's way differs at both points. Even in the Fourth Pythian he pours out, not a broad majestic river as does Homer, but a narrow stream that spreads here and there into shining lagoons: Jason in the market-place, Aeetes and Jason driving the plough, are pictures wrought in vivid detail, whereas Medea's flight receives but eight words, and it is actually uncertain whether he does or does not so much as mention the building of Argo.[53] Analogous treatment is observed in the other, far briefer, myths. And further, so indifferent is Pindar to rational presentation, to what every other ancient writer would regard as a vital feature of storytelling, namely, chronological order, that he usually sets his pictures in what appears random sequence.

Look now at a few of these pictures. The Sixth Olympian tells how Euadna, with child by Apollo, bore Iamos.

She, laying aside her girdle of purple and saffron, setting down her silver ewer, beneath a dark coppice brought forth a man-child in whom was the spirit of God. For her aid golden-tressèd Apollo sent the Fates and the gentle-souled Goddess of childbirth; and straightway from her womb amid the lovely birth-pang came Iamos to the light. In distress she left him upon the earth; but two grey-eyed serpents by Heaven's will cared for and nourished him with the innocent liquor[54] of bees. And when the king came driving his

chariot back from rocky Pytho, he inquired of all in the house concerning the child that Euadna had borne. "For," said he, "Phoebus
is the father that begot him, and he shall be above mortal men a
prophet among them that walk the earth; nor shall his generation
ever fail." Thus ran his tidings. But they swore that they had
neither heard nor seen aught. Yet had the child been born five days;
but he was hidden amid rushes in a great brake, his tender body
steeped in the yellow and purple sheen of violets.

There is Botticelli, translated into Greek! And now, beside
those lines, suffused with tender loveliness, set the Ninth
Olympian, tingling with a crisp tang as of an autumn morning upon quiet uplands. He tells of a little country town in
mid-Greece, whose patron-hero has himself but modest standing—Oïleus' son, the lesser Ajax; and his town's only wealth
is the beauty of her trees, her sole splendour the red blaze of
the thunderbolt stamped upon her coins. Leaving for once
his favourite method, a single myth greatly unfolded, Pindar
gives us a form suiting better the frugal mood of the whole
poem, four narratives, curt and spare, that seem to be delivered as well as acted in the morning of the world. Everything happens across an immense distance, yet sharply
outlined to the gaze in clear light and keen rain-washed at-
mosphere. Ancient cities and solemn mountain-ranges reveal
themselves across these airy spaces; we descry Poseidon's
trident beating upon Heracles' club in their grim conflict at
Pylos, and watch Pyrrha with Deucalion step down the empty
hillside, their hands filled with stones that bear God's blessing. These scenes impart a sense of unearthly quiet; for no
voice is heard. Even when Zeus is united with Opus' daughter
among the mountain-ridges, he utters no heartening prophecy; even of the fiery Achilles' exhortation to Patroclus in the
dread hour no word is reported directly, nothing but the
poet's description of his command. In all the narrative part
of his ode Pindar maintains this refusal of enrichment, this
tingling simplicity. What splendour would he have thrown,
in another mood, round his story of the Deluge, here dis-
missed in thirteen vigorous words! He compensates us by

what he so rarely bestows, a picture of the athlete's own
triumphant prowess. "Quelling each man by quick guileful
shifts of balance, himself unthrown, amid what shouts he
passed across the arena in the beauty of life's spring-time and
fair achievement!"[55]

All the other odes, likewise, save those of the smallest
compass, are ever and anon lit up by such vivid pictures.[56]
The dark scene of Coronis' mad offence is sweetly relieved by
a little pool of light: the girls who are playmates of the bride
love to sing for her arch ditties as evening falls. His own store
of songs he likens to a treasure-house, "which neither wintry
rain, savage army of the bellowing cloud, on its invading
march, nor the wind that lashes it with shingle from every
quarter, shall sweep into the sea's recesses"; or a brief sentence casts on us a spell of ancient majesty: "embowered
amid the dusky primeval mountains" is not only beautiful
but solemn, with a hint for us of Merlin and Broceliande.
Apollo himself fell in love with Cyrana when he found her
wrestling with a lion, the παρθένος ἀγροτέρα, *la belle sauvage*,
her loveliness hinted in one word, εὐώλενος—her arms were
beautiful. Borne away to Africa in his golden chariot, she is
greeted by silver-footed Aphrodite in that strange country of
heat and sand, whither she has been carried overseas in a
single day from her own shadowy mountains. The same delightful ode closes with the scene where Alexidamus led his
bride through the multitude of African horsemen who cast
upon them garlands of foliage and blossoms. Here is a vi-
gnette from the fighting at Troy that has been well compared
to a masterly vase-painting:[57] "Nestor's horse, wounded by
the bolts of Paris, hampered his chariot; and Memnon made at
Nestor with his mighty spear; and the aged Messenian's soul,
distraught, cried out to his son; and lo, his word was not cast
away upon the ground; that godlike man stood to it and
bought with his life the rescue of his father." When Heracles
sought out Telamon as a comrade in war, he found him feast-
ing amid friends: "Telamon bade Amphitryon's son, that

mighty spearman, to stand upon the lion's hide and begin the banquet with pouring forth of nectar; and Telamon the stalwart gave unto him the wine-filled goblet rough with embossèd gold. Then Heracles, holding up to heaven his invincible hands, uttered these words . . ."

The Seventh Isthmian, that enchanting blend of majesty and direct emotional appeal, calls to mind our most finely wrought Christmas carols: there is the same fervour and childlike awe, the same grave but triumphant proclamation of woe and suffering, the same brief yet adorably picturesque recital of old stories in all their artless and moving simplicity. The poet opens by hailing Theba, despite her sorrows, as the Blessèd, and straightway pours forth an exquisitely varied enumeration of no less than seven ancient glories whereon she may justly pride herself, among them a magical glimpse of Heaven's King standing at midnight before Amphitryon's gate, ready to bestow on mankind his greatest son, while the glory of his presence turns to gold the snow-flakes that descend upon him from the darkness.[58] The last splendid scene that comes upon his memory is the exploit of a Theban clan that marched far to the southward and by taking Amyclae brought relief to Sparta. That puts him in mind of recent Spartan ingratitude and evokes a marvellous phrase, ἀλλὰ παλαιὰ γὰρ εὕδει χάρις, "but grace of old time slumbereth now," which again recalls to him his own power of making grace and favour live eternally, raised to the perfect bloom of poesy. And so for Strepsiadas, too, let the festal song be heard: his victory in the games, his thews, his beauty and noble heart have given a share in the garland to his lost kinsman. . . . There the poet's mood changes to majestic sadness and proud regret for him who died in his country's defence: "thy youth's fair bloom sighed itself away amid the throng of the battle-front, where heroes stemmed that bitter fray with high heart in the desperate hour."

> εὐανθέ' ἀπέπνευσας ἁλικίαν
> προμάχων ἀν' ὅμιλον, ἔνθ' ἄριστοι
> ἔσχον πολέμοιο νεῖκος ἐσχάταις ἐλπίσιν.

This loss brought to Pindar grief beyond words, but now the sea-god has granted calm after tempest, for in his precinct Strepsiadas has found glory. The poet can sing again, with garlands upon his hair, quietly pursuing each day's happiness and shunning arrogant hopes too high for human frailty, warned by the downfall of Bellerophon who strove to enter the celestial conclave. Sufficient blessing for us if Phoebus grants at Pytho yet another garland, of fair bloom like his whom we have mourned.

Many other poets have excelled in picturesque writing, but none of their most graphic passages reminds us of Pindar; and that is true also of the narratives into which those scenes of his are built up. What unique flavour or dexterity or point of view sets him thus apart? Outside these odes we possess few lyrical narratives in Greek, yet enough for a fruitful comparison. Let us compare four masterpieces:[59] the last fight of the Twin Brethren in the Tenth Nemean, Theseus and Minos in Bacchylides, the sacrifice of Iphigenia in Aeschylus' *Agamemnon*, and the Phrygian slave's story in the *Orestes* of Euripides. At once we distinguish the second and fourth from the work of Aeschylus and Pindar; for though Bacchylides' narrative owes its power to lucidity, elegance, and charm, whereas Euripides with immense power depicts hysteria and uncanny adventure, both stories alike lead nowhere, being capable only—though that is much—of thrilling us by the incidents in themselves. But who would call the narratives in Pindar and Aeschylus interesting or even thrilling? They altogether transcend such praise. Where resides their astonishing power? They so narrate events, important and touching in themselves, that while we receive upon our imagination the full impact of those events, we are carried beyond them, and our soul gains a momentary vision of all life, the order of the Universe—*moenia mundi discedunt*. Bacchylides and Euripides have offered us excellent literature, Pindar and Aeschylus spiritual life. But what, again, is the difference between the last two? Anyone who wishes to write down "the reference" to Aeschylus will find that he cannot easily determine where "the passage" begins! There at once we light upon the main distinction. Aeschylus has woven his detailed story of a single human experience into a vaster whole. His lyric opens with those memorable stanzas concerning "Zeus, whoe'er he be" and his leadership of mankind through sorrow to understanding: then the story of Iphigenia's sacrifice at Aulis begins . . . When that scene of beauty and anguish closes, the lyric is not yet over, for we return to the earlier thought in those solemn words: "Justice with a weight of understanding cometh upon them that have suffered"—and the warning follows, that this lesson will be taught and learnt yet again in the deeds that are now to unfold themselves. Lovely shrinking Iphigenia and the king of men are placed in a stupendous perspective that includes God himself, His primeval wars and His eternal purpose. Aeschylus has reached this height because he is endowed not only with poetical genius but with spiritual genius also. Pindar has not so wrought; because, though he may be the other's peer in verse, he lacks that power to fathom deep mysteries. The play *Agamemnon* is not only about Zeus: it reads as if it were written by Zeus; the Tenth Nemean was written by a Dorian poet. That vision, then, of life and the Universe whereof we spoke is in Aeschylus not merely Greek, but human; in Pindar, though noble almost beyond praise, it is not Greek in the broadest sense, but Dorian, Dorian in the frugal majesty of its phrasing—"forthwith they devisèd a great deed," "he released the eye, then the voice, of bronze-belted Castor," and "together in the solitude they were consumed by fire"; Dorian too in its conception of Zeus, to whom Aeschylus looks as the soul's leader and saviour, but who in the dread hour of Pindar's imagination says "thou art my son," and reveals himself as a father after the flesh.

Pictures exist by throwing up a subject against its background. Pindar's effects (it was said earlier) are gained for the most part by envisaging a few glorious sights—heroic action, the radiance of sun and moon and gold, sparkling wine and flaming blossoms, the fair bodies of gods and goddesses or

godlike men and women—against a background null, un-
friendly, even sinister. To some few of his noblest or most
highly wrought passages this description does not apply, to
his openings perhaps in particular—those of the Sixth Olympian, "Golden be the pillars that we set in the fair-built portico of song"; or the Seventh, "As a man taketh in his wealthy
hand a goblet wherein foameth the dew of the vine . . ."';
or the Fifth Isthmian: "Mother of the Sun-God, Splendour
that bearest names manifold"; and we must be on our guard
against the danger of too sedulous manipulation and one-
sided statement which lies in wait for him who attempts the
explanation of beauty. Nevertheless, it is manifest that
Pindar often writes with a stately reserve, a certain spare,
even stern, dignity. This note is less obvious than in Lucre-
tius and Milton, more marked than in Sophocles and Virgil;
here Pindar is close kin to Dante. One of the ablest among
ancient critics, Dionysius of Halicarnassus, takes him as an
example of the "austere manner."[60]

This blend of austerity and loveliness is normally secured
(as we have just remarked) by a strongly differentiated background. A simple instance is the contrast of ἀγλαός, "radiant,"
and μέλας, "black," in his invocation (*Nem.* VII 1 ff.): "Hearken,
thou Giver of birth to children: without thee we have no
glimpse of sunshine or *black* night that we may win thy sister,
Youth of the *radiant* limbs." An astonishingly powerful instance is the contrast between a blaze of beauty and dark
cold irresponsiveness in the *encomium* for Theoxenus, where
the language has more affinity with Elizabethan "conceits"
than anything in the triumphal odes. "Whoso looketh upon
the rays that beam from those dazzling eyes and is not tossed
upon billows of passion, his black soul hath been forged in
cold flame from steel or iron, and Aphrodite's dancing gaze
rejecteth him."[61] Semele the beautiful, beloved of Zeus, was
consumed by the thunderbolt but taken up into Heaven, her
loveliness . . . unimpaired—as we should word it. How does
Pindar? Somewhat thus: "She liveth among the Olympians,
she that died amid the roar of thunderbolts, *long-tressèd*

Semele" (*Ol.* II 25 f.). Slighter examples can be observed in profusion: "malice requiting fair deeds" (*Pyth.* VII 15); "peace after wintry rain" (*Pyth.* V 10); Delos "a far-shining star upon the dark-blue earth" (fr. 78 = 87); the sun "a radiant star in empty Heaven" (*Ol.* I 6); the Locrian girl standing at her door "with eyes free from dread after hopeless miseries of war" (*Pyth.* II 19 f.). More striking is the vision of Apollo as he strode forth amid the devastation of a countryside and the glare from Coronis' funeral-pyre (*Pyth.* III 38 ff.). The fragmentary Second Paean commemorates men of Abdera in Thrace who fell in battle against a barbarian tribe. Its two most affecting lines offer a fine example of what we have now specially in mind. Pindar goes out of his way to mention the mountain, Melamphyllon, near which they fought. Why? Because the name means literally "with black foliage"; and that name he contrasts with the brightness of their courage. "Upon them came the supreme radiance when they fronted their foemen hard by the Dark-leaved Mountain."[62] Heroic action in prospect also, as in the past, gains splendour from the background of dark death. The youthful Pelops, ardent for a dread enterprise, exclaims (*Ol.* I, 81 ff.): "Great peril rejecteth the dastard. Since die we must, wherefore should a man sit in the dark vainly nursing old age bereft of fame, aloof from all that is noble?" Rarely can we find a narrative that owes none of its richness to this device—perhaps only that of Alexidamus in the Ninth Pythian: in the same ode, the entrancing story of Cyrana includes her struggle with a lion. Finally, two whole poems are conceived in this *chiaroscuro* vein, the exquisite brief Twelfth Olympian and the First Pythian, noblest of them all.

DICTION; SYMBOLISM

In the preceding lectures much has been said incidentally of Pindar's poetical excellence. We are now to consider this directly; and, first, the most obvious but not the only elements in the unique Pindaric brilliance: his vocabulary and the texture of his phrasing—in short, his style.

To describe the style of any poet is more useful than some believe, not because it imparts knowledge but because it quickens attention, thus deepening that blend of pleasure and illumination which art evokes. To carry this through well is extremely hard, but there need be no mystery-mongering; for, when all is said, poems consist of known words. We must use precision and detail, nothing daunted by the particular difficulties of a language both foreign and ancient: or if we are thus daunted, we should leave the whole matter untouched. Vague ecstasy is not criticism. It must have been weariness of such vapouring that inspired Voltaire's address: "Rise from the tomb, divine Pindar; thou who of yore didst celebrate the horses of sundry Corinthian or Megarian citizens, thou who ownedst the gift to speak much and say nothing; thou who didst skilfully modulate verses that no one understands and which (nevertheless) it is our duty to admire."[1] But for various reasons I shall not attempt elaborate discussion, seeking rather to give indications or clues to those who would follow this alluring study further.

First, then, the magic of Pindar's diction is due in no small measure to his native tongue itself, a speech so wonderful that even the most casual-seeming words show, when once they catch ear and eye, such urbane directness and clarity that we could almost wish to take them up and turn them in our fingers. Χορεύων ἐν Κέῳ ἀμφιρύτᾳ σὺν ποντίοις ἀνδράσιν (*Isth.* I 7 f.)—why is that delicious? Hardly in virtue of its meaning—that is given well enough by the unremarkable English "dancing with mariners in sea-girt Ceos." Little by its rhythm. Rather more by a tinge of quaintness in the last two words, ποντίοις ἀνδράσιν . . . "sailors" will not do; "mariners" is better, but too literary; "seamen" is too ordinary for ἀνδράσιν: perhaps the best version has been given by—of all un-Pindaric writers on earth—Dickens, who made Rogue Riderhood describe himself as a "waterside character." Another element is the pleasant variety of four datives, each with a different termination: Κέῳ ἀμφιρύτᾳ ποντίοις ἀνδράσιν. But, above all, the phrase delights us by its essential Greekness, a diction that seems washed in dew, utterly fresh yet so utterly *right* that it comes upon the mind more intimately even than our own everyday language. But such litheness and vivacity is normal in Greek literature down to the fourth century: with it Pindar blends his own brevity and force. Herein no one, no Greek even, resembles him; for Aeschylus, who stands nearest, uses greater strength, language more ponderous and less concise, a more widely questing imagination. Consider this simple idea: "It is easy for a wise man to requite every kind of effort with praise and thus do general good." That is a tolerable version of κούφα δόσις ἀνδρὶ σοφῷ ἀντὶ μόχθων παντοδαπῶν ἔπος εἰπόντ' ἀγαθὸν ξυνὸν ὀρθῶσαι καλόν (*Isth.* I 45 f.). Admirable!—not only because Greek is a graceful speech, but more in particular because Pindar has used peculiarities of his own, *slight* variations—that is the point: instead of "it is easy," he writes, omitting the verb, "a light gift," hinting at a picture; for "every kind of," he uses a single word corresponding to "multifarious"; for "praise" he substitutes "good speech"; and in ὀρθῶσαι we again find a picturesque touch—"to set upright"—whereas normal Greek would give εὐεργετῆσαι, "to benefit," simply.

If for clearness' sake we may sink to pedantic inaccuracy—no good writer "puts style into" his work, still less introduces it by instalments,—let us call the method just described the first process in style, which makes a sentence more handsome by "altering" single words. The next stage, in many Greek and Roman authors, is to give it elasticity, a ripple,[2] whereby a mere row of separate words becomes a fused and tempered unit of utterance. The sentence in its first stylized condition consists of (let us say) three grammatical masses, A B C: the "ripple" is secured by what technicians name hyperbaton—that is, by placing one word or more from B inside A, a word or more from C inside B. In poetry the fusion may be more intricate. Thus Virgil, instead of the obvious *tot oppida praeruptis saxis manu congesta*, writes *tot congesta manu praeruptis oppida saxis*. What Dryden calls his "golden" lines are but a special form of this: *impiaque aeternam timuerunt saecula noctem;* and the Horatian stanza beginning *te boves olim* is composed at the height of such virtuosity.[3] Pindar, too, uses this way of making a sentence one and flexible instead of leaving it a series of lumps. In the passage just quoted, εἰπόντα is set between ἔπος and ἀγαθόν: δόσις belongs in grammar to ὀρθῶσαι.

A third method he shares with few or none: an invariable employment of the sensuous word—the noun, the verb, even the preposition[4]—which forces us to visualize what we read. All poets, to be sure, have used this artifice: one of the greatest has placed sensuousness among the three qualities that mark poetry. But has any employed it so continually as Pindar? Open even Shelley at random:

> For as with gentle accents he addressed
> His speech to them, on each unwilling heart
> Unusual awe did fall—a spirit-quelling dart.[5]

We chance to have lit on something that strongly recalls Pindar. "Spirit-quelling dart" is precisely in his manner—δαμάσιφρον βέλος suggests itself. And we know how he would have worded the former half of the passage: *Pythian* IV 137 shows that in place of the colourless word "addressed" he would have hinted at a picture of one who pours ointment: "Jason with his soothing voice *distilling* gentle language," as Sandys well translates it. Keats' style is more sensuous than Shelley's; but consider the first line even of *Ode to Autumn:* "Season of mists and mellow fruitfulness." Perfection, yes; but it illustrates what we have in mind. "Fruitfulness" is an

abstract noun: Pindar would have written some such phrase
as ὀπώρας μᾶτερ, "mother of fruits." To enumerate examples
from these odes would be foolish: the difficulty is to find any
concept, capable of sensuous expression, not so expressed. His
most celebrated metaphors are only the most starry feats of
this instinct, and need small comment here. Concerning his
mixed metaphors there has been perhaps too much talk.[6]
When they are really mixed, when we read (*Pyth.* IV 273 ff.)
that to set an overturned city upon its base again is a sore
wrestle unless God becomes a steersman to the guides—then,
perhaps, we are right to censure him. Usually the metaphors
are not mixed after all, but only follow one another at a speed
too rapid for sluggish imaginations.

To read Pindar, then, above all to read him aloud, feels like
passing one's hand over a surface tingling with electricity.
All is alive: at times one could swear that the verse is full of
eyes as well as music; the effect no doubt, of picturesqueness
in a single word—there, and gone in a flash: instead of "bestow praises on this island" (*Isth.* VI 21), "sprinkle this
island with praises." Or a hundred times one sees out of the
corner of one's eye . . . something, that stirred quickly: then
one turns the head, and it is just a word, demurely grammatical, and nothing more. Much of this vivid, electrical,
effect is secured by shifts in the meaning or application of
words: the sentence must be a living creature (surely!), for its
members heave and quiver. His language is iridescent, one
topic shading off into another by use of phrasing exquisitely
ambiguous—a delight to those who yield themselves to his
Greek, a stumbling-block to those who translate each element
into English and then remark that the English elements clash.
Ol. VI 57 f. provides a good example: τερπνᾶς δ'ἐπεὶ χρυσο-
στεφάνοιο λάβεν καρπὸν Ἥβας, "when he gained the fruit of
delightful Youth whose garland is all gold." We must not exclaim: "A bungle! The only ἥβα which he could 'take' was
maturity, and that is an abstraction, possessing therefore no
garland, golden or not. If on the other hand the adjective
makes us think of the goddess Heba, he did not take her."[7]

That is the wrong frame of mind: we must surrender ourselves
to the words as they leap upon the ear: such a passage is the
grammatical analogue of those wherein he speaks of Libya
and Theba now as if they were deities, now as if they were
places.[8] In the last sentence of *Isthmian* VI he praises Lampon
as a man of integrity and an inspiration to others, adding
πίσω σφε Δίρκας ἁγνὸν ὕδωρ—"I will give him to drink of Dirca's
sacred water," meaning (no doubt) "I will pour forth in his
honour my Theban minstrelsy": but the next words refer to
the literal fountain of Dirca, for it springs "beside the fair-
built gate of Cadmus" . . . yet he says also that it was caused
to flow by the Muses. In *Pythian* I 81 ff., he begins by commenting on his own method in writing panegyrics, but the
language insensibly changes into admonition of Hiero.

We must not linger more than a moment upon another topic,
Pindar's metre and rhythm.[9] A Pindaric ode consists of
stanzas, sometimes all identical in structure, precisely as do
The Faerie Queene, In Memoriam, and countless other poems.
More often the stanzas are grouped in triads, a triad being
thus the largest possible unit—two stanzas (called the strophe
and the antistrophe) which are in shape identical, followed by
a third (the epode), resembling them but not repeating them;
if an ode contains more than one triad, the triads exactly
correspond. The metres are complicated and varied, reaching
the most opulent splendours which human speech has attained.
In this respect the Sixth Olympian perhaps excels all its
companions. The metre is one of those in which he has blent
the Homeric hexameter and that trochaic movement which
has been, time out of mind, the chief instrument of popular
poetry among Western nations. Thus the final verse of its
strophes and antistrophes seems to me Pindar's finest metrical
achievement; and the ninety-first, of all that he ever wrote,
is my especial favourite:

ἠϋκόμων σκυτάλα Μοισᾶν, γλυκὺς κρατὴρ ἀγαφθέγκτων ἀοιδᾶν.

In an earlier discussion, much was said against various
theories whereby unity was to be revealed in these odes, and a

promise was given that a new method of studying them would be described. It is now time to redeem that undertaking, to discuss a feature of Pindar's technique which appears, to one student at least, by far the most attractive element in his work, though it has hitherto gone almost, if not completely, unremarked. Whether it should or should not be acclaimed as the most notable quality of his art may perhaps be debated; but beyond question here lies the greatest difference between his work and that of all other poets—a difference of poetical method naturally corresponding to the difference of fundamental interest. He instinctively sets himself, as we have said, to create beauty. So, when he gazes upon his miscellaneous material—the circumstances of the victory, the athlete's career, family, and native town, contemporary events in general and any detail in particular which his client has requested him to include—he broods emotionally upon these until there arises in his imagination some sensible object round which these varied topics may crystallize. His favourite means of coördinating them so that they quicken one another with newly discovered kinship of significance and the thrill of relationship in beauty hitherto unguessed, of transforming a heap of facts into a radiant body, alive, nimble, and soaring, is to feel them all and portray them all in terms of this symbol, this familiar sight—a beacon-fire, it may be, a horse, a pebble, or a sapling—which confers upon them a unity not logical but aesthetic. Some touch, at least, of this image-making instinct will ever be found shaping the diction of poets; but Pindar is herein unique, that when his genius works at full power the instinct becomes a magnificent energy that dominates not merely phrases but the whole theme, which is thus seen to bear lineaments strange and fascinating, filled with novel light and hues, narrated accordingly in language coloured by this sensuous origin, so that we regularly come upon at least one word in the poem which cannot be understood fully or perhaps at all without reference to the symbol, and which therefore serves as a signpost or revelation of it.

Let us straightway look at an example of such a significant word. It is perhaps the simplest of all: we shall find more complex and thus far more convincing instances later. In any case, here is the manner in which I at least came to appreciate the Fourteenth Olympian more intensely. In the midst of this exquisite little poem, we read that the Graces revere their Olympian Father's everlasting glory. "Everlasting" is correct enough: it is the word used in Farnell's translation, for example. But literally αἰέναον means "ever-flowing." Why should God's glory be so described? That suggests further scrutiny of the whole poem, and of the circumstances from which it rose. At once we note the boy-victor's name: Asopichus, derived from Asopus, the name of the chief river in Boeotia, where stood the lad's native town Orchomenus. The symbol of the ode is Moving Waters, and at once we see why Pindar invokes the Graces as dwelling beside the stream on which Orchomenus stood, and why the very first words are: "Cephisian waters." The fair pastoral scene rises clearly before our gaze, drawing majesty from local sanctities, and awe from the august presences wherewith on one side they are associated. The song praises not the victor only, but those Graces who are queens of this ancient city, rich and powerful in days that were old in Homer's time, but now a tranquil little-regarded town amid green pastures and beside quiet waters, where horses graze near gleaming Orchomenus. Not only in Boeotian meadows do the Graces rule, but in Heaven also, ordering the joyous life of gods, setting their thrones beside Apollo and doing reverence to the Olympian Father's glory that *flows like a river from age to age.*

This doctrine, so uncompromisingly set forth, that symbolism gives the key to full appreciation of Pindar, may seem to many impossible of acceptance as ignoring his earnest and lifelong concern with ethics—a concern which led many scholars to find in some ethical idea the very explanation of a whole ode. Not so. Though it has been maintained in an earlier lecture that Dissen and many others have immensely overrated Pindar's importance as a moralist, his insistence upon ethics, however misguided, was nowhere denied; and it is not impossible for the symbol to typify some moral doctrine. But that matters nothing: it happens in the poet's private thought before he begins to create his poem: it explains, at most, only his choice of a myth. He is imaginatively concerned with a picture, which concern explains his way of telling the myth; and that is overwhelmingly the greater interest of those who go to him for his poetry. If anyone suspects confusion of thought here, let him recall Milton's purpose in writing *Paradise Lost*, and decide whether his perusals have brought him as much theological instruction as delight in exalted poetry. Thus heartened, we proceed to another ode, the First Pythian, the most instantly cogent example of Pindaric symbolism.

It celebrates ostensibly the victory gained in the chariot-race at Delphi by Hiero, tyrant of Syracuse, in 470 B.C.;[10] but its real concern is the city of Aetna,[11] recently founded by Hiero at the foot of that mountain. He made his son[12] Deinomenes king of the new city and was so eager to surround its beginnings with splendour[13] that when he gained this Pythian victory he caused himself to be announced to all Hellas not as Hiero of Syracuse but as Hiero of Aetna.

This ode is the most sublime of all lyrical poems: even less open to doubt is its supremacy as a masterpiece of poetical architecture, whereby thoughts, emotions, and interests that might seem utterly distinct are wrought into wondrous unity. Pindar has left us other poems as beautiful, none so noble. Bidden to celebrate the ageing and crafty prince, the youthful king, the newly founded city, he ponders also the achievements of Hiero and his brothers in conflict with barbarians, and the Dorian constitution just granted to Aetna, a limited monarchy, a western Sparta, with freedom for its burghers. Dominating the scene of this celebration towers the Pillar of Heaven, that great volcano which but a few years before had burst into dreadful activity. All these thoughts blossom and entwine themselves till he sees the picture, the symbol round which they may be assembled. Where another would think

and speak of the underlying idea, he sees and displays the
visual object which represents and unites all these events,
hopes, and prayers.

This symbol is the Lyre, that χρυσέα φόρμιγξ which his illustrious prelude directly addresses, as other preludes address
gods or goddesses. Its rhythm thrills Heaven with gentle bliss,
but whatever beings are sundered from God's love this music
fills with consternation, wherever they lurk by land or sea.
Thus at the outset Zeus and the other gods are proclaimed
lovers of the Lyre, his enemies as its enemies—creatures of
disharmony and chaos: at once it has grown into all that
Plato meant by μουσική, and more—the spirit of serenity,
order, concord throughout the Universe opposing and holding
in subjection whatever makes for turbulence, jarring discord,
the disruption of all.[14] Then the poet with magical dexterity
swings into the orbit of this cosmic thought today's human
festival. For of those fiendlike Titans, enemies of Zeus, is the
hundred-headed Typhos, imprisoned now by our own Sicily
and by the hill-ranges behind Cumae across the water; for
upon his shaggy bosom stands the heaven-reaching column,
crested with unmelting snows—Aetna, the forehead of this
fruitful land. Next rises a scene of sinister glory, belching
flame and smoke, the lava-stream that rolls beneath half-
dispelled darkness with a roar into the sea-levels: such is the
infernal rage of this monster, quelled yet writhing.[15] And here
the poet cries that in Zeus alone lies our hope, Zeus who rules
upon this mountain, the mountain whose name—and here
again he swings his mighty thought inward—Hiero caused to
be proclaimed in his victory at Pytho.

By so terrible a road do we arrive at the original reason for
this poem, Hiero's success, and at the enterprise on which he
has set his heart, a kingdom for his son. But now the eagle
towers anew, quitting the lad Dinomenes and his throne for
Hiero's doughty achievements in war, when he and his brothers culled a garland of renown fairer than any other among
Greeks can boast. That is no discursive weakness: Pindar will
have us bear in mind together all the strands of high dis-

course. Back to the new city, where again the spiritual music is heard, for here too peaceful concord must dwell—σύμφωνος ἡσυχία (v. 70)—the *voices* must blend in tranquil music, echoing that divine melody in Heaven wherewith the poem opened. This lesson is worded with an emphasis that must have caused the aged dynast to stir in his seat and glance uneasily.[16] "What you have said, O Hiero, you have said: let this fair beginning, the gift of a well-based polity, endure unimpaired"—such is the feeling that underlies these verses. They open (v. 61) with the proclamation that Hiero has founded this city with freedom God-built upon the laws of Hyllus the Regulator, and the strophe overflows with august names, bringing to memory those who founded and upheld the famed Dorian system of liberty under law. To clinch the matter comes again a prayer to Zeus: for ever may mankind report that such is the way of life for citizen and king beside the Restless Water.[17]

There follows a great passage extolling Hiero not merely as a conqueror but as a saviour of Greece. From all quarters of the earth barbarians had pressed to her destruction, Persians from the east, Etruscans from the north, Carthaginians from the south and west. Salamis he proclaims as the glory of Athens, Plataea as that of Sparta, while at the Himera Hiero and his brothers had beaten back another member of the same confederacy. Pindar sees plainly that Hellenic civilization and freedom have been ringed by foes: on every side powers of darkness were leagued against the union of liberty, law, and enlightenment, against everything symbolized by the Lyre, everything which Zeus championed in battle with the Titans. Their thwarted lust for ruin rages even now before our eyes in the mountain that but lately shot forth the fires of Typhos. Today the barbarian foemen bring to mind those savage creatures[18] against whom the King of Heaven had earlier moved to war.

Fired by these terrific thoughts, the poem blazes to the skies. Before he names the three battles, Salamis, Plataea, Himera, Pindar recalls to us, with an intensity astonishing

even for him, the fight where Hiero broke the sea-power of
Etruria (vv. 71 ff.):

λίσσομαι νεῦσον, Κρονίων, ἄμερον
ὄφρα κατ' οἶκον ὁ Φοῖνιξ ὁ Τυρσα-
νῶν τ' ἀλαλατὸς ἔχῃ, ναυ-
σίστονον ὕβριν ἰδὼν τὰν πρὸ Κύμας.

"Grant my supplication, O Son of Cronos! May the war-cry
of Carthaginian and Etruscan abide in quietness at home,
seeing that their pride by the shore of Cumae brought groan-
ing upon their ships." The battle of Cumae—Cumae named
earlier as part of the burden that imprisoned the defeated but
raging Typhos! The whole great region is volcanic—Vesuvius,
Stromboli, Aetna and their lesser neighbours link Syracuse
with Cumae by a chain of subterranean fires; Hiero triumphs
at Cumae over the enemies of sweet concord, and at the foot
of a volcano sets up a new home of order and harmonious
voices in the Dorian polity entrusted to his son. The voices:
Pindar prays not only that the barbarians may keep still at
home—ἄμερον, learning serenity in their own despite—but
that the *war-yell*, the ἀλαλατός, of Phoenician and Etruscan
may hold off: their savage cries are set against the "music"
of Hellas.[19] Yet again, when the leader of Syracusans tamed
them, casting their youthful warriors into the sea, that sea
into which rolled Aetna's lava-streams, the clamour rises:
"their ships groaned over their pride"—as was said elsewhere, "howl, ye ships of Tarshish!"

Of the final triad, two stanzas urge the dignity, tact, justice
and sincerity needed by a great ruler, and remind him of
"that fierce light which beats upon a throne." Whether these
maxims are meant for Hiero or for his son it is a little absurd
to discuss. The father would of course have much to say in the
government of Aetna; and Pindar cherishes a passionate desire that the new city shall live, not in the grip of an irrespon-
sible sultan, but under the guidance of a constitutional king.
In this way his personal advice is brought, like all the rest,
into the orbit of his great conception, civilization as the

world's music. And, these political exhortations delivered, though we pass to what seem quite personal concerns of wise lavishness and renown, the Golden Lyre is heard again in those beautiful lines that briefly contrast two other famous princes, Phalaris the Agrigentine, a name of horror throughout the West, and Croesus, whom Delphi and Delphi's loyal worshipper hold in grateful remembrance. Concerning Phalaris we hear only that he is beset by hostile *talk*, a last echo of the struggle between Heaven and the Titans; but the righteous and kindly Lydian wins melodious acclaim: "Lyremusic beneath the rafters welcomes him amid boyish voices to gentle fellowship." The Lyre is named at the close, as at the outset, joined now to youthful human song that breathes peace and friendship.

That symbolism is not only astonishingly fine, but quite obvious—so one would have said, but for Hermann's remarks which were quoted in the last lecture. Still, others[20] have naturally shown keener eyesight; in particular I am happy to own that a Swiss scholar, the amiable and acute Rauchenstein,[21] has in this ode anticipated all the separate points I had to make. So we need trouble less about Hermann, despite his vast erudition; for as a literary critic he stands in the lowest class. This award I base on a dictum in his *Opuscula*,[22] the most inept remark on poetry that ever found its way into print: "If we have rightly perceived what a poet, in view of the nature of his subject-matter, ought to say, we can easily perceive also how he has said it." That is, first you sit down and ask yourself "How should people write plays about Macbeth?" When you have got that clear, you decide: "Shakespeare bungled his *Macbeth*." One begins to understand why Voltaire said that Shakespeare was an imaginative savage whose works were fit only for London and Canada.[23]

Let me next offer two much slighter examples. That in the Twelfth Olympian is indeed very slight, but too pretty to omit, though three scholars, Boeckh, Heyne, and Gildersleeve, have already pointed to the picture. The notion that hopes disappoint is thus worded: "Oft up, oft down, hopes roll, cutting vain falsehoods." Why "cutting"? Why "up and down"? Ergoteles, the victor, lived at Himera, but was born in Crete, whence he had been driven by civil strife. Clearly the symbol is a sailing Ship, put in Pindar's mind by the exile's voyage from Crete to Sicily's northern coast. This figure is conveyed with marvellous skill by the rhythm, especially[24] by v. 6—one of the most haunting lines in Pindar:

πόλλ' ἄνω, τὰ δ' αὖ κάτω ψεύδη μεταμώνια τάμνοισαι κυλίνδοντ' ἐλπίδες.

No words ever written have better depicted the motion of a small sailing-ship: first the slow regular roll in the rhythm and rhyme of πόλλ' ἄνω τὰ δ' αὖ κάτω and the steady heave shown by the meaning of those two words ἄνω and κάτω, "up and down"; then a pause, and the quivering dip into more broken water, ψεύδη μεταμώνια; recovery, τάμνοισαι; then the slight shake, after which she "puts her nose into it" and the spray flies over the bows—κυλίνδοντ' ἐλπίδες. One must search long even in Virgil for anything to rival that!

The Seventh Isthmian, in honour of the poet's fellow-citizen Strepsiadas, relates among the achievements of Theba that she aided Sparta in her distress, putting it thus: ὀρθῷ ἔστασας ἐπὶ σφυρῷ (vv. 12 f.), "thou didst stand her upon an upright ankle"—"pulled her to her feet," as we say. The symbol is a War-horse: it stumbles in the fray, but its skilful rider helps it to recover. No sooner do we take that symbol than we see why, later in the ode, Bellerophon is selected as an example of audacity: because of Pegasus, his winged steed. And when the poet says (v. 19) that achievement is "yoked" to glorious streams of poetry, we see what dictated that otherwise harsh metaphor. Argos is called ἵππιον, "land of horses," and Iolaus receives the strange adjective ἱππόμητις, which (however) has no affinity with our "horse-sense," but means "with knightly heart," for the horse was even then, and even in non-Dorian Athens, as Aristophanes' play is of itself enough to prove, the sign of knightly prowess and ideals:[25] which of course is Pindar's reason for selecting the symbol.

Now we turn to a dazzling *tour de force*, the symbol which

gives that amazing Seventh Nemean whatever unity it possesses—the Triple Diadem. It deserves close attention, less because of the symbolism itself, which is fairly obvious and not too successful, than because it throws light on Pindar's conception of his art. The Triple Diadem is described in these gorgeous lines (77 ff.):

εἴρειν στεφάνους ἐλαφρόν· ἀναβάλεο· Μοῖσά τοι
κολλᾷ χρυσὸν ἔν τε λευκὸν ἐλέφανθ᾽ ἁμᾷ
καὶ λείριον ἄνθεμον ποντίας ὑφελοῖσ᾽ ἐέρσας.

"Twining garlands is a light employ. Strike up! The Muse, we know, weldeth gold and white ivory therewith, and lily-blossom culled from beneath the sea-foam." It is commonly[26] assumed that the whole of this describes Pindar's work. If so, we should be astonished by ἐλαφρόν. "An easy task"? It is needless to cite the passages in which Pindar tells us again and again, what we are quite ready to believe, that his odes are the achievement of genius toiling mightily.[27] The first sentence must mean "anyone can turn you out a set of complimentary verses"; and ἀναβάλεο, "strike up," is here a dignified analogue of our "Go ahead!" To this the next words offer a contrast, the powerful κολλᾷ, "welds," being set against the slight εἴρειν, "twine," and the three materials of the Triple Diadem utterly outbalancing στεφάνους, "garlands." "Any journeyman," he means, "will produce for you, without effort or inspiration, a string or so of poetical flowers; but the genuine Muse toils at her task, welding three elements into a solid and enduring crown. So you must not chafe if I have sung other things than you expected: a Pindaric ode is a richer, more variegated, work than you thought."

For we are not to accept the belief that these lines are but a vaguely rich description. That would be a mere bit of confectionery, which it is impossible to suppose that Pindar would have conveyed in language not only superb but definite: nothing could be less like the heady verbiage of dithyrambists. He unmistakably enumerates three definite and different things, which his Muse welds together; and he in-

tends something specific by each of them. No one will assert
that he means them literally; but before going further we
should see how the material Diadem appears to his imagination. Not only is it composed of splendid materials: it forms a
rich colour-scheme—gold, white, and red.[28] If proof is demanded, we find it in the phrase "white ivory": everyone
knows that ivory is white, but the adjective is inserted to
press the idea of colour upon us. In adding coral Pindar has
shown an exquisite adroitness which even he never surpassed.
The journeyman-poet can offer nothing but flowers, yet they
must be entwined even in the most august verse; and because
no goldsmith can weld ordinary blossoms to gold or ivory,
Pindar selects the only flower that can be thus treated, the
stone-like red blossom sought beneath the dew of the sea by
his divine Artificer herself.

This Diadem, we said, is the symbol of the Seventh Nemean. But it serves another purpose too. Just as the Lyre of
the First Pythian engendered the feeling and imagination of
the whole, but is saluted as a power in its own right; so here
the Diadem is meant by the poet for a picture of his own art.
Among the themes which exercised him while he wrote this
ode is the influence of poetry: here he analyses its power. The
gold is to be identified as the illumination, the poet's way of
viewing things. What is the coral? Flowers, as we saw: to the
poetic vision is added the grace of lovely words. And for what
does the ivory stand? For that glamour of poetry, the power
to bewitch, described earlier when he tells us concerning
Homer (vv. 22 ff.): "Upon his falsehoods and soaring skill is
shed a mysterious grandeur, and his poesy beguileth us with
seductive legends."[29] It is Homer himself who uses ivory to
symbolize untruth, when he sings that true dreams issue from
the gate of horn, false dreams from the gate of ivory. Pindar
has refined a little on this idea: after "lies," he goes on to
"mysterious grandeur" and perversions due to poetry. He
has in mind not so much lies as glamour in the old sense, a
sorcery that causes the eye to see what is not there, or fail to
see what is there.[30] Hesiod expresses the same idea when he

reports that the Muses themselves had said to him: "We know how to tell many falsehoods in the guise of fact; and, when we so desire, we know how to utter truths."[31] Yet Pindar is the very man who usually insists—who insists in this same ode—that he possesses the truth, and at times indeed that he will correct earlier versions of myth.[32] Why should he, of all poets, describe his art as containing the ivory of falsehood? Because at this moment of his career he finds himself forced to insist that it does and must somehow contain this "ivory." The seed of deception lies often not in the speaker but in the hearer. Apollo is ever truthful, but those who receive his oracles have many times left Delphi with error in their minds. Of Apollo's servants the same is true: what they sing is misunderstood, and Pindar, as we saw, here maintains that the Aeginetans mistook his purpose in the Sixth Paean. A deeply felt passage of our poem (vv. 23 ff.) insists on this: "The greatest multitude of men have a blind soul. For had it been that they could see the truth" Ajax would never have come to self-murder. That must have been the thought underlying a prayer in one of his fragments: "O sovereign Truth, foundation of high excellence, cause not my pledge to stumble against jagged falsehood."[33] How else could Truth cause his plighted word to stumble against the stone of falsehood, unless the truth itself can become deceitful through the stupidity of the heart to which it is offered? For him then, poetry is a blend of gold, coral, and ivory—of masterly conception, of verbal loveliness, and of a certain magic waywardness that, whatever his intent, misleads the multitude at times.

So much for the qualities of the Triple Diadem in itself. Less need be said about its influence as a symbol governing the structure of the whole ode. We observe at once that three topics, corresponding to the three elements in the Diadem, engage our attention throughout: praise of the boy-victor Sogenes, the power of song, and Pindar's alleged slander uttered at Delphi against Neoptolemus. This last topic, in all its implications, whether painful, sinister, or amusing, has been discussed earlier. Into the second, the power of song, we entered just now. As for the victor's praises, Pindar has put himself into an ungracious and rather absurd position, from which he extricates himself not unskilfully. Having seized on this occasion as an opportunity to put himself right with the Aeginetans in general, he writes a long and tortuous exculpation which allows him little space for the ostensible theme of his ode. Nevertheless, he finds room for a compliment very striking and by reason of its quaintness memorable: no doubt it was often quoted in the family with reverence or amusement, according to each man's sense of humour. Pindar claims that Heracles should persuade Zeus and Athena to bless young Sogenes and should himself confer lifelong strength and happiness upon the lad, with honour to his posterity; all because Sogenes lives between two shrines of this accommodating demigod!

Here then is the Triple Diadem, and here are the three elements which are joined into a crown of song. But is the blending satisfactory? Do we find the three subjects merging into a higher unity? No. There is in fact nothing but juxtaposition and a statement that unity has been wrought. The Diadem is not a normal symbol, rather a picture of tripartition. So Pindar himself seems to imply: his word κολλᾷ means fastening together, as by cement or molten lead, things that have each its own quality and retain it when joined. "I have made a splendid ode, but the three ideas in it have no natural connexion: they are combined by force, not blending imperceptibly, as I usually cause such elements to blend—you may see them still distinct from one another and detect the sutures." Indeed he more than hints (vv. 70 ff.) at an apology for his obtrusion of the Neoptolemus scandal. Thus, to speak pedantically, one attractive feature in this poem is that Pindar almost explicitly announces his method of symbolism by the external, heavy-handed way in which he has here forced it upon his work.

Certain more intricate but equally pleasant instances of symbolism shall be reserved for subsequent lectures. At present hear but one other. The Tenth Olympian is thus described by Farnell: "He is composing at the height of his powers, both of imagination and expression. Language and feeling are at white heat; the phrases are often arresting and strained, but never unnatural; the invocation of the thunderbolt of Zeus resounds with the crash of the elements; but the tense energy that animates most of the poem leaves room for grace and sweetness." And again: "that astonishing outburst about the thunder, perhaps the most daring and stormy verse that he ever forged." This passage (vv. 80 ff.) Farnell translates: "The thunder and the fire-forgèd shaft of Zeus, the awakener of the uproar in the heavens, the gleaming levinbolt, welded to Omnipotence." That eulogy, so far as it goes, is well deserved, yet the impression thereby conveyed is but partly true. Neither Farnell nor anyone else, I believe, has noted the symbolism of the Pebble and the manner in which that little picture is mirrored in the choice of myths and the very language. Even Gildersleeve, though he gives admirable notes on the opening passage, where the Pebble is actually mentioned, does not carry the matter through, asserting indeed that the lines (vv. 53 ff.) about Time shaming Pindar give "the key to the poem."

Hagesidamus, son of Archestratus, belonging to Western Locri in Italy, won the prize in the boys' boxing contest of 476 B.C.[34] The Eleventh[35] Olympian was composed for the same success, and probably at the moment; for, though admirable, it is very short: almost certainly it promises[36] a more elaborate poem, the Tenth Olympian, which we are now to consider. This he plainly did not send so promptly as he and others hoped, wherefore he confesses bluntly that he had forgotten his debt. The delay lasted perhaps several years.[37] This debt-idea explains his choice of a symbol, for pebbles were used by the Greeks in money-calculations. In the first thirteen lines Pindar elaborates the notion of his debt and what the Locrians in general, or Archestratus in particular, thought of his slackness in payment. This lengthy disquisition, and especially v. 13, "Precision rules the city of the Western Locrians," mean that he is half humorously, half maliciously,

twitting them with their business-like insistence that he
should produce the article which was overdue, perhaps already paid for. Locri, it should be remembered throughout,
was an important commercial centre.³⁸ The opening words are
a metaphor from bookkeeping: "Read the place in my heart
where Archestratus' son has been written down, the Olympian victor: for I owe him a sweet song but forgot it." In v. 4,
ὀρθᾷ χερί, "with accurate hand," alludes to an exact count of
the pebbles. His address to the Muse and to Truth means,
then: "Calculate exactly what I owe, thus enabling me to
destroy my ill-repute as a debtor, and a debtor to friends." He
proceeds: "The date on which payment was due, once so distant, has come upon me from afar and made me blush to
think how deep is my debt." Then comes mention of "interest": meaning, probably, special pains taken over this ode.
The sentence that follows (9 f.),

$$\text{ὀρᾶτ' ὦν νῦν ψᾶφον ἐλισσομέναν}$$
$$\text{ὀπᾷ κῦμα κατακλύσσει ῥέον,}$$

has often been misunderstood. The translation should be
somewhat thus: "Now mark how the flowing billow shall
wash away the rolling pebble." The point is a play on the two
usages of ψᾶφος, in a brilliantly effective phrase: the pebble-
calculation shall be obliterated by a flood of song. But the
metaphor alludes not to a beach or tides: what did Pindar
know of tides? He has in mind what was far more familiar,
described so vividly by Homer,³⁹ the work of the gardener
who irrigates his land, making a channel for the bubbling
water that thrusts along all the little pebbles in its course.
Next, κοινὸς λόγος is "the reckoning agreed," the entry in
which we are both mentioned, you as creditor, I as debtor.
And 'Ατρέκεια in v. 13 is not "Justice" (as Sandys translates)
but "Precision." The line, for all its dignity of wording, conveys what we might put colloquially: "these Locrians are the
last people with whom to play fast and loose." Throughout
this opening passage Pindar is arch.

Almost the whole poem is influenced by this symbolic Pebble and the accuracy for which it stands. The tale of Heracles' battles is based upon the idea of exacting a debt (vv. 28 ff.): "He killed Eurytus," we read, "that he might exact from overweening Augeas, less willing to pay than he to receive, the wage for menial service"—that is, in cleansing the Augean stables. And if we bear in mind what the poet has said earlier, we shall find still greater pungency in the lines (vv. 34 ff.) depicting Augeas' downfall:

καὶ μὰν ξεναπάτας
Ἐπειῶν βασιλεὺς ὄπιθεν
οὐ πολλὸν ἴδε πατρίδα πολυ-
κτέανον ὑπὸ στερεῷ πυρὶ
πλαγαῖς τε σιδάρου βαθὺν εἰς ὀχετὸν ἄτας
ἵζοισαν ἑὰν πόλιν.

"And lo, that cozener of guests, the Epeian king, no long time thereafter saw his country, full of riches, sink beneath cruel flame and smiting by the sword into a deep trench of ruin, his own city." "Trench"—ὀχετός? Why "trench"? For that, or "channel," conveys the true sense, not "gulf" or "pit," as some translate it. We must never blur Pindar's sensitive diction by asking ourselves what he should have written (to quote Hermann again) and then making him say it. The word, rightly taken, is at first puzzling,[40] but the truth is that once again we have met a twist of style which must be explained by the symbol and the use already made of it. Pindar might elsewhere have written only βαθεῖαν ἵζοισαν εἰς ἄταν, "sinking into deep ruin"; but his language here is coloured by what he has said about the debt, the pebble, and the flood of song, together with the ὀχετηγός—that is why he uses ὀχετός— the irrigator named in Homer's simile, which is at the back of his mind and which his language must recall to hearers familiar, like all Greeks, with Homeric poetry.

In the longer passage (vv. 43–77) which follows, concerning the institution of the Olympic festival by Heracles, emphasis lies not on debt but on the "precision" which the Pebble implies. There is a second and more exact account of Heracles' arrangements—"he marked off the sacred enclosure," and so forth.[41] A business-like list follows of winners in the six contests of that first festival. It is manifest that Pindar has not invented these names: nay more, he states with elaborate emphasis that the details he reports are the slow but accurate discovery of Time, which also (we remember) has brought his own debt to light (v. 7). Moreover, the preceding story, though not discreditable to Heracles, relates an exploit by no means so breath-bereaving as those more frequently related of him. He is no solitary champion, but leader of an army, which (whether he was present or not) suffered defeat at first. All this sounds like genuine history: we observe the ἀτρέκεια— the determination, already noted, to have the facts right at last. There seems no doubt that Pindar draws upon some work of antiquarian scholarship, which claimed by research to correct inaccurate tradition. That such a book appeared at so early a date may astonish us, but nothing else will account for his matter and manner: no odd picking up new facts from οἱ σοφώτεροι will serve—someone had published a book on "The Origins of the Olympian Festival."[42] It is, moreover, certain that he was a citizen of western Locri; for that state had otherwise no interest in the early history of Olympia, and it is unlike Pindar's method in these matters to introduce with so much elaboration the researches published by a citizen of some other state. He is paying a compliment to the victor's city which (as he says) studies the Muse.

Here let us pause in our survey. It is time that we dealt with a disquiet that may possess some minds when offered this doctrine. One may now and again begin to doubt whether our symbolism is really at work, since the power wherewith it comes upon the spirit seems to vary with the reader's mood, and one may be tempted to exclaim: "If the symbol dominates his most splendid work, why does he not tell us of that domination? If a Lyre or a War-horse is essential to the aesthetic unity of his poem, he must be clumsy or negligent, thus leaving us to discover, or fail to discover, a fact so momentous." To think thus is to mistake the manner in which poetry works upon us. That a poet cannot tell us everything is but a part of the matter: if he could he would not. Here is no accident or reason for lamentation: those who wish the full meaning set out in black and white, who cry "If that is what he intends, why does he not say so?" lose the essence of poetical art, and of all art. For the effect is such that by its nature it must steal upon us unawares, as if from ambush, most magically in those hours when, as Dante says, "our mind, more of a wanderer from the body and less thought-ridden, becomes in its visions almost prophetic":[43]

> la mente nostra peregrina
> più dalla carne, e men da' pensier presa,
> alle sue vision quasi è divina.

Goethe confessed to Herder concerning one of his poems: "it is all merely brain-work."[44] Who does not know that in ordinary social intercourse there is much advice, much information, that cannot be given in so many words but only by hints, not as a matter of kindness or tact merely, but because it is so tenuous that conveyance by direct language is downright impossible? In lyric poetry (at least) this must be so: the emotions conveyed are by their nature such that they enter one's consciousness indirectly, or not at all. Force upon them the shape of explicit syllables, and you make them too gross to enter the pores of the soul.

All that may be familiar enough: it is as old as the so-called Longinus' treatise *On the Sublime*;[45] but it needs to be remembered afresh whenever new poetry is discussed or old poetry studied in a novel manner. A very modern poet, Mallarmé, felt himself constrained to restate it when defending a new school. "The young fellows," he said, "are nearer to the poetic ideal than the Parnassians, who still handle their themes in the fashion of the old philosophers and the old rhetoricians, presenting subjects directly. I believe that, on the contrary, there should be nothing but allusion. The contemplation of subjects, the image taking wing from the reveries excited by them, are the song. The Parnassians, for their part, take full hold of a thing and display it; thereby, they lack mystery: they deprive the mind of that delicious joy—the belief that it is performing an act of creation."[46] Admirably said, but somewhat too loosely. The mind's delight in its own real or supposed act of creation arises from other artistic forms also: it is (for instance) the essence of wit that the hearer is induced to supply something himself and to thrill with a sense of collaboration. In poetry lies an element analogous to this, indeed, but conferring a nobler boon—not merely pleasure in one's own nimble intelligence, but a strengthening of the imagination.

Such mystery, then, sometimes hard to pierce, sometimes airy and alluring, must always hover between poem and reader. When, moreover, the poet belongs to another world than ours, employs an imagination no less original than opulent, and writes an alien language, the veil will often baffle any gaze but the most patient. And, further, students of this poet face an obstacle peculiar (it appears) to him among ancient writers. Pindar himself, in so many words, openly warns even his contemporaries that these poems are especially difficult; indeed, that they (or some of them) are puzzles. Let me cite again that passage of the Second Olympian (vv. 83 ff.) which declares: "Many keen arrows do I bear in the quiver beneath my elbow. For the wise they have a voice, but for the crowd they need interpreters."[47] That is proof, authoritative and emphatic, not merely that we are justified in employing our utmost subtlety upon the elucidation of his work, but that without such subtlety our efforts will often be in vain.

SYMBOLISM

(*Continued*)

THE PRECEDING LECTURE pointed to a new method of interpreting Pindar: namely, study of his symbolism; and offered a few easy examples of its working. Before we go on to more complex or subtle instances it may be well to face a somewhat embarrassing question: "If this doctrine is true, why has no one announced it before?" A complete answer cannot be offered, but sundry considerations may be found that will save us from the charge of implying that (like Homer's hero) we vaunt ourselves much better than our fathers. This new doctrine is by no means the only critical novelty that has been overlooked by brilliant, shrewd, or vastly learned men, to be noted by others in a later day. Horace, the *numerosus Horatius* as Ovid[1] called him, "the expert in metres," himself believed that Pindar's dithyrambs could not be scanned: today no one agrees with Horace. Countless readers have studied Pindar in a frame of mind which made it next to impossible that such a view as ours should occur to them: you may recall what was said in an earlier lecture about the harmful and long-continued severance of classical scholarship from genuine poetical criticism. Throughout the history of letters this inertia again and again has benumbed faculties otherwise active. Literature of a new type, an unfamiliar flavour, has often been misunderstood despite what now seem the plainest indications of its quality. One has but to recall the grotesque captions added to the Song of Solomon by King James's translators; Euripides' deadly lampoon on the Delphic oracle, which even Verrall's[2] skill has not yet succeeded in bringing home to some; the early opinions concerning Wordsworth's new themes and new diction; the chorus of abuse that greeted the first performance of Ibsen in London.

Further, although this doctrine has not been promulgated before, two adumbrations of it have been made. As long ago as 1885, Gildersleeve,[3] who must still be revered as greatest among Pindaric scholars, wrote: "Pindar's poems are constellations. There are figures in the heavens, a belt, a plough, a chair, a serpent, a flight of doves, but around them clusters much else. The Phorminx is the name of the constellation called the First Pythian." This *obiter dictum*, unfortunately nowhere elaborated, supplies vital help in few words, as was Gildersleeve's way. Questions of priority seem important to many; and it may be asked whether I owe my doctrine of symbolism to him. Frankly, I cannot say: it is now many years since I first studied his edition. On the whole, it is probable that I derived the idea from him. But he nowhere else, I believe, hints at it; and I have carried it into developments which I can only hope would have received his sanction. Again, we may point to certain sentences of Fraccaroli's invaluable *Prolegomeni*.[4] After translating the proem of the Sixth Isthmian—the Three Libations—he remarks that this image influences Pindar so strongly that it returns, to take the central place in his picture of Heracles' visit, and engenders secondary analogous phrases elsewhere in the ode— Αἴγιναν κάτα σπένδειν μελιφθόγγοις ἀοιδαῖς (8 f.) : νᾶσον ῥαινέμεν εὐλογίαις (21) : Χαρίτων ἄρδοντι καλλίστᾳ δρόσῳ (63 f.) : πίσω σφε Δίρκας ἁγνὸν ὕδωρ (74). All this, so far as it goes, gives us welcome endorsement. Fraccaroli, by the way, asserts that such effects do not spring from "an act of consciousness or will": how he became sure of this, we are not told. It seems more natural to believe that the symbol is definitely present in Pindar's mind, though we shall hardly suppose that he worked out the extent to which it should colour the diction. There grew in his imagination not a programme, but a picture, now more dimly, now more brightly present in all its colours.

We are next to study other instances of symbolism, more complex, if not more beautiful, than those considered in the preceding lecture. You will remark—and on this I would lay especial emphasis—that some of them provide what seems to me an irresistible proof that the symbol-theory is sound. If an ode has been proclaimed unintelligible in its whole drift, or if striking details have been given over as inexplicable by all commentators from the Alexandrians to our own day; and if this new doctrine reveals the whole poem as a unified work of art, the seemingly irrelevant items falling into place, may we not claim to have lit upon Pindar's conception of his topic and traced with some sureness the journey of his imagination? What have our commentators[5] reported of the Eleventh Pythian, to which we shall now turn? First a scholiast raises his familiar wail: "Pindar has wrought the panegyric excellently; but in the sequel he has employed a most irrelevant digression." Distinguished modern editors have said more. Boeckh writes: "Anyone who has determined to perform duly the office of an interpreter, will meet in scarcely any ode so much difficulty as this presents"; Mezger: "The explanation of the poem confronts a commentator with such difficulties as hardly any other contains"; Gildersleeve: "In most of the odes the meaning of the myth, its office as an incorporation of the thought, can, at least, be divined. Here the uncertainty of the date and the unusual character of the story combine to baffle historical interpretation"; Wilamowitz: "*Pythian* XI especially is one of the obscurest among his poems"; Farnell erupts as follows: "This ode is certainly unique among Pindar's works; for while it is marked by vigour and other characteristics of our poet, it is quite unpardonable; so wilful and amazing is the irrelevance of the greater part of it, an irrelevance which no commentator's learning or penetration can explain or excuse." You are now, I hope, prepared to be patient with one who attempts to unravel so tangled a skein! Though I might offer the explanation first and then show how it puts everything into place, I believe it will be more interesting if I ask you to follow my own explorations, made when I first seriously attacked this famous enigma. You all know Anatole France's *dictum* that criticism is an account of the soul's adventures among masterpieces. Let me tell you mine.

First hear an outline of the poem, which I will borrow from Gildersleeve. "Pindar calls on the daughters of Kadmos and

Harmonia to chant Themis and Pytho in honor of the victory
of Thrasydaios, which he won in the land of Pylades, the host
of Orestes. Upon this invocation . . . follows the familiar
story of Orestes, which ends here with the death of Klytaimnestra and her paramour, Aigisthos, a myth which hardly
seems to belong to a joyous *epinikion*. If Pindar had kept his
usual proportion, the story would have extended through the
third triad, but . . . he exclaims that he has been whirled out
of his course, summons the Muse to fulfil the promised task,
and praises the achievements of Thrasydaios, recounting how
the house had won in the chariot-race at Olympia and put to
shame their rivals at Pytho. Then, putting himself in the
victor's place, Pindar prays for a right spirit, for the love of
what is noble, for self-control in the midst of effort. Hence
the middle rank is best, not the lofty fate of overlords. But if
the height is scaled, then avoid insolence. Such a noble soul
is Thrasydaios . . . ; such Iolaos . . . ; such Kastor and Poly-
deukes, sons of the gods, who dwell one day at Therapnai,
one within Olympos."

I began with the story of Orestes' vengeance (vv. 17–37).[6]
It is beautifully done, especially the first sentence, a notable
specimen of Pindar's sweeping style; but (quite apart from
its relevance to the whole ode) it contains puzzling elements.
Why is the nurse of Orestes called Arsinoa? The question
seems trivial, but her name was reported by Stesichorus and
Pherecydes as Laodameia.[7] Other enigmas call for longer discussion.

On Orestes' conduct Pindar remarks only this (vv. 36 f.):
"But in later years with warrior hand he slew his mother and
laid Aegisthus low in blood." Detachment could not be more
complete. But the absence of comment need not greatly surprise us: the story is one element in a rather short ode, and
he cannot discuss everything—indeed he appears in the next
sentence (ἦρ', ὦ φίλοι κτέ.) to chide himself for saying even so
much.[8] But this silence emphasizes by contrast Pindar's precise questioning (vv. 22–25) about Clytaemnestra's reasons
for slaying Agamemnon: "Was it perchance the slaughter of

Iphigenia beside the Euripus, far from her homeland, that stung Clytaemnestra to launch wrath of heavy hand? Or did couchings in the night hours misguide her, o'ermastered by another union?" The words that I have translated last are usually taken to mean "overborne by a new love"—her passion for Aegisthus. But that involves a flat tautology: the view of Bergk and Fennell is certainly right:[9] "humiliated by another connexion on Agamemnon's part," namely his amour with the captive princess Cassandra, who therefore appears in no less than three separate passages of the myth, the others being "the Trojan damsel" (vv. 19 f.) and "the damsel of prophecy" (v. 33). That is astonishing,[10] and so is the silence of nearly all commentators[11] on Pindar's repetition. But there can be no question that for Pindar, at this moment, the "prophetic maid" is a chief element in the story. Why? There was my first perplexity, which perforce I left unsolved, and passed on.

After alluding to "the citizens' malicious tongues," he proceeds (29 f.):

ἴσχει τε γὰρ ὄλβος οὐ μείονα φθόνον·
ὁ δὲ χαμηλὰ πνέων ἄφαντον βρέμει.

"For prosperity bringeth jealousy in equal measure, but—." But what? That second line is the hardest in the poem. Still, if I am to discuss it, I must make shift to offer a provisional translation—"but he whose breath is of the earth murmureth obscurely." Scholars are divided in their interpretation. A good number think that the lowly man murmurs *against* the prosperous, in which case the whole passage will mean "prosperity bringeth jealousy in equal measure, but the censure of the humble is obscure"—that is, "disregarded," "ineffectual." If they are right, Pindar has written ineptly, for the logic of the passage forbids us to minimize such censure or malice. The other interpretation must be right, though it brings in a new perplexity. These two lines must contrast the lot of the great and that of the lowly: prosperity brings jealousy equal to itself, while the man of low station escapes jealousy because he is unobserved. Excellent, so far! But what are we to make of βρέμει, "murmureth" as I provisionally translated it? Had Pindar written ἄφαντος πέλει,[12] "*is* obscure," all would have been simple: the groundling by his obscurity escapes the vexations to which high fortune lies open. But how can βρέμει mean ἐστί? There is the great question, which, nevertheless, has rarely[13] been observed. Mezger writes "passes his life unnoticed," but unfortunately loses his hold and proceeds with "the humming tumult of the great multitude, in which no definite voice can be distinguished." Pindar says naught of any great multitude; Mezger has blurred the real point by admitting after all a reminiscence of the "obscure spite" notion. To sum up: βρέμει, which means "utters a hoarse indistinct noise," must by some mysterious transvaluation here be used to mean or imply merely "lives." "Is that possible?" I asked myself. "Can I see any door in the wall up to which I have insisted on walking?"

Turning aside, I came to Pindar's proclamation (vv. 52 ff.) of the more durable prosperity enjoyed by the middle class (τὰ μέσα) in the state, and μέμφομ' αἶσαν τυραννίδων—"I condemn the lot of princes": that is, despite their prestige, they make a poor bargain of life. For even here, where he shows some real conception of the community, he is concerned mainly with the bearing of this or that political creed upon the comfort and reputation of the man who entertains it.[14] Nevertheless, he expresses a genuinely political view, and the excellent phrase that follows, ξυναῖσι δ' ἀμφ' ἀρεταῖς τέταμαι, "the social virtues are my passion,"[15] reinforces his remark about τὰ μέσα: he believes in a polity where the citizens of middle standing coöperate; that is, in the virtues of a commonwealth as compared with monarchy or despotism. There follows a description of the "longer prosperity."[16] "(And thus) spiteful foes are avoided. If a man keeps himself from dread arrogance by gaining eminence in *them* (the social virtues) and by quietly cultivating *them*, he can move towards a fairer verge of black death, leaving to his sweet children that best of boons, the grace of good repute." "Fairer" means "fairer than that awaiting a despot." The citizen who modestly serves the common good wins a fairer lot upon the dark beach of death than Agamemnon found upon "the shadowy bank of Acheron" (v. 21)—those two phrases point the contrast.

The final stanza offers examples of men on whom this conduct bestows renown, Iolaus and the Twin Brethren who dwell in Therapnae and in Heaven on alternate days. These names endorse our view of the passage just cited: to wit, that it concerns the ξυναὶ ἀρεταί—the social virtues (in our modern phrase) or "noble coöperation," whereof Iolaus is in truth a fine exemplar, possibly the finest, for not only was he the trusty squire of Heracles: he is scarcely ever thought of apart from him. And if an even better instance can be found, it is the Twin Brethren who owe their strange immortality not to ἀρετά simply, but to noble comradeship.

Opinion has been almost unanimous[17] that Pindar here has in mind the politics of his own time. But to what feature thereof? The allegorizing school discovered orchidaceous blooms even more startling than their usual display: it suffices to mention that even the acute and wary Mezger[18] detected the Persian generalissimo Mardonius in the guise of Agamemnon, and in Cassandra the city of Thebes. Later scholars have remarked that such imaginings should be rejected, if for no other reason, because Pindar could not have hoped that any hearer would solve the charade, as Fraccaroli[19] calls it, and have wisely referred to real despotisms in Pindar's day. It is certain that he has in mind the despots of Sicily.[20] He had just returned to Thebes from Syracuse, and realized that his fellow-citizens looked on him with suspicion as a man who had gained wealth in foreign courts[21] and was perhaps an agent of the tyrants. They are indeed κακολόγοι πολῖται, "slanderous citizens," and he makes it his first business to set himself right with his own people as a simple member of the Theban community.

These two great passages, the Orestes-myth and the discussion of politics, fill most of our ode. Two others have not yet been discussed, each of which contains something mys-

terious. Why are heroines only, not heroes, summoned to the
Ismenion shrine? Why does Pindar, when recalling his Muse
from her vagaries to pursue only the task for which she has
been hired, use (it would seem) the most inappropriate phrase
conceivable? ἄλλοτ' ἄλλᾳ ταρασσέμεν, "to bustle hither and
thither" (v. 42), we protest, is precisely what he should forbid. To these difficulties are added the two which were postponed: βρέμει and the great importance allotted to Cassandra.
Finally, what bond connects the four portions: procession to
the Ismenion, Orestes-myth, praise of Thrasydaeus and his
family, political doctrine?

All these questions are answered by the symbol, to be discerned, as often, in the words that puzzle us most—ὁ δὲ χαμηλὰ
πνέων ἄφαντον βρέμει (v. 30). Here is yet another of those at
first sight impossible phrases which have been distorted (for
us foreign students) by the pressure of the symbols, and are
often, for that very reason, our most obvious guides to them.
The word βρέμει is after all quite natural from one point of
view: for, instead of using "live," or "exist," we may name
some characteristic and vital action of the person or creature
whereof we speak. Coleridge writes:

> Were it not better hope a nobler doom,
> Proud to believe that with more active powers
>   On rapid many-coloured wing
>   We thro' one bright perpetual Spring
>   Shall hover round the fruits and flowers,
> Screen'd by those clouds and cherish'd by those showers?

"Hover" of course does not precisely and emphatically suggest "we shall fail to settle on the fruit." The idea is: "We—as
insects—shall live happily"; and for "live" is set a word describing a familiar act of theirs.[22] So in our Pindaric passage:
the Greek is quite normal if we take it as alluding to the
"lowly life" of some creature that hums. The symbol, in fact,
of this ode is the Bee. That prophetesses were often called
"bees" is well attested: Pindar himself calls a response from
Delphi an "oracle of the Delphian bee."[23] To this symbol, it

may be surmised, he was led by an accident, that the goal of Thrasydaeus' festal procession was Apollo's prophetic shrine. The ancient habit of discovering significance in names worked strongly upon him, and Ἰσμήνιον suggested σμῆνος to his fancy—"a beehive," sometimes "a swarm of bees"—no less obviously than Ἑλένα suggested ἑλένας to Aeschylus or Αἴας αἰάζειν to Sophocles.[24] His fancy thus caught, constructive imagination takes control, and he writes of women only in these opening stanzas, simply because male prophets were never called "bees." No other reason can be adduced with any confidence for his invitation of heroines only to the Ismenion.[25]

If we reread the ode with our symbol in mind, we shall not only see fresh colour and force in single words or phrases: ὁμοθάλαμε (v. 2 b), Μελίαν (v. 4), ἐπίνομον (v. 7 b), ὁμαγερέα (v. 8), ἔκνιξεν (v. 23), πυρωθέντων Τρώων ἔλυσε δόμους ἀβρότατος (vv. 33 ff.), ἐδινήθην (v. 38), νεμόμενος (v. 55 b), γλυκυτάτᾳ (v. 57)—some of which, indeed, are very faint, while others have pungency: above all, the burning out of Troy's rich homes. More than this: we shall at length understand the emphasis laid on Cassandra in the myth: she was beyond compare the most famous μέλισσα of all. Not less welcome is the explanation, in this way only to be attained, of a sentence at first sight gratuitously bad. Ἄλλοτ' ἄλλᾳ ταρασσέμεν, which we translated "to bustle hither and thither,"[26] has engendered a crop of emendations which will not tempt us if we realize the symbol's presence. "Muse, since you have hired out your voice, it is just now your part to busy yourself with Thrasydaeus," etc. As βρέμει can imply "live" when said of a bee, ἄλλοτ' ἄλλᾳ ταρασσέμεν can imply "perform your normal function"—but, again, only when applied to a bee. Pindar compares himself thereto, as in ἐδινήθην (v. 38), "I swung about." It is important to notice that the symbol is strongly felt here, for otherwise it would be absurd to write ἄλλοτ' ἄλλᾳ exactly when he is calling his Muse back from her roamings.[27] Without the symbol the passage is wantonly obscure and worse,[28] as the ruthless translation of Morice reveals: "'Tis thine on various themes to ply the vagrant tongue!" ἄλλοτ' ἄλλᾳ does not mean "vagrant," but "round and about one bush or mass of flowers."

The Bee-symbol governs, inspires, and explains this whole ode, complex but not confused. Receiving a commission to celebrate a Theban boy, Pindar decides to use this opportunity of a Theban ode to justify himself in Theban eyes concerning that affection for despotic governments which his Sicilian visit was thought to have inspired. On these two facts his sorcery begins to work—sorcery, we call it, for who can here confidently expound cause and effect, or tell where study ends and the sudden swoop of genius begins? To strengthen what he means to say concerning politics, he first relates a myth that reveals sin and sorrow dogging the most illustrious of all Greek dynasties. In that story Cassandra plays a part—the prophetess, the Bee . . . from that picture all the poem radiates. Even the substitution of Arsinoa for Laodameia is now explained: the name means[29] "sagacious," suggesting the wise insect. Pindar himself is a bee—he said something like that twenty-four years ago, in his earliest ode[30]—and now his swaying minstrelsy hovers busily round Thrasydaeus and his father. In the Orestes-myth, his lowly man is figured as a bee, and what more natural, since the best life for a citizen is found, not in arrogant and selfish splendours, but in ξυναὶ ἀρεταί, those communal virtues whereof the bee is Nature's best exemplar? So we move in festal procession rejoicing round the happy lad as he steps along with his garland to the shrine of the Hive, our own Ismenion.

Far-fetched? Too complicated? Such questions depend for their answer upon the feeling of each reader, as he cons yet again the strange sumptuous fabric of these verses. Two things, at least, must surely be granted: first, that Pindar did not fling out a handful of topics pell-mell; second, that had he made his symbolism entirely clear and unmistakable, he would have half-ruined his ode, since the delight of such things resides not least in the eager questing of those for whom it was composed.

There ends the most complicated demonstration that I shall lay before you: that is how I worked out the ode for myself. Our next example, though both charming and a little quaint, presents far less elaboration. Elaboration . . . Often, perhaps, I may give the impression that Pindar deliberately[31] made his odes difficult. That is the worst of using language at all! In his symbolic poetry is some entirely conscious intellectual construction, some entirely instinctive pressure of imagination: to say how much of each, would be charlatanism in any critic, but the words I use must (alas!) be intellectual instruments only.

The Sixth Olympian was written for Hagesias, a citizen both of Syracuse in Sicily and of the Arcadian town Stymphalus; he won the race with a team of mules, probably in 468 B.C. The ode appears to have been performed first at Stymphalus, later at Syracuse. In vv. 12–17 we read: "For thee, Hagesias, that praise is ready which long ago Adrastus justly pronounced straightway for the prophet Amphiaraus, Oecleus' son, when the earth engulfed him and his bright steeds. And thereafter, when the seven death-pyres were finished, Adrastus spake at Thebes this word: 'I mourn the star of my army, both a good prophet and a good spearman.'" Pindar alludes to the expedition of the Seven Champions against Thebes, led by Adrastus: all seven fell in the assault and Adrastus pronounced funeral orations upon them. This famous legend occurs often in ancient literature: the full story was related in a lost epic, the *Thebais*, which Pindar here follows. Now, the praise which (he tells us) was uttered by Adrastus when the earth engulfed Amphiaraus is taken by the scholiast and practically all moderns to be the words "I mourn," etc. But ἔπειτα, which I have translated "thereafter," and which cannot mean anything else, makes it clear that Pindar describes two occasions and two distinct utterances by Adrastus.[32] If further proof is needed, we observe that the occasions are differently described: "when the earth swallowed him," and "when the seven pyres had been finished." Again, the funeral speech containing "I mourn," etc. was

delivered "at Thebes"; Amphiaraus fled from the city and
was engulfed at Oropus. Adrastus may or may not be supposed by Pindar to have witnessed his disappearance, but
"at Thebes" at least suggests a different place for the lament
of v. 16. Finally, the hitherto unexplained ἀπὸ γλώσσας, which
I translated "straightway," is best understood as implying
"extempore," unlike the quoted words, which are to be regarded as more deliberate and studied: no doubt Pindar's
hearers knew that they formed part of a set funeral oration.[33]
In any case, ἔπειτα makes the matter certain. What, then,
did Adrastus say at first? Why does Pindar not quote it? Can
it have been materially different from the reported second
utterance? If not, why so carefully bring in two similar
eulogies?

Next, the famous story, which we examined in an earlier
lecture,[34] how Euadna bore Iamus, is preceded by an account
of Pitana who bore Euadna herself (vv. 29 ff.): "She, as
legend tells, lay with Poseidon, Cronos' son, and bore a child,
Euadna of the violet tresses. Beneath the folds of her raiment
she hid her unwedded travail, and when the final month was
come sent handmaidens bringing the babe to Eilatus' hero-
son, that he might rear it." This brief passage is so completely
cast into the shade by the radiant and tender loveliness of
the narrative which follows, that its strangeness has gone
almost unnoted.[35] The situation of Pitana and the situation
of Euadna being closely similar, we should have expected
Pindar to take one of two courses: either to say no more
than: "Pitana bore Euadna to Poseidon, and Euadna, in her
turn . . ." with the full development which we then find; or
else to give Pitana's story with charm, indeed, and some
elaboration, but from a quite different point of view—a picture corresponding to Euadna's, yet in no sense a duplicate
of it.[36] But he has done neither, offering us a brief uncoloured
description that reads like a prosaic though inexact condensation of the Euadna narrative—a preliminary sketch or
"note" for it, one might almost say, unaccountably left in
the completed ode. In all other respects the Sixth Olympian

is not only glorious but also richly and carefully elaborated. This blunder, if we choose to call it so, must be the outcome of conscious art. Why has Pindar allowed himself to make it?

Now set these passages, that concerning Adrastus and that concerning Pitana, side by side. Both exhibit exactly the same astonishing oddity—each describes, with emphasis yet briefly, an occurrence that anticipates another told at length. The effect of these two repetitions is exactly that which we receive when we gaze at some object while pressing our eyelid slightly with a finger. Either of the repetitions should surprise us:[37] together they convince us of some definite pattern in the poet's imagination.

We cannot, that is, fail to observe a governing idea of duality,[38] of persons, things, events, arranged in pairs. Pindar's symbol is the Two Anchors of v. 101; to this he has been led by the unusual fact, which appeals strongly to his imagination, that Hagesias has two citizenships, two homes, the rustic Arcadian township and Syracuse, the rich and puissant Western city. So does his festal song make its progress from one home to the other, οἴκοθεν οἴκαδε ποτινισόμενον; and the whole poem shines with reflexions, of thought or legend or emotion. Amphiaraus is both a good seer and a good warrior. Pitana is set beside Euadna. The infant Iamus is fed by two serpents; in mid-Alpheus he prays to both Poseidon and Apollo, receiving "a double treasure" of soothsaying. Heracles founds both a festival and a mighty ordinance of athletic contests. The poet himself has a double endowment,[39] genius in song and the power to inspire others; his first injunction falls into two parts; the second bids his choir-master make mention both of Syracuse and of Ortygia.[40] Then at the close appear the Two Anchors that hold the ship fast in a night of storm, together with a prayer that Heaven may grant fair fortune in this home and in that. This sense of dualism presses so strongly upon the poet that when it is not obvious in the legends he invents it:[41] that is the only possible explanation of the strange shape assumed by the Adrastus and Pitana narratives.

We come now to the illustrious Second Olympian, which
has been more discussed than any other Pindaric ode because
of that great passage concerning the life after death whereon
we touched in the third lecture. It is at least equally important artistically, being a most profound and opulent example
of the symbolic manner. The occasion was peculiar and splendid. Thero, tyrant of Acragas, or Agrigentum, in Sicily, won
the chariot-race at Olympia in 476 B.C., a year that marks the
zenith of Pindar's accomplishment, no less than five of his
odes being dedicated to successes won at this festival. Thero's
victory was sung not only in this Second Olympian, but in the
Third also, which formed part of the official rejoicing, whereas
the Second belonged to a more intimate celebration, and
dwells on private interests as well as public.

In vv. 53 f. we read that wealth brings varied opportunity—then follows a phrase describing how it does so: βαθεῖαν
ὑπέχων μέριμναν ἀγροτέραν. I must not beg any questions by
attempting a final translation at present: very roughly indeed
he says: "holding underneath (something or someone) a deep
anxiety, or study, or care, which is ἀγροτέρα." What is the
implication of ἀγροτέρα? It regularly means "connected with
the open country" (ἀγρός), often with a secondary notion of
"hunting" (ἄγρα). But too many have blurred this strong,
even picturesque, sense: three most excellent Pindarists,
Mezger, Fraccaroli, and Gildersleeve, are contented to write
"grievous care" and the like. It seems to have been widely
felt that good manners cannot attribute to a monarch "deep-
seated ambition that hunts in the wild"; we are thus left
wondering why Pindar used a word which he did not mean
and left us to smudge its significance away.

A second expedient is to call the Greek corrupt. Wilamowitz, far too vigorous to condone dilution of a rich word,
issued the following manifesto. "μέριμναν ἀγροτέραν is simply
nonsense, utter nonsense. Schroeder retains it in his text, but
I observe from his note that ἀβροτέραν ['daintier,' 'more
luxurious'], an easy and inevitable emendation, was proposed
by Stadtmüller, presumably before me (*Hermes* xliv 445).

1

2

3

4

The only important thing is that the truth shall be recognized, but one's personal gratification is undimmed by the fact that others also, others already, have shown the insight; and not seldom the efforts of many are needed to make it prevail."[42] This emotion seems excessive when expended on the substitution of an allegedly obvious for an allegedly nonsensical word: why should a copyist have rejected the former for the latter? In any case βαθεῖαν μέριμναν ἀβροτέραν, which can mean nothing but a deep-rooted passion to outdo everyone else in luxury, is utterly out of key with its context, and indeed with the whole poem.

There remains a third way: to *hear* Pindar's own words. His language is often shot with merging colours; and in this place, eager to show its full sense, he calls attention to such iridescence by the word ἔτυμος, which at times means not so much "genuine" as "etymologically correct,"[43] and here points to etymology explaining ἀγροτέραν. In Greek writing of Pindar's day the despot's name, Θήρων, had exactly the same spelling as the verb θηρῶν, "hunting,"[44] and in pronunciation there can have been small difference. The man's wealth and greatness fire him—that is the implication of ὑπέχων: holding a torch beneath fuel—to behave as the Hunter which his very name calls him. Such playing upon names is too familiar to need illustration: Pindar himself provides at least three examples,[45] and the present idea may perhaps be seen at work on the later coins of Thero's city, where the hunting eagles fly with a hare in their talons. (See Plate I, 2, facing p. 130.) He is the mighty Hunter, whose wealth and noble character kindle deep in his heart a yearning that drives him forth into the wild. Instead of enticing him to restless refinements of luxury (as the wretched ἀβροτέραν would imply), they inspire him with a passion for adventure, spurring him on as a champion of Greece against those Carthaginian hordes whom he overthrew at Himera.

This word-play by no means exhausts the importance of Thero's name, for quite literally it contains the symbol round which the poet's ideas have crystallized. Here and there turns of diction occur which perplex us somewhat, though pulling few readers to a complete halt. Fate sends good fortune "swinging aloft" (vv. 21 f.):[46]

> ὅταν θεοῦ μοῖρα πέμπῃ
> ἀνεκὰς ὄλβον ὑψηλόν.

Sorrow "falls heavily" by the force of greater boons (vv. 23 f.):

> πένθος δὲ πίτνει βαρὺ
> κρεσσόνων πρὸς ἀγαθῶν.

Fate brings, not only heaven-sent bliss, but somewhat of grief also, by a *rotation* at another time (vv. 35 ff.):

> οὕτω δὲ Μοῖρ', ἅ τε πατρώϊον
> τῶνδ' ἔχει τὸν εὔφρονα πότμον, θεόρτῳ σὺν ὄλβῳ
> ἐπί τι καὶ πῆμ' ἄγει, παλιντράπελον ἄλλῳ χρόνῳ.

This last passage, if not the other two, refers plainly to the motion of a wheel. Here, then, we find indicated for the first time in literature that most familiar and most impressive of all metaphors—the Wheel of Fortune,[47] more precisely indicated, though still without the later elaborations, by Sophocles: "Sorrow and joy wheel round for all men, even as the revolving course of the Great Bear."[48] This Wheel, which (as we are to see) by a simple yet magnificent symbolism makes the whole Universe visible for a strange moment of apocalypse, is pictured for us in Thero's own name, the initial letter being written[49] ⊕, a picture of the ancient four-spoked wheel.[50]

To see the shape of a letter as a simple picture was common enough before the invention of printing; and this attractive play of the imagination appears now and again even in our own day. The Pythagorean fancy was best known, which used Υ to represent the path of life, offering after a while the choice of routes to good and to bad. In Euripides' *Theseus*[51] an illiterate man who had seen the name "Theseus" spelled it by describing each letter as the picture of some familiar object: *sigma*, for instance, is a tress of hair. Two pretty examples from French nineteenth-century verse are given in Professor W. B. Stanford's delightful book, *Greek Metaphor*. De Musset, in his *Ballade à la lune*, writes:

> C'était, dans la nuit brune
> Sur le clocher jauni,
> La lune
> Comme un point sur un i.

Paul Maurice tells Victor Hugo that

> Les tours de Notre-Dame étaient l'H de ton nom.

The colophon of an English publishing firm is with diverting dexterity so designed that the letters E M represent an owl perched below the crescent moon. Dante has drawn vivid effects from a device of this kind. With characteristic quaintness and pungency he says that a cadaverous visage told its humanity by its lineaments—that is, *omo* thus written (or drawn):

> Parean l'occhiaie anella sanza gemme.
> chi nel viso degli uomini legge 'omo'
> ben avria quivi conosciuta l'emme.

"Their eye-sockets seemed rings without jewels: whoever reads 'omo' in the faces of men would well have recognized therein the m."[52] This artless play of fancy is developed into sublimity when in the *Paradiso*[53] he describes how the blessed souls marshal themselves so as to form the words DILIGITE IUSTITIAM QUI IUDICATIS TERRAM, and how the final letter changes into the shape of the Imperial Eagle.

Pindar throughout this poem sets himself to console Thero for his sorrows by impressing upon him the law of human life, that grief and joy come upon us with inevitable alternation. Throughout the poem: for even the verses which speak his disdain for those who croak against the divine bird of Zeus (Pindar himself) point also at the detractors who in his final stanza are said to vent crazy spite upon Thero's grandeur.

This alternation he displays with august power and variety:
Semele died amid the roar of the thunderbolt, but lives now
in Heaven, her beauty unimpaired; Cadmus dwells in the
Island of the Blest, his griefs all put away; Laius' house sank
in a horror of bloodshed, yet Thersander survived therefrom
to win honour; the pioneers who came overseas endured much
in their hearts before they won a sacred dwelling-place beside
the stream; the whole race of men meets now pain, now bliss,
in earthly life and in the long trial of soul after the death of
the body. *Tu vero dubitabis et indignabere?* Here, at least,
Pindar's thought is no less clear than majestic; but, according
to his wont, he reinforces thought by sovereign imagination;
that is, by this symbol of the Wheel.

But why choose a presentation of Fortune's vicissitudes
hitherto unknown in poetry or (so far as appears) in popular
maxims? Why not some other more familiar, such as the
veering winds[54] that he so often mentions in brief comparison?
We need not look far to discover his reason: the Wheel comes
to him directly from that religion of mystery (so often called
Orphic[55]) whose eschatology he here sets forth. We have no
need to discuss at length[56] this celebrated passage, on which
so many scholars have dilated. It does not include—that is
Pindar's way—explicit allusion to the Wheel of Human Life,
that κύκλος γενέσεως or cycle of birth, death, and rebirth, from
which the completely purified alone escape to dwell with the
gods at last. But the purgatorial system typified thereby is
described in vv. 68 ff.:

> ὅσοι δ' ἐτόλμασαν ἐστρὶς
> ἑκατέρωθι μείναντες ἀπὸ πάμπαν ἀδίκων ἔχειν
> ψυχάν, ἔτειλαν Διὸς ὁδὸν παρὰ Κρό-
> νου τύρσιν.

"All they who dared, through a threefold sojourn on both
sides of the grave, to keep their souls utterly from sin, journey along the road of Zeus to the Tower of Cronos." That is
all, in this eschatological passage, concerning alternation; but
he is unmistakably repeating the doctrine of the mysteries,

and therefore must still have the Wheel in mind. Pythagoras, according to later tradition,[57] had already asserted that "the soul, passing through the Wheel [or "cycle"—κύκλος] of necessity, is imprisoned at various times in various animals." Empedocles,[58] Pindar's younger contemporary, took over this figure into his physical speculations, describing as a wheel of change that alternate dominance of Φιλότης and Νεῖκος, Love and Strife, which makes up the rhythm of the Universe. Closer to our theme are the Campagno Tablets,[59] found at the excavation of graves near Naples, Orphic documents of high importance, one containing this verse among others: "I have flown forth of the grievous burdensome Wheel." It was made in the fourth century B.C., but the poem reads like a debased form of an earlier version, which may well be supposed at least as old as our ode. Also in the fourth century, a South Italian painter decorated a splendid vase,[60] now in Munich, with a scene from the Underworld, in which Orpheus, leading three of the Blessed, approaches the palace where Pluto and Persephone are seen with two wheels suspended above their heads. (See Plate II, facing p. 146.)

Pindar often moralizes, but rarely in his epinicians does he go beyond this to muse on religion, the government of the Universe, and a future life; and what we find, however august, is brief, save here. This memorable pageantry is unsuited to the ostensible occasion, but becomes legitimate, nay, magnificently apposite, if we read the Second Olympian as composed for a half-private rendering and an audience fit though few.[61] It has been thought[62] that Pindar aims his description at one auditor exclusively, Thero himself, to whom this high discourse would come with particular urgency; for, as he died a natural death only four years later, we may believe him well advanced in age when he listened to this ode. But were there no others in Acragas attached to these beliefs?

Acragas, more than any other city west of Delphi, was steeped in religion: her temples, built by Thero, are still counted among the wonders of Europe. Pindar describes the arrival of Thero's ancestors in language (vv. 8 f.) that recalls the travel-worn Israelites' entry into their promised land: "After suffering much in their hearts, they won a holy abode beside a stream." On this a scholiast remarks that in Acragas stood "a temple of Athena possessing unusual sanctity"; but the whole city, he adds, was bestowed by Zeus on Persephone as a gift at her unveiling when first she returned from the realm of Pluto; Pindar elsewhere[63] salutes it as "the seat of Persephone," and in one of his *encomia* relates how Thero's forebears set out from Rhodes and dwelt in a high city, "offering up full many gifts to the Immortals."[64] For us the most impressive fact of all is that in Acragas dwelt the brilliant philosopher whom we mentioned a moment ago, Empedocles, the fragments of whose dirges tingle with a passionate sense of personal relation to God and of damnation through sin.[65] It is a natural surmise that Pindar found in Acragas a number of persons dedicated to a religious life, a congregation, a *thiasos*, which would assemble to hear his poem: perhaps the youthful Empedocles stood among that company and drew inspiration from these solemn verses.

Can we know anything more about those people? Perhaps a little. Much as this ode has been discussed, one element in it has been ignored: the prominence assigned to goddesses and women. Cronos is described (v. 77), with astonishing emphasis,[66] as "husband of Rhea who hath her throne above all other thrones." In v. 12 Zeus is called "son of Rhea." Next (vv. 25 ff.) comes the great salutation of a woman, Semele; but why therein is Pallas named beside Zeus and the ivy-garlanded son of Semele—Pallas who has elsewhere no relation whatever to that story? Merely, one surmises,[67] because she is a female divinity. The deification of Ino follows. That Memnon is described (v. 83) as "the Dawn-Goddess' Ethiopian son" may be thought unimportant, but no one can deny emphasis to the reason for Achilles' appearance in the Happy Island (vv. 79 f.): "Achilles his mother brought, when she had by prayer won over the heart of Zeus."[68] For all this some cause must have existed, and it is natural to suppose that whatever interest in religion Thero cherished was shared by women of Acragas, and in particular by one very near the prince, a great lady who stood for much in the life and history of the island during those troubled years—Demareta,[69] Thero's own daughter, married first to Gelo, tyrant of Syracuse, later to Polyzalus, his brother and Hiero's. To her Pindar has perhaps directly alluded in the words (v. 53) ὁ πλοῦτος ἀρεταῖς δεδαιδαλμένος, "wealth adorned with virtues," for the verb usually means, and always implies, skilful handicraft. "Wealth cunningly adorned by *aretae*" may put us in mind of the Demareteion, the silver coin issued by her husband Gelo in 479 B.C., only three years before the date of this ode, to commemorate the victory of Himera, and named not after him, but after his wife.[70] (See Plate I, 3, facing p. 130.) That magnificent coin attracted Pindar's admiration, and he hints at it in this imperial phrase.

Whether his great picture of death, judgment, and far-off blessedness reveals a sincerely held creed of his own or but proclaims a doctrine held by others is a question on which scholars disagree. But it has in truth no importance. What the man Pindaros of Thebes, now so long dead, himself believed matters to none of us: we are concerned only with the verse that has survived him. Therein we discern, among more obvious features, a strange piece of literary history. The Orphic Wheel is by no means an emblem of life's vicissitudes, in the ordinary sense of that phrase; but Pindar symbolizes them by a quite novel picture, Fortune's Wheel, suggested to him by the mystic symbol which is part of his theme and quite different from the other, save as portraying alternation. Thus the fancy, speech, and literature of mankind have derived one of their still most favoured metaphors from a religion now obsolete, which attracted, if only for a marvellous hour, the eye of a creative genius.

SYMBOLISM

(*Concluded*)

IN THIS LECTURE we shall conclude what is now to be said about Pindaric symbolism, opening with one final master-piece of this method; then discussing more concisely four poems that are less important for their symbolism but are on other grounds attractive; finally we shall endeavour to answer an obvious question or two concerning later poetry.

The Seventh Olympian extols the uniquely renowned Diagoras of Rhodes, who won the prize for boxing in 464 B.C. This is the poem which so deeply impressed the Rhodians that they set it up in letters of gold on the wall of a temple dedicated to Athena.[1] Here is an outline of its content. 'As a man gives a goblet of wine at a marriage-feast, so do I send forth my song, hymning Diagoras and the island of Rhodes. His ancestor Tlepolemus slew a kinsman, wherefore the Delphian oracle bade him seek a new home. Thus he came to Rhodes, upon which Zeus sent a shower of gold when Athena was born from his head. The Sun-God warned the citizens to be first to worship her and make her their patroness. But they forgot to bring fire, and their sacrifice failed of entire success; nevertheless she taught them marvellous arts. When Zeus divided the earth, all gods received a portion—save the Sun-God, who was absent. But he cared nothing, for he chose and received a land not yet known, this island, which was then growing up from the sea-floor. There he was united with the nymph Rhodos and begot three sons, who founded the three Rhodian cities. At home and throughout Greece Diagoras has won many victories—a great athlete, a great man.'

In this ode commentators have found but one serious diffi-culty. All three myths—the story of Tlepolemus, the Rho-dians' sacrifice, the partition of the earth—superbly told as they are, sound yet a sinister note: shadows fall across the brightness; how are we to explain this quality in a poem of

congratulation?[2] The settlement of Rhodes is traced directly
to homicide committed by the founder; her citizens fail by
their own mysterious forgetfulness to secure the full blessing
of Athena; the partition of the Earth by Zeus is, at first sight,
vitiated by the absence of the Sun-God. Yet Pindar carefully
informs us that his story is authoritative: "For them whose
lineage begins with Tlepolemus full gladly will I proclaim in
truer form the current story."[3] For once we can observe the
method of his revision, for this "current story" is what we
find, and Pindar's hearers found, in Homer. The Catalogue
in the Second Book of the *Iliad* (vv. 653 ff.), reporting that
Tlepolemus brought nine ships to Troy from Rhodes, describes his earlier career. Not only is the name of his mother
different—Astyocheia in Homer, Astydameia in Pindar—and
his victim Licymnius ageing, an invidious detail which Pindar omits: much more notable, whereas the Catalogue says
that Tlepolemus, having slain Licymnius, quickly built
ships and fled by sea, because Licymnius' surviving kin
threatened him, the ode mentions no threats but relates that
he consulted Apollo and was commanded to seek a new home
overseas. It may be added here that when Pindar reports (vv.
77 ff.) the institution of games in Tlepolemus' honour, scholiasts accuse him of error, the games being dedicated to the
Sun-God, not Tlepolemus. But the "correction" is a mistake:
Boeckh has remarked that Pindar could not give among Rhodians a false account of contemporary Rhodian contests; and
Wilamowitz[4] points out that games for Tlepolemus are
attested by an inscription of the second century B.C., whereas
Sun-games date only from the foundation of the later city
called Rhodes.

Pindar, then, well knew at each point exactly what he was
doing. Why has he done it? The symbol, when found, will
make all clear, as usual. But, first of all, this perhaps is the
best place to note a passage whose difficulty seems to have
escaped notice.

Helios, the Sun-God, asks Zeus and Lachesis to swear that
when the Island emerges into the light of day it shall be his

domain. Then (vv. 68 f.): τελεύταθεν δὲ λόγων κορυφαὶ ἐν ἀλαθείᾳ πετοῖσαι. The literal translation is: "And the tops of
words were accomplished, falling in truth." What are we to
make of that? First, the phrase λόγων κορυφαί, "tops of
words,"[5] has been too often taken as meaning "the chief
points of his (or their) speech." That is absurd: are we to
suppose that Zeus, Lachesis, and Helios blundered about
details? The phrase can mean nothing here but "consumma-
tions consisting in words"—and what that, in turn, means we
cannot exactly tell: it must wait until we find the key to the
whole ode. Secondly, all scholars take τελεύταθεν, "were accomplished," and ἐν ἀλαθείᾳ πετοῖσαι, "falling in truth," as
equivalent, both of them, to our "were fulfilled." This is no
less intolerable than the other. Repetition of thought, we all
know, need not be avoided; indeed it is often an excellent
rhetorical device: but dexterity is needed if the tautology is
not to offend, as in Sandys' version: "were fulfilled and fell
out truly." No: τελεύταθεν undoubtedly means "were fulfilled": therefore "falling in truth" must mean something
else. And further, πίπτω "to fall," when it does mean "happen," is applied elsewhere to events themselves, not to fulfilment of promises about events; so that our phrase should (it
seems) imply that *the conversation* "really happened," which
is foolishness. What, then, does the whole sentence mean?
What is "their crowning parley was accomplished, falling in
truth"? For the moment we cannot tell.

This masterpiece of Pindar's genius is notable also as
the best evidence of the loss sustained by reading him in the
wrong way.[6] We should *hear* the whole poem, to the best
of our ability, as a Greek would hear it. But many of us insist on
translating it into a different language and then listening to
our own version. Everyone speaks of the Island as "Rhodes."
But to Pindar and all who heard his ode it meant The Rose.
This was no subtlety, as we may allege in the etymology of
Αἴας from αἰάζω and the like. No Greek could ávoid the identification here; and a rose appears upon the coins of the Island.
(See Plate I, 4, facing p. 130.) It is a charming fact that,

whenever Pindar mentions the name, he uses a case which makes the Island indistinguishable from the Flower. Here glows the most obvious, and the most delightful, symbol to be discovered in his work, giving richness and unity to the whole sequence of myths.

Pondering the island-home of Diagoras, Pindar is led by its beautiful name to see it under the similitude of a Rose, and thus conceives his radiant picture of that favoured spot, the one tiny region which for the Sun-God outshone all other earthly domains, as a divine plant growing up from the sea-floor into the sunlight. With this picture before him he studies the whole mass of Rhodian story until it too is shaped after the image of the growing rose-tree, but a tree that grows as no tree known now to man, from a dark bed beneath salt water. That is why he sings that the island "blossomed" (βλάστε, v. 69), not "emerged"; and not from "the water of the sea" (Sandys) or "the watery main" (Myers) or "gulfs of sea" (Billson), but from ἁλὸς ὑγρᾶς—which may seem at first a feeble or inept phrase. For, since ἅλς, literally "salt," so often in poetry means "sea," why add ὑγρᾶς, "moist"? Because that addition, by giving the idea of water, forces us away from the derivative sea-notion in ἅλς back upon the word's literal meaning: he inserts ὑγρᾶς precisely to prevent us from taking ἅλς as "sea." Why? To emphasize salt, because in salted earth no tree can flourish—so you would think. Pindar's Rose is no plant of every day: it grows in his quickening imagination to a symbol of our life, of sorrow turned into joy, of a miraculous burgeoning from a spot without fertility or sunlight into final radiance and sovereign beauty.

That is why all the stories clustering round the Rose-Island are narrated in a manner so unsuited (at the first glance) to a poem that proclaims the gorgeous destinies of the Sun-God's descendants, and in particular the success of Diagoras and his illustrious kin. For, in all three, radiance is preceded by gloom. If we ask why Pindar consented thus to write, why he yielded, even more notably than was his habit, to the attraction of light and shadow thus interfused, we must realize that (however natural our curiosity) we pass thereby from the realm of poetry to biography. Boeckh[7] makes a good case for supposing that Diagoras' family, the most eminent in Rhodes, the Eratidae, who had once been kings there, were now in danger of losing what influence and power they retained, under pressure of the commons, abetted by the Athenian democracy. "Avoid dangerous foreign friends! Support the Eratidae, whose glory is your glory!" Boeckh points to the emphatic and repeated mention of the cloud that comes over men's wits, and sees there a warning to the Rhodians against political folly.[8] This is far more attractive than the guess of Dissen, that Diagoras had accidentally killed one of his opponents.[9] But such explanations, however correct, are beside the point. The critic's business is not what happened to Diagoras in the past, but what happens to Pindar's thoughts and emotions in the poem, just as readers of Meredith's *Phoebus with Admetus* have no need to lament if they do not know why the god was exiled.

These three legends, the story of Tlepolemus, the institution of fireless sacrifice by the Rhodians, the partition of Earth among the gods, maintain this insistence upon gloom beside sunshine, joy following pain. " 'Tis this bewilders the questing mind—what today and in the end is the highest boon for man's winning." But we should observe also adroit graduation in treatment of the hero, of the nation, of the god. Concerning the hero we read that he began with murder[10] done in wrath—"with a staff of hard olive-wood he smote and slew Licymnius": that which at Olympia was the token of glory became at Tiryns an instrument of bloodshed. But before that stanza is finished the gloom begins to lighten: "he came to the god and sought his oracle." Next, the nation's misdeed is less, but startling. Despite the Sun-God's warning to his sons, that they should be the first to honour the newly born Athena with sacrifice and so make her their patroness, they omitted to bring fire with them to the precinct which they assigned her on their acropolis. The poet's astonished comment on that mysterious forgetfulness is emphatic, indeed, but less so than the corresponding passage (vv. 31 f.) on Tlepolemus:

αἰ δὲ φρενῶν ταραχαὶ
παρέπλαγξαν καὶ σοφόν.

Of the Rhodians he writes (vv. 45 ff.):

ἐπὶ μὰν βαίνει τι καὶ λάθας ἀτέκμαρτα[11] νέφος,
καὶ παρέλκει πραγμάτων ὀρθὰν ὁδὸν
ἔξω φρενῶν.

"*Distraction* of soul" has been succeeded by "a cloud of *forget-fulness* that comes upon man in baffling wise and plucks from his soul the right course of action." Then follows the rich solace. Pindar leaves us to remember that Athena became protectress of another city and dilates majestically upon the lessons in handicraft that she gave the Rhodians. What, finally, of the god himself? This plan of narrative demands some offence or weakness; but how can that be found in one called (v. 60) so emphatically "the holy god"? Yet Pindar contrives something that will serve. When Zeus and the rest portioned out the earth, Helios was *absent:* in this strangely working imagination the Sun-God himself goes through his hour of eclipse. Yet so it was that in the end he received as his share the jewel itself of earth. Was ever island so marvellously praised, even when Shakespeare wrote of "this precious stone set in the silver sea"? The absence of Helios results in overwhelming glory: the god, rejecting all other lands that he views in his daily path across the heaven, is content to wait until his Flower raises her head above the waves.

The stories are narrated out of chronological order so that this august culmination may find its due place at the close: it was no casual whim[12] that led the poet to set forth a descending scale of guilt and a crescendo of glory. Browning has written of growth "tree-like through pain to joy"; that thought receives from Pindar vivid hues and motion in this progression of legend. So much is clear: and we are tempted to ask whether his symbol fills the poem, to look for the magic tree in every sentence. Nevertheless, obvious reasons forbid us to expect that any Pindaric ode will fit a scheme with all its edges. So here. The long list of Diagoras' victories lies outside the area dominated by the symbol. Much more surprising is the Goblet wherewith this poem so splendidly opens. For once, we find two symbols in a single ode—two separate acts of poetic conception. We are to note that his πρόσωπον τηλαυγές, "façade far-gleaming" (to quote the Sixth Olympian), is wrought out for itself, bearing small structural relation with the sequel, less like the portico of a Greek temple than the narthex at Vézelay in Burgundy. This exordium shows in miniature the same peculiarity of expression that we discern in the rose-strophes. Why does he trouble to write (v. 7) νέκταρ χυτόν, "flowing nectar"? Is not all nectar fluid? The adjective is obtruded in order to press upon us a comparison between this foaming goblet presented by the bride's father to the bridegroom, a gift that passes from one home to the other, and the nectar of poesy "poured abroad" by Pindar— his song travels far, across the sea.

Rose-symbolism explains his orchestration of the legends, yes; but should we not expect to find verbal allusions to it, clear or faint? No doubt; but hardly two readers will agree entirely in their identification of these. Slighter allusions may possibly be observed in κορυφὰν κτεάνων (v. 4), καρπὸν φρενός (v. 8), ἀμπλακίαι κρέμανται[13] (vv. 24 f.), σκληρᾶς ἐλαίας (v. 29), σπέρμα φλογός (v. 48), κλέος βαθύ (v. 53). Such things are shadowy; but now, and only now, can we deal with the passage which we found unintelligible and which must remain so unless read (thus to put it) as rose-language—τελεύταθεν δὲ λόγων κορυφαὶ ἐν ἀλαθείᾳ πετοῖσαι. Pindar does of course intend "their words were fulfilled," but he voices his meaning thus curiously because of his preoccupation with the beloved Rose-tree. Translation therefore becomes even harder than usual. The least poor is, perhaps: "The summit of speech came to perfection, being set in truth." The gods' converse reaches maturity as the plant reaches full efflorescence:[14] τελεύταθεν λόγων κορυφαί. Next, ἐν ἀλαθείᾳ πετοῖσαι, a phrase (as we saw) apparently tautological, now becomes rich and effective.

πετοῖσαι is here not "falling," but "being placed" or "being set":[15] it alludes to the planting of seed, and ἀλάθεια is the soil that receives it. We note what may still surprise us, that the summit—the culmination—of the speech, its flower, is thereby (it seems) identified with the lowest part, even the seed;[16] the summit being placed in a certain soil: and we may hazard yet another version—"To flower came the crown of their parley, for it was planted in truth"; the "truth" here being the soundness and rightness of the conditions wherein they spoke, in particular the Sun-God's love and the future glories of the Island. The length and elaboration of this comment, it is important to remember, arise from the repellent and cumbrous verbosity in which anyone flounders who seeks to "explain" quintessential poetry in words at all.

A moment ago we observed that the exordium of this ode had nothing to do with the Rose-tree, but contained an elementary symbolism of a Goblet. There is of course no overwhelming reason that the symbol should govern a whole ode: it may influence only those portions upon which the poet's imagination has worked most freely; and, since his task usually includes a catalogue of athletic successes, he writes at times under a prosaic preoccupation. Let us, then, glance at certain odes in which the symbolism, though often charming, is certainly not pervasive, but usually needed—if we may put the matter from our modern point of view—in order to explain knotty phrases like the τελεύταθεν sentence over which I made such a pother.

Let us begin with the Eighth Isthmian. When Themis declares that the mortal Peleus, not the gods Zeus or Poseidon, must wed Thetis, she says (v. 49): "in the hero's arms she must loose the bridle of maidenhood." That is a strange variant of the usual language: Greeks spoke of untying the girdle. A scholiast condemns it as "harsh and in falsetto."[17] Farnell's comment is a warning against the impatience which flings uncritical censure upon poetry that baffles the first glance. After quoting the scholiast, he proceeds: "We should be inclined to blame the phrase as wrong from the point of view

of ethos: a girdle is a guard or a defence to the chaste woman:
it is only a 'bridle' or 'curb' for the wanton. And Themis
ought not to speak so of Thetis. Probably Pindar did not
realise the full import of his phrase." No doubt all poets nod
on occasion, but the assumption of such negligence should be
our last resource, not our first. Themis, poor goddess, of
course meant no offence; but why is "bridle" substituted for
"girdle"? We cannot answer without assuming that here, as
so often, the symbol presses upon the diction so that it is . . .
distorted, if we care to say so. Pindar's idea, or rather his
picture, is a Broken Chain,[18] a bond that is loosed.

And why? This ode was written soon after the defeat of the
Persian invasion, and is dominated by thought of that mighty
deliverance.[19] Its opening stanzas voice the poet's relief that
"some god hath turned aside the stone of Tantalus which
hung overhead." His language has nothing in it of triumph,
only of release—hence the symbol. "Freed from sorrows" (v.
6), he writes; "ceasing from hopeless evils" (v. 10); "hath
ended sore distress" (v. 14). It was by no means inevitable,
however natural, that the triumph of Hellas should be so
viewed. Other aspects were equally obvious: for example, the
glorious achievement, at Salamis, of that very Aegina which
he celebrates; and at the same moment an even greater poet
was pondering these events as manifestation of God's judgment upon Persian *hubris*. But Pindar's own city had sided
with the invader, and for him relief overshadows pride.

We pass to the story of Thetis' marriage. That myth is told
to glorify an Aeacid, Achilles; and surely no more sublime
and more touching eulogy exists—the unparalleled achievements of Thetis' son are in reality but the poor faint glimmer
of the overwhelming majesty and power that would have
been his had she mated with Zeus.[20] But Pindar, while secur-
ing this blend of grandeur and pathos, has shaped his narrative to meet another purpose also, inventing (as it appears),
and from any other standpoint needlessly, the story that not
only did Zeus seek to wed Thetis, but that Poseidon was his
rival, that they quarrelled, and that Themis intervened[21] to

arrange their dispute. Here then is emphasized the Chain that is to be broken: not only must the wish of Zeus be quelled, but the rivalry; and so it is that at the end of her address to the gods she uses not only the word for "release" (λύοι), but a phrase for virginity which repeats the picture of a bond or chain. From that marriage sprang Achilles, who served his country with peerless bravery and success.

Served his country? That is language no modern reader—and few ancient readers—of the *Iliad* would use concerning Achilles. *Iura negat sibi nata*: he has less sense of the public good than any man in the epic. But Pindar's account is un-Homeric in tone: one who had seen no other report than his would suppose (for example) that Achilles captured Troy. The lines are stately, but they have received a peculiar twist: everything is true—that is, nothing actually contradicts current legend,—but the poet's preoccupation has shaped the diction so as to imply that Achilles breaks through restraints and thereupon and thereby confers benefits. His first exploit (vv. 54 f.), "He it was that encarnadined the Mysian plain vine-clad, sprinkling it with Telephus' dark gore," is so described as to carry a hint of enriching the vine-yield. Next (v. 56),"for Atreus' sons he bridged their return home," is no natural description of Achilles' exploits before Troy: as everyone knew, much remained to be done after he fell. But Pindar insists on regarding Achilles as a benefactor. He makes him *release* Helen (v. 57), as if she had been a virtuous lady carried off by force and pining for a rescuer. Finally, observe that the Trojan War is described as a bond or entanglement: ῥύοντο (v. 58),"they sought to hold him back," is reinforced by the names of his opponents here mentioned —Memnon, "the withstander"; Hector, "he who restrains."

In the Eighth Pythian we note first vv. 21 ff., where instead of saying that Aegina is the home of the Graces, he writes that Aegina *falls* not far from the Graces. Why? Commentators tell us that he has in mind the fall of dice, but to transfer the "falling" to the person who throws the dice, or on whose behalf they are thrown, seems grotesque, if not impossible; moreover there is no other hint of dice in the ode.²² We must, as usual, suspend judgment and look for similar words and ideas elsewhere. There are two allusions to falling. In vv. 81 f., which describe the youthful wrestler's success, he writes: "Upon four bodies didst thou fall from on high," where "fall" is entirely natural; "from on high" may seem unneeded and in fact exaggerated. Sandys does not care to translate it "from aloft," but "heavily," which is an evasion. The other passage is vv. 92 ff.:

ἐν δ' ὀλίγῳ βροτῶν
τὸ τερπνὸν αὔξεται· οὕτω δὲ καὶ πίτνει χαμαί,
ἀποτρόπῳ γνώμᾳ σεσεισμένον.

"Mortal happiness groweth in a brief time; but as briefly it falleth to the ground, shaken by a change of mood"—or, perhaps, "by an estranged will." At first we think we see the familiar metaphor of a flower that blossoms quickly and as quickly loses its petals, but something strange and more sinister enters with the last phrase. Whose is the change of mood? We gain illumination from vv. 76 ff., which is quite clear in purport, though the metaphor may baffle us again: the altered, estranged, will is God's: "Those things lie not in man's power: it is God that dispenseth them, who casteth aloft now one, now another, and bringeth another below his hands."²³ In both places the idea is identical: are the metaphors the same also? Let us add a third passage, equally obscure. Of the victor's success Pindar exclaims: τράχον ἴτω... ἐμᾷ ποτανὸν ἀμφὶ μαχανᾷ, "let it run forward, winged by my art" (vv. 32 ff.). Why should it merely run, if it has wings?

When we set these three passages side by side, hoping that they will explain one another—joy growing up but falling because shaken with a change of temper; God casting one man aloft, another down; achievement winged yet walking or running,—the symbol is quickly seen. It is a Captive Bird, tied by a cord, which its master now tosses aloft for a brief flight, anon with a whimsical twitch of the hand—ἀποτρόπῳ γνώμᾳ σεσεισμένον—pulls down to earth. The aged poet,

watching the delighted victor who stands at the opening of
his own life, ponders the fragility of human joy: "creatures
of a day . . . yet what glory for a moment!" The lad seems to
soar on wings, ὑποπτέροις ἀνορέαις (v. 91), but how soon his
pinions will sink! Life is playing with him, like the Love-God
of Propertius' fancy, who suffers his victim to run and flutter
for a while, then checks him with the hand's sudden pressure²⁴
—a fancy elaborated by Shakespeare:

> 'Tis almost morning; I would have thee gone:
> And yet no farther than a wanton's bird,
> Who lets it hop a little from her hand,
> Like a poor prisoner in his twisted gyves,
> And with a silk thread plucks it back again.

Now we can better understand why Pindar writes that Aegina
"falls" near the Graces: he half unconsciously sets down a
word dictated by the symbol. Now, also, we account for
ὑψόθεν, "from on high," in v. 81: the wrestler falls, indeed,
upon his antagonist, but not from "on high"; yet it is on high
that the Captive Bird hovers in its brief hour.²⁵

Concerning the Eighth Nemean one is at times inclined to
say that its most delightful feature is the changes of style
that so exquisitely follow the poet's variations of thought or
feeling. His first triad recalls the manner of Correggio, showing the same spiritual elegance, the same enchanting reverie
that feels religion in a lover-like mood. It is not Shelley or
William Watson, but a Boeotian Greek, who sings of the
Loves "even as those who brought home to the fold Aphrodite's boons, hovering o'er Zeus and Aegina as they embraced,"
and whose verse casts a brief gleam on the dim languorous
figure of Cinyras, beloved of Apollo and meek priest of Aphrodite, as he is described in the Second Pythian, here said to
dwell opulently "long ago in Cyprus of the sea"—another
island than this Aegina of our present eulogy, but yet a land
that by its name recalls the Cyprian goddess no less clearly.
In this mood Pindar rightly calls his song a Lydian head-
band embroidered with music, rejoicing in the airy tune and

a fancy so wayward that, when he kneels in supplication to Aeacus for the city that he loves and her folk, he forgets what it is that he would ask and his prayer is lost to us. Later in the poem this tone, though braced somewhat by a sense of life's urgency, is heard again, for we can hardly say where fact ends and metaphor begins:

αὔξεται δ' ἀρετά, χλωραῖς ἐέρσαις
ὡς ὅτε δένδρεον ᾄσσει
ἐν σοφοῖς ἀνδρῶν ἀερθεῖσ' ἐν δικαίοις τε πρὸς ὑγρὸν
αἰθέρα.

"Prowess gaineth increase, as when beneath freshening dews a tree leapeth into the buxom air, exalted among men that are wise and righteous."[26] How strong a contrast all this makes with his picture of Odysseus the backbiter and the mischief he wrought, the peerless service of Ajax amid the rocking tussle of war, his rejection when he contended against Odysseus for Achilles' arms, and his last wrestle with death! This grim close-fibred language is Rembrandtesque: "In furtive ballot the Greeks served Odysseus' turn; and Ajax, robbed of the golden armour, wrestled with bloody death. Verily, unlike were the wounds those twain tore in the foes' warm flesh, reeling under the man-defending spear, now over Achilles newly slain, and in other toils of slaughterous days. So long ago, it seems, calumnious hatred was known, that keepeth pace with wheedling talk, that uttereth guile and malicious insult."

Such violent contrast in tone is anything but a mere exercise in virtuosity, for Odysseus thereby confronts another man who rose to power by qualities the precise opposite of his. From the union of Zeus and Aegina, so tenderly touched on (as we saw), sprang the ancestor of Achilles and all other Aeginetan worthies, Aeacus, whom Pindar presents as a figure of unearthly grandeur. How strange a prelude to the birth of the puissant Dorian prince and lawgiver are those exquisite opening lines that thrill with the beauty of youth and the ardour it awakes! Still more unexpected perhaps are the hovering Loves that attend his parents: they suggest Moschus or the *Anthology* rather than the Eagle of Thebes. When he passes to the ἀναξίαι, the dominance, of Aeacus, we see that it had something emotional and spiritual: he caught the imagination of Greece, so that men from North and South gathered to him by no military or political compulsion, but were drawn by his charm, ἀβοατί—he did not strive nor cry. Concerning his arbitraments we are told nothing directly, but in simple, haunting, words that "many prayed earnestly to look upon him." In this serenely majestic description ἀναξίαις is the most effective word of all, its sense being at once august and vague,[27] while the plural hints that upon each man who drew near to him Aeacus cast a separate and peculiar spell of authority.

This opposition between radiance and darkness Pindar presses upon his hearer by placing both men in situations as similar as he can find. Each gathers a following. To Aeacus they flock with unbidden fervour: ἀβοατί, ἤθελον, ἑκόντες; Odysseus employs his own arts, sinister arts: πάρφασις, αἱμύλοι μῦθοι, and the rest. Everyone feels also the contrast between the love, the tender charm, wherefrom Aeacus arose, and the scenes of carnage that preceded the Judgment of the Arms. That here too a connexion by contrast is intended, those apparently irrelevant words in v. 4 show: "for *every* deed." Both before and after this phrase the thought seems to be all of *eros*, as sexual love, but the poet inserts here a brief reminder that the word can be used more generally. That has its importance for Deinis, the youthful victor whom the ode celebrates;[28] yet it points also at the base ambition of Odysseus which results in "rotten glory."

But, after all this, where is the symbolism?[29] The Eighth Nemean belongs to that fairly large class of odes in which symbolism works indeed, but not profoundly: on only a very few and perhaps unimportant matters shall we be at a loss if we miss the symbol altogether. It is a Sapling, of whose fresh beauty and quick growth the young athlete puts Pindar in mind, the Sapling described in that iridescent passage which we quoted a few moments ago. Now, twice in the account of Odysseus the same strange verb is found. In v. 25 we read "to shifty falsehood a huge reward". . . not "is offered," but (literally) "is extended aloft." Then the bitter description of backbiting malice, which also we cited, continues "it doeth violence to the noble, but of obscure men it . . . extendeth aloft a rotten glory." That verb is pressed upon these two passages by the symbol: you will recall that the Sapling is "exalted" (ἀερθεῖσα). It spreads fine tendrils through the early stanzas: ἔβλαστεν (v. 7) "blossomed" is used of Aeacus' birth; the island of Aegina here receives the name Oenone, "Vineland" (v. 7); ἄωτοι (v. 9), almost equivalent to our metaphorical use of "flower," may be noted in passing; prosperity is "planted" like a tree (v. 17); and the wealth of Cinyras ἔβρισε (v. 18), which suggests a tree laden with fruit.

We now reach the last of all the odes whose symbolism is to be discussed in these lectures: the Second Isthmian, not only delightful but unique in Pindar's extant work. You will recall Thero, prince of Acragas in Sicily, for whom the Second Olympian was composed—the ode of the Wheel-symbolism.[30] Thero's brother Xenocrates won the chariot-race in the Isthmian Games of 476 B.C. or earlier. This Second Isthmian is addressed, not to the victor Xenocrates, but to his son Thrasybulus, and some years after the event, for Xenocrates is dead,[31] and Thero himself is not even mentioned. We conclude, then, that this poem was written after 472 B.C., in which year the tyrant died and the tyranny itself collapsed. Evidently Pindar wrote for some anniversary celebration by the victor's son Thrasybulus, who was now—and here is the important fact—a private citizen under the newly established democracy.

It is a vivacious and most charming ode, for Pindar very light, even playful. Editors (alas!) have made an uneasy business of it. They hardly conceal, for instance, their dislike of Pindar's airy verses (39 ff.) on Xenocrates' hospitality in the old aristocratic days: "Never at his guest-frequented table did the favouring breeze furl a sail: nay, in summer days he

voyaged to Phasis and in winter sailed to the coast of Nile."
These jovial lines, which (like a good deal else in the ode)
read as if Pindar had just dined well, have caused grave commentators much heart-searching. Some dilate on the fact that
the voyage from Sicily to Phasis is longer than that to the
Delta and therefore suits the summer months;[32] another laments that the passage is in bad taste and the imagery
baroque.[33] It is simply a trifle light-headed, recalling (for less
austere readers) that fine scene of farce in Heywood's *English
Traveller*, where the roisterers go to sea (so they wrongly suppose) in or on the dining-table. A scholiast seems to have
enjoyed prophetic vision of that excellent affair: "Xenocrates
when regaling his guests went to sea with the sail of his table."
It is clumsily put, as is often the way of scholiasts, but the
worthy fellow has seized Pindar's idea.

This poem, in fact, is a verse-epistle half playfully disguised
as a triumphal ode. Scholars have naturally recognized this,
yet they will not allow Pindar, as they are delighted to allow
Horace, the mood of a letter-writer. But if we refuse to enter
into his spirit, we shall miss not only all enjoyment but his
very meaning into the bargain. Why spend solemn discussion upon v. 24: "methinks they had enjoyed some deed of
hospitality"? Probably—we do not know, and neither does
Pindar, as πoυ and τι make plain—probably the man had
given these heralds an excellent dinner; and so they gave him
"a great reception" when he won the race, or rather (to translate Pindar) "when he fell into the lap of golden Victory,"
which again has a somewhat boisterous tone. The same lack
of austerity marks the phrase (v. 8) describing songs written
for money—"with faces silvered over";[34] the aphorism (v. 11)
"money, money makes the man"; perhaps even the metre of
the last verse in each triad. In v. 35 he writes a hopelessly
jumbled phrase, "oh for a long javelin-cast with the quoit!"
which cannot be tolerably explained except as a smiling
parody of his own manner. No less significant is the secular
mood of the opening stanza, where Aphrodite and the Muses
are nothing but figures of speech.

Arnold Bennett has stated as "the universal rule for a successful career in British art" that if a man paints a good picture of a policeman he must go on painting policemen for
twenty years. Pindar so often uses a majestic style that when
for once he takes a holiday scholars drag him back into his
authenticated position. Knowing that Thrasybulus' father is
dead and the tyranny has fallen, they insist on discovering
sorrow here, and sad glances at the great old days for ever
gone, though Xenocrates' death may have occurred many
years before, and Thrasybulus may have vastly preferred life
under a democracy to the chances of having his throat cut as
a member of the tyrant's house. Even the judicious Fraccaroli[35] has said that our ode should really be placed among
the dirges. Wilamowitz[36] writes that "recollection of the past
is essentially the content." Earlier, Leopold Schmidt[37] in-
geminated "Ichabod!" over vanished blitheness and glory:
"Thrasybulus had seen to it that an expression of lamentation
for this should reach Pindar, who replied in a poem which has
come down to us as the Second Isthmian Ode." It was a
strange Jeremiah who wrote that lovely first stanza, so buoyant, so filled with the gracious memory of light-hearted love-
songs thrown off with careless ease in the olden time! Read
with an open mind, the Second Isthmian will seem not inconsistent with the other two poems to Thrasybulus—the Sixth
Pythian and the *Encomion*:[38] it commemorates the father's
victories in no spirit of brooding, but with mannered elegance.

Only from this point of view can we solve two acknowledged
difficulties in the subject-matter of the first eleven lines. Why
mention love-songs? Why this elaborate description of the
hireling Muse?

First, then, for the splendidly urbane verses with which he
opens:

οἱ μὲν πάλαι, ὦ Θρασύβουλε, φῶτες, οἳ χρυσαμπύκων
ἐς δίφρον Μοισᾶν ἔβαινον κλυτᾷ φόρ-
μιγγι συναντόμενοι,
ῥίμφα παιδείους ἐτόξευον μελιγάρυας ὕμνους,
ὅστις ἐὼν καλὸς εἶχεν Ἀφροδίτας
εὐθρόνου μνάστειραν ἁδίσταν ὀπώραν.

Here is Mr. C. J. Billson's admirable translation:

> When men of old, O Thrasybulus, drove
>> In the bright Muses' chariot, and caressed
>>> The lyre's loud strings, they lightly let a shower
>> Of mellow notes go forth to pierce the breast
>>> Of any youth whose beauty's perfect flower
> Moved Aphrodite on her throne of love.

We need suppose no allusion to any passionate feeling (past or present) of Pindar for Thrasybulus: that phrase, "the men of old," cannot refer to their own younger days. Even so the love-element is not vital to his thought, or there would be no connexion with what follows—"poetry" (in general, not love-poetry in particular) "has become a paid profession." His point is that early poets pursued not a business but an un-exacting occupation, for its own sake; and he mentions love-lyrics because love was in fact a main topic of theirs—not of his own. So might a poet of our time, who wrote of religion or war or politics, exclaim: "We poets of today have a hard time —forced to think of publishers and contracts: how different from the Elizabethan who would dash off a sonnet to his mis-tress' eyebrow and then go a bat-fowling!"

So far, well. Such a prelude must lead to comment on the poet's career in Pindar's own day. But instead of any lament about the change in popular taste, or sordid rivalries, or the difficulty of finding new themes, he produces this outburst, which has surprised and distressed so many, that the Muse is covetous and insists on fees: "In those days the Muse was not avaricious or a hireling, nor did men purchase from honey-voicèd Terpsichore soft-syllabled minstrelsy with silvered countenance. But today she biddeth us observe the saying that cometh nigh to real truth—uttered by the Argive, bereft at once of possessions and of friends: 'Money, money maketh the man.' " Our surprise is pardonable, but our dismay rather absurd; because all the talk[39] about Pindar's indelicacy in asking payment, either for this ode or for any other, has no apparent foundation. We are left by him quite in the dark about his reasons for this lament; and if we are to guess, why not guess something more reasonable than that Pindar submitted a versified bill without mentioning the amount due? My own conviction is that Thrasybulus, whose fortunes are depressed under the newly established democracy and who is (as we learn from the Sixth Pythian) himself a poet,[40] now seeks to improve his income by the composition of odes; and that Pindar, whose livelihood depended on the same profession, offers him half-jocular sympathy.

The symbol crystallizes this conception. Once again we light upon a puzzling phrase (v. 38) which should have halted all who own a feeling for style:[41] ἱπποτροφίας τε νομίζων ἐν Πανελλάνων νόμῳ. "Devoted to horse-training in the manner of all Greeks." The original contains a jingle, νομίζων νόμῳ, which all editors would have punctually censured had it occurred in Bacchylides. Looking further, we note v. 47, ταῦτα ἀπόνειμον, the expected sense whereof is "hand this poem (to my friend)": but ἀπονέμω is not "give," rather "assign," "allot." Why the unlikely verb νέμω, which appears no less awkwardly in v. 22 also, where we read that a charioteer "allotted" his hand to all the reins?

Our answer is ready. The symbol of this ode is νόμος, the noun derived from νέμω: that is why Pindar with rather forced and otherwise inexplicable jocularity drags it into v. 38, twice to all intents and purposes: νομίζων ἐν Πανελλάνων νόμῳ. But why νόμος? What visible object can represent "law" or "custom," the familiar meaning of that word? As soon as we ask whether νόμος could be concrete, we recollect that it was so in the Greek of Sicily, where Pindar's friend and his family dwelt. The Sicilian poets Epicharmus[42] and Sophron[43] use this word for a coin—the very topic which has exercised us so much in the second and third stanzas. The symbol, then, is a Silver Coin, the emblem of this new materialistic age whereof Pindar loudly complains. We now understand more clearly the description ἀργυρωθεῖσαι πρόσωπα, "with faces silvered over": the first word suggests ἀργύριον, "money," whereas χρυσωθεῖσαι, "gilded," would not; χρυσός, "gold," and its cognates being so frequent, and so frequently metaphorical, in these poems, and therefore less noticeable. Pindar believes that Thrasybulus is obsessed by the need of hard cash, and therefore not only writes without reserve on that topic but allows it so to colour his diction that in two, if not three, places he cannot be understood unless one feels the influence of the symbol.

This and the two preceding lectures have dealt with the symbolism of a good many odes. Consideration of the rest is here omitted, partly because, as Corinna told our poet himself, one must scatter seed with the hand, not with the whole sack; partly, again, because some poems are too slight to admit such elaboration; a very few longer odes appear to contain no symbolism, a fact which need cause no surprise; in at least one ode, again, the demonstration of this technique demands a more complicated and lengthy disquisition than suits oral delivery.[44] Before quitting this whole theme, however, we should attempt to answer one more question, both obvious and engaging. Is such symbolism as Pindar's to be found in other lyric poets? It is at first sight astonishing that —so far as my own reading justifies the generalization— hardly more than a single instance can be found. But surprise will diminish when we remember that Pindar's chief use of this device is in the presentation of myth; and lyrics that contain a narrative are very few. In fact, I can point to but one poem in French (for example) relevant to our purpose: Victor Hugo's *Moïse sur le Nil*, which tells the story of Pharaoh's daughter. That admirable poem contains, indeed, little else; still, in the last lines one may perhaps see a hint of the Pindaric symbolism:

> Un berceau va sauver Israël,
> Un berceau doit sauver le monde.

But what of those later French poets whose very title suggests this technique of Pindar—the Symbolistes? Normally, a symbol is a concrete thing employed to remind us of emo-

tions or ideas, not by imitating them of course, but purely by
convention. The Stars and Stripes do not look like the United
States, or a sceptre like monarchy; yet in everyone those
symbols at once evoke political and spiritual thoughts or
feelings. Now, Mallarmé and the rest do resemble Pindar
herein, that their symbols are not instantly familiar as a national flag or a wedding-ring is instantly familiar: the poet's
symbol is his own, to be newly seized and appreciated by
hearers of one particular poem. Beyond this, no likeness whatever can be found between Pindar and the Symbolistes. To
describe these latter fully in a phrase or two is impossible,
since they differ not only in talent and temper but also in
theoretic details. Nevertheless, of all the Symbolistes this at
least can be said, that their chief interest lies in the expression
of their psychological experiences as they face the mystery of
life and the Universe, particularly of what we now term the
unconscious. They are called symbolists not so much because
they employ those special symbols to which I have just
alluded, as because they study the sensuous world as shadow-
ing forth another world beyond it. A French critic has said
that, for them, "every object contains something beyond its
bare self and becomes the symbol of an idea. Symbolist art is
like Helmholtz's resonators which isolate the overtones of a
musical note and make them perceptible in isolation. In like
manner it discloses the secret resonances which respond to the
object in the recesses of the receiving mind."[45]

Nothing in all this applies to Pindar. He is entirely ignorant of what has been called "the torment of the infinite":[46]
indeed, it would be no bad definition of all classical artists (to
whatever epoch they belong) that "the torment of the infinite" never assails them. You have heard much about the
symbolic Bee in his Eleventh Pythian. A French symbolist
also might well have written a poem called L'Abeille, though
I am not aware that any did so. As we saw, Pindar uses the
Bee as a means of imposing coherence upon the various facts
which he thinks fit to treat in the compass of one poem. The
Bee is nothing more than a beautiful and brilliant device

whereby details, on any other showing hopelessly disparate, are drawn into close and vivid relation. Our French poet would follow a method utterly different. Both in thought and in composition, he would begin with the Bee, and then write of it indirectly, using language that would completely bewilder ordinary readers and ordinary entomologists, since for him the creature would be only a starting-point of reverie about his own deepest emotions, his groping after the ultimate unknown.[47] Pindar, in fact, reverses the modern process: with him the symbol exists for the sake of the objective theme; with the Symbolistes, the objective theme is valued only as a symbol of the idea. Nevertheless, that strangeness of phrases or single words, which again and again we have noted as produced by his symbols, cannot but bring Mallarmé to mind, perhaps most strongly in the statement discussed a few moments ago, that Aegina *falls* not far from the Graces.

Only one modern poem known to me exhibits the genuine Pindaric technique—Matthew Arnold's *Westminster Abbey*, an elegy upon his friend Arthur Penrhyn Stanley, Dean of Westminster. Throughout, he thinks of Stanley as a spiritual light that illumines his generation, and sets this thought, more explicitly (it must be owned) by far than is Pindar's way, in the very forefront of his poem.

> What! for a term so scant
> Our shining visitant
> Cheer'd us, and now is passed into the night?
> Couldst thou no better keep, O Abbey old,
> The boon thy dedication-sign foretold,
> The presence of that generous inmate, light?—
> A child of light appear'd;
> Hither he came, late-born and long desired,
> And to men's hearts this ancient place endear'd;
> What, is the happy glow so soon expired?

This spiritual light, this φέγγος as the Greek lyrist would have named it, becomes a symbol dictating the language and—here comes the most finely Pindaric quality—the choice of myths. Myths, we have noted, are exceedingly rare in modern lyrical poetry; but this poem actually contains two, both most beautiful. As for the diction, we find indeed none of those enigmas that have so often first daunted, then helped, us in Pindar. But the idea of light is almost omnipresent, and in one place the word "mists" is chosen where we might have expected "depths."

> The Saviour's happy light
> Wherein at first was dight
> His boon of life and immortality,
> In desert ice of subtleties was spent
> Or drown'd in mists of childish wonderment,
> Fond fancies here, there false philosophy!

But the myths are by far the most relevant to our purpose. Immediately after the opening stanza he tells how, when the Abbey was first built and awaiting consecration, one night a fisherman was bidden by a stranger to row him across the Thames towards "the Pile, huge in the gloom." Soon the church was suddenly "glorified with light"; the stranger returned, and, blessing his humble ferryman, thus spoke:

> At dawn thou to king Sebert shalt relate
> How his St. Peter's Church in Thorney Isle
> Peter, his friend, with light did consecrate.

The other myth, aglow with the same unearthly radiance, tells of the wandering goddess Demeter and that "charm'd babe of the Eleusinian king" on whom she sought to bestow immortality by cradling him in fire. She was discovered, and her plan thwarted. Then follows the noblest stanza of all.

> The Boy his nurse forgot,
> And bore a mortal lot.
> Long since, his name is heard on earth no more.
> In some chance battle on Cithaeron-side
> The nursling of the Mighty Mother died,
> And went where all his fathers went before.
> —On thee, too, in thy day
> Of childhood, Arthur! did some check have power,
> That, radiant though thou wert, thou couldst but stay,
> Bringer of heavenly light, a human hour?

So much, then, for symbolism. "But," you will ask, "apart altogether from that, what of Pindaric influence in general? Are not many modern lyrists indebted to him, even if they have failed to realize and follow his symbolic technique?" Let me end this lecture by briefly answering that wider question,[48] so far as my reading permits.

We may disregard nearly all the greatest moderns. Nowhere in Milton, Wordsworth, Coleridge, or Keats, nowhere (I think) in Goethe, scarcely in Leopardi,[49] and (save possibly for that one passage about the cradle) nowhere in Hugo, can Pindar's influence be discerned. The only feature that they possess in common with one another and with him is high lyrical excellence; if we are to call Keats Pindaric (as he has been called), we must assert that Fielding resembles Jane Austen because both are fine novelists. Nevertheless—not to mention the very peculiar position of Matthew Arnold, as just described—there is one great poet who avowedly, and with at least a measure of success, did imitate Pindar: namely, Gray. But even here we must be on our guard. To most of his odes our first remark applies: fine as they are, no genuinely Pindaric element can be detected in them. The exception, of course, is the gorgeous *Progress of Poesy*, one of the very few compositions from which a Greekless student may gain some conception of the Pindaric manner. Yet the connexion is somewhat mechanical, consisting (where it is clearest) in obvious borrowing: those celebrated opening stanzas are almost a translation from the First Pythian. The remainder, especially his descriptions of Milton and Dryden, is glorious, but contains nothing that (to me, at least) recalls the ancient master, save the splendid line which for a moment rivals his noble sonorousness and strong-winged movement "thro' the azure deep of air":

With necks in thunder clothed, and long-resounding pace.

No doubt he uses the triad of stanzas—strophe, antistrophe, and epode; but that was employed by other Greeks than Pindar, being in fact the invention of his predecessor Stesichorus. Congreve also uses it, and Akenside and Mason, who are none the more Pindaric for that.

The last-named three writers belong to another class: the numerous poets or poetasters who have produced nothing in the least deserving to be called Pindaric, but who, haunted by the shadow of a mighty name, have bequeathed to posterity shelf upon shelf loaded with polysyllabic and many-hyphened bombast. Among them we must not include the estimable Klopstock, though one German scholar has seen fit to inform the world that "Pindar tends towards the Klopstockian style."[50] That is merely fantastic: no likeness at all exists between the two; Klopstock's writings contain no evidence that he knew anything more of his alleged forerunner than that he was a fine lyrist; and he actually believed that Pindar's odes follow no rhythmical scheme.[51] Again, Congreve's odes are distressingly bad, though he deserves credit for his well-informed and sensible *Discourse on the Pindaric Ode*. Voltaire's essays in this kind have (to be sure) no value; but he was not writing seriously: we have noted earlier[52] his contempt for our poet. Von Platen is, I believe, unique. His Pindaric odes certainly deserve attention from students of the Greek, as the only poems which to the last detail reproduce metres actually used by Pindar. This labour and dexterity, however, have met with small success, owing to the essential differences between Greek and German: we fail to hear the original melody and sweep of rhythm.

For the rest, we are confronted by a mass of affectation, noise, and pomposity, all the more repellent because professing to imitate the glories of a sovereign artist: it affects us as would a man who played Bach on a cracked trumpet. We need glance at only a few of these writers who have for one reason or another attracted special attention, in societies more familiar with Latin than with Greek.

French poetry can show very few men who rival the illustrious Ronsard.[53] But Pindar's quality and methods, save indeed that on occasion he indited compliments and told strange legends, were completely hidden from him. Therefore, when in an evil hour he sought to follow Pindar, he committed deplorable futilities:[54]

> Par un miracle nouveau,
> Pallas du bout de sa lance
> Ouvrit le docte cerveau
> De François, grand roy de France.
> Alors, estrange nouvelle:
> Tu nasquis de sa cervelle.

He salutes the Queen of France with this jewel:

> Quelle dame a la pratique
> De tant de Mathematique?

Chiabrera, sometimes hailed as the first Italian to pindarize published only mediocre lucubrations, not even based on study of the Greek, but on Latin versions thereof and on Ronsard. Guidi, though proclaiming that he attempts "the methods of the Theban Singer" and that "not Pindar alone is dear to the gods," produced nothing worth consideration. Boileau's *Ode on the Taking of Namur* is almost supernaturally bad, as Landor[55] demonstrated with his usual vigour. So are Cowley's ventures in this kind, written (it seems) on a theory that all one needs is to grow excited and write lines of unequal length: his recipe for ode-making contains this oafish sentence:[56]

> Let the Postillion Nature mount, and let
> The Coachman Art be set.

Beattie, in his *Ode to Peace*, well exemplifies the belief, widely held in eighteenth-century England, that poetry is achieved by the wholesale personification of abstract ideas, and lyric poetry by inserting anatomical or other horrors couched in a gentlemanly falsetto:

> How startled Phrenzy stares,
> Bristling her ragged hairs!
> Revenge the gory fragment gnaws;
> See, with her griping vulture-claws
> Imprinted deep, she rends the opening wound!

These and a thousand other ghastly outbreaks spring from one cause only. The writers, some of whom—especially Ronsard, Congreve, and Boileau—were in other moods and other styles undoubted masters, failed utterly and unaccountably to recognize their exemplar's unique blend of poetic virtues. It was this blindness alone that allowed them to essay a task hopelessly beyond the power of the most gifted among them. Until a poet arises who shall combine the merits of Milton, Swinburne, and Hugo with the tongue of Dante and Leopardi, the world must wait in vain for a second Pindar.

PINDAR ON THE ART OF POETRY; CONCLUSION

PINDAR was the earliest European literary critic. He did not, it is true, offer definitions of poetry: such things belong to a later age, an age of methodical thinking. But no poet in ancient Europe showed himself so deeply concerned with the psychological and the professional aspects of his art: that is, first, the quality and causes of inspiration—precisely *how* a man comes to write poetry; second, the methods of lyrical composition. On these topics he should interest us profoundly, not only because he writes with graceful terseness, but also because he eschews the nebulous.

To the question, how a man comes to write poetry, we receive from him answers that vary in depth and value. The most obvious cause is the subject proposed to him by his client. He not merely consents, and eagerly: the theme ... I was at point to say, the theme makes him a poet. This would be a shallow explanation of such a passage as that in the very first stanza (*Ol.* I 7 ff.) of our collection: "the Olympian contest, whence riseth the hymn's manifold utterance that besetteth the heart of a wise poet."[1] He again and again speaks of song as if it existed before the poet began his task; still, that is but a natural and pleasant confusion between subject and poem. In the stanza following that just quoted he declares that the charm of Pisa and the victorious steed have laid upon his mind the spell of "delicious study." This φροντίς, this study, he calls elsewhere[2] a passion, an ἴυγξ, the word used for that fever of love which in the Fourth Pythian fires Medea. Another cause is Pindar's own spirit, as we may translate θυμός, which in one place[3] "urges *me*," by a familiar distinction between a man and his mind, soul, or passions. The third source of inspiration is "Heaven"—the Muses, the Graces, Apollo, and more vaguely θεοί, "gods"; δαίμων, "divinity"; even πότμος, "fate." The descriptions of this are numerous and, as showing his religious mood, important; but they offer no account of the means whereby the divine power impinges upon the human, an omission not surprising. These three causes of inspiration—the theme, Pindar's soul, and divine assistance—are naturally to be thought of as combined, and Pindar now and again says as much. In *Olympian* IX 26 the poet's genius works upon the Graces' garden. Again (*Isth.* V 19 ff.), the Graces and the merits of the Aeacidae join to feed Pindar's heart with minstrelsy. In another place (*Nem.* III 9) he invokes the Muse to bestow on him abundance of song from his own mind; and in *Nemean* IV 7 f. he phrases the same thought more notably: "Whatsoever utterance the tongue, with the Graces' blessing, draweth from the deeps of the soul."[4]

And next, with regard to what we called the professional aspects of his art, we are first to notice the places where Pindar insists on the poet's responsibility to Truth. These are impressive by their number and by their emphasis:[5] though he by no means takes the tone of those Roman poets who regarded the title *doctus*, "learned," as their greatest honour, he repeatedly professes to speak with exactness on points of history, and to correct others. Αὔξεται καὶ Μοῖσα δι' ἀγγελίας ὀρθᾶς (*Pyth.* IV 279): even inspiration cannot dispense with accuracy. Indeed it is vital that the Muses' servant should report τὸ ὀρθόν, "what is correct," because the magic of his verse enables him to create opinion, true or false. Thus the Tenth Olympian opens with a long account of ἀτρέκεια, "precision," as practised both by the Locrians and by Pindar. His catalogue (*Ol.* X 64 ff.) of those who won prizes at the first Olympian Festival is but the most notable among the evidences of his wish to impart exact information about long-past events. Even from his favourite Hesiodic poems he will diverge in the details of myth;[6] and he avowedly gives the lie to all earlier narrators when he offers in the First Olympian his version of what happened to Pelops on Mount Sipylus. His language there concerning error shows by its careful elaboration[7] that he has closely studied this aspect of his art.

The sense runs practically thus: "Legends with artful embroidery of falsehood obliterate the correct version and thus pervert history." In his ardour for Truth he writes even of Homer with equivocal praise, because he used his inspiration, his technical skill, and his grandeur to impose falsehood upon posterity.[8] Nevertheless, Pindar's truth was not always our truth. Like Plato, he saw great virtue in a γενναῖον ψεῦδος, "a glorious lie," tending to edification; like Aeschylus, he would alter a legend to suit his conception of the gods and their conduct.[9]

We have already found occasion to discuss a surprising but on the whole attractive habit of his: to insert in an official ode matter which (on the face of it) concerns few people or none besides himself. Among such passages are certain descriptions of his own technique. Apart altogether from the many incidental praises of his work, from the remarks about "correctness" and "truth," and from what I have called the "hush-passages," there are a few places which definitely discuss his own method of writing. They do not cover the whole ground, naturally; but they throw invaluable light on it. Indeed, compared with the boyishly engaging confidences of Keats' *Endymion*, they are notably businesslike.

He more than once proclaims the novelty of his method. What is that method? He often calls it his τεθμός, his "ordinance," "rule"—one might almost say "formula." In the Fourth Nemean he explains that "from delivering the long story in full I am prevented by the ordinance and the hurrying hours."[10] Similarly the First Isthmian says that "my song, because it hath brief compass, is bereft of power to utter" all the successes gained by his client.[11] Towards the close of his long narrative in the Fourth Pythian he cuts things short with the words: "time closeth in upon me";[12] in the First he speaks of "summarizing"[13] his topic; in the Ninth, of "brevity."[14] None of these remarks, needless to say, means a genuine apology: indeed, more than once he observes that such conciseness is a merit.[15] Still, they do not carry us far: strictly in themselves, they are mere excuses for omitting details, reasons for stopping short, much as Dante prosaically interrupts himself at the close of the *Purgatorio*:

> Ma perchè piene son tutte le carte
> ordite a questa cantica seconda,
> non mi lascia più ir lo fren dell'arte.

"But because all the sheets designed for this second lay are filled, the bridle of the art suffers me not to go further." There "the bridle" is clearly no more than his plan of giving thirty-three *canti* to each of the three regions—the most rudimentary "scheme" imaginable. His brother-poet's "ordinance" or "system" must be more complicated than that,[16] something subtler than the mere abbreviation so far noted, or he would not thus emphasize its novelty.

What artistic reason, then, what artistic result, has this abbreviation? Here at length we touch the heart of the matter. Pindar himself proclaims that his odes—some, if not all— have a secret, that they need enlightened study by . . . experts, we might almost say. Let me quote that vital passage yet again. "Many are the swift arrows in the quiver beneath my elbow: for the shrewd they have a voice, but for the multitude they need interpreters."[17] One fact is unmistakable: that we may with no misgiving attribute to him a deliberate appeal, in some aspects of his work, to a small instructed circle. Three passages describe this "ordinance."

In the First Pythian we read: "If thy utterance hitteth the critical moment, twining together in brief space the cords of many themes, less blame followeth from mankind; for tiresome satiety blunteth lively expectation."[18] That is, the Pindaric conciseness is not mere omission. The critical moment is chosen, and the rest omitted; then the selected matter, which shows (as we put it) many facets, is so presented as to give the essence of a long story. In this First Pythian, for once, we have no myth; and the allusion is to the attack of barbarism upon Greece. Instead of telling the whole in outline, Pindar selects the καιρός—here, three *decisive* battles: Salamis, Plataea, and Himera.

Secondly, he hurries over the last phases of his Argonaut-story because "to travel along the highroad would make my journey long: for the time closeth in upon me; and I know a certain short path."[19] Here is the same thought, less pungently expressed. Instead of following out the traditional details, he will attain his goal by a short cut, giving the gist briefly. Observe that by saying "a *certain* short path" he indicates some definite artifice, not mere omission.

Thirdly, in the Ninth Pythian we find the best description. "Great achievement is ever fertile in legend; but to embroider a small part taken from a long theme is fit hearing for the cultured. The critical moment of a story renders its essence no less well."[20] The rope of many cords and the short cut were not so perfectly clear: now we have the embroidery of an essential part for the delectation of connoisseurs. In this ode the method has been employed upon the story of Cyrana; her struggle with the lion and her arrival in Libya are superbly wrought up, but we are told little more of her.

That is Pindar's "novelty"; that is his "ordinance." Why has he invented it, and why should it be relished by connoisseurs? To both questions we shall give the same reply. First, the conditions in which, normally, triumphal odes were performed denied him the amplitude enjoyed by his predecessors in choral lyric. But also—and this I think a weightier reason,—being endowed with a strongly individual genius, Pindar insisted upon evolving a new method. He worked in strong reaction against his great predecessor Stesichorus, whom Quintilian[21] compares with Homer; saying, indeed, that he sustained on his lyre the weight of epic poetry. Pindar invented the brief ode—not merely an ode shortened by omissions, a feat too simple for boasting; but an ode shortened by a new manner of handling narrative. Instead of telling the whole story in detail according to the now familiar manner which Stesichorus had inherited from Homer, he selected a highly significant portion and elaborated that by picturesque detail and direct moral comment, giving it structure and climax. As Aeschylus stood to Homer, so stood

Pindar to Stesichorus,[22] whose account of Orestes filled two books, whereas Pindar in the Eleventh Pythian writes but twenty-four lines on that story. In short: Pindar invented dramatic lyric.[23] This method applies only to a part, but the finest part, of his triumphal odes—the myths: of course, for the rest of his material would defy such treatment. Some of the phrases that we have quoted, especially βαιὰ ἐν μακροῖσι ποικίλλειν, "to embroider a small part taken from a long theme," suggest a man who is trying to say "dramatic lyric" but cannot: fully awake to literary values, he is yet no modern trained in critical technicalities. He preferred the phrases which he has used, and which well describe what Aeschylus did to the epic.[24] It is an attractive thought that Pindar learned something from the early tragedies of Aeschylus[25] and from comedy, then taking shape in the hands of Epicharmus,[26] who had long been active in Sicily when Pindar visited that island. In any case, he broke strongly away from tradition,[27] as attested by what we learn of Stesichorus and by what we now read in Bacchylides, whose Fifth and Sixteenth odes may reasonably be taken as examples of the fashion which ruled choral lyric when Pindar arose.

Now, further: does he say anything about the structure of a whole ode? In the Tenth Pythian we read:[28] "Superb hymns of praise hasten like a bee now to this theme, now to that." This alludes, indeed, to the variety of topics; but we cannot say that it points to any novelty in the handling of them. Two far more striking passages, however, do so unmistakably. In the Seventh Nemean he describes his ode as a Triple Diadem. "The Muse weldeth gold and white ivory therewith, and lily blossom culled from beneath the sea-foam."[29] About this we said much in an earlier lecture; among other things, that the Triple Diadem, as a symbol, refers to the threefold subject-matter in that ode: his client's merit, the power of song, and Pindar's alleged bad behaviour towards Neoptolemus. In the Third Nemean he writes: "Lo, I send unto thee this draught of minstrelsy, mingled honey and white milk, suffused with blending water."[30] This Triple Draught points to the three stages in the presentation of each topic: Achilles as a child, Achilles as a man, his father Peleus; the three virtues which should mark the three ages of ordinary men; and perhaps the three places, Nemea, Epidaurus, and Megara, which in the final verse are named as witnessing the exploits of his client. The symbols themselves, in both passages, describe the poet's method—a clear hint that it is his invention: a hint reinforced by the contrast drawn between his Triple Diadem and the work of others.

Such then was the change in choral lyric wrought by Pindar's original genius. Did he "found a school," as he appears to boast in the Fourth Pythian?[31] Not in the full sense that he was succeeded by·poets who imitated and developed his methods: there is no trace of Pindaric influence upon the subsequent lyrists[32] who devoted themselves to the popular dithyramb and the music therewith associated. No development of the epinician ode appeared, and the genius of Greek poetry threw itself into drama. Nevertheless, in his own day, Pindar, as he claimed, had followers, and two or three poems by these now stand among his works. Which are they?

The Fifth Olympian has been suspected since Alexandrian days. Psaumis of Camarina, a little town in Sicily, won the mule-car race in 452 B.C., and the brief Fourth Olympian, which celebrates this victory, is unquestionably Pindar's. The Fifth Olympian, even briefer, celebrates the same victory. Did Pindar write it? The scholiasts report that the original copies did not contain it, but that in Didymus' commentary it was stated to be Pindar's work.[33] Modern scholars have argued elaborately for and against Pindaric authorship, but the negative must be regarded as proved. 'If Pindar did write the Fifth as well as the Fourth Olympian, he was consenting to do his work all over again in order to meet objections raised by Psaumis: can we believe this? Moreover, we have here two poems of fairly equal length, neither of which contains anything that could not have appeared in the other. That does not apply to the other instances of two odes upon the same victory—*Ol.* II and III, *Ol.* X and XI, *Pyth.* IV and V. Since

Pindar had not dealt with whatever glories Camarina and Psaumis' family might be supposed to possess, Psaumis looked about for a man who would compose an ode celebrating these. Some poetaster of the town was commissioned, who supplied local colour and closely imitated Pindaric language.'[34] What small interest his poem possesses for us is confined to the curious prophecy (v. 14) of New York: "Swiftly he weldeth together a lofty-limbed forest of steadfast chambers."

Now let us consider the Third and Fourth Isthmians. It matters little whether we take them for two poems or one. Melissus, a Theban, won in the *pancration* at the Isthmus and in the chariot-race[35] at Nemea. The so-called Fourth was composed to celebrate the Isthmian victory, but before it was delivered Melissus gained the other success, whereupon the so-called Third was written, in the same metre, and prefixed to the original ode.[36] In one of the best manuscripts the two are set out as a continuous poem.

The authenticity of this work as a whole[37] has never yet been disputed, but I find myself compelled to reject it. Arguments that this or that passage is "much below Pindar's normal style" should of course be eschewed: the only evidence worth adducing is opinions or statements or turns of diction which it appears downright impossible to accept as Pindaric.

First, then, certain passages show a somewhat crude, yet winning, sense of fun. Melissus was full of tricks, as our author with much relish demonstrates, comparing him (IV 51) to a fox that turns over and fights on its back against a swooping eagle. On this he comments with smiling cynicism that if you wish to quell your opponent you must stick at nothing[38]—a doctrine that would have made Rob Roy lift his eyebrows, not to mention Bossuet, with whom Pindar has been elaborately compared;[39] it has distressed scholars even in our own large-hearted epoch.[40] Next, he dilates in no timid phrase on the victor's "paltry presence," driving his malicious point home by the contrasting use of a truly gigantic adjective—'Ωαριωνείαν, no less. Here a scholiast, mindful, no doubt, of Aesop's Lion and Mouse, strains himself to excuse "Pin-

dar," as thus: "To have courage and an exceedingly fine body
hints at harm, because (mark you) Orion, who was of that
description, set his desire on what was above him and attempted violence upon Artemis."[41] We may believe, if we can,
that Melissus the Boeotian realized all this massive innuendo.
Then comes the climax, one of the most surprising passages
in Greek poetry: to comfort the victor for his few inches, his
lively eulogist reports that Heracles too was short in stature!
The unhappy scholiast quotes Herodorus' testimony that
Heracles was seven feet high;[42] but he should have left the
sentence alone. It is of course banter, pure and simple, but
banter of which Pindar was incapable: when he pokes fun at
his patrons, he is vastly more delicate than this. At one point
our Unknown allows himself a chuckle, where he tells us (v.
43) that Homer has left material for others to sport withal—
ἀθύρειν, which means "to have fun" or (in more stately passages) to do a thing in gamesome mood, as the boy-Achilles
"made great deeds his sport."[43] And he himself sports with
language, indeed shows gross literary taste, when he writes
(v. 72) that the smoke of sacrificial incense *kicks*[44] the sky!

Other passages, in perfectly serious vein, are no less puzzling if we are to suppose that Pindar wrote them. At the
close of III, after mentioning life's vicissitudes, he ends: "the
sons of gods, indeed, suffer no wounds." If any man on earth
knew better, Pindar did: the poet who described the funeral
of Achilles and the slaying of Cycnus cannot have written
that sentence.[45] Further, here only in the Pindaric *corpus*, we
come upon a thought which is so familiar to us that we fail to
notice it, but which appears to have been quite outside Pindar's range.[46] For him, as an earlier lecture maintained, success alone counts: a man who fails is thereby proved not to
have God's blessing, and thereby again not to have goodness.
But here we discover a clear statement that a man may deserve success and yet fail. In vv. 35 ff., commenting on "the
inscrutability of fortune," he writes: "For she giveth now of
this, now of that; a stronger man is oft caught and tripped by
the skill of weaker men." This, reinforced by an allusion[47] to

Ajax' death, is a plain acknowledgment that failure proves nothing about desert. τέχνα, which we translated by "skill"—that is, of the athlete or warrior,—can mean "device," and there is (no doubt) a side-allusion to the trickery of Odysseus, as in the two passages where the genuine Pindar discusses the Trial of the Arms. But the fundamental cause here assigned for Ajax' failure is inscrutable fate, which has nothing to do with Heaven's grace, according either to Pindar or to this poet.

Needless to say, not all or most of our discussion means that the ode is bad. One or two among Pindar's own odes are not so good: in particular, this poet writes with great beauty and pathos of the revived Cleonymid fortunes (IV 19 ff.):

> νῦν δ' αὖ μετὰ χειμέριον ποικίλα μηνῶν ζόφον
> χθὼν ὥτε φοινικέοισιν ἄνθησεν ῥόδοις
> δαιμόνων βουλαῖς.

"But now, by Heaven's will, after the gloomy winter the earth (as it were) in her patterned months once more has bloomed with purple roses." A few lines further on, this idea recurs in language most vigorous and winsome:

> ἐκ λεχέων ἀνάγει φάμαν παλαιὰν
> εὐκλέων ἔργων· ἐν ὕπνῳ
>   γὰρ πέσεν· ἀλλ' ἀνεγειρομένα χρῶτα λάμπει,
> Ἀοσφόρος θαητὸς ὣς ἄστροις ἐν ἄλλοις.

"He arouseth from her bed the old-time Renown of their glorious deeds, for she had fallen on sleep; but she hath shaken off slumber, and the skin of her flesh gleameth, even as the Dawn-Bringer, fair to behold among the other stars."

Are not those passages as beautiful as many a Pindaric passage? And cannot we find, moreover, a good deal that reads exactly like his work? What of these lordly verses (IV 44 ff.):

> τοῦτο γὰρ ἀθάνατον φωνᾶεν ἕρπει,
> εἴ τις εὖ εἴπῃ τι· καὶ πάγ-
>   καρπον ἐπὶ χθόνα καὶ διὰ πόντον βέβακεν
> ἐργμάτων ἀκτὶς καλῶν ἄσβεστος αἰεί.

"Noble speech goeth onward and its voice liveth for ever. Across the fruitful earth and over the sea moveth an effulgence of fair achievement that Time shall never quench." Fine, to be sure, in the Greek, but we cannot say that it bears the unmistakable signature of Pindar: Bacchylides wrote much that is equally admirable. Beyond doubt this poem contains a good deal that suggests the master, or it would never have been accepted by Alexandrian scholarship.

Our poet, then, was eminent among those many to whom Pindar "showed the way of poesy." And he was a Theban, to all seeming. The novel number and the novel description that he gives of Megara's sons (IV 69 f.),[48] while of course no proofs for or against Pindaric authorship, show that the author was familiar with details of domestic Theban tradition. So close does he stand to Pindar that more than once he copies the very phrase:[49] compare IV 11 f. and *Ol.* III 43 ff., two passages about the Pillars of Heracles; IV 61 ff. and *Nem.* III 22 ff., Heracles in the western Mediterranean; IV 65 f. and *Nem.* I 71 ff., Heracles' marriage to Heba. The suicide of Ajax in IV 38 f., as we have said, is partly reminiscent both of *Nem.* VII 25 ff. and of *Nem.* VIII 27 ff. Commentators on these passages are wont to say that Pindar repeats himself. That position it is of course impossible to impugn decisively; but are we not surprised to find him repeating himself so often in the course of one ode? This fact, together with the stunted Heracles, the smoke that kicks Heaven, the unwounded sons of gods, and the cynical morality, should convince us that we here possess work by an accomplished disciple of Pindar, whose *style noble* he admired and imitated remarkably well, though with here and there a crudity of expression and a touch of *grotesquerie* that distinguish him from his exemplar. And he is less sure of himself. Whereas at IV 23 he calls his work "a wondrous song,"[50] in a moment he confesses himself no better than earlier poets. Still, he has refuted in advance Horace's comment[51] on those who imitate Pindar: the wax-bound wings falter at times, yet he completes his flight.

But concerning disciples Pindar himself has little to say, being more concerned with rivals and detractors. Even in the period of his highest repute he finds need to speak with vigour and haughty defiance of malicious opponents. All this would make an exciting chapter in the annals of literary criticism, if only we possessed more details. Even the Alexandrian editors, however, were but scantily informed: the scholiasts who draw upon them are content to remark incessantly "here he hints at Bacchylides," or "at Simonides," or "at Simonides and Bacchylides": it is a vague affair of personal jealousies.[52] We may, indeed, reasonably conclude that the scholiasts (so far as they go) are right, partly because their Alexandrian authorities knew as a rule what they were talking about, partly because we have a little direct evidence. Simonides[53] took a fling at poetic novelties: "Not yet doth the new wine outface last year's gift of the grape: this is an empty-headed tale of boys." The Alexandrians held, and justly, that in *Ol.* IX 47 ff. Pindar is contradicting this when he writes: "Arouse for them the pealing march of poesy; and, while thou praisest old wine, praise song-blossoms that are newer." Again, a famous outbreak in the Second Olympian (vv. 86 ff.) most probably points at Simonides and Bacchylides: "The true poet is he that knoweth much by genius; they who have but learned, violent in their random babble, like a pair of crows, utter baffled clamour against the divine bird of Zeus." Pindar himself is the eagle. The verb for "clamour," being in the dual number,[54] must allude to two persons, and (moreover), as the dual regularly implies, a pair. Far the most likely opponents of Pindar who could be thus coupled are Simonides and his nephew. *Nem.* III 80 ff. is similar, except that it contains no dual: "Swift is the eagle among birds, and swooping from afar he seizeth at once the gory prey in his talons; but the croaking daws feed on low-lying ground."

So much, at least, can be found concerning Pindar's rivals. There is also strong evidence that he suffered detraction from people who, whether themselves poets or not, censured him on artistic grounds, in what he calls φθόνος, or spite. So in *Ol.*

VIII 54 f. he says that if he has gone out of his way to praise the victor's trainer, he hopes that spite will not fling a jagged stone at him. Another passage, *Nem.* VIII 20 ff., carries the idea further, giving a reason for such malice: "Lo, I halt my nimble feet, taking breath before utterance. For many things have been spoken in many ways; to submit new inventions to the touchstone for assay importeth vast danger, since a man's words are a dainty morsel to the malicious." There is the rub—novelty, which we have maintained to be, not the new versions of myth, as some hold, but the dramatic method of constructing such versions, whether new or not; we shall soon observe that a certain clique upbraided him with another kind of novelty. In both cases the complaint was that he had deserted professional tradition, which explains his taunts at what we meet so often in the history of the arts under such familiar names as "hide-bound conventionalism," "the dead weight of tradition," and so forth.

His detractors, then, are persons of culture, indeed, but bred on school-tradition and hating originality because themselves bereft of it. He never names them, and we should be wise to distinguish these doctrinaires from the truly great Simonides and the admirable Bacchylides, about whose quarrel with him, if quarrel it was, we know in fact almost nothing, save indeed that Simonides scoffed at the "new wine." The doctrinaires fall under trenchant, if not truculent, reproach in three notable passages. *Ol.* IX 100 ff. proclaims: "That which nature giveth is ever best; but many a man hasteth after fame with excellence that resteth upon teaching alone." *Nem.* III 40 ff. runs: "Through inborn glory a man hath mighty weight; but whoso hath acquired only instruction, dim light is his: now to this, now to that his spirit turneth; never cometh he forth with decisive step, and to no purpose his heart tasteth of enterprises without number."[55] But it is in the Fourth Nemean that Pindar's concern with his professional affairs and with the art of poetry reaches its most emphatic and splendid expression: moreover, a curious and winning ingenuity has combined—nay, interwoven—these topics with the ostensible subject of the whole ode; which, accordingly, we shall now examine.

Timasarchus of Aegina won the boys' *pancration* at the Nemean festival perhaps in the year 473 B.C.,[56] when Pindar was forty-five years old. The ode seems at first not so much a magnificent poem as a poem that contains magnificent passages. We gaze with astonishment at so much varied richness heaped together in less than a hundred lines: nowhere has Pindar more lavishly displayed his regal blend of majesty, vigour, and beauty, his unsurpassed skill in painting a picture with a few magical strokes. In vv. 52 f., we might fancy that Theocritus had begun to rewrite Thucydides: "Where kine-pasturing headlands slope downwards from Dodona until at last they thrust far into the Ionian Channel." Later (vv. 69 f.) he extends the prospect and, like Thomas Hardy in *The Dynasts*, reveals the outline of a continent: "From Cadiz towards the darkness none may pass: turn back thy sails again to the mainland of Europe." Yet the ode as a whole looks at first incoherent: the pearls have no thread, and lie strewn in disorder. This confused effect is due, as so often, to our observing the poem from a wrong angle: we fail to realize in full Pindar's preoccupation with his own affairs.

It is at least plain that an attack had been levelled against his poetry; if we study this, and his reply, we shall find that the ode has a definite shape, a unity of thought. Let us begin then with the high-hearted lines that most clearly allude to his enemies, vv. 36–43:

> ἔμπα, καίπερ ἔχει βαθεῖα ποντιὰς ἅλμα
> μέσσον, ἀντίτειν' ἐπιβουλίᾳ· σφόδρα δόξομεν
> δαΐων ὑπέρτεροι ἐν φάει καταβαίνειν·
> φθονερὰ δ' ἄλλος ἀνὴρ βλέπων
> γνώμαν κενεὰν σκότῳ κυλίνδει
> χαμαὶ πετοῖσαν. ἐμοὶ δ' ὁποίαν ἀρετὰν
> ἔδωκε Πότμος ἄναξ,
> εὖ οἶδ' ὅτι χρόνος ἕρπων πεπρωμέναν τελέσει.

"Although the deep sea-brine holdeth the space between"—that is, between me and Aegina, where my friends and enemies dwell,[57]—

"nevertheless make head against conspiracy: all shall loudly aver that I have come home in sunlight triumphant over foes. Another man with spiteful eyes fumbleth in the dark a barren doctrine that falleth to the ground; but, as for me, well I know that time in its course shall carry to the destined fulfilment whatever excellence Fate our lord hath given."

Who is ἄλλος ἀνήρ, "another man," and what is it that he does? Postponing for the moment his possible identity with the δάϊοι, "the foes," we must note that ἄλλος contrasts him with Pindar: "Another man bungles, but I go on from strength to strength." The opposition is plain; and the phrase "spiteful eyes" suggests that the "other man" is a poet, or poets. Next, what is this γνώμα κενεά which he fumbles in the dark and lets slip through his fingers? Farnell says: "empty barren maxims, foolish art-maxims." That seems entirely right as comment, though not as translation:[58] γνώμα means here "opinion," but it is in fact an opinion about poetry. The man fumbles with unsound notions that end in a fiasco: he is a stupid blundering doctrinaire whose poems fail. Contrasted with this soars Pindar's sovereign genius, a gift of inborn validity which develops with the sureness of fate.

Here we must pause, for clearness' sake, to say what can be said about our postponed query, the relation between ἄλλος ἀνήρ, "another man," and the δάϊοι, "the foes." It is less likely that Aegina at this time contained a whole coterie of poetical doctrinaires, than that ἄλλος ἀνήρ alone is a theoretician and a spiteful rival poet, who has infected a number of persons with dislike of Pindar: he "has a following." It seems probable that the group is hostile not only to Pindar but also to his friends the Theandridae, to which family the boy-victor belonged, and members of which, as we learn from a few rather charming remarks,[59] had won local repute as musicians and poets.

A moment ago we spoke of Pindar's soaring confidence in his destiny. Here we touch the central thought of his poem, for he compares himself to his own favourite heroes, and in particular to Peleus. Indeed, though we look in vain for the normal symbol, we find it replaced by these Aeacids, who are, in more than one sense, a prototype of the poet. This note is struck first in vv. 30 ff.: "Unskilled in battles would he show himself, whoso understood not that tale: for it is meet that he who doeth aught should suffer also." So ends the stanza that relates the overthrow of Alcyoneus, and it is next to incredible that so elaborate a comment should be written only about such a familiar fact as the destruction of an evil-doer by Heracles. Pindar has his own foes also in mind, with whom he is prepared to deal ruthlessly.

More impressive is the comparison with Peleus. In vv. 60 f., we read that Chiron saved Peleus "and carried through the destiny fated by God"— καὶ τὸ μόρσιμον Διόθεν πεπρωμένον ἔκφερεν. The sentence seems over-emphatic, if not padded. Was it not enough to say that he brought Fate to fulfilment?[60] Why add Διόθεν? Above all, why add πεπρωμένον to μόρσιμον? He has over-elaborated an obvious thought to remind us of the language that he has used concerning himself in vv. 41 ff.: πότμος there corresponds to μόρσιμον here, ἔδωκε Πότμος ἄναξ to Διόθεν, πεπρωμέναν to πεπρωμένον, τελέσει to ἔκφερεν. Peleus is thus made a prototype of Pindar: the hostility of Hippolyta and Acastus[61] prophesies of the Aeginetan detractors, and the ἐπιβουλία, the conspiracy, against which the poet exhorts himself to make head, is answered by the δόλιαι τέχναι, "artful plots," and the λόχος, "ambush" (vv. 56 ff.), set up by treachery against Peleus. He in revenge subjugated Iolcus πολεμίᾳ χερί, "with warlike hand," just as Pindar at the close threatens to do fierce and resistless battle with his own enemies.

Since he compares himself with Peleus and his kin, we should expect to find that the legends concerning them throw light upon the hostility felt for Pindar. The charge brought by Hippolyta against Peleus having no such application, we look elsewhere among the mythical parts of the ode, and speedily notice a fine analogue of those "digressions" so often condemned by the scholiasts, and (as it now appears) by the Aeginetan doctrinaires. The Aeacidae are widely scattered: Telamon went to Troy, Teucer reigns afar in Cyprus, Ajax dwells in Salamis, Achilles haunts a gleaming island of the Euxine, Thetis rules in Phthia, Neoptolemus in Epirus beside the narrow Ionian Sea, Peleus met strange adventures in the North. This picture of the Aeacid Dispersion explains Pindar's comparison of himself with the Aeacid Peleus. His notion of waging controversy about artistic methods is peculiar to him, as we have seen in other odes. Here he offers a masterpiece in this kind, by far the most complete, though anything but explicit. He is, indeed, at pains to avoid the explicitness which a prose-critic naturally seeks, for he remains a poet, beautifully and adroitly interweaving his controversial matter with the Peleus-myth and the Nemean victor's family concerns. In a plain paraphrase his contention is: "Pedants censure me for what they style my digressions. But this so-called incoherence is a splendid device: I touch on many themes, just as the Aeacids filled every quarter of Greece with their sovereignty and their exploits; but I thus create the noble unity of a whole poem, just as they formed one glorious family. What is more, by genius I shall outface enemies and comfort friends, as did Peleus of old by his prowess."

Thus does he set himself right with his friends, his pedantic opponents, and posterity. Remarking, as we have seen, that the soul of a true poet is in the hands of God, he shows no misgiving or the faintest intention to profit, or to suffer, by criticism. His own specific for immortality is no theory of literature, but Heaven's blessing on original genius (vv. 6 ff.): "Speech hath a longer span of life than any deed, whatsoever utterance the tongue, with the Graces' blessing, draweth from the deeps of the soul."

With that proclamation concerning the origin and virtue of poetry let us conclude our attempt to depict this greatest among lyric poets. His renown has been less than he deserved. He receives, indeed, homage from the greatest of all ancient and of all modern intelligences:[62] Plato quotes him with admiration in the opening of his *Republic*; Goethe tells a friend that some of Pindar's lines have gone through his heart like swords. But only a few years after his death, Eupolis, the distinguished comic playwright of Athens, complained that Pindar's work had "fallen on silence through popular indifference to beauty."[63] That he has been a great name rather than a great influence or a great source of delight to the world at large, is due to several causes, most of which have already been noted: the nature of his immediate themes, the difficulty of his language, his political and social loyalties, and his symbolic method, a superb invention which, though at once the chief glory of his poetry and its key, has proved too subtle for general recognition.

But we moderns face another obstacle, no less formidable, which surrounds most of the finest Greek poetry. We must not be misled by the fact, the deeply significant fact, that the whole vast accumulation of Occidental literature, from its epic beginnings beside the Aegean Sea down to whatever books were published this morning in Boston or Oxford, is united by unmistakable kinships. An educated American or Englishman of our day can, it is true, take up the *Aeneid* or *Don Quixote*, *Medea* or *Hedda Gabler*, Plato's *Apology* or the *Funeral Orations* of Bossuet, and find them not alien, only different enough from his own life and prejudices to provide boundless interest. The cosmology of Dante cannot dismay the scientist, or his religion the Protestant; no economist who rejects Aristotle does so through despair of understanding him; and Tacitus, for all his splenetic temper, will (in Gibbon's phrase) instruct the last generations of mankind. Yet this magnificent progress includes an early stage that is unlike the usual preliminaries of great epochs or activities. It is not weak, but immensely powerful. It is not tentative, but opens with the *Iliad* itself. It shows no adolescent jerkiness or uncertainty in aim and method: each of its poets, whether as profound as Aeschylus, as bitter as Archilochus, dashing and buoyant like Alcaeus, or grimly didactic like Hesiod and Parmenides, wields his pen with entire confidence in himself and in the authenticity of what he has to say. Each writes like a prince, or like a prophet who is the instructor of princes.

Nevertheless, no sooner do we begin to consider those shining generations, not by themselves but as a portion of world-
history, than we find them primitive, inchoate in thought,
however consummate their imagination and art. It was not
until the middle of the fifth century before Christ that the
contours of Western civilization began recognizably to emerge,
in the Age of Enlightenment, as some have called it, when
the reign of intelligence was inaugurated by the great sophists
and established by Pericles, Anaxagoras, and Socrates.

Earlier Greeks lived, worked, and wrote in the dawn of
Europe, with barbarism pressing upon every side and not yet
expelled from their own cities. Our civilization was still in the
making: those great commonplaces, justice, loyalty, the need
of clear thought and sound action concerning government,
morals, and religion, were yet upon the anvil. Splendid intui-
tions, heroic behaviour, were jostled by utter crudity of mind
and baseness in act. As early as the *Iliad* we observe this pre-
cariousness in the meeting of Priam and Achilles, who converse in dreadful oscillation between noble humanity and
frank savagery. Late in this period Themistocles, the greatest
realist of his day, offered human sacrifice before the Battle of
Salamis. Despite the sins and follies that disgrace succeeding
ages, it remains true that after the fifth century this pre-
cariousness of all that is noble, wise, and constructive grew
less: the world rode on a more even keel. Greece became intelligible to the modern mind; and Xenophon was the first
Hellene who could have felt himself at home in any cultivated
family of eighteenth-century Europe or America. Him we
understand perfectly, and Demosthenes; indeed, all later
authors (save Aristotle), if hard, are hard only in exact proportion to the difficulty of their topics: this is probably true
even of that manifold genius, Plato himself. Later, in Plutarch the European Idea finds complete and conscious expression. When we consider that Pindar belongs to the early
epoch, we shall no longer marvel that, as Goethe said of
Byron, "he is great only when he writes poetry: as soon as he
reflects, he is a child";[64] that his utterance bears no trace of

that logical structure which dates from the sophistic age; that metaphor is his natural language and myth his substitute for argument; that in politics and ethics he shows no hint of self-criticism and no more sense of the common good than Homer's chieftains; that, finally, he combines with this simplicity an imperial power of song and lives in passionate dedication to beauty. After his death it was no longer possible to think like a child and sing like an archangel.

If anywhere in these lectures my tone has been dogmatic, that was only for clearness' sake. My aim has been, not to dictate opinions, a folly which any true student of Greek must abhor, but to communicate an enthusiasm deep, enduring, infinitely precious. If anyone has heard me with interest, I would have that interest refresh his eagerness for independent study, for original appreciation and criticism. Such criticism, if indeed original, must often remain a private affair, because so personal that if published it might seem bizarre. But to ourselves it is all the more attractive for that very reason, replete with joy and enlightenment, since we have discovered—or so we fancy—exactly why a great passage or a great book enchants us. May I take leave to exemplify what I mean by private criticism, and make a clumsy but sincere attempt to show just why those words in the Fourth Nemean, which I translated a moment ago "from Cadiz towards the darkness none may pass," Γαδείρων τὸ πρὸς ζόφον οὐ περατόν, fill me with exultant rapture? First, we hear a solemn statement that we stand on the edge of the possible, the final horizon, and all men feel a thrill in reaching the limit of a great expanse. This is emphasized by the statement that darkness lies beyond. The dark is called ζόφος, bringing up thoughts of Homer's ποτὶ ζόφον ἠερόεντα and then of his Odysseus, who voyaged into that distant gloom and found the world of ghosts. From this, thought takes wing to Dante's sublime story in the twenty-sixth canto of the *Inferno*, how that same Odysseus' ship made its way so far south across the outer sea that he descried the Mountain of Purgatory before the waters closed upon him and his company. In Γαδείρων the

three long syllables suggest the stern effort which is to be
unavailing, and the labials of πρός, ζόφον, περατόν are a faint
mutter of discouragement, a notion reinforced for me by
sudden recollection of the same device, more exquisitely employed (it is true) by Sophocles:[65]

> ἀνδρί τοι χρεὼν
> μνήμην προσεῖναι, τερπνὸν εἴ τί που πάθοι.

In the first word again, by some freak of the mind—perhaps
the similar sound of αἴρων, "raising," and Pindar's own words
elsewhere[66] about hoisting a sail to the yard-arm,—the syllables εἴρων call up a picture of tall masts raking at the dark
clouds, masts of adventurers, the pirates suggested by περατόν.
Finally I recall how I myself once sailed in mist towards
Cadiz out of that very west here named as inaccessible, and
dimly saw Gadeira's walls and spires, beneath which men
must be moving on their humdrum tasks along secluded
streets and in cheerful shops or taverns set upon what Greeks
thought the uncanny limit of the world. All this comes upon
my spirit in a tumult of awe and glorious realization whenever
I read Γαδείρων τὸ πρὸς ζόφον οὐ περατόν.

As you smile at this, remember that it is all *true*—such is
one reader's experience, as student, as traveller, as human
being. Consider too that, while no other reader will have
exactly the same experience, everyone will nevertheless have
his own; and that this difference explains why we vary in our
enthusiasm for great lines of poetry. Be sure, finally, that
unless we are to abjure discussion of great lines, this artless
manner is the only sound, the only illuminating, way to appreciate them for oneself, the only safe basis of a criticism
that is to be developed for communication to a public great
or small.

No other reader, I said, will meet exactly the same experience. We all recognize the same beauty, but though it utters
to everyone the same syllables, to each it modulates them
with an accent reserved for him alone among all the sons of
men. There is in the *Odyssey* a passage,[67] marvellous even in

that best-loved of all poems, where Menelaus reminds Helen
of the night after the Wooden Horse, filled with Greek heroes,
was brought into Troy. She suspected that they lurked within
it and thought to lure them out."Thrice didst thou walk round
the hollow ambush, passing thy hands over it, and didst name
severally the Greek chieftains, imitating the voice of each
man's wife." Those words are beyond any comment of mine;
but we may let them serve as intimation of the magic whereby
Beauty is at once universal and yet private to each man's
bosom.

SYMBOLISM IN THE SECOND PYTHIAN

ALTHOUGH the symbolism of this ode is interesting both by its magnificence and by the light it throws on passages otherwise puzzling, demonstration of it is too complicated for oral delivery. It was therefore postponed to this place.

Vv. 89–92 run thus:

> ἀλλ' οὐδὲ ταῦτα νόον
> ἰαίνει φθονερῶν· στάθμας
> δέ τινος ἑλκόμενοι
> περισσᾶς ἐνέπαξαν ἕλ-
> κος ὀδυναρὸν ἑᾷ πρόσθε καρδίᾳ,
> πρὶν ὅσα φροντίδι μητίονται τυχεῖν.

We may dispense with examination of the many attempts to explain στάθμας κτἑ., for most or all of them contain their own refutation, being notably far-fetched[1] and even so not accounting for all the elements in the sentence. (But the idea that στάθμα means "a balance," since it has the approval of such distinguished scholars as Schroeder[2] and Wilamowitz,[3] should be mentioned. No clear evidence[4] can be quoted that στάθμα ever meant this: they seem to have confused it with σταθμός, which does mean "balance.") Three facts, if considered together, will clear the passage up.

First, the only meanings of στάθμα (στάθμη) in classical Greek are the literal, a "plumb-line," a "cord" for marking or measuring; a "line" drawn by means of it (as we use a ruler); and the metaphorical, "system," "constitution," as in *Pyth.* I 62: Ὑλλίδος στάθμας . . . ἐν νόμοις.

Second, ἐνέπαξαν ἕλκος καρδίᾳ can mean nothing but "stabbed their own hearts woundily": sores and cuts on the chest are out of the question. But the sentence is fully[5] metaphorical; otherwise the φθονεροί would die, which is an unsuitable idea, for the passage demands woeful disappointment.

---

[1] My own "emendation" of στάθμας into σπάθας (*Class. Quart.* IX, p. 5) is to be rejected with the rest.

[2] *Pythien*, p. 23.

[3] P. 292, note 2. (For explanation of such references see N.B. at the head of the Notes.)

[4] In Pollux, IV 171, Bethe reads σταθμά with most of the MSS.

[5] I.e., it is not true that whereas the στάθμα-idea in general is a metaphor, inside the metaphor all is literal—that people who did in fact στάθμας ἕλκεσθαι would really kill themselves.

Third, the regular⁶ assumption that περισσᾶς here means "excessive" is a mistake. περισσός no doubt often means "bigger than it ought to be," but it also often means "bigger than might have been expected"—that is, not "excessive," but "immense." Further, though "excessive" is a frequent sense in Attic, the early non-Attic writers never use it; in the three⁷ other Pindaric passages where περισσός (or περισσῶς) appears, the meaning is not "excessive(ly)" but "very great(ly)."

All the "covetous" and "self-aggrandizing" explanations must, then, be forgotten, and all the "cord" theories hitherto offered. The στάθμα περισσά is a vast ordinance, the ordinance of God⁸ who has just been named—χρὴ δὲ πρὸς θεὸν οὐκ ἐρίζειν. Nor is it surprising that he adds τινός, for he is using a novel and impressive metaphor: στάθμα τις περισσά is "the vast mysterious dispensation of Heaven." To this phrase ἑλκόμενοι is attached—with what purpose? He means that the φθονεροί rebel against the divine government, precisely as he has already implied, in simpler language, that they πρὸς θεὸν ἐρίζοντι, and as he will imply next moment, in language that happens to be familiar to us, that they ποτὶ κέντρον λακτίζοντι, developing the idea of φέρειν ζυγόν, a metaphor with exactly the same intention as στάθμα. The whole passage from v. 88 to the close enforces the wisdom, and the necessity, of submission to the divine government—here in one of its manifestations, as we shall find. ἑλκόμενοι is chosen to express this rebellion, because the στάθμα against which some strive is literally a kind of rope, just as in English "beat" can express rebellion if it forms part of the phrase "beat against the bars." The result of such revolt is anguished defeat for the malcontent; and for this Pindar says ἐνέπαξαν ἕλκος because the inevitability of the punishment gains emphasis by the assonance of ἕλκος and ἑλκόμενοι.

---

⁶ The only exception I have noted is in Hermann's *De Officio Interpretis* (*Opusc.* vii, p. 121): "περισσά autem στάθμα recte dicta, sive potentiorem funem, hoc est, funem tractum a validioribus, sive proprie maiorem partem funis intelligi placet."

⁷ *Nem.* VII 43, frr. 99 a (110), 204 (216).

⁸ Here I find myself anticipated by Gundert, who writes (p. 93): "Mit Gott, der bald den, bald jenen erhöht, soll man nicht rechten (86/9). Die Neider, die unzufrieden und blind für dieses Gebot an der gottgefügten Ordnung zerren, treffen sich selber, ehe sie ihr ziel erreichen." But he nowhere expands this idea. Tycho Mommsen, in a note on his translation ("am unmässigen Zeil geschleppt") writes of "a mania for a principle," which is "die Ergebenheit an die Tyrannen." So also Meinel (pp. 9 ff.), who sees here an allusion to Polyzalus. Schadewaldt (p. 329) does indeed say that the thought of God's justice is the "Inbegriff des Mythos," but surprisingly finds (p. 332) the unifying idea of this ode to be that "tyranny is sanctified by the divine justice."

The symbol of the Second Pythian, then, is a Measuring-line, suggesting ordinance, regulation. In popular morality, the system is that summarized by μηδὲν ἄγαν, which (as he says elsewhere[9]) wise men have praised περισσῶς; as sanctioned and directed by God, it is the dispensation that organizes the Universe.

Only thus can we understand the following lines about φθονεροί. Pindar has evidently been attacked by calumniators who seek to oust him from his position in Hiero's esteem. It was to be expected that a man of his genius and religious temper would not always content himself with personal attack and defence, but would sooner or later view his own quarrel *sub specie aeternitatis*. After proclaiming (vv. 89 f.) that Heaven exalts now these, now those, he continues ἀλλ' οὐδὲ ταῦτα νόον ἰαίνει φθονερῶν, and calls them rebels against God. They chafe under the divine Rule—that aspect of it which is seen in fortune's vicissitudes and which he has earlier so sensibly voiced (vv. 49 ff.): "Heaven exalts me today, you tomorrow: if the envious had but the wisdom and the decency to wait, their turn would come." That explains οὐδὲ ταῦτα in v. 89[b]: not even this—the fact that their day will come—satisfies the φθονεροί: they refuse to wait, and twitch petulantly at the concord of the Universe, to their own confusion and woe.

Turn now to the myth. In the full course of his story concerning Ixion's attempt upon Hera, Pindar stays to deliver the moral. What does he say? That wickedness is hateful? That this sinner was insanely bold? No: something less obvious (v. 34): χρὴ δὲ κατ' αὐτὸν αἰεὶ παντὸς ὁρᾶν μέτρον—"a man should always take the measure of each thing by his own stature." μέτρον reminds us of στάθμα: Ixion broke the Rule, the pattern or system. His son Centaurus, too, is not plainly condemned as wicked, but viewed with horror for his abnormality, his offence against the norm: ὑπερφίαλον—he was monstrous in his lust;[10] μόνα καὶ μόνον—like his mother, he was unique; and he was without honour, not ἐν θεοῖς but ἐν θεῶν νόμοις—he sinned against the *laws* of Heaven.

Thus our symbol not only gives pungency and force both to the myth, as here told, and to Pindar's defiance of his assailants: its presence in both these themes draws the whole work into a unity. Yet that is but a somewhat formal unity; for the detractors sin against the Rule by impatience of the vicissitudes which it im-

---

[9] Fr. 204 (216).
[10] Not in his shape: the centaur-form was the result of his lust.

poses, whereas Ixion's sin against it, we are clearly told, is ingratitude—by the behests of Heaven he cries from his wheel that one should requite a benefactor with kindly recompense (vv. 21 ff.). We know that Pindar is put in mind of gratitude by Hiero's own experience—the beautiful little passage about the Maid of Locris proves so much beyond doubt; and it is tempting to join the two portions of the ode more closely by a surmise that Pindar's enemies sought to discredit him by persuading Hiero that he was ungrateful to the prince. But for that no evidence exists. Even the scholiasts, who are obsessed by Bacchylides and in their notes on the latter part of the ode name him repeatedly as the calumniator whom Pindar has in mind, nowhere report the substance of his calumny.

A parallelism of phrasing that cannot be accidental links the passages that describe Ixion's delusion and the delusion escaped by Rhadamanthys: in each there occur words that are not perfectly natural but are suited to recall the other description. Nephela is a ψεῦδος, a word more fitted to the ἀπάται that fail to betray Rhadamanthys. Instead of saying that Rhadamanthys does not *listen* to ἀπάται, we read that οὐ τέρπεται, more suited to γλυκύ and μεθέπων in the Ixion-passage. Other parallels or contrasts there are which in neither place arouse any surprise, but they deserve mention. καλὸν πῆμα is answered by καλός, αἰεὶ καλός. Παλάμαι are mentioned in both passages. The μαινόμεναι φρένες of Ixion are strongly opposed to Rhadamanthys' φρενῶν καρπὸς ἀμώμητος, and ἀνάτα ὑπεράφανος to εὖ πέπραγεν.

Pindar seems, then, to have indicated this contrast in order to strengthen that unity which is conferred, but not too forcibly, by the presence of the Measuring-line in both portions of the ode.

THE FIFTH ISTHMIAN

PHYLACIDAS of Aegina, Lampon's son, was successful in the *pancration*, probably in 480 B.C., the year of Salamis. The exact date of the ode is not known: Gaspar places it in 480; Fraccaroli and Farnell early in 479, before the victory at Plataea;[1] Wilamowitz in 476, just before Pindar left for Sicily. This is the third ode written by him for Lampon's sons.[2]

Few of these poems vary so much in the reader's estimation from perusal to perusal. Some commentators have called it admirable, others weak and jejune. It contains admirable poetry—the superb opening address to Theia, and the brief allusion (vv. 49 f.) to Salamis where "the Lord sent forth slaughter like much rain; and, even as the hail, from men beyond number fell blood"—but also much that sounds mechanical and forced.[3] It will, however, be best to comment first on all the noteworthy passages in order, whatever kind of interest belongs to each.

i) The significance of Theia has been much debated, but little need be said here after the noble sentences of Wilamowitz,[4] eloquently supported by Farnell.[5] Hesiod[6] had merely named her as the mother of Helios, Selene, and Eos, and we hear nothing else of her as a deity. Pindar took the name as representing, better than any well-known name, the majestic Splendour that gives value and glory to mortal achievement and the beautiful things of our world. καί in v. 2 implies "not only in Heaven, but also on earth."[7]

ii) vv. 4 ff.

> καὶ γὰρ ἐριζόμεναι
> νᾶες ἐν πόντῳ καὶ ὑφ' ἅρμασιν ἵπποι
> διὰ τεάν, ὤνασσα, τιμὰν ὠκυδινή-
> τοις ἐν ἀμίλλαισι θαυμασταὶ πέλονται.

Does this allude to battle or to athletic contests?[8] The language suits both reasonably well. The first idea finds support in what

---

[1] Salamis is mentioned in vv. 48 ff. as the scene of naval victory; but the words that follow have been taken to imply that the Persian land-force was still intact.

[2] The others are the Fifth Nemean, for Pytheas, and the Sixth Isthmian, for this same Phylacidas.

[3] "Egli suppliva con la retorica quella passione che gli mancava per davvero." (Fraccaroli, p. 691.)

[4] Pp. 201 f.   [5] I, pp. 271 ff.   [6] *Theog.* 371 ff.   [7] Fraccaroli, p. 687.

[8] The idea of commercial rivalry, set forth by Mezger and others, seems inadmissible in view of θαυμασταὶ and the allusion to chariots.

follows, ἔν τ᾽ ἀγωνίοις ἀέθλοισι κτέ., where τε should imply change of topic. In favour of the second view we observe that boat-races were well known,[9] that ἄμιλλα suggests rivalry rather than war,[10] that θαυμασταί points the same way, and that the ἀγώνια ἄεθλα next mentioned allude in fact to skill of hands and feet (which is shown in boxing and running), and thus allow the earlier phrase also to mean athletics—rowing and driving. The truth is, Pindar has left the choice open between these two explanations.[11]

iii) In the muster-roll of heroes, when he reaches the Aeacidae, we read (vv. 35 ff.):

> τοὶ καὶ σὺν μάχαις
> δὶς πόλιν Τρώων ἔπραθον, σπόμενοι
> Ἡρακλῆϊ πρότερον,
> καὶ σὺν Ἀτρείδαις.

σὺν μάχαις is at first sight absurdly flat; yet few commentators seem to have felt misgiving. A scholiast, who paraphrases with ταῖς ἑαυτῶν συμμαχίαις,[12] possibly read σύμμαχοι; this would not account for καί and clumsily anticipates σπόμενοι κτέ. Bury, followed by Farnell, reads συμμάχοις. This is hardly better than the vulgate, for (like other suggestions) it infelicitously emphasizes the σπόμενοι clause, which so far as it goes diminishes the Aeacid achievement and is of course inserted (*after* their exploit has been mentioned—δὶς πόλιν Τρώων ἔπραθον) in accordance with Pindar's custom of enlarging a narrative by details that are in strictness not needed. If the vulgate is sound—and certainly it has not that hangdog look which invites correction—we must contemplate the whole ode till we find some point of view from which καὶ σὺν μάχαις becomes intelligible.

iv) In v. 38, ἔλα νῦν μοι πεδόθεν, the last word is explained by some as "drive onward," by others as "drive up away from earth." πέδον means "the ground," but often in the sense of "the spot"—the place where one is standing. Hence either translation satisfies Greek usage. But the first is very flat—Dissen has to reinforce it by unwarrantably translating "perge iam ab origine."[13] We should

---

[9] See Neil's note on Ar. *Knights* 554 f.

[10] Sandys in his translation is constrained to insert "of battle."

[11] It is delightful to find Dissen (of all people) describing E. Schmid, whom he follows in the war-idea, as "homo non tam ineptus quam multi censent" (*ap.* Boeckh, II 2, p. 513).

[12] Friese was led by this scholium to propose τοὶ καὶ συμμάχαις, "auxilio suo." That is open to the same objection as σύμμαχοι and brings in a ἅπαξ εἰρημένον.

[13] *Ap.* Boeckh, II 2, p. 518. He adds "Nam πεδόθεν h.e. [I do not know what these letters mean] est ἐξ ἀρχῆς." Even if this were true, it would not suit the context.

therefore accept the more spirited explanation "soar from the ground."

v) Praising Aegina (v. 44) as διαπρεπής, he continues:

τετείχισται δὲ πάλαι
πύργος ὑψηλαῖς ἀρεταῖς ἀναβαίνειν.

The obscurity here is increased by the difference of the meanings which Pindar attaches to ἀρετά—prowess, and the success obtained by it.[14] Still, it seems plain that ἀρεταῖς should be joined not to τετείχισται but to ἀναβαίνειν, because with the former construction ἀναβαίνειν would read awkwardly by itself at the end. Therefore the outline is: "has been built for ἀρεταί to climb." Whatever that may be supposed to mean, it at least suggests (ἀναβαίνειν being a kind of progress) that ἀρεταί here are virtues, forms of greatness, not successes. ὑψηλαῖς then will mean "high-climbing," no doubt with a secondary sense of "exalted," "noble." This helps to explain πύργος as a lofty place on which one stands conspicuous afar. It is "a lofty station"; and at this point our passage is parallel with fr. 201 (213):

πότερον δίκᾳ τεῖχος ὕψιον
ἢ σκολιαῖς ἀπάταις ἀναβαίνει
ἐπιχθόνιον γένος ἀνδρῶν
δίχα μοι νόος ἀτρέκειαν εἰπεῖν.

Next, is πύργος subject or predicate—"a tower has been built" or "Aegina has been built as a tower"? The preceding sentence, which calls Aegina διαπρεπέα νᾶσον, rather strongly supports the latter view. We thus reach the sense: "From of old she hath been built as a tower for their lofty prowess to climb." If you are an Aeginetan, any prowess you show will be more conspicuous, because (in our more homely phrase) you stand on your father's shoulders.

vi) After his brief mention of Salamis, he says (v. 51): ἀλλ' ὅμως καύχαμα κατάβρεχε σιγᾷ. Why? Even if, as some would have it, Plataea had not yet been fought, here was a glorious achievement nevertheless.

vii) The most obscure passage of all is vv. 56 ff.:[15]

οὗτοι τετύφλωται μακρὸς
μόχθος ἀνδρῶν οὐδ' ὁπόσαι δαπάναι
ἐλπίδων ἔκνισ' ὄπιν.

---

[14] See Lecture III, pp. 48 f.
[15] The only variation of the MSS. is between ἔκνιξ' and ἔκνιζ', both of which are against the metre. A good many editors therefore read ἔκνισ', as above.

Of many explanations the simplest is as follows. The subject of
ἔκνισε is ὁπόσαι δαπάναι—"the thought, 'how great is the cost.'"
Ἐλπίδων depends on δαπάναι: "the expense involved by their hopes"
of success in the athletic contests—a frequent thought in these
poems.[16] ὄπιν is their zeal for that success, and ἔκνισε means
"stabbed,"[17] that is, "quelled." So much has been set forth by
others. But why say "stabbed," and why ὄπις, an unlikely[18] word
for zeal? Bury made the valuable remark that ὄπις "is chosen for the
sake of its supposed etymological connexion with ὄψομαι, ὄψις,
ὄππα." Hence the choice of κνίζω as the word for quelling: the expense did not stab and injure their far-seeing eye, that eye whereto
τετύφλωται also alludes, which gazes upon Θεία and the radiance
of achievement. In that thought lies the symbolism of this ode,
though the symbol seems unimportant, and indeed for us serves
only to make the present passage clear. The Eye is suggested to
Pindar by Θεία, whom he connects with θεάομαι.

Our discussion has left two problems unsolved: καὶ σὺν μάχαις in
v. 35, and καύχαμα κατάβρεχε σιγᾷ in v. 51. To put these side by side
is almost to explain them both. Their difficulty, and the strained
tone heard in most of the poem, puzzle us only because of our own
preoccupation. We extol the victory of Salamis as a splendid feat of
arms, an effective blow at the barbarian invader who threatened
the very life of Greece. So felt and wrote Pindar's contemporaries,
Herodotus and Aeschylus. But Pindar did not share this exultation.
For us, the most repellent fact in early European history is the help
which some Greek states afforded the invader; and among them
was Thebes. What did Pindar think? Certainly in the Eighth
Isthmian he uses concerning the Persian menace language that we
should expect from a patriot, a man of honour, brains, and decency.
But that ode was written after the enemy had been finally and
overwhelmingly defeated. Here, even if we hesitate to affirm that
he endorsed the behaviour of Thebes and actually wished for a
Persian success[19] which would strengthen the Theban oligarchy,

[16] Cp. e.g. Pyth. I 90, V 106, Isth. I 42.
[17] Not "fretted away" as Sandys and others. The normal meaning is here in
point—ἐλύπησαν (schol.).
[18] The nearest usage is in Pyth. VIII 71 f.: θεῶν δ' ὄπιν ἄφθονον αἰτέω—"ungrudg-
ing favour."
[19] Mezger (p. 346) writes: "Dass Pindar dabei nur ihren blutigen Charakter und
die Tapferkeit der Aegineten hervorhebt, aber eben so wenig ein Wort der Aner-
kennung für die Athener findet, als für die Sache, der sie an jenen glorreichen Tage
zum Sieg verholfen haben, lässt deutlich genug erkennen, dass er mit seinen Sym-
pathien noch auf Seite der Perser stand und nur halb widerwillig das Lob spendete.
Wie er in späterer Zeit dachte, zeigt die Ol. 76, 3 gedichtete erste pythische Ode."

we must acknowledge that he plainly does two things. First, he minimizes Salamis. (Marathon, we recall, is mentioned thrice in his works, never with any hint of the battle.) Secondly, he implies, at this moment of all moments, that success in the Great Games is comparable to defeating the hosts that threaten Greek freedom.

The first of these two statements is proved by καύχαμα κατάβρεχε σιγᾷ. His "reason" is that "Zeus grants this and the other"; that is, apparently, since misfortune may come, do not be too proud of success. Such warnings occur frequently in his panegyrics, but elsewhere they are uttered only after the praise has been magnificently pronounced: here the eulogy is slight and curt—it is in fact one word, ὀρθωθεῖσα.

The other statement finds confirmation in several passages. Pindar has not only been commissioned to celebrate Phylacidas' success at the Isthmus: he has also (it appears) been instructed to extol the recent victory at Salamis, in which ἤκουσαν Ἑλλήνων ἄριστα Αἰγινῆται ... ἀνδρῶν δὲ Πολύκριτος Αἰγινήτης:[20] at any rate he sets out to exhibit war and athletics as the two great means of glory, and the stiffness felt almost throughout is due to the fact that his heart is not in the comparison.

This unwilling and mumbled eulogy of martial valour helps us to interpret the curious phrase καὶ σὺν μάχαις in v. 35. It lays a clumsy emphasis on something distasteful that has nevertheless to be said. "They—*yes, in battle as well as in athletics they distinguished themselves*—they twice sacked Troy, first as allies of Heracles, later with the Atridae." We see now why the first strophe has been variously explained. The original plan of the first dozen lines was to proclaim that Theia grants renown in war and in the Games; but Pindar edges away from this and blurs the distinction, writing so that the whole passage can be taken of athletics, as we saw. Look next at the uneasy diction of the second strophe. "If Aegina hath set her face towards a clear road of heaven-sent deeds, grudge not to mingle in song the fitting vaunt in recompense for her toil." We really must do this, he seems to say—"for good warriors gained repute among heroes also." Is it an exaggeration to say that he excuses himself for praising the men of Salamis by a reminder that heroic fighters have made prowess in war perfectly respectable? Hardly, in view of καὶ σὺν μάχαις and his statement (vv. 26 ff.) that the warriors of heroic days were praised in song: why should he not

[20] Herod. VIII 93.

set his teeth[21] and do the same for those who conquered at Salamis? After a brief and mechanical list of men slain by Achilles comes the tower-passage and Salamis, of which he is content to remark that "the land of Aias was saved from falling by her sailors,"[22] with a curt though fine description of the slaughter. Having urged that this meagre "boast" be "drenched with silence" because Zeus bestows varying fortunes, he continues (vv. 53 ff.):

> ἐν δ' ἐρατεινῷ
> μέλιτι καὶ τοιαίδε τιμαὶ καλλίνικον
> χάρμ' ἀγαπάζοντι. μαρνάσθω τις ἔρδων
> ἀμφ' ἀέθλοισιν γενεὰν Κλεονίκου
> ἐκμαθών.

The τιμαί are honours gained in athletics, as the next sentence shows: καί means that the Games are to be set on a level with the naval victory. Pindar is now on more secure ground, and completes this astonishing poem without further embarrassment.

---

[21] "Di ciò che non può tacere parla a denti stretti"—Fraccaroli, p. 695, meaning renown in war. (Fraccaroli sets out much the same views as are given above.)

[22] Sandys.

APPENDIX C

METRE AND RHYTHM

THIS SUBJECT is so complicated, the doctrines from time to time in fashion have differed so greatly, the importance of appreciating this side of Pindar's work is nevertheless so manifest, that it seems needful to add here a statement as brief, lucid, and correct as may prove possible. To treat the whole subject with anything like completeness would mean writing a treatise lengthy, labyrinthine, and at a hundred points controversial. The following pages are meant to serve two purposes only: first, to enable the student to hear the structure of a Pindaric strophe—and that is the most important reason for discussion of metre and rhythm; second, to satisfy the curiosity which many must feel concerning the varied length of our printed lines and the numerous endings in a half-word followed by a hyphen. Knowledge of more elementary scansion is here assumed—everything that one needs in order to understand the metre of Homer and the non-lyrical parts of dramatic poetry.

It is well to distinguish metre and rhythm at the outset, though this cannot be done without anticipating what will be discussed later. Metre is the arrangement of words into a series of recognizable feet which are either the same or obviously akin. Rhythm, by means of a repeated ictus-pattern, breaks up metrical material into groups. Metre can be perfectly exhibited by a dead monotonous delivery: rhythm is exhibited by utterance with "expression."

A Pindaric ode consists of stanzas resembling one another, sometimes identical, in scansion. The Sixth Pythian has six stanzas all of exactly the same pattern: for example, the first lines of the successive stanzas,

ἀκούσατ'· ἦ γὰρ ἑλικώπιδος Ἀφροδίτας
τὸν οὔτε χειμέριος ὄμβρος ἐπακτὸς ἐλθών
σύ τοι σχέθων νιν ἐπὶ δεξιὰ χειρὸς ὀρθάν

and so forth, have all the same arrangement of quantities: ∪ − ∪ − ∪ ∪ ∪ − ∪ ∪ − ∪ − −. The second lines in each, again, all show ∪ − ∪ − ∪ ∪ −. Such complete identity is rare. The normal arrangement is a triad, the first and second stanzas (called respectively "strophe" and "antistrophe") being identical as just described, while the third, the "epode," has a pattern similar but not the same. That is, if strophe and antistrophe are largely (let us say) dactylic,

[197]

the epode is dactylic too; but the dactyls and other elements do not show the same pattern. In the Third Nemean, the first lines of strophe, antistrophe, and epode are respectively (e.g.):

> ξανθὸς δ' 'Αχιλεὺς τὰ μὲν μένων Φιλύρας ἐν δόμοις
> κτείνοντ' ἐλάφους ἄνευ κυνῶν δολίων θ' ἐρκέων
> ὄφρα θαλασσίαις ἀνέμων ῥιπαῖσι πεμφθείς

The first two show $--\cup\cup-\cup-\cup-\cup\cup---\cup-$: the third, $-\cup\cup-\cup-\cup\cup---\cup--$. An ode may contain only one triad, as the Fourth Olympian, or more: the Fourth Pythian extends, far beyond all others, to thirteen triads. If there are more triads than one, all the strophes and antistrophes follow (almost[1]) exactly the same model, and all the epodes (almost[1]) exactly a different model of their own.

But the Pindaric stanza is too large a unit for the ear to appreciate definitely. If we are to grasp its metre and rhythm, we need to perceive its elements and gain a sense of structure by observing their interdependence. Five such elements have been discerned, which are, in ascending order of size: syllable, foot, colon, verse, and period. Two of these shall not be discussed here: the syllable, because (as was said above) knowledge of quantity, elision, synizesis, and the like[2] is assumed; the period, which is a group[3] of verses, partly because its size and structure are so often doubtful, but above all because for us moderns it is a matter of ink and paper only, and means nothing to our tongue or ear.

We shall first, then, consider the strophe (etc.) merely as a collection of feet. *Isth.* VI 23 runs thus[4] in all the editions:

> καὶ πέραν Νείλοιο παγᾶν καὶ δι' 'Υπερβορέους.

As to the quantities there is, fundamentally, no question:

$$-\cup---\cup---\cup\cup-\cup\cup-$$

But disagreement arises about the feet. Here are two utterly divergent scansions by scholars who have at different times exercised

---

[1] Apart from verse-endings (see below) we find, very rarely, in one stanza a short syllable "corresponding" to a long in the others. Attempts to eliminate these anomalies by emendation are not convincing. In performance they would no doubt be masked by the music.

[2] Apparent hiatus is frequent in Pindar, as in Homer, if we neglect the digamma. Most editors unfortunately do not print it.

[3] Usually three or four in a stanza: there may be more, or (occasionally) but one. There is no necessary structural kinship between period and period as such.

[4] In wording. Bowra and Puech divide into two lines, a consideration which at present does not concern us.

influence. J. H. H. Schmidt, whose methods are now almost univer-
sally rejected, offers this:[5]

$$- > \ | -- | - > \ | -- | -\cup\cup \ | -\cup\cup \ | -\bar{\Lambda} \ |$$

Schroeder gives:[6]

$$-\cup-- \quad -\cup-- \quad -\cup\cup- \quad \cup\cup-$$

The latter looks simple enough: he is making as many quadri-
syllabic feet as he finds possible.

Schmidt's arrangement is more surprising: the spondees and dactyls are familiar, but what are $->$ and $-\bar{\Lambda}$? The latter means that
the final foot is catalectic, $\bar{\Lambda}$ indicating a pause to complete it.
Schmidt uses Λ for a pause equivalent to one short,[7] $\bar{\Lambda}$ for a pause
equivalent to two shorts, and $\dot{\Lambda}$ equivalent to three; voice-utter-
ance and music being accommodated to these lengths. Further,
$->$ means (according to circumstances) either that a spondee is
accelerated so that it counts as a trochee, or that a trochee is retarded so as to equal a spondee. Here καὶ πέ- and -οιο are retarded
trochees. Why all this? It is a fundamental doctrine of Schmidt
that each foot in a verse must be equal in length to all the others.
Here the majority of feet are plainly of four "times" (χρόνοι); that
is, equal to $\cup\cup\cup\cup$: the others must be made to agree. Hence the
final long syllable is reinforced by $\bar{\Lambda}$, not Λ, and the trochees are
retarded to $->$.

A like situation obtains in other metres. *Pyth.* VI 5,

Πυθιόνικος ἔνθ' ὀλβίοισιν Ἐμμενίδαις,

is scanned by Schroeder

$$-\cup\cup-\cup- \quad\quad -\cup-\cup-\cup\cup-$$

and by Schmidt

$$-\cup\cup \ | -\cup \ | \ \llcorner \ | -\cup \ | -\cup \ | -\cup\cup \ | -\Lambda \ |$$

The metre being at least predominantly trochaic, he imposes at any
rate a quasi-trochaic scansion upon the whole—by two devices.
First is the use of τονή: that is, a long syllable is protracted to equal

---

[6] *Kunstformen* I, p. 423. At two places he gives $||$, not $|$ as above, but $||$ refers
to cola, and can be ignored for the present.
[6] In his *editio maior* of Pindar. He uses gaps instead of $|$ to indicate foot-division.
[7] Thus a catalectic trochaic verse would be shown with $| -\Lambda |$ as the last foot.
(Λ is a capital lambda, the first letter of Λεῖμμα.)

three shorts (⌊).[8] The other device is to regard Πυθιό- and Ἐμμενί-
as accelerated or "cyclic" dactyls, each equivalent in total[9] length
to a trochee, this equivalence being indicated by ‿∪ ∪. It will be
remembered that a spondee can count as a trochee, being marked
–>. Thus Schmidt scans *Nem.* IV 5,

γυῖα, τόσσον εὐλογία φόρμιγγι συνάορος,

$$ -\cup \mid -\cup \mid \smallsmile\cup\cup \mid -> \mid \smallsmile\cup\cup \mid -\cup \mid -\Lambda \mid $$

Another artifice whereby he secures this uniformity is Hermann's invention, "anacrusis" (ἀνάκρουσις, "striking up")—a preliminary syllable or two syllables standing outside the verse-
scheme,[10] like grace-notes. *Nem.* I 4, Δάλου κασιγνήτα, σέθεν ἀδυεπής,
he scans:

$$ - \vdots -> \mid -- \mid -\cup\cup \mid -\cup\cup \mid -\overline{\Lambda} \mid $$

One advantage gained hereby is that Schmidt avoids recognition of
the astonishing and rare "acephalous" verse, in which the first syllable is apparently missing. The sixth verse of the strophes and
antistrophes in *Ol.* VI run (e.g.):

συνοικιστήρ τε τᾶν κλεινᾶν Συρακοσσᾶν, τίνα κεν φύγοι ὕμνον

Schroeder insets this scansion:

$$ \cup-- \quad -\cup-- \quad -\cup-- \quad -\cup\cup- \quad \cup\cup-\overline{\cup} $$

Anacrusis and τονή enable Schmidt to give a "normal" verse in
dactylic metre:

$$ \cup \vdots \sqcup \mid \sqcup \mid -> \mid -- \mid -> \mid -- \mid -\cup\cup \mid -\cup\cup \mid -- \mid $$

The reader may well ask why space has been given to exposition
of a system rejected today by the overwhelming majority of metricians; especially when, quite apart from such authority, several of
Schmidt's expedients appear (to put the best face on it) artificial.
The answer goes to the root of the whole subject. A Pindaric
stanza is so complicated that many, conceivably most, moderns
cannot grasp its structure unless its delivery is governed by some

---

[8] Or, if we are concerned with four-time metre, a long syllable may be protracted
to equal four shorts. That is indicated by ⊔. In reading aloud, the voice should of
course dwell for an appropriate time on such syllables.

[9] The long and the first short are understood each to lose some length.

[10] So, in tragedy, older editions print φεῦ or ἔα at the beginning of an iambic verse
which contains six feet without it.

principle which reveals a considerable degree of uniformity.[11] A considerable degree: not, of course, exact and therefore monotonous uniformity. If we recite these two consecutive verses of Euripides:[12]

ἢ οὐκ ἀξιόχρεως ὁ θεὸς ἀναφέροντί μοι
μίασμα λῦσαι; πῶς τις οὖν ἔτ' ἂν φύγοι;

or these of Virgil:[13]

... Magna satis, dubito haud equidem implorare quod usquam est.
Flectere si nequeo Superos, Acheronta movebo,

we render two lines of very different quality, but we utter also the same six-foot metre. So too in these odes, if we read aloud a strophe following Schmidt's pattern, we shall *hear structure*. The schemes put forth by Schroeder and others of his school may be far more scientific; they may be intelligible; undoubtedly they look more reasonable on paper: but if we accept them, many odes disintegrate into a chattering chaos. In the following summary, therefore, we shall use the familiar two- and three-syllable feet as far as possible; but we shall, for reasons to be given at the proper place,[14] decline to use Schmidt's > invariably.

Pindar employs the following feet:

1. Trochee: εἰ δ' ἄεθλα γαρύεν   (*Ol.* I 3) $-\cup \mid -\cup \mid -\cup \mid -\Lambda \mid$
2. Iambus:[15] ὁδῶν ὁδοὶ περαίτεραι   (*Ol.* IX 105) $\cup - \mid \cup - \mid \cup - \mid \cup - \mid$
3. Spondee (only in combination with other feet):

θαύμασον οἷον ἀταρβεῖ νεῖκος ἄγει κεφαλᾷ μόχθου καθύπερθε νεᾶνις

(*Pyth.* IX 31)

$-\cup\cup \mid -\cup\cup \mid -- \mid -\cup\cup \mid -\cup\cup \mid -- \mid -\cup\cup \mid -\cup\cup \mid -- \mid$

4. Dactyl (only in combination with other feet): see no. 3 above.
5. Tribrach (only as resolution of trochee):

ἐπὶ γὰρ ἰοχέαιρα παρθένος χερὶ διδύμᾳ   (*Pyth.* II 9).

$\cup\cup\cup \mid \cup\cup\cup \mid -\cup \mid -\cup \mid -\cup \mid \cup\cup\cup \mid -\Lambda \mid$

---

[11] Cp. Dion. Hal. *de Comp. Verb.* XXVI: οἱ μελοποιοὶ πολυμέτρους τὰς στροφὰς ἐργα- ζόμενοι καὶ τῶν κώλων ἑκάστοτε πάλιν ἀνίσων τε ὄντων καὶ ἀνομοίων ἀλλήλοις ἀνομοίους τε καὶ ἀνίσους ποιούμενοι τὰς διαιρέσεις, δι' ἄμφω δὲ ταῦτα οὐκ ἐῶντες ἡμᾶς ὁμοειδοῦς ἀντίληψιν λαβεῖν ῥυθμοῦ πολλὴν τὴν πρὸς τοὺς λόγους ("prose") ὁμοιότητα κατασκευά- ζουσιν ἐν τοῖς μέλεσιν.

[12] *Orestes* 597 f.

[13] *Aen.* VII 311 f.

[14] See p. 208, note 27.

[15] Schmidt scans iambi as trochees with anacrusis: e.g., in the example given above, $\cup \;\vdots\; -\cup \mid -\cup \mid -\cup \mid -\Lambda \mid$

6. Cretic[16] (or paeon,[17] frequently resolved):

    ἀλλ', ὦ Κρόνιε παῖ 'Ρέας, ἕδος 'Ολύμπου νέμων   (*Ol.* II 12)

    – ⋮ –∪∪ | –∪– | ∪∪∪ | –∪– |

7. Bacchius (very rare):

    ἰανθεὶς ἀοιδαῖς (*Ol.* II 13). ∪–– | ∪–– |

8. Anapaest (rare):

    καὶ παρὰ Κασταλίᾳ, πατέρα τε Δαμάγητον ἀδόντα Δίκᾳ   (*Ol.* VII 17)

    –∪∪ | –∪∪ | –∪∪ | ∪∪– | ⊔ | –∪∪ | –∪∪ | –Λ̄ |

9. Dochmius (very rare):

    σύ τοί νιν κλυτᾶς (*Pyth.* V 6) ∪––∪–

10. Epitrite (see p. 208).

At this point it is well to explain why a series of feet is often called monometer, dimeter, trimeter, or tetrameter[18] instead of dipody, tetrapody, hexapody, octapody, respectively. When the number of feet is even, they are by many metricians counted in pairs, each pair being a unit, called "metron" ("measure"). For the two feet in a metron are not, after all, exactly equivalent: there is a stronger ictus[19] upon the stressed syllable of the first foot than upon the stressed syllable of the second foot. Thus the metron is the smallest genuine unit of *rhythm*. In the present summary it has not been found necessary to say more on this subject; but it seemed useful to explain words so often used as "dimeter," etc., and also the dots which, in Gildersleeve's edition, serve to mark the stronger ictus.

All that we have so far done is to organize the syllables into feet, but that is far from adequate as demonstration of structure. What larger units can we find, between the foot and the whole stanza? Amid all the perplexities and confusions one vital fact stands plain and undisputed. The stanza is divided for us by a number of pauses, made either by hiatus or by a *syllaba anceps*. We may confidently break up the strophe into the masses thus indicated. They are called "verses"—*versus*, στίχοι. Though στίχος is often translated by "line," this latter word should, in discussions of metre and rhythm, be

---

[16] The cretic is a genuine single foot, not | –∪ | ⌊ |, for it is often resolved into –∪∪∪ (e.g., in the Parodos of the *Acharnians*) which cannot = –∪⌊, for then ⌊ would equal ∪∪.

[17] The paeon is a long and three shorts, called first, second, third, or fourth paeon according to the position of the long. Thus –∪∪∪ is a first paeon, ∪∪∪– a fourth paeon.

[18] This terminology is applied only to feet equal to four shorts or less; and among them not to the dactyl, which is always scanned by feet only. Thus the dactylic hexameter consists of six feet.

[19] Ictus is voice-stress: thus the first syllable of "April" and the second of "July" have the ictus.

carefully distinguished from "verse." A line is a purely mechanical division of writing or print, fixed by the width of the paper: its length has nothing to do with meaning, grammar, style, metre, or rhythm. But a verse is a rhythmical mass: it must be so, or Pindar would not have marked its close by such licenses as these two. Now and again a verse will just fill a line, but that coincidence means nothing.

It is to be observed that, though in each strophe every verse ends with the end of a word, neither hiatus nor *syllaba anceps* is necessarily found there in *each* strophe. As in the Homeric verse, each verse (being a separate unit) can at the poet's convenience end with one or both of these licenses, but very often does not. One instance will show how this principle works. The first strophe of *Pyth.* VIII is usually printed thus:

Φιλόφρον Ἡσυχία, Δίκας
ὦ μεγιστόπολι θύγατερ,
βουλᾶν τε καὶ πολέμων
ἔχοισα κλαῖδας ὑπερτάτας
Πυθιόνικον τιμὰν Ἀριστομένει δέκευ.
τὺ γὰρ τὸ μαλθακὸν ἔρξαι τε καὶ παθεῖν ὁμῶς
ἐπίστασαι καιρῷ σὺν ἀτρεκεῖ.

Not one of these verses is marked by a pause. But examine the other stanzas. In v. 28 we find ἐμπρέπει followed by εἰμί—hiatus: therefore τὰ δὲ καὶ ἀνδράσιν ἐμπρέπει must be a verse, and so its metrical equivalent Φιλόφρον Ἡσυχία Δίκας also must be a verse. Our next item ends at θύγατερ, because Ἐπίγονοι in v. 42 is followed by ὧδε. Similarly the verse-endings at πολέμων and ὑπερτάτας are proved by hiatus at v. 50 and v. 44 respectively. Our fifth portion closes with a long syllable, but at the same place (v. 32) we see τράχον, the final syllable of which is short by nature and is not lengthened by a succeeding consonant, for the next word is ἴτω. Just so φίλτατον (v. 13) followed by ἑκόντος proves a verse-ending at ὁμῶς in our first strophe.

This method enables us to set out all the strophes and antistrophes in the Eighth Pythian—and many others—in a satisfactory form. But not, for example, the epodes of that poem, since the pauses give us (e.g.) this as one verse: τόξοισί τ' Ἀπόλλωνος· ὃς εὐμενεῖ νόῳ Ξενάρκειον ἔδεκτο Κίρραθεν ἐστεφανωμένον. This occasionally happens even in long odes, and is naturally to be expected in the shortest, since there are very few stanzas to help one another

out. Even the Fourth Pythian, despite its length, is left with this as
the second verse of the strophe—and of course exactly similar
masses in the other twenty-five corresponding stanzas:

στᾶμεν, εὐίππου βασιλῆϊ Κυράνας, ὄφρα κωμάζοντι σὺν Ἀρκεσίλᾳ

These verses strike us at once as unsatisfactory. Why, precisely?
That they are too long for a "line" matters nothing. We can print to
the margin and add the casual residue in the next line, as is done for
example by Sandys and Farnell. Boeckh was so averse to any sort
of break in these long verses that he chose a quarto instead of an
octavo format[20] for his famous edition, and triumphantly printed
στᾶμεν κτέ. right across his noble page, unsullied by any hyphen.
But that concerns page-setting, not the art of poetry. The all-
important fact is that such a verse is *too long for a single utterance:*
too long, that is, for a *rhythmical* unit. We thus reach the most interesting, perhaps the most vital element in Greek lyrical composition,
the colon, κῶλον, the "limb" or "member." These verses must be
divided into cola, so that we may pronounce them with ease and
expression. Those verses which satisfy us in the Eighth Pythian,
and elsewhere, are satisfactory because they are identical each with
a single colon. These longer verses must be divided into two or
more cola, not merely to make artistic delivery convenient, but to
make it possible.

The long verse, then, must be divided into two—possibly three—
parts. How are we to know where the division is to be made? We
cannot answer "more or less in the middle, as in prose," since our
division must, for symmetry's sake, come at the same point in all
the corresponding verses throughout the ode. We must therefore determine it in view of what is common to all the verses. The following natural rules will singly or in combination settle nearly all the
divisions of long verses.

1. Read the whole poem aloud, so that the cola already certain (i.e., the short
verses) may help to give the lilt.

2. Expect division after a syllable or foot which clearly slows down the rhythm:
i.e., ∟ or ⊔ or a spondee.

3. If a word-ending occurs regularly at the same place throughout, it probably
ends a colon.

4. Cola tend to contain the same number of feet.

---

[20] *Praefatio*, p. XXX. Gildersleeve, in theory, does the same, but his page is
narrower; therefore his lengthy verse often continues into a second line.

If a colon thus obtained ends (in any verse of the ode) inside a word, we must then print the whole verse so as to show this, insetting the second colon (and the third, if any) so as to show that neither colon is a separate verse; e.g., *Ol.* I 17 will appear thus:

ἄνδρες ἀμφὶ θαμὰ τράπεζαν.

ἀλλὰ Δωρίαν ἀπὸ φόρμιγγα πασσάλου

The first colon ends with a word-ending, but its predecessor in the first strophe does not:

ἄλλο θαλπνότερον ἐν ἀμέ-
ρᾳ φαεννὸν ἄστρον ἐρήμας δι' αἰθέρος.

Let us now see what we can do with a few long verses, using the rules just given.

Pyth. IV 233:

εἶχετ' ἔργου· πῦρ δέ νιν οὐκ ἐόλει παμφαρμάκου ξείνας ἐφετμαῖς.[21]
–∪ – – | –∪∪ | –∪∪ | – – | –∪ | – – | –∪ – – |

Rule 2 gives us division after the spondee, and surely our ear agrees. We then mark colon-endings in our scheme by double lines,

–∪ – – | –∪∪ | –∪∪ | – – || –∪ | – – | –∪ – – ||

and print[22] the verse:

εἶχετ' ἔργου· πῦρ δέ νιν οὐκ ἐόλει παμφαρμάκου ξείνας ἐφετμαῖς.

Isth. VI 50.

ἀρχὸν οἰωνῶν μέγαν αἰετόν· ἀδεῖα δ' ἔνδον νιν ἔκνιξεν χάρις.
–∪ – – | –∪∪ | –∪∪ | ⊔ | –∪ | ⊔ | –∪ – – | –∪ – Λ̄ |

Here ⊔ occurs twice, and Rule 4 points to colon-ending after the earlier:

ἀρχὸν οἰωνῶν μέγαν αἰετόν· ἀ-
δεῖα δ' ἔνδον νιν ἔκνιξεν χάρις.

Ol. X 3.

ἐμᾶς γέγραπται· γλυκὺ γὰρ αὐτῷ μέλος ὀφείλων ἐπιλέλαθ'· ὦ Μοῖσ', ἀλλὰ σὺ καὶ θυγάτηρ
∪ :–∪ | – > | ∪∪∪ | – > | ∪∪∪ | – > | ∪∪∪ | – > | ⌞ | –∪∪ | –∪∪ | –Λ |

---

[21] For the scansion | –∪ – – |, not | ⌞ ∪ | – – | or – > | – – | see below, p. 208.
[22] So Schmidt, Puech, Schroeder, and Bowra; Christ does not divide at all.

In all the other nine strophes a word ends where ὀφείλων ends here.
Therefore, by Rule 3:

> ἐμᾶς γέγραπται· γλυκὺ γὰρ αὐτῷ μέλος ὀφείλων
> ἐπιλέλαθ'· ὦ Μοῖσ', ἀλλὰ σὺ καὶ θυγάτηρ

But this ode is very difficult: while Schmidt and Bowra divide as
above, Christ, Puech, and Schroeder have other arrangements.

Nem. I 7:

> ἅρμα δ' ὀτρύνει Χρομίου Νεμέα τ' ἔργμασιν νικαφόροις ἐγκώμιον ζεῦξαι μέλος.

$$-\cup--\ |-\cup\cup\ |-\cup\cup\ |\ \sqcup\ |-\cup--\ |-\cup--\ |-\cup--\ |-\cup-\overline{\Lambda}\ |$$

By Rule 2 we shall make a division after ⊔ : that is, after Νεμέα τ'.
So Christ, Schroeder, and Bowra divide. But Schmidt and Puech,
agreeing with respect to Νεμέα τ', make a further division after the
first syllable of ἐγκώμιον, probably because they find the proposed
second colon too long:

> ἅρμα δ' ὀτρύνει Χρομίου Νεμέα τ'
> ἔργμασιν νικαφόροις ἐγ-
> κώμιον ζεῦξαι μέλος.

Nem. III 83:

> τίν γε μέν, εὐθρόνου Κλεοῦς ἐθελοίσας, ἀεθλοφόρου λήματος ἕνεκεν

$$-\cup\cup\ |-\cup\ |-\cup\ |-\cup\cup\ |\ L\ |-\cup\ |-\cup\cup\ |\ L\ |-\cup\ |\cup\cup\cup\ |-\Lambda\ |$$

Rule 2 points to division at either the first or the second L ; but
Rules 1 and 4 suggest that to cut after ἀεθλοφόρου would make the
cola disagreeably unequal. We decide therefore on:

> τίν γε μέν, εὐθρόνου Κλεοῦς ἐθελοί-
> σας, ἀεθλοφόρου λήματος ἕνεκεν

This is printed by Christ,[23] Schroeder, Puech, and Bowra; Schmidt
divides at both places, producing three cola.

Ol. XIII 6:

> ἐν τᾷ γὰρ Εὐνομία ναίει κασίγνηταί τε, βάθρον πολίων ἀσφαλές.

$$-\ :\ -\cup\ |-\cup\cup\ |\ L\ |\ L\ |-\cup\ |\ L\ |\ L\ |-\cup\cup\ |-\cup\cup\ |\ L\ |-\cup\ |-\Lambda\ |$$

The frequency of τονή is somewhat embarrassing:[24] we shall do best

---

[23] He prints a short dash after ἀεθλοφόρου, which is his method of indicating
τονή—a great help in reading aloud.

[24] We can of course twice write – > in place of L L, which will lead us to the
colon-division of Christ and Puech. A slight objection to doing so is that we thus
make two cola of five, instead of six, feet; and the latter number is more usual.

by a division after the third, thus giving an equal number of feet to both cola (Rule 4):

> ἐν τᾷ γὰρ Εὐνομία ναίει κασί-
> γνηταί τε, βάθρον πολίων ἀσφαλές.

This arrangement is used by Schmidt, Schroeder, and Bowra; Christ and Puech divide after the next ∟, κασίγνη-.

It will have been noticed that not all editors follow the divisions which we have offered for our specimen long verses. One more instance will demonstrate the situation still more clearly. *Nem.* VII 2 is thus variously arranged:

> i) παῖ μεγαλοσθενέος, ἄκουσον,
>   Ἥρας, γενέτειρα τέκνων· ἄνευ σέθεν   (Schmidt).
> ii) παῖ μεγαλοσθενέος, ἄκουσον, Ἥ-
>   ρας, γενέτειρα τέκνων· ἄνευ σέθεν (Christ and Schroeder).
> iii) παῖ μεγαλοσθενέος, ἄκου-
>   σον, Ἥρας, γενέτειρα τε-
>   κνων· ἄνευ σέθεν   (Puech).
> iv) παῖ μεγαλοσθενέος, ἄκουσον, Ἥρας, γε-
>   νέτειρα τέκνων· ἄνευ σέθεν   (Bowra).

This comparison might suggest the comment that Pindaric scansion is merely a muddle: such a welter as the foregoing has no value, hardly any meaning, for others than addicts of metric and rhythmic, not of poetry. But we can at least do here what it is a student's business to do everywhere: namely, limit the area of confusion. Such extreme divergences are almost confined to the logaoedic[25] odes, which engross about one-half of the whole; and even there they are not frequent. "Logaoedic" means "compounded of prose and verse": it is applied to lyrics consisting of cyclic dactyls and trochees, and points to the unwelcome truth that such writing at times does not sound clearly like verse. Some of it has no definite lilt or swing—no genuinely appreciable rhythm, at least to modern ears: that is precisely why the cola, when not indicated by pauses, are (as we have seen) difficult to determine. But there are other types of ode.

A very small number are written in the cretic (or paeonic) metre —*Ol.* II, *Ol.* X (in part), and *Pyth.*V (in part). Here again metricians

---

[25] The reader need not be startled by this name, long regarded as a sign of ridiculously obsolete views. Connoisseurs of labels will be interested to note that the word is becoming respectable again: it is used by at least two recent authorities, Puech (1922) and Koster (1936). These intrepid scholars even talk of dactyloepitrites (see below), renamed by Schroeder (*Nomenclator*, pp. 15 ff.) "Chalcidian."

differ, but the fact that we have to deal with a longer foot makes arrangement easier. In *Ol.* II 26,

κεραυνοῦ ταννέθειρα Σεμέλα, φιλεῖ δέ νιν Παλλὰς αἰεί,

we plainly hear the cretics -οῦ ταννέ-, -θειρα Σεμέ-, λα φιλεῖ, and end the colon after φιλεῖ, leaving two bacchii as the next colon to complete the verse.

But the third class has vastly more importance than the paeonic: the dactylo-epitrite,[26] to which half the odes belong, including nearly all the finest, for instance *Ol.* VI, VII, *Pyth.* I, IV, IX, *Nem.* X. Pindar being a most difficult poet, and his scansion being highly complex, it is marvellously good fortune that the greater part of his noblest work should be the easiest to follow in language and the easiest to appreciate in its metre and rhythm. If we look into our five authorities at *Pyth.* IV 2, we remark that no less than four agree in this division:

στᾶμεν, εὐίππου βασιλῆϊ Κυράνας,
ὄφρα κωμάζοντι σὺν Ἀρκεσίλᾳ

This glorious rhythm delights us even when we come upon it fresh from the Homeric hexameter. It presents, indeed, a blend of the "heroic" rhythm and the perennially beloved trochaic, a union of majesty and flexible charm that suits to perfection Pindar's aims and style. The verses are compounded normally of dactyls, spondees, and epitrites. This last name is given to the sequence – ◡ – –, sometimes so marked, sometimes as | ∟ ◡ | – – | with Gildersleeve, sometimes as | – > | – – | with Schmidt.[27] ἐπίτριτος means "showing the ratio of 4 : 3"; and, if we regard this sequence as a genuine trochee *plus* a genuine spondee, those two feet (counted in *morae* or shorts) have the values of 3, 4.

A dactylo-epitrite verse may be simple or may show anacrusis, τονή, and catalexis. An entirely epitrite verse, without dactyls, may occur among dactylo-epitrite verses. Resolution is rare.

Pyth. I 1:

χρυσέα φόρμιγξ, Ἀπόλλωνος καὶ ἰοπλοκάμων
– ◡ – – | – ◡ – – | – ◡◡ | – ◡◡ | – Ᾱ ||

---

[26] See last note.

[27] Both Gildersleeve and Schmidt mark as they do in order to gain equality between the two feet of which they regard the epitrite as consisting. I have preferred to take the whole as a quasi-foot, so that the second part of it may not be confused with the spondee which is a pendant to a dactylic sequence in this rhythm. Accordingly, I dispense with both > and ∟, since, if – ◡ – – is regarded as a unit, there is no need to equate the first and the second parts of it.

Nem. I 6:

αἶνον ἀελλοπόδων μέγαν ἵππων, Ζηνὸς Αἰτναίου χάριν
$-\cup\cup\,|-\cup\cup\,|-\cup\cup\,|--\,||-\cup--\,|-\cup-\overline{\Lambda}\,||$

Isth. I 1:

μᾶτερ ἐμά, τὸ τεόν, χρύσασπι Θήβα
$-\cup\cup\,|-\cup\cup\,|--\,|-\cup--\,||$

Nem. V 24 b:

χρυσέῳ πλάκτρῳ διώκων
$-\cup--\,|-\cup--\,||$

Pyth. IX 8:

ῥίζαν ἀπείρου τρίταν εὐήρατον θάλλοισαν οἰκεῖν
$-\cup--\,|-\cup--\,|-\cup--\,|-\cup--\,||$

Ol. XII 16:

εἰ μὴ στάσις ἀντιάνειρα Κνωσίας σ' ἄμερσε πάτρας
$-:-\cup\cup\,|-\cup\cup\,|--\,|-\cup--\,|-\cup--\,||$

Nem. XI 16:

καὶ τελευτὰν ἀπάντων γᾶν ἐπιεσσόμενος
$-\cup\,\llcorner\lrcorner\,|-\cup--\,|-\cup\cup\,|-\cup\cup\,|-\overline{\Lambda}\,||$

Nem. I 69:

ἔνεπεν· αὐτὸν μὰν ἐν εἰρήνᾳ τὸν ἄπαντα χρόνον
$\cup\cup\cup--\,|-\cup--\,|-\cup\cup\,|-\cup\cup\,|-\overline{\Lambda}\,||$

Pyth. IV 16:

Διὸς ἐν Ἄμμωνος θεμέθλοις
$\cup\cup\cup--\,|-\cup--\,||$

Nem. V 6 a:

οὔπω γένυσι φαίνων τερείνυς
$-:-\cup\cup\cup-\,|-\cup--\,||$

Ol. XI 4:

εἰ δὲ σὺν πόνῳ τις εὖ πράσσοι, μελιγάρυες ὕμνοι
$-\cup-\cup\,|-\cup--\,|-\cup\cup\,|-\cup\cup\,|--\,||$

The anapaest is rare.[28]

Finally, the relation between these various rhythms and the topics which Pindar handles—more accurately, his personal feeling about them—is a fascinating study[29] that lies outside a business-like summary. It must suffice to note a few striking effects. Logaoe-

[28] See *Ol.* VII 17 (p. 202, above).
[29] Professor Thomson's *Greek Lyric Metre* contains much that is delightful, ingenious, and stimulating on this subject.

dics vibrate with a wayward charm as the festoons of tangled
rhythm fall upon the ear—

> ἦ θαυματὰ πολλά, καί πού τι καὶ βροτῶν
> φάτιν ὑπὲρ τὸν ἀλαθῆ λόγον
> δεδαιδαλμένοι ψεύδεσι ποικίλοις ἐξαπατῶντι μῦθοι.[30]

The Dorian majesty of dactylo-epitrites has been exemplified in
single lines: its full grandeur is to be felt and heard by reading aloud
a whole triad of the Fourth Pythian. But Pindar has known how to
infuse tenderness into this austere rhythm. The Eleventh Olympian
is written for a boy-victor, and there is no mistaking the art which
has touched it with gentle grace by the final dactyls and by a
double trochee here and there instead of an epitrite.[31]

> τέλλεται καὶ πιστὸν ὅρκιον μεγάλαις ἀρεταῖς.

His theme in the Ninth Pythian is love, and his subtlety here calls
for and exquisitely repays our closest scrutiny. V 25,

> ὕπνον ἀναλίσκοισα ῥέποντα πρὸς ἀῶ,

has a tremulous beauty which sets it apart from the companion
verses, such as εἰ δὲ χρὴ καὶ πὰρ σοφὸν ἀντιφερίξαι and has caused it
to be savaged by muscular critics. The rhythm hesitates and checks,
then sweeps into assured dactyls, like the breathing of this girl who
stirs in sleep and then springs to vivid action. The opening epitrite
contains irrationally an extra short syllable—that is all, but a masterpiece of minute skill. Again, in the third lines of strophe and
antistrophe Pindar has written what looks impossible: for instance
the tender and tranquil little picture of Aphrodite (v. 11),

> ὀχέων ἐφαπτομένα χερὶ κούφᾳ.

It is best to regard the first foot as an unexpected but welcome third
paeon—welcome, because it suffuses the else severe rhythm with
feminine grace. And after this winsomeness of variety, the strophes
close with the unbroken roll of

> ῥίζαν ἀπείρου τρίταν εὐήρατον θάλλοισαν οἰκεῖν.

For Cyrana was not only a lovely bride, but a huntress of lions and
worshipped by a great nation.

---

[30] *Ol.* I 28 ff.
[31] E.g., in v. 6 the second syllable of ὅρκιον is short.

NOTES

N. B.: For full titles of works quoted, see under authors' names in the Bibliography. If no title is quoted, reference is to the first (or only) work given in the Bibliography under the author's name.

References to, and quotations from, Pindar normally point to Dr. C. M. Bowra's Oxford Text; fragments are given first with Bowra's number, next with Schroeder's.

NOTES TO LECTURE I

(pp. 1–21)

[1] *Convivio* I vii 84 ff. "Anche lo Latino l'avrebbe sposte a gente d'altra lingua, siccome a Tedeschi e Inglesi e altri: e qui avrebbe passato il loro comandamento. Chè contro al loro volere, largo parlando dico sarebbe sposta la loro sentenza colà dove elle non la potessono colla loro bellezza portare. E però sappia ciascuno, che nulla cosa per legame musaico armonizzata si può della sua loquela in altra trasmutare, senza rompere tutta sua dolcezza e armonia."

[2] Eckermann, Jan. 10, 1825. "Und dann ist wohl nicht zu leugnen, dass man im allgemeinen mit einer guten Uebersetzung sehr weit kommt. Friedrich der Grosse konnte kein Latein, aber er las seinen Cicero in der französischen Uebersetzung ebensogut als wir andern in der Ursprache."

[3] *Hypatia*, chap. viii.

[4] Coleridge, however, quotes (chap. xviii) the first few lines of *Ol.* II which Cowley "composed for the charitable purpose of *rationalizing* the Theban Eagle," and a version of his own, "as nearly as possible word for word." Those who heard these renderings agreed that Cowley's was mad, but that Coleridge approached "the style of our Bible in the prophetic books." To me, both seem perfectly lucid, if stilted; and Cowley's the better.

[5] The most extreme instance of this mania is a bulky work on Walter Pater, which gives only thirteen pages to his style, but records that his cat died in 1904, at the age of fifteen, and that his Pomeranian had passed away long before, in 1896, only eighteen months after αὐτότατος.

[6] Lucian, *Adv. Indoct.* 15. Τὸ Αἰσχύλου πυξίον, εἰς ὃ ἐκεῖνος ἔγραφε, σὺν πολλῇ σπουδῇ κτησάμενος καὶ αὐτὸς ᾤετο ἔνθεος ἔσεσθαι καὶ κάτοχος ἐκ τοῦ πυξίου, ἀλλ' ὅμως ἐν αὐτῷ ἐκείνῳ μακρῷ γελοιότερα ἔγραφεν.

[7] In the Fourth Pythian, many have supposed that Pelias and Jason *definitely* represent Arcesilas and Damophilus. The objection to this view is not that it violates history or common sense, or does injustice to Pindar's own wishes about Damophilus: the objection is *aesthetic*, for the narrative contains nothing for the appreciation of which those identifications are needed.

[8] Wilamowitz (p. 441) regards a dream as the only possible explanation. Coppola (p. 209) actually reports that Pindar *says* it was a dream; so does Perrotta (pp. 111, 143, 212); Cerrato even puts "in sogno" into his translation. Friederichs (p. 54) and Fraccaroli (p. 459) suppose, still more feebly, that the notion of Alcmaeon "came into the poet's mind" as a theme of song.

[9] P. 132 (note 256).

[10] P. 168.

[11] *Ol.* II 79 ff.: 'Αχιλλέα τ' ἔνεικ', ἐπεὶ Ζηνὸς ἦτορ
λιταῖς ἔπεισε, μάτηρ.

[12] P. 136.

[13] P. 196; so p. 223: "sotto il cielo stellato."

[14] *Wanderers Sturmlied, sub fin.*

[15] His edition of Pindar, published in 1616, emends the text in more than six hundred places.

[16] P. 362 (ed. of 1934).

17 The first example that comes to hand happens to be provided by Drachmann, the distinguished editor of the Pindaric scholia. Reviewing Schadewaldt's *Aufbau*, he writes (*coll.* 1098 f.): "In dem 7. nemeischen Gedicht hat Sch. das Stück über Odysseus und Aias (v. 20 bis 30) dahin zu erklären versucht, dass Pindar zwischen der Verkennung des Aias durch die Achäer und seiner eigenen Verkennung durch die Ägineten eine Parallele zieht . . . Vor allem muss man fragen, wie in aller Welt die Ägineten . . . diese Parallele hätten ziehen können. Es wird hier, wie so oft in den früheren Pindarerklärung, gegen den Grundsatz gesündigt, dass man nicht ohne zwingenden Grund einer Aussage einen Sinn beilegen soll, den ihr Empfänger nicht verstehen konnte." "Grundsatz"—there is the disastrous error, that in literature, as in science, a thing is completely true or completely untrue. Why should not Pindar have *more or less* definitely intended what Schadewaldt says, and been *more or less* indifferent whether the Aeginetans took the point or not?

18 Προοίμιον (Drachmann III, p. 287): προκοιλιοῦσθαι τὸ σῶμα τοῦ μέλους τῇ παρεκβάσει δίκην προγάστορος.

19 Cp. Lecture V, note 1.

20 Προοίμιον (Drachmann III, p. 289): τὸ λαβυρινθῶδες τῆς ἐν αὐτῷ φράσεως καὶ τοῖς πολλοῖς ἀδιόδευτον ἀπευθύνουσι καὶ τὰς ἕλικας περιοδεύοντες ἕως καὶ ἐνδοτάτου εἶτ' αὖθις ἀνελίττουσι καὶ οἴκοι κατ' ἔμφρονα νοῦν ἀποκαθίστανται.

21 For example, L. V. Schmidt (p. 444) places *Nem.* VIII among "the most valuable" odes because it affords a glimpse into Pindar's *Lebensgang*.

22 I may spare myself the ungrateful task of producing examples here: it suffices to quote Wilamowitz' own words in the first paragraph of his Conclusion (p. 463): "Seine Welt ist uns ganz fremd; ihre Sitten, ihr Dichten und Trachten für uns reizlos, wo nicht anstossig. Er selbst ist kein reicher Geist . . . All das Grosse, an dem unsere Seele hängt, ist ionisch-attisch; aber von diesem Wesen mag er nichts wissen; nicht nur Odysseus, Homer selbst ist ihm antipathisch. Fremdartig ist uns selbst seine Kunst nicht minder in dem, was ihm eigen ist wie in dem gegebenen Stile." He proceeds, it is true, to express his love for Pindar; nevertheless, the words just cited show how he was handicapped by biographical and pseudo-scientific methods. That Pindar looked askance at Homer, as that Byron despised Wordsworth, matters, in the realm of poetry, nothing whatever.

Now and again I shall be forced to insist, not only that Wilamowitz' attitude has spoiled his perspective, but also that what must be termed his intellectual arrogance has led him into deplorably magisterial verdicts on passages that need for their understanding more patience, caution, and sympathy than he cared to bestow. It is all the more incumbent on me to avow my admiration and reverence for the greatest Greek scholar that the world has seen.

23 Fr. 183 (193).

24 *Pyth.* V 75 f. Jebb (*Encyc. Brit.*) remarks that the Aegeidae, tracing their descent from Aegeus, belonged to the Cadmean element in Thebes and so to the older nobility: that is, "the circle of families for whom the heroic myths were domestic records." Pindar "had a personal link with the memories which everywhere were most cherished by Dorians, no less than with those which appealed to 'Cadmean' . . . stock."

25 Προοίμιον (Drachmann III, p. 296): . . . . τῷ Πινδάρῳ . . . γενομένῳ ἐπὶ ἄρχοντος Ἀβίωνος κατὰ τοὺς χρόνους Αἰσχύλου, ᾧ καὶ συγγεγένηται, ὁμιλήσας καὶ ἀπονάμενός τι καὶ τῆς ἐκείνου μεγαλοφωνίας.

[26] Farnell, who develops it with vigour (I, pp. 359 f.), seems to go astray here.

[27] Fr. 9 in Bowra. Schroeder (fr. 29) prints it as the first stanza of the hymn to Zeus written for the Thebans, whereon Wilamowitz (pp. 189 ff.) makes attractive but ill-founded comments. Bowra seems to me fully justified in keeping his frr. 9 and 10 separate. Fr. 10, Schroeder's 30, quoted in Lecture II (pp. 22 f.), is the opening of what must have been a magnificent poem: I cannot believe, and see no genuine evidence to suggest, that such a hymn opened with the prentice-work that I have quoted.

[28] Plutarch, De Gloria Ath. 347 f. Ἡ δὲ Κόριννα τὸν Πίνδαρον . . . ἐνουθέτησεν ὡς ἄμουσον ὄντα μὴ ποιοῦντα μύθους, ὃ τῆς ποιητικῆς ἔργον εἶναι συμβέβηκε, γλώσσας δὲ καὶ καταχρήσεις καὶ μεταφράσεις καὶ μέλη καὶ ῥυθμοὺς ἡδύσματα ὑποτίθεται· σφόδρα οὖν ὁ Πίνδαρος ἐπιστήσας τοῖς λεγομένοις ἐποίησεν ἐκεῖνο τὸ μέλος Ἰσμήνιον . . . [fr. 9 = 29] δειξαμένου δὲ τῇ Κορίννῃ, γελάσασα ἐκείνη τῇ χειρὶ δεῖν ἔφη σπείρειν ἀλλὰ μὴ ὅλῳ τῷ θυλάκῳ· τῷ γὰρ ὄντι συγκεράσας καὶ συμφορήσας πανσπερμίαν τινὰ μύθων ὁ Πίνδαρος εἰς τὸ μέλος ἐξέχεεν.

[29] The scholiast on Aristoph. Ach. 720 reports that Pindar in the first book of his partheneia used ἀγοράζειν with the meaning ἐν ἀγορᾷ διατρίβειν.

[30] Fr. 15 (Diehl): μέμφομη δὲ κὴ λιγουράν
        Μουρτίδ' ἰώνγα,
        ὅτι βανὰ φοῦ-
        σ' ἔβα Πινδάροι πὸτ ἔριν.

[31] Aelian XIII 25. Πίνδαρος ὁ ποιητὴς ἀγωνιζόμενος ἐν Θήβαις ἀμαθέσι περιπεσὼν ἀκροαταῖς ἡττήθη Κορίννης πεντάκις. ἐλέγχων δὲ τὴν ἀμουσίαν αὐτῶν ὁ Πίνδαρος σῦν ἐκάλει τὴν Κόρινναν.

[32] Farnell, I, p. 363.

[33] Herod. IX 69.

[34] By Coppola, p. 155, and Gaspar, p. 151.

[35] Herod. IX 1.

[36] P. xii. Fraccaroli (p. 11) offers a striking parallel. "I re di Persia, non altrimenti che gli imperatori medievali, favorivano i principi, e i principi vedevano in loro la propria salvaguardia: i Ghibellini non erano un partito meno Italiano dei Guelfi, tranne durante il periodo della prima Lega Lombarda, nè i Medizzanti erano meno Greci dei loro avversari, tranne il tempo dell' invasione. L'una volta e l'altra vinse la parte migliore, e la vittoria fu una fortuna per la patria e per l'umanità; ma fu piuttosto una forza inconsciente e prepotente che trasse il popolo alla lotta, che non un consiglio savio e calcolato sulle probabilità di uscirne con qualche vantaggio."

[37] IV 31, 5. οὐδὲ γὰρ Θηβαίους ἐπαινοῦμεν κατὰ τὰ Μηδικά, διότι τῶν ὑπὲρ τῆς Ἑλλάδος ἀποστάντες κινδύνων τὰ Περσῶν εἵλοντο διὰ τὸν φόβον, οὐδὲ Πίνδαρον τὸν ἀποφηνάμενον αὐτοῖς ἄγειν τὴν ἡσυχίαν διὰ τῶνδε τῶν ποιημάτων [fr. 99 (109)]:
        τὸ κοινόν τις ἀστῶν ἐν εὐδίᾳ
        τιθεὶς ἐρευνασάτω
        μεγαλάνορος Ἡσυχίας τὸ φαιδρὸν φάος,
        στάσιν ἀπὸ πραπίδος ἐπίκοτον ἀνελών,
        πενίας δότειραν, ἐχθρὰν δὲ κουροτρόφον.

[38] Fr. 65 (77): ὅθι παῖδες Ἀθαναίων ἐβάλοντο φαεννὰν
        κρηπῖδ' ἐλευθερίας.

[39] Isth. V 48 ff. For Isth. V as a whole see Appendix B.

⁴⁰ XVI, Ἠΐθεοι ἢ Θησεύς,is a paean written to be sung by a chorus of Ceans at Delos (cp. Jebb, *Bacchylides*, p. 223). And what in Greek is so Tennysonian as the Eagle of V 16 ff.?

⁴¹ The frenzy to find parallels, imitations, etc., is astonishingly exemplified by the otherwise well-poised Schmid, who suggests (p. 549, note 11) that if Napoleon had not protected Haydn's house in Vienna, we might have thought Alexander's action a legend based on the sparing of Antenor's house when Troy was taken by the host of Agamemnon (Strabo 608).

⁴² Pausan. IX xxiii 4.

⁴³ Fr. 106 (120, 121).

⁴⁴ *Ol.* VI 93 ff.—"perhaps by Hieron's own order" (E. A. Freeman, II, p. 539). For *Ol.* VII, cp. Lecture VII, pp. 138 ff.

⁴⁵ See the *Inscriptio* (Drachmann I, p. 195): ταύτην τὴν ᾠδὴν ἀνακεῖσθαί φησι Γόργων ἐν τῷ τῆς Λινδίας Ἀθηναίας ἱερῷ χρυσοῖς γράμμασιν.

⁴⁶ Pausan. IX xvi 1.

⁴⁷ But in one poem he at least extolled Sparta. Plutarch, *Lycurgus* 21, reports: Πίνδαρος δέ φησιν [fr. 189 (199)].

ἔνθα βουλαὶ μὲν γερόντων
καὶ νέων ἀνδρῶν ἀριστεύοισιν αἰχμαί,
καὶ χοροὶ καὶ Μοῖσα καὶ Ἀγλαΐα.

⁴⁸ The extant Ode III. Dornseiff (*Pindar*, p. 134) explains εὐθύγλωσσος in *Pyth.* II 86 thus: "Ich, Pindar, würde bei jeder Staatsform frei reden, also tue ich es auch unter deiner Tyrannis." Despite the sumptuousness of *Pyth.* IV (not to mention V), when Arcesilas two years later gained an Olympian victory, the commission for the ode celebrating it was not—so far as appears—given to Pindar.

⁴⁹ It should be mentioned that the phrase μετὰ τριῶν κτέ. (v. 60), and some other details, would not have troubled recent commentators had they been aware that the whole matter of Tantalus' punishment was settled by Comparetti in 1873. Jurenka (on v. 58) refers to the article, but makes practically no use of it: Fraccaroli (pp. 176 f.) alone saw its importance. Wilamowitz (p. 236) gives the phrase up as inexplicable. Farnell, *ad loc.*, uses his favourite explanation, that Pindar "is in a hurry."

I offer a summary of the article. The fourth πόνος is immortality [this had already been noted by Rauchenstein (*Comment. Pind.* II 11)], πόνον being in apposition with βίον; the other three are thirst and hunger (indicated by νέκταρ ἀμβροσίαν τε) and of course the stone. Sisyphus and the others have nothing to do here, for *Tantalus is not in Hades*: we have been misled by the Homeric account in *Od.* XI 583 ff., where the stone is not mentioned. Homer's version is unique. The story followed by Pindar is that which Athenaeus reports (281 b) from ὁ τὴν τῶν Ἀτρειδῶν ποιήσας κάθοδον:Tantalus, being granted fulfilment of a wish, asked "to live in the same way as the gods," and Zeus in anger at his greed allowed him to come to their table but hung a rock over his head so that he could not enjoy the victuals. It is to this form of punishment that εὐφροσύνας ἀλᾶται refers: εὐφροσύνα means "enjoyment" and suits the heavenly banquet, but could not describe life in Hades, even without the stone. Thus Tantalus' μέγας ὄλβος itself becomes a punishment. (Plato, to be sure, in *Crat.* 395 D, mentions both the stone and Hades, but that does not affect the interpretation of our passage: probably he read it as all moderns did before Comparetti, with memory of Homer.)

⁵⁰ Mahaffy (p. 223) asserts that Pindar "often preaches the suspicion, the jealousy, and the selfishness which we find in Theognis." The first two faults are certainly not preached by him; moreover the Pindaric temper and manner differ completely from the Theognidean.

⁵¹ Cp. V. 99: ἑξηκοντάκι δῆμφοτέρωθεν. The scholiasts say (no doubt rightly) τριακοντάκις ἐν ἑκάστῳ ἀγῶνι: but Pindar, determined to give full value, makes it sound like sixty at each. One can well believe that this egregious family used similar ambiguity in conversation.

⁵² Vv. 44 ff. The sea-pebble sentence explains the much debated δηρίομαι κτὲ. The sense is: "I am at odds with many (admirers of your family) about the number of your victories. They each give a *definite* (however great) figure: my view is that these successes transcend arithmetic altogether."

⁵³ Pindar often surprises us by the readiness and explicitness with which he voices his personal thoughts, but nowhere has he equalled this. What follows is also crisp. Then we find a sentence which, at first hearing, sounds like normal Pindaric piety; if looked at with attention, it proves either meaningless or so casual as to approach blasphemy (vv. 105 f.):

> εἰ δὲ δαίμων γενέθλιος ἕρποι,
> Δὶ τοῦτ' Ἐνυαλίῳ τ' ἐκδώσομεν
> πράσσειν.

Why state conditions? Willy-nilly, men must leave the future to Zeus. And what has Enyalius to do here? Mezger (pp. 460 f.), referring to Ares' title ἵππιος and the Pegasus-story which has preceded, thought that Xenophon aimed at the prize for horse-racing. Christ (*ad loc.*) and Wilamowitz (p. 369) suggest that he proposed to compete in the hoplite race at Olympia.

⁵⁴ The poem is so classified in Bowra's text (fr. 107) and Schroeder's (fr. 122), but the category is not certain; Christ (*ad loc.*) and Fraccaroli (p. 315) call it a *scolion*. The lines quoted are vv. 13 ff. Some have thought that the Ἰσθμοῦ δεσπόται are deities, but λέγοντι surely disproves this. Athenaeus (XIII 574 B) paraphrases: ἠγωνία ποῖόν τι φανήσεται τοῖς Κορινθίοις τὸ πρᾶγμα.

⁵⁵ The word is ἑκατόγγυιον, which Wilamowitz (p. 375) takes as meaning fifty girls: ". . . die Summe der φορβάδες κόραι angegeben wird, spasshaft durch ihre hundert Beine." But is not the precise intention of the adjective "a hundred sets of limbs"? (So Jebb on *Oed. Col.* 718 f.).

⁵⁶ Coppola (p. 159) takes the passage in easier mood. "Il lettore aveva cominciato a leggere l'ode con un sorriso; a questo punto, il sorriso si accentua; Pindaro si scopre, fa egli stesso l'obiezione che ogni lettore poteva fare, e rende così la situazione ancora più leggera e arrischiata."

⁵⁷ *Pyth.* XI 41 f.; *Isth.* II 6 ff.

⁵⁸ The scholiasts report that elsewhere Pindar assigned the invention of this to Naxos, and elsewhere again to Thebes: an example of the facility wherewith he adjusted himself to suit his patrons.

⁵⁹ Fraccaroli (p. 318), feeling this, has made a great deal more out of the αἰετός than would occur to most people.

⁶⁰ Trireme, Wilamowitz, p. 372; vases, Boeckh II 2, p. 214; commerce, Dissen, ed. min. *ad loc.*

⁶¹ It must be owned that the MSS. give ψυχρᾶς, but Schroeder's ψυχρῶν appears certain: αἰθέρος would hardly have two adjectives, κόλπων none.

NOTES TO LECTURE II

(pp. 22-43)

1 See Boeckh's introduction to his scholia-volume; Wilamowitz' *Textgeschichte*; Sandys (*Hist.* I) under "Pindar," "Zenodotus," "Aristophanes," "Aristarchus," and "Didymus"; Schmid (pp. 621 ff.), who quotes (p. 621) the view of Feine and Horn that Aristophanes was eclipsed by Aristarchus. Aristophanes (*ca.* 257–*ca.* 180 B.C.) was the third head of the Alexandrian Library, Aristarchus (220–145 B.C.) the fourth.

2 Didymus (65 B.C.–10 A.D.), the celebrated χαλκέντερος who wrote nearly four thousand books, produced an edition based on, but often sharply criticizing, his predecessors. The invaluable "scholia vetera" (admirably edited by Drachmann) are founded on Didymus. The "scholia recentia" were written by Triclinius in the fourteenth century. All my references are to the "vetera."

Metrical scholia are regularly supplied, but they have little or no value. The *inscriptiones*, or brief headings which give dates, etc., are very useful. A good example of the manner in which scholiasts quote Pindaric scholars, and of what those scholars discussed, is provided by the various scholia on *Ol.* I 23 (35). ἱππιοχάρμαν· τὸν τῇ ἱππικῇ χαίροντα. καλῶς τὸ ἐπίθετον τῷ βασιλεῖ διὰ τὸ ἱπποτροφεῖν, ἵνα δείξῃ ὅτι οὐ τύχης γέγονεν ἔργον τὸ τῷ Φερενίκῳ χρήσασθαι, ἀλλ' ἐπιστήμης καὶ τῆς περὶ τὸ πρᾶγμα ἐπιμελείας. ἔνιοι δὲ ἀναγινώσκουσι παροξύνοντες τὴν παραλήγουσαν συλλαβὴν τοῦ Συρακουσίων καὶ τὴν ἐσχάτην τοῦ ἱππιοχαρμᾶν περισπῶσιν, ἵν' ᾖ Συρακοσίων ἱππιοχαρμῶν. τὸν γὰρ Ἱέρωνα οὐκ εἶναι Συρακούσιον ὅτε ἐνίκα. κτίσαντα γὰρ αὐτὸν τὴν Κατάνην καὶ προσαγορεύσαντα Αἴτνην ἀπ' αὐτῆς Αἰτναῖον αὐτὸν λέγουσιν. εὐήθεις δέ φησι Δίδυμος τούτους· τότε γὰρ ὁ Ἱέρων ἦν Συρακούσιος καὶ οὐδὲ ἦν Αἰτναῖος, ὥς φησιν Ἀπολλόδωρος. ὁ δὲ Ἀριστόνικος ἀξιοπίστως Αἰτναῖον ὄντα Συρακούσιον ὀνομάζεσθαι. γράφεται καὶ ἱππιοχαρμὴν Συρακουσίων καὶ συντάσσεται οὕτως. ἐτυμολογεῖται δὲ ἢ ἀπὸ τοῦ ἵππου καὶ τοῦ χαίρω ἢ ἀπὸ τοῦ χάρμη ἢ μάχη.

3 Delos: fr. 78 (87), Strabo X 485; justice: fr. 70 (81), Aristides ii 70; next world: fr. 114 (129), Plutarch, *Consol. ad Apoll.* 35, p. 120 and *De Lat. Viv.* 7, p. 1130.

4 Some twenty types of lyric poetry were distinguished by Alexandrian scholars: see Smyth, pp. xxiv ff.

5 I take χρύσεαι ἀέρος κόμαι almost literally, as in the (apparently) quite similar passage, *Iliad* XIV 350 f. But Dornseiff (p. 20), quoting Ovid, *Met.* VI 113, takes the phrase as meaning Zeus' approach in fire. Schmid (p. 608, note 2) thinks that it means lightning.

6 From the astonishing *Persae* (Diehl II, pp. 136 ff.) one brief extract (6 d, vv. 102 ff.) may suffice: στόματος

δ' ἐξήλλοντο μαρμαροφεγ-

γεῖς παῖδες συγκρουόμενοι.

7 *De Vet. Orat.* 1073 f.: παραδείγματα δὲ αὐτῆς [sc. τῆς ἀρχαίας καὶ αὐστηρᾶς ἁρμονίας] ποιητῶν μὲν καὶ μελοποιῶν ἥ τ' Αἰσχύλου λέξις ὀλίγου δεῖν πᾶσα καὶ ἡ Πινδάρου, χωρὶς ὅτι μὴ τὰ Παρθένεια καὶ εἴ τινα τούτοις ὁμοίας ἀπαιτεῖ παρασκευάς· διαφαίνεται δέ τις ὁμοία κἂν τούτοις εὐγένεια καὶ σεμνότης ἁρμονίας τὸν ἀρχαῖον φυλάττουσα πῖνον.

The κεχωρισμένα παρθενείων (*Vit. Ambr.*, Drachmann I, p. 3, and schol. 139 a on *Pyth.* III 98) are supposed by Schmid (p. 575) to have been composed for Pindar's own cult of Pan and Rhea (*Pyth.* III 77 f.).

8 Προοίμιον (Drachmann III, p. 303): περιάγονται μάλιστα διὰ τὸ ἀνθρωπικώτεροι εἶναι καὶ ὀλιγόμυθοι καὶ μηδὲ πάνυ ἔχειν ἀσαφῶς κατά γε τὰ ἄλλα.

9 P. lxxxi. Not only the Greeks of the Alexandrian age, but the Greeks of later antiquity, had small interest in such local cults as evoked these poems. Further, Wilamowitz writes (p. 3): "Die erhaltenen vier Bücher waren die letzten der antiken Gesamtausgabe; ein Grammatiker des zweiten Jahrhunderts n. Chr. hat sie für den Schulunterricht ausgewählt und erklärt." (So also his *Einl. in d. griech. Tragödie*, p. 184).

10 In order to express Olympiad chronology in years b.c.: multiply the number of the Olympiad by 4; to the product add 0, 1, 2, 3 according as the year is the first, second, third, or fourth of the Olympiad: then subtract the number thus gained from 780. The remainder gives the year b.c. in which the Olympic year *began*, two b.c. dates being required to include the whole of the Olympic year.

11 See the *Chronicle* of Eusebius (Karst, pp. 90 ff.). It exists only in an Armenian version of the Greek; Karst gives a German translation of the Armenian. That Eusebius took the list over from Sextus Iulius Africanus was first asserted by Scaliger (Gelzer I, pp. 161 f.). The latest Olympiad in the list is the 249th, which occurred in Africanus' lifetime; Eusebius, who flourished a century later, remarks at the close: "Bis zu diesem haben wir das Olympiadenverzeichnis vorgefunden."

12 *Quaest. Conviv.* II 2 639 E: καὶ τὸ τοῖς νικαφόροις [*sc.* in the Games—see the context] εἰσελαύνουσι τῶν τειχῶν ἐφίεσθαι μέρος διελεῖν καὶ καταβαλεῖν, τοιαύτην ἔχει διάνοιαν, ὡς οὐ μέγα πόλει τειχῶν ὄφελος ἄνδρας ἐχούσῃ μάχεσθαι δυναμένους καὶ νικᾶν.

13 VI vii 4, 5. Δωριεῖ δὲ τῷ Διαγόρου παρὲξ ἢ Ὀλυμπίασιν Ἰσθμίων μὲν γεγόνασιν ὀκτὼ νῖκαι, Νεμείων δὲ ἀποδέουσαι μιᾶς ἐς τὰς ὀκτώ· λέγεται δὲ καὶ ὡς Πύθια ἀνέλοιτο ἀκονιτί . . . καὶ ἐναυμάχησεν ἐναντία Ἀθηναίων ναυσὶν οἰκείαις, ἐς ὃ ὑπὸ τριήρων ἁλοὺς Ἀττικῶν ἀνήχθη ζῶν παρὰ Ἀθηναίους. οἱ δὲ Ἀθηναῖοι πρὶν μὲν ἢ Δωριέα παρὰ σφᾶς ἀναχθῆναι θυμῷ τε ἐς αὐτὸν καὶ ἀπειλαῖς ἐχρῶντο· ὡς δὲ ἐς ἐκκλησίαν συνελθόντες ἄνδρα οὕτω μέγαν καὶ δόξης ἐς τοσοῦτο ἥκοντα ἐθεάσαντο ἐν σχήματι αἰχμαλώτου, μεταπίπτει σφίσιν ἐς αὐτὸν ἡ γνώμη καὶ ἀπελθεῖν ἀφιᾶσιν, οὐδὲ ἔργον οὐδὲν ἄχαρι ἐργάζονται.

14 *Tusc. Disp.* I 11 46. *Hanc sententiam significare videtur Laconis illa vox, qui, cum Rhodius Diagoras, Olympionices nobilis, uno die duo suos filios victores Olympiae vidisset, accessit ad senem et gratulatus: Morere, Diagora, inquit; non enim ad caelum adscensurus es.*

Under the 62nd Olympiad Eusebius relates (*ut sup.*, p. 94) that Milo of Croton won six Olympian, six Pythian, ten Nemean, and nine Isthmian victories; under the 157th Olympiad (p. 99), that Leonides of Samos won twelve Olympian victories in four Olympiads.

15 *Il.* XXIII 262–897; *El.* 680–756; *Idyll* XXII 80–134.

16 Jaeger's *Paideia* insists on this view: see especially pp. 271–291 (first edition), or Highet, pp. 204–221. The subject is discussed in Lecture III, pp. 46 f.

17 That is, the reverse of a model or pattern; cp. Lecture III, pp. 47, 66.

18 *An Hymne in Honour of Beautie*, v. 133: "For soule is forme, and doth the bodie make."

19 Forman, p. 68.

20 *Pyth.* IV 131; *Nem.* IX 51 f.; *Nem.* VII 53.

21 *Nem.* VIII 2 f.

22 *I wandered*, v. 1; *Aen.* XI 68; *Purg.* I 25.

23 The references for this and the next seven allusions are the following: *Ol.* VI 35 ff., *Ion* 881 ff. and 936 ff., *Nem.* IX 23, *Pyth.* XII 16, *Nem.* I 68, *Pyth.* VI 54, *Pyth.* IV 114.

24 *Nem.* X 35 f., perhaps the only bombastic passage in Pindar:

γαίᾳ δὲ καυθείσᾳ πυρὶ καρπὸς ἐλαίας
ἔμολεν Ἥρας τὸν εὐάνορα λαὸν ἐν ἀγγέων
ἔρκεσιν παμποικίλοις.

25 I can recollect no passage in classical Greek literature that reveals any appreciation of specific precious stones as beautiful in themselves. Engraved gems were of course well known and highly prized, but in virtue of the engraving: Polycrates' famous emerald was a σφρηγὶς τὴν ἐφόρεε χρυσόδετος, σμαράγδου μὲν λίθου ἐοῦσα, ἔργον ἦν δὲ Θεοδώρου τοῦ Τηλεκλέος Σαμίου (Herod. III 41). We find nothing of the allusiveness so frequent in English—"his eyes like carbuncles," "the natural ruby of your cheeks," "as pearls from diamonds dropp'd," etc. But though precious stones somehow failed to catch the imagination of poets, it is of course true that they were known, esteemed, carefully cut and mounted. Pliny's last book (*Nat. Hist.* XXXVII) is rich in detail. A useful summary is given by K. Sittl (pp. 192–195). But on one interesting point he strangely contradicts Pliny: "Der antike Geschmack unterschied sich von dem unsrigen; der Diamant tritt sehr zurück." Pliny grows lyrical for a moment on this (4, 55): *Maximum in rebus humanis, non solum inter gemmas, pretium habet adamas diu non nisi regibus et iis admodum paucis cognitus.*

26 An anonymous writer in the *Quarterly Review*, 1886, p. 177. He is said to have been R. Y. Tyrrell.

27 Wilamowitz (p. 458), after rightly praising the Danae-fragment of Simonides as "ein wunderbares Bild, an dem das Ethos eben so entzückt wie das Farbenspiel," unaccountably proceeds: "So etwas hat Pindar einmal auch, bei der Geburt des Iamos Ol. 6,38; es ist aber das einzige Mal, denn das Malerische reizt ihn nicht." It is true that Plutarch (*de Mus.* 20) implies that Pindar did not use χρῶμα, but he is talking of music and couples him with Simonides.

28 Villemain, p. 19.

29 V. 209: δίδυμαι ζωαί. The scholiasts remark that this detail comes from Pindar's "fantastic imagination," προστερατεύεταί τι, and call it διθυραμβικόν, "affected" or "in falsetto."

30 This assumption, that love entered human life at a specific moment as the gift or invention of a specific person, witnesses to exactly the same imaginative process as the *Oresteia* (and probably the *Supplices*-trilogy also). Such conceptions are perhaps the most impressive of all the proofs that Greeks possessed an instinct, as well as a talent, for drama.

31 The same device is used in the *Prometheus Vinctus*, but with much less vivacity as with more grandeur. Cp. my *Greek Tragedy*, p. 96.

32 Pathetic attempts to make the Argonautic expedition commonplace and sensible may be found quoted in Miss J. R. Bacon's learned and useful *Voyage of the Argonauts*, pp. 42–66. On p. 103 she reports: "It is held by many authorities that, if there was an Argo at all, she sailed no further than Lemnos, or at best, the Hellespont." (The "authorities" would probably prefer "at worst.") Jack's beanstalk was no doubt but five feet high.

Needless to say, both romance and the complete idea of chivalry are found in Morris' *Life and Death of Jason*.

[33] Romantic touches are of course numerous, despite the old opposition of Classical and Romantic. As for the Golden Fleece, Apollonius Rhodius has romance, but not chivalry: see especially III 1204 ff., IV 395 ff.; and Valerius Flaccus' fine invocation (I 76 ff.) reminds us of Pindar:

> tu sola animos mentesque peruris,
> Gloria; te viridem videt immunemque senectae
> Phasidos in ripa stantem iuvenesque vocantem.

Flaccus' *sua arma precatus* (II 512) recalls αἰδεσθέντες ἀλκάν. But by far the nearest approach in ancient literature to the full conception of chivalry is made by Xenophon's *Cyropaedia*. In real life its best, though an imperfect, realization was the career of Alexander.

[34] Christ rightly says: "fortitudinem tamquam deam reverebantur." Jurenka (p. 1059) finds this phrase so "sonderbar" that he alters it to αἶν' ἐσθέντες ἀλκάν, "als Nachahmung des homerischen θοῦριν ἐπιειμένοι ἀλκήν."The value of this horrible "emendation" is that it shows how an accomplished scholar may be misled if he has the wrong frame of mind.

[35] *Il.* V 530.

[36] This version, by Dr. A. S. Way, is the likeliest that I have seen. One must own that it hardly satisfies, which is no doubt inevitable. But, apart from the perfection of Pindar's whole phrase, there is a difficulty seldom noted: have we really a word for ἥβη? "Youth" refers to the same period of life, but from a different angle. One who has youth is not yet a man; one who has ἥβη is no longer a boy. Greeks spoke of reaching ἥβη; we never speak of reaching youth.

[37] His daughter Arete taught her son his grandfather's philosophy; the younger Aristippus was hence called μητροδίδακτος (Diog. Laert. II 86) and the word may remind us of Pindar's ἐν Μοίσαισι ποτανὸς ἀπὸ ματρὸς φίλας (*Pyth.* V 114).

NOTES TO LECTURE III

(pp. 44–71)

¹ Though such distinguished scholars and writers as Professor Gilbert Murray (pp. 112, 116) and Sir Richard Livingstone (pp. 140–146) have expressed this opinion, nearly all others who have written on Pindar hold the opposite view. Among them I must single out, if not for apology, yet for regretful mention, Professor D. M. Robinson; because, strongly as I disagree with his belief that Pindar was "a poet of eternal ideas," I owe much to the learned and vivacious book so entitled.

² See frr. 4, 7, 10, 37 (Diehl); cp. Schmid, pp. 508 f., and Bowra (*Gk. Lyr. P.*), pp. 345 f.

³ *Flor.* II i 21: τοὺς φυσιολογοῦντας ἔφη Πίνδαρος ἀτελῆ σοφίας καρπὸν δρέπειν— fr. 197 (209). Cp. *Ox. Pap.* V, p. 841 (fr. 42, Schroeder, p. 540):

τ]υφλα[ὶ γὰ]ρ ἀνδρῶν φρένες,
ὅ]στις ἄνευθ' Ἑλικωνιάδων
βαθεῖαν ἐλθ[. . .]των ἐρευν[ᾷ σ]οφίαις ὁδόν.

⁴ Fennell, *Olympian and Pythian Odes*, pp. xx f. Matthew Arnold also had written (p. 8): "In the Greece of Pindar and Sophocles . . . the poet lived in a current of ideas in the highest degree animating and nourishing to the creative power; society was, in the fullest measure, permeated by fresh thought, intelligent and alive." It is hardly an exaggeration to retort that there was no such thing as "the Greece of Pindar and Sophocles."

⁵ Diels, p. 78: πρῶτος ἔφη ἐκλείπειν τὸν ἥλιον τῆς σελήνης αὐτὸν ὑπερχομένης κατὰ κάθετον, οὔσης φύσει γεώδους.

⁶ A scholium on Aratus 283 includes the words τὸν παρὰ Πινδάρῳ ἑκατοντόργυιον ἀνδριάντα, ἀφ' οὗ τῆς κινήσεως τῶν ποδῶν τὸν Νεῖλον πλημμυρεῖν. (Fr. 294 b = 282.)

⁷ *Ol.* III 44 ff., *Nem.* III 20 f. So also *Isth.* IV 11 ff. (but see Lecture VIII, pp. 172 ff.). Contrast Herod. IV 42, 152, 196 (this last is the germ of the famous simile which closes Arnold's *Scholar-Gipsy*).

⁸ I mean, of course, original composition; and take this opportunity to record my admiration for Jebb's version of *Abt Vogler* and Headlam's of *The Wisdom of Solomon XVIII*.

⁹ Since Jaeger's justly famous work bears the name "Paideia," he naturally enlarges on the minutest traces of educational practice or theory. But unless we have in mind the "educational value" of all great poetry as such—thereby reducing what was a definite theme of research to a mere cloud—no educational element at all exists in Pindar. But his definite maxims are education? Not so, unless a collection of Biblical texts is theology. Do we not find maxims in numberless writers who are baldly sententious without any spark of inspiration? On these lines, Tupper is a more important "educator" than Pindar. True education teaches us, not what to think, but how to think.

This conception of him as a teacher of Greece is held by Schmid also. On pp. 547 f. he paints an attractive picture of a mighty reformer whose voice summoned the Greek aristocrats to a crusade against democratic vulgarity. That is pure fancy; and one observes that Schmid's copious (and invaluable) footnotes suddenly cease, at just this point, to supply references to Pindar himself. Nevertheless, this idea leads him to an excellent remark (p. 564) about the "Aristokratisierung der Tyrannis," for which, of course, clear evidence exists, especially in *Pyth.* I. But that is politics, not education.

[10] P. 284: "So führt Pindars stetes Gedenken an die Vorfahren ... eine ganze Philosophie mit sich voll tiefer Besinnung über Verdienst, Glück und Leid im Wechsel der Generationen eines mit den höchsten Erdengütern gesegneten, mit den edelsten Gaben ausgestatteten, von den höchsten Ueberlieferungen getragenen Menschentums."

[11] P. 285: "Seine Helden sind gegenwärtig lebende und ringende Menschen. Er stellt sie in die Welt des Mythos hinein ... in eine Welt idealer Vorbilder, deren Glanz auf sie überstrahlt und deren Lob sie strebend zu gleicher Höhe emporziehen und ihre besten Kräfte wecken soll. Das gibt dem Mythengebrauch bei Pindar seinen besonderen Sinn und Wert."

[12] P. 601 and note 3. His ten examples are not convincing, except the last (see next note). Ixion illustrates contemporary history, rather than *vice versa*. The Bellerophon passage is not a myth, but a few words to justify the simple idea of τερπνὸν ἐπάμερον διώκων κτὲ. For Antilochus see note 14. To quote *Nem.* X in this connexion is almost absurd. No doubt the myth deals with brotherly love; but who has ever thought of it as a piece of exhortation? It is a sublime story wrought for its own sake into an ode that has no particular concern with it. The Paean IV instance is extremely slight: "Ceans love their modest home: so did Euxantius." *Nem.* I is a strong example of something very rare in Pindar—the great man's service to his fellows; but I see no hint that the eulogy of Heracles should be taken as advice, rather than a compliment, to Chromius (cp. note 89). Rhadamanthys (*Pyth.* II) has nothing to do here: see *A.J.P.* LXII 3, pp. 340 ff. Tantalus (*Ol.* I) is introduced mostly as prelude to Pelops and his experiences. As for Cinyras, I cannot divine the intention of these tantalizing little passages.

[13] *Isth.* VII 32 ff. is of course undeniable. My emendation, indeed, of 'Αμφιάραον to ἀντιφερίζων (*A.J.P.* LXIII 4, pp. 460 f.) makes the case even stronger.

[14] Vv. 28 f.:   ἔγεντο καὶ πρότερον 'Αντίλοχος βιατὰς
νόημα τοῦτο φέρων,

that is, the command to honour parents (v. 27) which, we have already (vv. 19 f.) heard, was obeyed by Thrasybulus. Note κ α ὶ πρότερον.

[15] Gundert, p. 20: "Dabei gehen wir von einigen Dichten aus, in denen nicht die Deutung des Tuns überhaupt, sondern jeweils ein besonderes Leiden zu der Erkenntnis führt, wie der Mensch sein Schicksal zu überwinden habe." (The odes referred to are *Isth.* VIII, *Pyth.* III, and *Ol.* II.)

[16] Coppola, p. 227. He compares Pindar to Plato, "poichè anche in Platone lo stesso problema della virtù è risoluto, si può dire, nello stesso modo che in Pindaro. Platone non crede alla virtù naturale, ma crede alla virtù dono di dio: la virtù non s'insegna, ma un dio ce la dona e un dio ce la toglie." What utterance of Plato can be twisted into a seeming confirmation of the last phrase?

[17] Fraccaroli, p. 163: "L'uomo più forte, dice altrove, N. IX 15 ... pone fine alla giudizia di prima: cioè a ciò che prima era giusto toglie la sanzione che lo rendava tale." But *Nem.* IX 15, κρέσσων δὲ καππαύει δίκαν τὰν πρόσθεν ἀνήρ, surely means nothing so monstrous: δίκα here is equivalent to the Attic δίκαια, "rights"; and so both Sandys and Farnell translate it.

[18] Untersteiner, pp. 64 ff.: "Un'altra corrente spirituale aveva determinato il corso dei pensieri di Pindaro: il verbo di Apollo ... Questo Dio non aveva insegnato

agli uomini la speranza che è tormento e turbamento dello spirito, ma aveva fatto balenare la luce dell'idea, nella quale sola essi potevano trovar pace delle contradizioni dell'esistenza. Le antinomie del mondo e della vita, la tenzone eterna del l' Uno e dei Molti ..." etc.

[19] *Ol.* VIII 68 f., *Pyth.* VIII 85 ff., fr. 216 (229).

[20] *Ol.* VII 10, ὁ δ᾽ ὄλβιος, ὃν φᾶμαι κατέχοντ᾽ ἀγαθαί. *Pyth.* I 99 ff.:

τὸ δὲ παθεῖν εὖ πρῶτον ἀέθλων·
εὖ δ᾽ ἀκούειν δευτέρα μοῖρ᾽· ἀμφοτέροισι δ᾽ ἀνὴρ
ὃς ἂν ἐγκύρσῃ καὶ ἕλῃ,
στέφανον ὕψιστον δέδεκται.

[21] E.g., *Pyth.* VI 23 ff. The grandiloquence contrasts queerly with the platitude.

[22] Dornseiff (*Pindar*, p. 14) offers a portentous list of German words for *areta*. "Für Pindar heisst arete Glanz Adel Ehre Trefflichkeit Kraft Männlichkeit Fähigkeit gute Familie Vorzug Leistung Hochsinn Glück Reichtum Gedeihen Ruhm, das alles schwingt immer in dem Worte mit." Cf. Plutarch, *Quomodo adul.* etc., 24 CD: σφόδρα δὲ δεῖ καὶ τοῖς ἄλλοις ὀνόμασι προσέχειν, κατὰ πολλὰ πράγματα κινουμένοις καὶ μεθισταμένοις ὑπὸ τῶν ποιητῶν. οἷόν ἐστι καὶ τὸ τῆς ἀρετῆς κτὲ.

[23] Or, in the plural, specific kinds of excellence. In *Ol.* I 89, the men who are called ἀρεταῖσι μεμαλότες include Atreus and Thyestes (though no names are given)— with allusion, doubtless, to their courage.

[24] E.g., *Ol.* IX 100, τὸ δὲ φυᾷ κράτιστον ἅπαν : *Nem.* X 30, οὐδ᾽ ἀμόχθῳ καρδίᾳ προσφέρων τόλμαν παραιτεῖται χάριν: *Pyth.* I 41, ἐκ θεῶν γὰρ μαχαναὶ πᾶσαι βροτέαις ἀρεταῖς. Schmid (p. 591) well summarizes Pindar's full opinion, without, however, realizing (so far as appears) its irrationality. "Für Pindaros ist das καλὸν ἔργον die durch göttliche Gnade mit Erfolg gesegnete Tat eines ἀνὴρ ἐσλός oder ἀγαθός, der durch gottgefälliges Leben und williges Erdulden von Mühe und Gefahr ἀρετή erwiesen und sich des Erfolges würdig gemacht hat; da muss der Neid verstummen und auch die Musenkunst muss solche Tat zum Vorbild für die Zukunft auf den Leuchter stellen."

[25] In *Ol.* IX 100 ff. (see last note) they are indeed all mentioned together, if ὤρουσαν be taken (as well it may) to indicate effort. But they are not combined in the same person.

τὸ δὲ φυᾷ κράτιστον ἅπαν· πολλοὶ δὲ διδακταῖς
ἀνθρώπων ἀρεταῖς κλέος
ὤρουσαν ἀρέσθαι·
ἄνευ δὲ θεοῦ σεσιγαμένον
οὐ σκαιότερον χρῆμ᾽ ἕκαστον.

[26] That is, in the case as here put, and usually in the actual cases treated by Pindar. Where he does assign a reason for what I have called "God's grace," it is the favouritism of a particular god, given for reasons cogent but quite mundane. See below, p. 55 and note thereon.

[27] E.g., *Nem.* XI 37 ff.

[28] Scholars have tended to exaggerate Pindar's contempt of learning or school training. The passages are but three:

Ol. II 86 ff.:   σοφὸς ὁ πολλὰ εἰδὼς φυᾷ·
μαθόντες δὲ λάβροι
παγγλωσσίᾳ κόρακες ὡς ἄκραντα γαρύετον
Διὸς πρὸς ὄρνιχα θεῖον.

Ol. IX 100 ff. (quoted in note 25).

Nem. III 40 ff. (the present passage):

συγγενεῖ δέ τις εὐδοξίᾳ μέγα βρίθει.

ὃς δὲ διδάκτ' ἔχει, ψεφεννὸς ἀνὴρ

ἄλλοτ' ἄλλα πνέων οὔ ποτ' ἀτρεκεῖ

κατέβα ποδί, μυριᾶν δ' ἀρετᾶν ἀτελεῖ νόῳ γεύεται.

It is impossible to believe that Pindar seriously decried all professional training: in these passages he probably girds at the Stesichorean school (see Lecture VIII, pp. 169 f.). Nevertheless his contemporary Epicharmus might seem to be directly attacking him for insistence on φυά and depreciation of διδαχή: ἁ δὲ μελέτα φύσιος ἀγαθᾶς πλέονα δωρεῖται, φίλοι. (Lorenz, p. 261: Kaibel, fr. 284, reads δωρεῖται φίλοις.) Cp. Democritus fr. 33 (Diels): ἡ φύσις καὶ ἡ διδαχὴ παραπλήσιόν ἐστι. καὶ γὰρ ἡ διδαχὴ μεταρυσμοῖ τὸν ἄνθρωπον, μεταρυσμοῦσα δὲ φυσιοποιεῖ. Similarly Euenus fr. 9 (Diehl):

φημὶ πολυχρονίην μελέτην ἔμεναι, φίλε, καὶ δή

ταύτην ἀνθρώποισι τελευτῶσαν φύσιν εἶναι.

[29] See the magnificent passage, *Nem.* VIII 25 ff., and the less remarkable *Nem.* VII 25 ff. The other Ajax-passage, *Isth.* IV 35 ff., though in itself important (see Lecture VIII, pp. 173 f. and note 46 thereon), is not considered here, because I regard that ode as unauthentic (*ibid.*, pp. 172–175).

[30] Note (e.g.) σαθρόν in *Nem.* VIII 34 b.

[31] *Pyth.* III 86 ff. Fr. 117 (134), εὐδαιμόνων δραπέτας οὐκ ἔστιν ὄλβος, cannot be quoted against this assertion, as we do not know the context. The whole passage may well have meant: "To be εὐδαίμων signifies permanent ὄλβος; and thus no mortal is εὐδαίμων." Anyone convinced that no human happiness has permanence might well say, "Blessed is he whose joys have no wings."

[32] Wade-Gery and Bowra, p. xxiv.

[33] *Pyth.* III 77 ff., on which the scholiast writes: ἐγειτνία τῇ Πινδάρου οἰκήσει Μητρὸς θεῶν ἱερὸν καὶ Πανός, ὅπερ αὐτὸς ἱδρύσατο.

[34] P. 182. Nevertheless we hear that Pindar told of the gods' metamorphoses into ἄλογα ζῷα (fr. 81 = 91)—but Rose in *C.Q.*, April, 1930, pp. 107 f., gives good reason for rejecting this—and that he mentioned the incident of Hera, Hephaestus, and the trick chair [fr. 295 (283)].

[35] In his account (*Eum.* 1–19) of the manner in which the Delphic oracle came under the control of successive deities, Aeschylus openly contradicts common "knowledge" (cp. Verrall *ad loc.*). As for Pindar, a useful conspectus and discussion will be found in van der Kolf. Dornseiff (*Pindar*, note 54, *Pyth.* III) has a good remark about the bribery of Asclepius. "Ursprünglich hat Zeus den allzuglücklichen Arzt getötet, um die Menschen nicht unsterblich werden zu lassen, wie er aus ähnlichen Gründen den Prometheus unschädlich gemacht hat. Wie Koronis, so konnte für Pindars empfinden auch Asclepios nicht schuldlos von der Gottheit bestraft worden sein." (Illig also, e.g. on p. 63, holds that Pindar moralizes his myths.) Dornseiff is perfectly right about Asclepius: the passage is a slighter instance of what is discussed on pp. 62 f.—Pindar's groping towards a moral view of divine behaviour. The Coronis-passage (*Pyth.* III 8–23) is by no means so certain an example: Pindar's variations seem intended only to strengthen this incident as a warning against τὸ αἰσχύνειν τὰ ἐπιχώρια (v. 22).

[36] Fraccaroli (p. 162) remarks that Pindar in *Ol.* I 28–52 rejects the myth "non

tanto perchè sia immorale, quanto perchè è brutto e indecoroso far cannibali i Numi; quello *bello*, che vi sostituisce, non ci rappresenta però i Numi moralmente più puri: la correzione di Pindaro sta tutta nell'apparenza esteriore."

[37] Fr. 50 (61)—Schroeder's reading:

τί ἔλπεαι σοφίαν ἔμμεν, ἃν ὀλίγον τοι
ἀνὴρ ὑπὲρ ἀνδρὸς ἰσχύει;
οὐ γὰρ ἔσθ' ὅπως τὰ θεῶν βου-
λεύματ' ἐρευνάσει βροτέᾳ φρενί·
θνατᾶς δ' ἀπὸ ματρὸς ἔφυ.

[38] *Nem.* VI 1 ff. The pattern of the thought here has not always been clearly shown. That ἓν ἀνδρῶν, ἓν θεῶν γένος means not two different γένη but the same, is now agreed:* it follows, then, that we should place a comma, not a colon after γένος, since ἐκ μιᾶς δὲ πνέομεν ματρὸς ἀμφότεροι merely reinforces the first clause. Then the strophe twice expresses the greatness and the lowness of mankind, ἔν . . . ἀμφότεροι corresponding to ἀλλά τι . . . ἀθανάτοις, διείργει . . . οὐρανός corresponding to καίπερ . . . στάθμαν.

[39] *De Comp. Verb.* 22—fr. 63 (75).

[40] Fr. 61 (Schroeder, pp. 546 f.).

[41] Aristides II 142—fr. 12 (31).

[42] Apart from the frequent mention of thunder and lightning as wielded by Zeus, and the earthquakes caused by Poseidon, which are not striking in this connexion, there are but two passages. In fr. 98 b (Schroeder, p. 554) we read that θεός can bring unsullied radiance out of black night and cast eclipse upon brilliant sunshine. In *Ol.* IX 52 f. the flood is suddenly banished Ζηνὸς τέχναις.

[43] Where this notion comes into view, it is denied (but without emphasis): in *Ol.* VII 61 f. Helios rejects Zeus' offer to cast lots anew; in *Nem.* V 37 Zeus gives Thetis to Peleus γαμβρὸν Ποσειδάωνα πείσαις.

[44] Are we to include fr. 48 (57)?

Δωδωναῖε μεγασθενές,
ἀριστότεχνα πάτερ . . .
δαμιοργὸς εὐνομίας καὶ δίκας.

That is clear and striking. But did Pindar write thus, and (if so) as one passage? The testimony is defective and confused: see Schroeder's apparatus. Plutarch *adv. Stoic.* 1065 might, perhaps, be taken to imply that Pindar voiced the complete idea of a well-governed Universe—a Stoic θεῶν καὶ ἀνθρώπων ἄστυ κοινόν. But it is not certain that he said nearly so much: indeed, Plutarch *may* here be quoting from him no more than the word ἀριστοτέχνας. In *praec. reip. ger.* 807, ἀριστοτέχνας and δημιουργὸς εὐνομίας καὶ δίκης are used to describe, not Zeus, but ὁ πολιτικός. Moreover, if Pindar wrote what is suggested in *adv. Stoic.* 1065, it is surprising that so impressive an utterance is nowhere fully quoted or discussed. On the whole, we cannot venture to use the passage (or passages).

[45] *Ol.* VIII 25 ff.:   τεθμὸς δέ τις ἀθανάτων καὶ
τάνδ' ἁλιερκέα χώραν
παντοδαποῖσιν ὑπέστασε ξένοις
κίονα δαιμονίαν.

_____

* Fennell remarks: "As the Greek for 'one' occurs thrice in the space of so few words, each and all of the three would seem to be intended to emphasize the idea of unity."

Aeginetan righteousness is a frequent theme with Pindar. Here he calls it heaven-sent. What of καί? It seems never to have been really explained. Dissen *ad loc.* says it compares Aegina with Olympia. Why? Fraccaroli (p. 265) suggests that the "general eulogy" applies *also* to Aegina: that is no way to congratulate the favourite island. We seem forced to conclude that the justice of Aegina corresponds on earth to the divine τεθμός; but καί is a very slight, even casual, method of expressing so magnificent a thought.

⁴⁶ See Appendix A.

⁴⁷ Cp., e.g. *Ol.* I 75 f., III 39 ff., VI 57 ff., VII 41, *Nem.* III 64 f., X 49 ff., 80. Schmid (p. 584, note 11) is impressed by *Nem.* X 54, καὶ μὰν θεῶν πιστὸν γένος: "eine von Pind. zuerst . . . genannte Eigenschaft der Götter, die eine bemerkenswerte Versittlichung des Gottesbegriffs bedeutet—bei Homer ist sie in Gebeten (εἰ ποτέ τοι usw.) noch sehr schüchtern und zweifelnd berührt." But what of Athene's loyalty to Odysseus in the *Odyssey*? *Nem.* X seems to me only an example of that kindness in return for hospitality which I mention in the text: the Dioscuri had been guests of Pamphaes.

⁴⁸ See, further, Lecture VII, pp. 148 f. and note 25 thereon.

⁴⁹ *Nem.* V 14 f.

⁵⁰ Staehlin (p. 192) juggles with Pindar's narrative in order to justify Zeus. (His article is otherwise able and attractive.)

⁵¹ V 60: Ἴδας ἀμφὶ βουσίν πως χολωθείς.

⁵² It must be noted (though this, of course, is not confined to Pindar) that the woman's consent is always taken for granted—so much so that the poet does not even trouble to allege that she was pleased. This strikes one especially in the Ninth Pythian, which gives so beautiful a picture of Cyrana. The contrast between Euadna's experience in *Ol.* VI and Creusa's in *Ion* has been noted in Lecture II (p. 33).

⁵³ *Pyth.* IX 84 ff., *Nem.* X 11, *Isth.* VII 5 ff. On the third passage see Lecture IV, p. 89 and note 58.

⁵⁴ P. 219. The poet's comment on Asclepius is (to be sure) vague: χρὴ τὰ ἐοικότα πὰρ δαιμόνων μαστευέμεν κτὲ. See, further, note 35 above.

⁵⁵ Frr. 152 (169), 70 (81). See Plato, *Gorgias* 483 c–484 c, for Callicles' doctrine, which Perrotta (p. 214) says that Pindar would have rejected with horror. When the stronger was Heracles?

⁵⁶ Herod. VIII x 5. Ὁρᾷς τὰ ὑπερέχοντα ζῷα ὡς κεραυνοῖ ὁ θεὸς οὐδὲ ἐᾷ φαντάζεσθαι, τὰ δὲ σμικρὰ οὐδέν μιν κνίζει; ὁρᾷς δὲ ὡς ἐς οἰκήματα τὰ μέγιστα αἰεὶ καὶ δένδρεα τὰ τοιαῦτ' ἀποσκήπτει βέλεα; φιλέει γὰρ ὁ θεὸς τὰ ὑπερέχοντα πάντα κολούειν . . . οὐ γὰρ ἐᾷ φρονέειν ἄλλον μέγα ὁ θεὸς ἢ ἐωυτόν.

⁵⁷ *Paean* VI 92 ff.: μόρσιμ' ἀναλύεν Ζεὺς . . . οὐ τόλμα. This is the same confusion as that of the *Aeneid*. In *Nem.* VII 44 ἐχρῆν is exactly like Herodotus' use of ἔδεε, e.g. in V xxxiii 2; both words mean nothing.

⁵⁸ *Isth.* I 39 f. I borrow "natal star" from Farnell.

⁵⁹ Of the many scholars who have discussed them it may suffice to name Rohde (II, pp. 204–222) and Farnell (I, pp. 335–338; II, pp. 459 ff.).

⁶⁰ Fr. 116 (131). Cp. Aesch. *Eum.* 104 f.

⁶¹ Smyth, p. 376.

⁶² Vv. 56–80. See, further, Lecture VI, pp. 134–137, and note 56 thereon.

⁶³ Fr. 114 ab (129, 130).

⁶⁴ See Lecture VI, pp. 134 f. Fr. 127 (133) seems to stand apart from the other eschatological passages.

> οἷσι δὲ Φερσεφόνα ποινὰν παλαιοῦ πένθεος
> δέξεται, ἐς τὸν ὕπερθεν ἅλιον κείνων ἐνάτῳ ἔτεϊ
> ἀνδιδοῖ ψυχὰς πάλιν, ἐκ τᾶν βασιλῆες ἀγαυοὶ
> καὶ σθένει κραιπνοὶ σοφίᾳ τε μέγιστοι
> ἄνδρες αὔξοντ'· ἐς δὲ τὸν λοιπὸν χρόνον ἥροες ἁ-
> γνοὶ πρὸς ἀνθρώπων καλεῦνται.

The first two clauses undoubtedly mean "purgatory," an idea far more nebulously—if at all—expressed in *Ol.* II 68 ff. For the παλαιὸν πένθος see Rose, pp. 79 ff. and in *Harvard Theol. Rev.* The rest appears to be a very tentative blend of two ideas—deification and the cycle of existences.

Scholars discussing Pindar's eschatology have talked much of Orphism. Since the publication of Linforth's book, the word must be used with greater care: see Lecture VI, note 55.

⁶⁵ Fr. 121 (137 a):

> ὄλβιος ὅστις ἰδὼν κεῖν' εἶσ' ὑπὸ χθόν'·
> οἶδε μὲν βίου τελευτάν,
> οἶδεν δὲ διόσδοτον ἀρχάν.

⁶⁶ That the eschatological passages report Pindar's own beliefs is emphatically affirmed by Rohde (II, pp. 215 f.). "Dass Pindar, der stolze, eigenrichtige, sehr bewusster Weisheit frohe, mit dem Vortrage solcher, populärem Bewusstsein so fremdartiger Lehren sich lediglich fremden Wünschen gefügt, fremden Glauben gefällig sollte Ausdruck gegeben haben, das ist undenkbar. Es ist der Inhalt eigener Ueberzeugung, selbsterrungener Einsicht, in die er gleichgesinnten Freunden, in geweiheter Stunde, einen Blick eröffnet." Wilamowitz (pp. 460 f.) is equally emphatic on the other side. "Diese Lebensregeln sind ganz menschlich; keinerlei Götterglaube spielt hinein. Und so ist es auch mit dem Tode. Unser letztes Kleid ist die Decke des Grabes. Nur die Heroen sind zu neuem Leben erhöht. Der Mensch lebt nur weiter in seiner Nachkommenschaft und daneben im Liede, das sein Gedächtnis, die Ehre seines Namens erhält. Theron und andere mögen an die Seelenwanderung für die Auserwählten und ein Gericht im Jenseits glauben, die eleusinischen Mysten sich ihrer Hoffnungen getrösten: Pindar stört sie nicht, trägt ihnen zu ihrer Erbauung ihre Glaubensideen vor, wie er den Rhodiern eine Göttergeschichte erzählt, die nur für Rhodos Geltung haben konnte. Aber sein eigner, apollinischer Glaube wird dadurch nicht berührt."

What really matters is the light thrown upon Pindar's artistic conscience by his readiness to voice contradictory views.

⁶⁷ *Ol.* X 91 ff. Cp. *Nem.* VIII 30 ff.

⁶⁸ *Pyth.* V. 96 ff. Cp. *Ol.* VIII 77 ff., XIV 20 ff., *Nem.* IV 85 ff.

⁶⁹ To these may be added *Pyth.* III 54 ff.: cp. note 35 above.

⁷⁰ Perhaps the best example is Soph. *Ant.* 308 ff.:

> οὐχ ὑμὶν Ἅιδης μοῦνος ἀρκέσει, πρὶν ἂν
> ζῶντες κρεμαστοὶ τήνδε δηλώσηθ' ὕβριν,
> ἵν' εἰδότες τὸ κέρδος ἔνθεν οἰστέον
> τὸ λοιπὸν ἁρπάζητε.

⁷¹ Gildersleeve, however, asserts (p. cvi) that ἔραται is subjunctive instead of optative because the purpose "is good for all time."

[72] Jaeger, pp. 272 f. (Highet, pp. 204 f.), admirably describes Pindar's archaism of feeling, especially about the nobles.

[73] Fr. 65 (77).

[74] Fr. 64 (76).

[75] Fr. 235 (43).

[76] Pyth. X 71 f.

[77] Pyth. V 75 f.: Αἰγεῖδαι, ἐμοὶ πατέρες. I cannot accept the view that ἐμοί refers to the chorus-leader. The question is well discussed by Farnell ad loc.

[78] It would be an exaggeration to allege that he has no standards at all. The best support for that view would be ἄλλο δ' ἄλλοισι νόμισμα, σφετέραν δ' αἰνεῖ δίκαν ἕκαστος. But that is a fragment (203 = 215), so that we do not know its setting; and δίκαν may well have the meaning "custom" (cp. νόμισμα).

[79] Herod. IX 80: Παυσανίης δὲ κήρυγμα ποιησάμενος μηδένα ἅπτεσθαι τῆς ληΐης, συγκομίζειν ἐκέλευσε τοὺς Εἵλωτας τὰ χρήματα . . . ἐνθαῦτα πολλὰ μὲν κλέπτοντες ἐπώλεον πρὸς τοὺς Αἰγινήτας οἱ Εἵλωτες, πολλὰ δὲ καὶ ἀπεδείκνυσαν, ὅσα αὐτέων οὐκ οἷά τε ἦν κρύψαι · ὥστε Αἰγινήτησι οἱ μεγάλοι πλοῦτοι ἀρχὴν ἐνθεῦτεν ἐγένοντο, οἳ τὸν χρυσόν, ἅτε ἐόντα χαλκὸν δῆθεν, παρὰ τῶν Εἱλωτέων ὠνέοντο.

[80] P. 33.

[81] Ol. IX 29 ff. This is one of the "hush-passages," to be discussed in Lecture IV, pp. 80 f.

[82] Pyth. VI 28–46. There has been too much humming and hawing over this comparison. Jurenka, Wien. Stud. XIX, pp. 75 f., sensibly remarks on Ol. VI: "Pindarum qui sano iudicio legerit cum bellatore (sc. Amphiarao) Agesiam ea de causa componi cognoscet, quod Olympiae curru vicerat . . . eiusdem carminis v. 86, ubi poeta carmina epinicia se pangere dicit ἀνδράσιν αἰχματαῖσι, vides eodem ornari epitheto victores Olympiacos quo ab Homero bellatores ornantur."

[83] Iliad XII 447 ff.

[84] Herod. VIII 26. Neither the historian nor the Persians show any surprise at this notable anticipation of Sir Francis Drake's game of bowls. It was the olive-garland alone that impressed Tritantaechmes: παπαῖ, Μαρδόνιε, κοίους ἐπ' ἄνδρας ἤγαγες μαχεσομένους ἡμέας, οἳ οὐ περὶ χρημάτων τὸν ἀγῶνα ποιεῦνται, ἀλλὰ περὶ ἀρετῆς.

[85] See Appendix B, pp. 194 ff.

[86] Cp. Ol. IX 89, XIII 110, Pyth. VIII 79.

[87] El. 387 ff.:
αἱ δὲ σάρκες αἱ κεναὶ φρενῶν
ἀγάλματ' ἀγορᾶς εἰσιν· οὐδὲ γὰρ δόρυ
μᾶλλον βραχίων σθεναρὸς ἀσθενοῦς μένει.

[88] Fr. 2, 20 ff. (Diehl):
σμικρὸν δ' ἄν τι πόλει χάρμα γένοιτ' ἐπὶ τῷ,
εἴ τις ἀεθλεύων νικῷ Πίσαο παρ' ὄχθας·
οὐ γὰρ πιαίνει ταῦτα μυχοὺς πόλιος.

[89] Cp., e.g., Ol. VII 93 f., Isth. II 37 ff. Dr. B. R. English rightly says (p. 93): "Alcibiades remains the greatest exponent of Pindar's political philosophy"— though "philosophy" is too grand a word.

Schmid, however, will have it that Pindar insists on the aristocrat's public duty, ascribing to the poet "ein neues Ideal des aristokratischen Menschen" (p. 615). See note 9 above. The most remarkable passage is on p. 594. "Die egotistisch-materielle Herrenmoral mit ihren Methoden von List und Gewalt und ihrer brutalen Kriegsfreudigkeit billigt er nicht, sein Herrscherideal zeigt soziale, sein Bürgerideal altruistische Züge." That is misleading, because "social traits" can be more and less constructive: Schmid would no doubt be justified if hospitality and the like, so often mentioned by Pindar, were what he meant. But his oft-repeated doctrine, that Pindar seeks to evangelize the nobles, goes far deeper, and rests on nothing but the mistaken belief (see notes 11 and 12 above) that the myths are patterns of life offered to the poet's athletic clients. As for altruism, the forty-odd passages where the faintest allusion to it can be even suspected are nearly all slight remarks on hospitality and helping friends. But altruism means something beyond dinner-parties or gifts: it is helping others through self-sacrifice. In four places only can we reasonably say that we discern it. The ξυναὶ ἀρεταί of Pyth. XI 54 ff. are, no doubt, striking, but they are "social virtues" of a more humdrum kind—coöperation by men of enlightened self-interest: see Lecture VI, pp. 122 f., 126. In Pyth. III 47 ff., the list of Asclepius' normal feats as a physician fill a strophe. But does Pindar mean to dilate on his "services to suffering humanity"? There occurs no word of praise, and the passage is probably meant as a mere prelude to his fatal exploit in the antistrophe: these impressive details are but a tribute to Asclepius' father Apollo and his teacher Chiron. Nem. X offers an example of brotherly love so impressive that to call it altruism is almost inept. But the First Nemean, at least, provides an unmistakable picture of altruism. Heracles' achievements (vv. 62–68) mean a life devoted to well-doing at the price of immense personal risk and unexampled toil—though (it must be owned) no word of this description can be found in Pindar except καμάτων (v. 70). Next, whatever we think of the pattern-doctrine, there can be no doubt that Chromius is presented as resembling Heracles; so that we find a contemporary of the poet receiving from him the implication of altruism. Such awkward phrasing is necessary, for Pindar even here, in the passage that best supports Schmid's view, does not plainly voice it. Still, he certainly means it. Observe vv. 53 ff., where the common lack of altruism is vigorously described and (more-over) quite "unnecessarily" introduced. At least as arresting are vv. 32 f., where the usual φίλοις ἐξαρκέων is reinforced by words that express a sense of human fellowship and sympathy—κοιναὶ γὰρ ἔρχοντ' ἐλπίδες πολυπόνων ἀνδρῶν.

An excellent remark of Schmid's (p. 593) may be noted here, that in Pyth. II 21 ff. Pindar, for the first time in Greek literature, exalts gratitude by showing Ixion punished for the lack of it.

90 Figures, not characters. He says that he is no maker of statues (Nem. V 1), but something of the statuesque marks all his persons. We never feel that we know them as real people, only as splendid creatures to whom wonderful things happen, by whom impressive deeds are performed. Dionysius of Halicarnassus (De Vet. Scrip. Cens. V) includes ἠθοποιία in his list of Pindar's merits, but it is difficult to see why he does this, with Homer, Euripides, and Menander at his elbow.

91 Pater, at the height of his feline deftness, makes a beautifully indirect attempt to portray Sparta itself as an ancient blend of Eton and Kensington in the 1880's. (Plato and Platonism, pp. 206, 208, 219, 220 ff.)

92 Coppola, p. 62: "Libera è per lui la città dove il potere è nelle mani dei nobili."

93 See Coppola, p. 219. After the astonishing comment on Tantalus etc. and "la tremenda giustizia di dio" already quoted (p. 57 and note 54), he proceeds: "Ecco perchè l'interpretazione lirica del mito l'abbiamo cercata sempre nelle

gnome, e sempre ve l'abbiamo trovata." On the same extraordinary page he compares Pindar with Prodicus the sophist, and takes the word σοφός (which Pindar applies to himself) as meaning, apparently, "philosophical." "Io non sostengo che Pindaro sia un sofista; dico solo che egli è un poeta σοφός, che egli è poeta del mondo dorico e che la grande sua arte ha il suo centro ideale e morale oltra che politico nelle norme dell'etica dorica. Egli è, forse, vicino al precursore di Socrate, Prodico di Ceo …"

Illig reaches the same position by another path. On p. 74, after describing the myth of *Nem.* X, he remarks: "Hier ist in einem anschaulichen Bild alles gesagt, und doch genügt es Pindar nicht. Er gibt Polydeuces die Gnome in den Mund, die nur er aussprechen konnte: οἴχεται τιμὰ φίλων τατωμένῳ φωτί· παῦροι δ' ἐν πόνῳ πιστοὶ βροτῶν καμάτου μεταλαμβάνειν. Für unser Gefühl durchbricht sie die objektive Einheit der Bildgestaltung. Für Pindar ist die Gnome die letzte, im Grunde einzig adäquate Form, die im Mythos beschlossene Norm zu offenbaren und zur Geltung zu bringen."

[94] See Lecture IV, pp. 75 f.

[95] Perrotta, p. 154: "Un'affermazione così vigorosa non è più una massima, è un sentimento; e questo passo di Pindaro, infatti, può esser paragonato ai versi più profondamente religiosi di Eschilo, a certi cori delle *Supplici* o dell'*Agamennone*."

[96] In the *Cypria* (fr. 5 Kinkel) Castor was mortal, Polydeuces immortal; in *Hom. Hymn* XVII 2 Castor is a god; Hesiod (fr. 91 Rzach), according to the scholium on *Nem.* X 150 a, ἀμφοτέρους Διὸς εἶναι γενεαλογεῖ. Pindar is no doubt following the *Cypria*, though the scholiast just mentioned reports his authorities as ἕτεροι τῶν ἱστορικῶν. In any case, there can be no doubt that he gains a magnificent effect by making Polydeuces ignorant of his origin, concealing it at first from the hearer also and the reader. In v. 73 he names Tyndareus as Polydeuces' father. (Christ would ruin this effect by reading παῖς Ζηνός in v. 66 instead of Λήδας παῖς.) That Polydeuces cries πάτερ Κρονίων (v. 76) matters nothing: Pindar in his own person has said Ζεῦ πάτερ (v. 29). The god's address puts it beyond question that Polydeuces has always supposed himself sprung from a mortal father: ἐσσί μοι υἱός alone could, of course, be no more than the heartening reminder of a fact already familiar; but the added *explanation* τόνδε δ' ἔπειτα κτέ. proves that Zeus now reveals something hitherto unguessed.

NOTES TO LECTURE IV

(pp. 72–93)

1 See p. 79 and note 34.

2 Humboldt translated fifteen odes—three of them only in part—with metrical correspondence of strophes, antistrophes, and epodes quite in Pindar's manner; without, however, reproducing his actual schemes. This latter feat, I believe, has been performed by von Platen alone: see Lecture VII, p. 162.

Hölderlin's translations have attracted more attention than Humboldt's, but must be counted inferior, for they follow Pindar's word-order so closely that they strike even German readers (I gather) as unnatural, if not unintelligible. Nevertheless, he at times reflects with astonishing success the sheen and majesty of Pindar's diction. In at least one original poem (*Der Rhein*, 46 ff.) he uses not only the Pindaric tone but also one of the Pindaric beliefs:

> Ein Rätsel ist Reinentsprungenes. Auch
> Der Gesang kaum darf es enthüllen. Denn
> Wie du anfingst, wirst du bleiben,
> So viel auch wirket die Not
> Und die Zucht, das meiste nämlich
> Vermag die Geburt,
> Und der Lichtstrahl, der
> Dem Neugebornen begegnet.

3 Some readers will be surprised that in what follows no use is made of Schadewaldt's *Aufbau*. Eulogistic reviews by Drachmann and Robertson have caused me to study it yet again, but its merits remain hidden from me. The book suffers from a failure to understand what a poet is and does; also, from a failure to realize what a critic is and should do. With regard to Pindar, a critic's business is to answer questions raised by his odes: Schadewaldt asks questions answered by his odes. The numerous examples are mostly too long to quote, but a brief and milder specimen (p. 316) may serve. "Diese Beobachtungen lehren mit aller Deutlichkeit, wie der objective Programmpunkt in die subjective Einheit des Hauptgedankens eingegangen ist und von der persönlichen Absicht seine besondere Gestalt erhalten hat."

Illig, his disciple, resembles him in spirit and manner. But, whereas Schadewaldt's stand-by is a given normal scheme for writing epinicia (e.g., p. 280), Illig's point, with respect to structure, is "Ringkomposition": an ode at the close turns back to its beginning (pp. 57, 59, 61). Further, he adheres to the doctrine, discussed in Lecture III, that the myths supply moral patterns (e.g., pp. 7 f.).

4 Cp. Lecture VIII, pp. 167–170.

5 Pp. 81 ff.

6 Pp. 24 ff. He finds the Terpandrian system in all but "six odes of quite narrow compass (O. 4. 11. 12. 14., P. 7, N. 2)" and *Nem*. XI, which is no epinician.

7 Westphal, p. 80. Cp. Bethe's text of Pollux (IV 66), and a good discussion of the νόμος in Smyth, pp. lviii ff.

8 Mezger, who in his commentary gives a scheme for each ode, offers on pp. 29 f. three special examples, which one may suppose him to think the best: *Pyth*. X, the earliest ode; *Isth*. V, which "gehört der Blüthezeit des Dichters an"; *Ol*. XIII, written in 464. In the first, the ἀρχά has twenty-three lines from a total of seventy-

two, three more than the ὀμφαλός; of the eight parts named on p. 24, one is missing from *Pyth.* X, three from *Isth.* V. As Farnell remarks (II, p. xxvi), "the freedom of the odes of Pindar refuses this Procrustean framework." But I cannot accept his verdict (*ibid.*) that Mezger's work is "valueless." No doubt the νόμος-theory and the catchword-theory must be rejected, but his annotations on the text are admirably sensible, terse, and lucid.

9 For a discussion of *Pythian* XI see Lecture VI.

10 Perrotta, p. 120: "La sagacia dell'interprete moderno riesce, poi, a svelarci quello che il poeta antico, non si sa perchè, avrebbe nascosto con tanta cura." On the other side, Croiset writes (p. 331): "Sa pensée secrète se trahit par l'influence qu'elle répand ... elle est comme le pôle invisible vers lequel le mouvement de l'inspiration entraîne l'artiste et ses auditeurs; mais jamais, ou presque jamais, elle ne s'offre clairement aux regards dans la nudité sévère que la prose préfère à toutes les parures," etc.

11 Wilamowitz, *Isyllos*, p. 173: "auch bei Pindar gilt diejenige disposition, die der schriftsteller selber angibt, und es ist torheit, besser als er selber wissen zu wollen, was er gewollt hat."

12 Cp. note 35 on Lecture VI.

13 Croiset (pp. 315-327) gives an acute and interesting account of theories promulgated by his predecessors.

14 Hermann, *Opusc.* III (*De Sogenis ... quinquertio*).

15 *Opusc.* VIII, p. 111.

16 Dissen on *Pyth.* II: "Ut summam sententiam carminis etiam definitius explicemus, illud Pindarus laudat, ut ὄλβος et σοφία coniuncta sint" (*ed. min.*, p. 182); on *Nem.* VIII: "Censeo . . . fundamentum carminis oppositione amoris et invidiae contineri" (*ibid.*, p. 469).

Frequently, however, Dissen offers, not pallid maxims but a mere description of Pindar's most obvious official purpose. For instance, on *Isth.* II (p. 535): "Laudat poeta in Xenocrate optimarum virtutum societatem," etc.The "vera sententia" of the Fourth Pythian itself is this (p. 218): "Fortunae regiae, divinitus datae, hereditariae, nunc etiam Pythia victoria ornatae, adde, Arcesilae, etiam moderationis, lenitatis, clementiae virtutem; sis mitis, ut Iason fuit, in summo iure. Sic enim, nec alio modo, deorum favorem conservabis qualem Iason habuit et regnum vaticiniis oraculisque genti tuae datum."

17 Hermann, *Opusc.* VII, pp. 111 f.

18 Pp. 328-345. The passage quoted is on p. 332.

19 Coppola, p. 160: "Tutto Pindaro, anche il Pindaro delle immagini, può essere inteso solo se si tiene conto di questa unità la quale si sintetizza in sentimenti estetici armonicamente governati da un sentimento etico che è tragica eredità di una civiltà che scompare a poco a poco."

20 *Id.*, p. xiv. The "good formula" wherewith to define the unity of Pindar's poetry is "non idea lirica, non idea poetica nè idea musicale, le quali formule hanno avuto fortuna meritatissima e hanno certo contributo a rendere sempre più intelligibili veri termini della poesia pindarica, ma idea etica e interpretazione etica del mito." For Jaeger see Lecture III, pp. 46 f. and notes thereon.

21 After a baffling allusion to "the metaphysical sense of the *ego*" (p. 160), he proceeds to discuss certain examples, such as Rhodes in *Ol.* VII, but fails to say anything not obvious at the first glance.

234 NOTES TO LECTURE IV (PAGES 76–79)

22 *Art poétique* II, p. 72.

23 Dornseiff, p. 113. "Die Schönheit ist durchaus die des Fragments. Man sieht plötzlich ein leuchtendes Bild, hört einen Klang, der einem bleibt. Aber den Gedankengang eines längeren Gedichtes genau zu verfolgen, ist fast unmöglich . . . Nicht weil es zu tief wäre, sondern alles ist zu undisponiert."
The whole error lies in the word "Gedankengang." So Trezza (pp. 9–20), discussing Hermann's "idea poetica" and Croiset's "idée lyrique," insists on talking about "the abstract idea." This quest for Pindar's "thought" has sadly harmed the study of his work. Trezza does indeed (p. 16) mention "simbolismo," which will sound attractive to any who accept the doctrine of the next three lectures; but it proves to be Tycho Mommsen's "historical symbolism."
How vastly better is Hölderlin's brief remark (III, p. 267): "Es [sc. das lyrische] ist eine fortgehende Metapher Eines Gefühls"!

24 Perrotta, p. 115.

25 *Id.*, p. 116.

26 *Id.*, p. 118. "Come riesce Pindaro a fondere elementi così diversi ... ? Un'ode pindarica riesce ad essere una vera unità? Per porre il problema, bisogna distinguere, prima di tutto, non tra 'unità oggettiva' e 'unità soggettiva,' come faceva il Boeckh, non tra 'programma' e 'intenzioni soggettive,' come vuol fare ora lo Schadewaldt, ma unicamente tra unità estetica e unità logica. E quella che veramente deve importare a chi voglia giudicare la poesia di Pindaro, è naturalmente l'unità estetica."

27 *Id.*, p. 127.

28 *Id.*, pp. 121 f.

29 *Id.*, pp. 126 f.: "... un trittico maraviglioso in cui rifulge come solo poche volte altrove il genio del poeta."

30 *Id.*, p. 144: "Come si vede, è questo un povero, per quanto artificioso, legame." Friederichs (p. 90) makes an unconvincing attempt to show a genuine connexion.

31 Cp. Lecture VII, pp. 144 f.

32 P. 89.

33 Pp. 124 f.

34 Dornseiff, *Pindars Stil*, p. 133. "Der Anfang muss schön sein—darauf ist Pindar stolz: O 6, P 7, N 4—, dann wuchert und kriecht das übrige unzentriert irgendwie weiter. Europäisches vorbereitendes Hinarbeiten auf einen grossen poetischen Höhepunkt, d.h. jede Steigerung fehlt. Meist ist der Anfang pompös und das Ende trocken. Das ist archaische Kompositionskunst, vor der attischen zentrierten Weise."
Cp. Coleridge, *Anima Poetae*, p. 168: "The odes of Pindar (with few exceptions, and these chiefly in the shorter ones) seem by intention to die away by soft gradations into a languid interest, like most of the landscapes of the great elder painters. Modern ode-writers have commonly preferred a continued rising of interest."
Had pseudo-Longinus (περὶ ὕψους XXXIII 5) this feature, or the digressions, in mind when he wrote his famous sentence: ὁ δὲ Πίνδαρος καὶ ὁ Σοφοκλῆς ὁτὲ μὲν οἷον πάντα ἐπιφλέγουσι τῇ φορᾷ, σβέννυνται δ' ἀλόγως πολλάκις, καὶ πίπτουσιν ἀτυχέστατα? Almost certainly he means the digressions, which were a frequent topic of ancient criticism, and which Horace (*Odes* IV iv 18–22) lamentably tries to imitate.

[35] The most striking example is *Pyth.* III 27 ff., where Apollo learns of Coronis' misdoing. Instead of adding only πάντα ἴσαντι νόῳ, Pindar writes:

κοινᾶνι παρ' εὐθυτάτῳ γνώμαν πιθών,
πάντα ἴσαντι νόῳ· ψευδέων δ' οὐχ
ἅπτεται, κλέπτει τέ νιν
οὐ θεὸς οὐ βροτὸς ἔργοις οὔτε βουλαῖς.

This extreme elaboration would have puzzled all modern readers but for the scholium 52 b (v. 29). It reports that Artemon praised Pindar for rejecting the story in Hesiod (fr. 123 Rzach)—that is, the Coronis-*Eoee*—where Apollo learned this news from the crow. The tautology, then, implies: "Phoebus knew this by his own powers: yes, his own—for I reject the Hesiodic version, which is absurd. How could such a god need help in such a matter?" (παράλογον γὰρ τὸν ἄλλοις μαντευόμενον αὐτὸν μὴ συμβαλεῖν τὰ κατ' αὐτοῦ δρώμενα, as Artemon remarked.) See also Wilamowitz, *Isyllos*, pp. 57 ff.; Schroeder, *Pythien*, p. 26.

In *Pyth.* IX, the conversation between Apollo and Chiron has features which, says Dornseiff (*Pindar*, p. 110), mark revolt from the *Eoeae*. Certainly the supposition (despite the scholiasts' silence) is attractive, that the *Eoee* contained the god's questions; and that Pindar, finding these irrational (for the same reason as in *Pyth.* III), puts his objections into Chiron's mouth.

Occasionally we come upon brief phrases—some easy enough in themselves, some obscure—whose relevance it is hard to explain. These I take to be condensations of longer passages in narratives which Pindar used, made by their brevity puzzling for us who have not the originals. An excellent instance is *Ol.* X 51, where, after describing Heracles' dedication of the Altis, he proceeds:

καὶ πάγον
Κρόνου προσεφθέγξατο· πρόσθε γὰρ
νώνυμνος, ᾶς Οἰνόμαος ἄρχε, βρέχετο πολλᾷ
νιφάδι.

The last three words no modern commentator has explained, and the fumbling of the scholiasts proves that the ancients too were at a loss. I suggest that Pindar's authority—and the details of vv. 64 ff. show that he is following some chronicle—contained an account of the district, and to this the snowfall was somehow genuinely relevant. (See note 42 on Lecture V.) So in *Pyth.* IV, μία βοῦς (v. 142), Κόλχοισιν βίαν μεῖξαν Αἰήτα παρ' αὐτῷ (vv. 211 f.), τέλεσαν ᾶν πλαγαὶ σιδάρου (v. 246) and ἐσθᾶτος ἀμφίς (v. 253) are obscure as they stand; but we know that the third book of the *Eoeae* treated the Argo-legend (cp. Hesiod frr. 51, 54, etc., Rzach). Cp. note 7 to Lecture VI.

The Pindaric scholia only thrice refer to the *Eoeae* by name: *Pyth.* IV 36 c (= 20), IX 6 a (= 5), *Isth.* VI 53 a (= 37); but their references to "Hesiod" often mean the *Eoeae*.

[36] This kind of passage must not be confused with repudiation of a story as false, as in *Ol.* I 28–35, 52 f. In the four places quoted, Pindar says, actually or in effect: "I have made a mistake in embarking on this true story."

Nor, of course, should *Pyth.* X 4, τί κομπέω παρὰ καιρόν; be taken as a "hush-passage." He has *finished* the preceding theme, and the question is a rather clumsy way of passing on to the victor. This earliest ode has more than one such bit of coltishness, and we had better not try to emend: certainly none of the suggestions in Schroeder's *apparatus* is at all convincing.

[37] Didymus remarked (say the scholiasts) that Pindar combines three separate combats: εἴη δ' ἂν ὁ Πίνδαρος τὰ καὶ τόποις καὶ χρόνοις διεστῶτα εἰς ἕνα καιρὸν ἄγων, ἕνεκα τοῦ μειζόνως ἢ ὡς ἔσχε ταῖς ἀληθείαις τὸν Ἡρακλέα ἐπαινεῖν. Pindar does not actually say that all three gods attacked Heracles together; but the repetition of ἤρειδεν makes his intention clear. Practically everyone, therefore, understands him to mean: "It is κατὰ δαίμονα that men are ἀγαθοί (and σοφοί). Consider the astounding prowess of Heracles. He could not have shown it save by the support of Heaven."

Farnell, however, regards this view as "mere fooling" (II, p. 69). According to him, the idea is: "We are all dependent on God for our valour and wisdom; for how could it have been true that Heracles successfully defied gods in battle? Let us reject that story as impious." That is quite perverse. First, the accumulation of details—ἀμφὶ Πύλον σταθείς and the like—implies strongly that the tale confirms, not contradicts, the original thesis: they would be omitted from a story which was quoted only to be rejected. Second, Farnell accepts elsewhere (I, p. 52) Didymus' report that the myth, in this form, is Pindar's invention. But that fact instantly destroys his interpretation, which implies that the story of Heracles' fight against the Three was already familiar. We cannot believe that Pindar invented an impious legend, related it, and then exclaimed: "Away with this legend! It is impious." Farnell does indeed see and state this objection (ibid.), but he signally fails to meet it. No doubt there already existed "certain mythic elements that could be combined into such a story"; but if Pindar, intending repudiation, did so combine them, he showed not only the "audacity" and the "carelessness" which Farnell confesses on his behalf, but an incompetence too startling even for pity.

[38] This is the most striking passage of the four; it has, however, received scant notice, and no solution. Heimsoeth (p. 23) finds the hardihood to declare it the necessary bridge—"das nothwendige innere und äussere Zwischenglied"—between the praying Aeacids and the further aim, Peleus' wedding on Mount Pelion. As if that were the only way to get him out of Aegina! Does not Pindar elsewhere show himself capable of dispensing with a "Zwischenglied" altogether?

[39] Fraccaroli (pp. 136 f.) explains the "hush-passages" as an imitation of familiar talk. "Il mito di regola generale si introduce riassumendolo dapprima complessivamente e brevemente e poi svolgendolo nei particolari ... Questo avviene nel parlar popolare e nel parlar famigliare: così si comincia a narrare un avvenimento o un aneddoto, specialmente se chi parla è agitato da una particolare commozione; vi si accenna, poi lo si dilinea nelle sue particolarità: la sintesi sensibile è sempre anteriore all'analisi intelligibile. E così fa Pindaro costantemente. E ch'egli ci presenti nel mito una intuizione e non una riflessione. oltre di questo procedimento nell'esporlo, lo prova anche quest'altro fatto, che qualche volta messosi a svolgere in un quadro particolareggiato il primo schizzo della sua idea, proceduto un po'innanzi lo corregge, accorgendosi che così, come essa s'era presentata alla prima, non poteva andare." (He instances Ol. I 26 ff. and Ol. IX 35 f.) I cannot believe that Pindar carried "naturalness" so far. Fraccaroli thinks that he really changed his mind, and withdrew statements, in a lyric just as in casual talk. My explanation goes quite far enough: that as a literary artifice he merely pretended to do so. A first-rate orator will often "correct" his own language, for an excellent and obvious reason; Pindar employs the same device, but more elaborately, and for reasons less obvious.

⁴⁰ See Lecture VIII, pp. 167–170.

⁴¹ *Herc. Fur.* 673–686, one of the finest things he ever wrote, unmistakably alludes to himself, and contains a perfect description of his art:

> οὐ παύσομαι τὰς Χάριτας
> Μούσαις συγκαταμειγνύς,
> ἁδίσταν συζυγίαν.

⁴² *Pyth.* VIII, vv. 67 ff.:

> ὦναξ, ἑκόντι δ' εὔχομαι νόῳ
> κατά τιν' ἁρμονίαν βλέπειν
> ἀμφ' ἕκαστον, ὅσα νέομαι.

So Bowra, except that in the first line he reads τ' (= σ') after Wade-Gery. But δ' seems unexceptionable and gives a favourite Pindaric word-order, as in (e.g.) *Ol.* I 36. The second line offers more perplexity: are we to read κατά τιν or κατὰ τίν?* The former gives a clumsy phrase, for τινά adds nothing to ἁρμονίαν, whether we take κατά as governing it or as belonging by tmesis to βλέπειν (so Schroeder), the compound καταβλέπειν then governing τιν' ἁρμονίαν. Read therefore κατὰ τίν—and what is that? Farnell takes τίν as dative (so regularly in Pindar), and the whole phrase as meaning "in harmony with thee." The sense is excellent, but the word order extremely harsh: Farnell calls it a tmesis, but tmesis elsewhere separates preposition and verb (not noun) as in his "parallel," *Ol.* IX 35 f.: ἀπό μοι λόγον τοῦτον, στόμα, ῥῖψον. We seem compelled to make κατά govern τίν as accusative—a construction not otherwise found in Pindar, but used by Corinna (fr. 12 Diehl)—"according to thee": that is, "in allegiance to thee," almost "following thee," which is Farnell's meaning, attained by another route. Next, ἁρμονίαν is governed by βλέπειν, which gives a phrase not "comic"† but beautiful: "to have concord‡ in one's glance" is (helped by its context) a fine equivalent of such an English phrase as "to keep one's life in focus." The last verse is clear: literally, "in regard to each of all the steps I take"—"in all my ways."

⁴³ Vv. 89 f., ἀρχαῖον ὄνειδος ἀλαθέσιν λόγοις εἰ φεύγομεν, is usually taken to mean "whether in very truth we have escaped the old reproach" (Sandys). ἀλαθέσιν λόγοις seems too emphatic for so simple a thought as "truly." Farnell's "whether on a true account we shake off" has more vigour. But it seems better to understand φεύγω here in the sense "I am put on my trial," though I can quote no non-Attic parallel. ἀλαθέσιν λόγοις will then be more natural: "whether our accusers speak truth."

⁴⁴ See Lecture VIII, pp. 165–171, 176–181.

⁴⁵ See Lecture VI, pp. 119–126.

⁴⁶ Cp. Farnell II, p. 342. See Lecture VII, pp. 152–157.

---

* Farnell *ad loc.* has not noticed that Schroeder's emendation, κατ' ἐμίν, is withdrawn in his *Pythien*.

† Farnell *ad loc.* Possibly he is misled by the well-known examples in Aristophanes; but cp. *Ol.* IX 111 (ὁρῶντ' ἀλκάν), *Pyth.* II 20 (δρακεῖσ' ἀσφαλές), *Nem.* IV 39 (φθονερὰ βλέπων), Aesch. *Septem* 498 (φόνον βλέπων). Or it may be that he is too much amused by his own version "to look tuneful," which does not correspond to the Greek.

‡ This meaning, which is attached to the word here by most commentators, is strictly unparalleled; but *Iliad* XXII 255, where it means "covenants," "agreements," and Aesch. *P.V.* 551, "order," "dispensation," of Zeus, seem reasonably close.

47 The onslaught upon Neoptolemus has been a fruitful theme of discussion—much of it obsolete because written before 1908, when the newly discovered fragments of the Sixth Paean were published (*Ox. Pap.* V, p. 841). The scholium 94 a (v. 64) remarks: οὐ μέμφοιτο ἂν οὖν με 'Αχαιὸς ἀνὴρ ἐπὶ τῷ δοκεῖν μικρολόγον παρεστακέναι τὸν Νεοπτόλεμον, ὅτι εἶπον αὐτὸν περὶ κρεῶν μεμαχῆσθαι καὶ διὰ τοῦτο ἀπολωλέναι. καθόλου γὰρ ἀπολογεῖσθαι βούλεται περὶ τοῦ Νεοπτολέμου θανάτου πρὸς τοὺς Αἰγινήτας. ἐκεῖνοι γὰρ ἠτιῶντο τὸν Πίνδαρον, ὅτι γράφων Δελφοῖς τὸν Παιᾶνα ἔφη ἀμφιπόλοισι μαρνάμενον μοιριᾶν* περὶ τιμᾶν ἀπολωλέναι. ἀπολογούμενος γάρ τι ἀντεισήγαγε τοῦτο ὁ Πίνδαρος, ὅτι οὐκ ἔφησε περὶ χρημάτων γεγονέναι τῷ Νεοπτολέμῳ τὴν μάχην, ἀλλὰ περὶ τῶν νομιζομένων τιμῶν τοῖς Δελφοῖς. This is an utter muddle, no doubt combining two or more separate and incompatible notes. περὶ κρεῶν . . . ἀπολωλέναι is precisely what Pindar says in the ode: why should not the Achaean say that it makes Neoptolemus μικρολόγον? The "defence" offered to the Aeginetans is ridiculous. Nothing about χρήματα occurs in the ode or in what we possess of the paean, the Neoptolemus-passage of which closes before our text ends: χρημάτων is perhaps due to a reading χρεῶν for κρεῶν in v. 42, which would allude to the story that Neoptolemus came to demand of Apollo a fine for causing Achilles' death. The rest of the answer, περὶ . . . Δελφοῖς, merely repeats the statement which is said to have annoyed the Aeginetans. A far better scholium, on v. 102 (150 a), quotes Aristodemus, the pupil of Aristarchus: μεμφθεὶς ὑπὸ Αἰγινητῶν ἐπὶ τῷ δοκεῖν ἐν Παιᾶσιν εἰπεῖν τὸν Νεοπτόλεμον ἐπὶ ἱεροσυλίᾳ ἐληλυθέναι εἰς Δελφούς, νῦν ὥσπερ ὑπεραπολογεῖται εἰπών, ὅτι οὐχ ἱεροσυλῶν ἐτελεύτησεν, ἀλλ' ὑπὲρ κρεῶν φιλοτιμηθεὶς ἀνῃρέθη. This at least makes sense, but arouses strong suspicion that the paean was lost even in the best days of Alexandrian scholarship; for there is no allusion to sacrilege in our part of the paean. Pindar may have returned to the subject later; but the important fact is that the paean, as we have it, provides an excellent reason for the annoyance expressed by the Aeginetans.

Aristodemus' ἱεροσυλία attracts one more than the other reasons offered. But it is highly improbable that Pindar mentioned it, for the paean shows that Apollo intended Neoptolemus' death and that the dispute at Delphi was merely a way by which the god's purpose was fulfilled. Aristodemus was probably thinking of Eur. *Androm.* 1095.

On the whole story of Neoptolemus at Delphi see Frazer's masterly note (II, pp. 254 ff.) on Apollodorus *Epit.* VI 14.

My own view of the correct reading in 31–35 is given in *A.J.P.* LXIV, pp. 325 f.

48 Schol. 56 a (v. 37), 150 a (v. 102).

49 Fr. 235 (43), vv. 4 f.:

τῷ παρέοντι δ' ἐπαινήσαις ἑκὼν
ἄλλοτ' ἀλλοῖα φρόνει.

50 V. 35: Πριάμου πόλιν Νεοπτόλεμος ἐπεὶ πράθεν. It is delightful that Bornemann (*Philol.* XLV, p. 604), who never saw the paean, thought these words flat after 'Ιλου πόλιν (v. 30). He thus became a perfect witness to Pindar's guilty conscience: Priam *must* be named, in pretended agreement with the paean.

51 Vv. 22 f.:   ψεύδεσί οἱ ποτανᾷ τε μηχανᾷ
σεμνὸν ἔπεστί τι· σοφία δὲ κλέπτει παρ-
άγοισα μύθοις.

---

* Drachmann prints μοιριᾶν, but records a variant μυρίαν: the editors of the papyrus print [μ]υρ[ιᾶν].

[52] Dissen's vast learning can find no other evidence for them. Farnell's quotations (*Cults* IV, pp. 426 f.) suggest that Pindar has arbitrarily turned an entertainment of god-guests into a reception of heroes.

[53] *Pyth.* IV 244 ff. Most scholars take it that the dragon is compared to *a* ship: Gildersleeve rightly sees an allusion to Argo.

[54] *Ol.* VI 46 f.: ἀμεμφεῖ ἰῷ μελισσᾶν. Farnell's note is excellent, as a matter of diction: he points to the Aeschylean use of reversing or correcting adjectives. But a scholium (78 g on vv. 46 ff.) does even better: the serpents duly ejected venom; which, however, miraculously changed into honey: ὡς ἐπὶ δρακόντων δὲ τὸν ἰὸν εἶπεν· ἀποβάλλει γὰρ ὁ δράκων ἰόν· βουλῇ δὲ θεῶν ὡς μελισσῶν ἄνθος ἡδὺ γίνεται καὶ οἷον ὡς μέλι.

[55] *Ol.* IX 91 ff.; cp. Lecture II, p. 29.

[56] The references for this paragraph are: Coronis, *Pyth.* III 17 ff.; treasure-house, *Pyth.* VI 10 ff.; "embowered . . . ," *Nem.* VI 43 f.; Cyrana, *Pyth.* IX 26 ff., 6, 17 ff., 121 ff.; Nestor, *Pyth.* VI 32 ff.; Telamon, *Isth.* VI 37 ff.; "from the darkness," *Isth.* VII 5 ff.; ἀλλὰ παλαιὰ κτὲ., *ibid.* 16 f.; "youth's fair bloom," *ibid.* 34–51.

[57] Schroeder *ad loc.* (*Pythien*, p. 62): "Man hat den Eindruck wie von einem Vasenbilde, und zwar einem meisterlichen."

[58] In Lecture III, p. 57, the Amphitryon-story was described as "a uniquely atrocious affair." But only definite and modern moral ideas were there in view: here we are concerned with an artless state of mind for which all that the gods do is *ex hypothesi* right.

[59] *Nem.* X 55–90, Bacchylides XVI, *Ag.* 205–249, *Or.* 1369–1502.

[60] Cp. Lecture II, note 7.

[61] Fr. 108 (123): τὰς δὲ Θεοξένου ἀκτῖνας πρὸς ὄσσων
μαρμαρυζοίσας δρακεὶς
ὃς μὴ πόθῳ κυμαίνεται, ἐξ ἀδάμαντος ἢ σιδάρου κεχάλκευται μέλαιναν καρδίαν
ψυχρᾷ φλογί, πρὸς δ' Ἀφροδίτας ἀτιμασθεὶς ἑλικογλεφάρου . . .

[62] Paean II 43 f. (Schroeder, p. 531): κείνοις δ' ὑπέρτατον ἦλθε φέγγος
ἄντα δυσμενέων Μελαμφύλλου προπάροιθεν.

NOTES TO LECTURE V

(pp. 94–116)

¹ Ode XVII, stance 1:

> Sors du tombeau, divin Pindare,
> Toi qui célèbras autrefois
> Les chevaux de quelques bourgeois
> Ou de Corinthe ou de Mégare;
> Toi qui possédas le talent
> De parler beaucoup sans rien dire;
> Toi qui modulas savamment
> Des vers que personne n'entend,
> Et qu'il faut toujours qu'on admire.

The poem is described by its author as "Galimatias Pindarique," and is more than half playful throughout; one gibe points at the celebrated "digressions":

> Car ta muse est accoutumée
> À se détourner en chemin.

Voltaire, like so many others, will casually mention Pindar as a great poet, e.g., in *stance* ix, where he addresses Van Haren as "Démosthène au conseil, et Pindare au Parnasse"; his own nineteenth ode (the least bad) he calls "pindarique." But in a letter to Chabanon (March 9th, 1772), where he discusses Pindar and Horace at some length, he calls the former "votre inintelligible et boursouflé Thébain"; and, writing to La Harpe (April 19th, 1772), he expresses "doubt whether in all the Greek odes a better couplet can be found than the second of this famous song:

> Recevez ma couronne,
> Le prix de ma valeur;
> Je la tiens de Bellone,
> Tenez-la de mon cœur."

That defies comment.

² The difference between a sentence of genuine prose and a mere series of verbal lumps can best be indicated by quoting Kipling (*His Private Honour*, in *Many Inventions*): "The men did their work and gave him very little trouble, but just when they should have been feeling their feet, and showing that they felt them by spring and swing and snap, the elasticity died out, and it was only drilling with war-game blocks. There is a beautiful little ripple in a well-made line of men, exactly like the play of a perfectly-tempered sword. Ouless's half-company moved as a broom-stick moves, and would have broken as easily."
Georg. II 156, I 468; *Odes* I x 9 ff. One delightful type of such interlacement is discussed in Conway's article. Starting from simple things like *nunc tempus equos, nunc poscere currus* (*Aen.* IX 12), he works up to various attractive instances and, above all, for the first time correctly explains Ar. *Ach.* 717, κἀξελαύνειν χρὴ τὸ λοιπὸν κἂν φύγῃ τις ζημιοῦν . . .

⁴ E.g., in *Nem.* V 2: ἐπὶ πάσας ὁλκάδος ἔν τ' ἀκάτῳ.

⁵ *The Revolt of Islam*, XI xiv. We have one passage, in the Sixth Paean (fr. 40 vv. 137 ff., Schroeder, p. 539) which is absolute Shelley (cp. Lecture II, p. 23).

⁶ The metaphor most often discussed and blamed for intolerable harshness, that celebrated "whetstone upon the tongue" (*Ol.* VI 82) has, I hope, at last been explained and justified (*Cl. Phil.* XXXVI, pp. 394 ff.): the verse means nothing

more offensive than "in addition to my power of song, I have high repute as a trainer of others in music."

[7] Wilamowitz (*Isyllos*, p. 166) fails to appreciate the iridescence of the language here: "Pindars rede ist eben grade in dem, was so besonders klingt, durchaus conventionell: ein durch jahrhundertlange übung gefestigter stil ist ihre voraussetzung." Where in earlier poetry do we find such a turn of style as this?

[8] Cp. Lecture II, pp. 35 f.

[9] See Appendix C.

[10] The date has at last been fixed by the list of victors in *Ox. Pap.* II, p. 85, which shows that the Pythian Games began in 582 B.C. The *inscriptio* says that this victory was gained at the 29th festival.

[11] It was the former (and future) Catana, with new settlers.

[12] According to Wilamowitz (*Hier. u. Pind.*, p. 1277), the *tyrannis* had been to a considerable degree a joint power (cp. 79^b, παίδεσσιν . . . Δεινομένεος): that is why (p. 1278) Hiero gave Aetna to his son, to be his own special and, as it were, private affair, not part of a family domain. Cp. note 16 below.

[13] Aeschylus also helped: ἐλθὼν τοίνυν ἐς Σικελίαν, Ἱέρωνος τότε τὴν Αἴτνην κτίζοντος, ἀπεδείξατο τὰς Αἴτνας, οἰωνιζόμενος βίον ἀγαθὸν τοῖς συνοικίζουσι τὴν πόλιν. (Vita, 9.)

[14] Cp. Horace, *Odes*, III iv 42-80, especially the stanza beginning *vis consili expers*.

[15] This superb passage and the equally famous description in Aesch. *P.V.* 351 ff. are compared by Fraccaroli (pp. 356 ff.), who believes that Aeschylus is working "after the example" of Pindar. "Aeschylus' picture is more interesting, Pindar's more sublime." Gellius (XVII 10 8, borrowed by Macrobius, *Sat.* V 17 7 ff.) quotes Favorinus' comparison of Pindar's passage with Virgil's (*Aen.* III 570 ff.), much to the latter's disadvantage.

[16] Boeckh (II 2, p. 226) thinks Hiero was present at the celebration. Wilamowitz (*Hier. u. Pind.*, p. 1280) thinks not: he believes (*ibid.*, p. 1279) that Hiero was sincerely set upon the Dorian στάθμη, and tried to establish it in the West of Sicily.

[17] V. 67, Ἀμένα παρ' ὕδωρ. It seems likely that Pindar, whose mention of the name looks emphatic (though the Amenas was an insignificant stream), takes it to mean "restless," and contrasts it with the stability in politics for which he prays. To this ἔτυμον in the next line points, meaning not merely truth but etymological exactness. See note 43 to Lecture VI. Headlam (*loc. ibi cit.*, pp. 150 f.) incidentally implies that our διακρίνειν ἔτυμον λόγον ἀνθρώπων does not allude to etymology. But if ἔτυμον here means no more than "correct," it is only padding.

[18] Fraccaroli (p. 350) notes the statement of Plutarch (*Apophth. Reg. et Imp.* 175), that in the conditions of peace made after Himera the Carthaginians agreed to cease the custom of human sacrifice. Though this can scarcely be credited—for how could Gelo make sure that the undertaking was fulfilled?—it provides a notable comment on Greek opinion about the meaning of the conflict. Fraccaroli rightly goes on to mention Phalaris.

[19] A scholium excellently notes: χαριέστατα ἐκ τοῦ θορύβου τὴν τῶν βαρβάρων ἀκοσμίαν ὑπεστήσατο, ὡς καὶ Ὅμηρος (*Il.* IV 436): ὡς Τρώων ἀλαλητὸς ἀνὰ στρατὸν εὐρὺν ὀρώρει.

[20] E.g., Dissen, Mezger, Croiset (pp. 341 ff.), Schroeder, Gildersleeve, and Schoder.

[21] Pp. 145-151. Rauchenstein was rector of the canton school at Aarau in Switzerland a hundred years ago, and a hearty enthusiast for Pindar, whom he long taught to his highest class. In 1843 his *Einleitung* appeared, a pamphlet which

duly begins with a section entitled "Ob und wie Pindar auf Gymnasien zu lesen sei"; for the school "programmes" of the two following years he wrote *Commentationes Pindaricae*. His old-fashioned, leisurely, even amateurish air must endear him to anyone who wades long through the marshes of research "literature." In his preface to the *Commentationes* he complains: "Editionem Schneidewini ne nunc quidem accepi." (Not "nondum," observe!) The work itself opens with a detailed and vigorous account of a Swiss shooting-match, which culminates in a super-Livian picture of the marker's ecstatic gambols whenever a bull's-eye is scored. How enraptured would Scott have been to meet in Anne of Geierstein's country a schoolmaster fit to exchange snuff with Jonathan Oldbuck!

22 VII, p. 114 (*De Officio Interpretis*): "Apparere ex his puto, si id, quod debuerit poeta pro rei quam tractandam recepit natura dicere, recte perceptum sit, facile etiam quomodo id dixerit perspici posse."

23 Letter to Saurin, Dec. 4th, 1765: "Je ne peux vous savoir mauvais gré de vous être un peu moqué de Gilles Shakespeare. C'etait un sauvage qui avait de l'imagination. Il a fait beaucoup de vers heureux, mais ses pièces ne peuvent plaire qu'à Londres et au Canada."

24 The metre is dactylo-epitrite, which demands a long syllable instead of τά in v. 6: cp. the corresponding v. 12 (ἀντικύρσαντες). Erasmus Schmid accordingly proposed ταί for τά, and was followed by Heyne. But such discrepancies undoubtedly occur (though seldom) in Pindar, and here the irregularity is justified by his wish to represent the ship's motion.

25 Cp. Lecture II, pp. 39 f.

26 Schmid (p. 605) and Dornseiff (*Pindar*, p. 38) understand the passage as here explained; save that the latter translates ἀναβάλεο by "das schiebe hinaus!" Cerrato writes: "ἀναβάλεο = 'exspecta paullisper' Heyne e Boeckh—Tu riceverai una corona ben più nobile, più degna—Heyne, Cookesley, Turner"; and in his translation gives: "Intessere corone è facile; ma tu attendi un momento, chè la Musa mia una te ne vuole comporre d'oro."

27 Croiset, however (p. 276), has no misgiving: "Pour lui, cette tache difficile n'est qu'un jeu." Of the numerous passages contradicting this, it suffices to quote *Ol.* II 83–90, X 97, *Pyth.* IV 247 f., *Nem.* III 76–82, VI 53–59, *Isth.* VIII 5–9.

28 It is clear that the coral must be red: otherwise the colour-scheme would be spoilt, since ivory and white coral are so much alike. Pindar does not mention its colour because (so far as the meagre evidence goes) not only was the red kind more highly prized: in his day it was probably the one kind known in Greece. Theophrastus, nearest to him in date of our authorities, has never heard of white coral (*De Lapid.* 38): τὸ γὰρ κουράλιον . . . τῇ χρόᾳ μὲν ἐρυθρόν, περιφερὲς δ᾽ ὡς ἂν ῥίζα· φύεται δ᾽ ἐν τῇ θαλάττῃ. Others speak of the red as at least more familiar. Pliny reports (XXXII ii 11): *probatissimum quam maxime rubens;* Dioscorides (*De Mat. Med.* V 121): ἄριστον δέ ἐστι τὸ πυρρὸν τῇ χρόᾳ. Dion. Perieg. 1103 says of the Indian Ocean: πάντη γὰρ λίθος ἐστὶν ἐρυθροῦ κουραλίοιο. Further, λείριον is no obstacle, for red lilies were known, or heard of. Theophrastus (*Hist. Plant.* VI vi 3) writes: . . . καὶ ἔτι δὴ μᾶλλον ἡ τῶν κρίνων [sc. χροιά], εἴπερ δή, καθάπερ φασίν, ἔνια καὶ πορφυρᾶ ἐστίν. Dioscorides (*ut sup.* III 106) says: φασὶ δέ τινες καὶ πορφυρᾶ ἄνθη κρίνου γίνεσθαι. Pindar's description of coral as a flower agrees with the universal ancient opinion, that it was a plant which turned into stone when taken out of the water: cp. Pliny (*ut sup.*), *forma est ei fruticis, colos viridis, bacae eius*

candidae sub aqua ac molles, exemptae confestim durantur et rubescunt . . . aiunt tactu protinus lapidescere, si vivat.

[29] For Homer's "lies" cp. Lecture IV, p. 86 and note 51, Lecture VIII, p. 167 and note 7.

[30] *Od.* XIX 562 ff.

[31] *Theog.* 27 f.: ἴδμεν ψεύδεα πολλὰ λέγειν ἐτυμοῖσιν ὁμοῖα,
ἴδμεν δ', εὖτ' ἐθέλωμεν, ἀληθέα μυθήσασθαι.

[32] Cp. *Ol.* I 36, VII 21, IX 35 ff., and Lecture III, pp. 52 f., 55 f.

[33] Fr. 194 (205): Ἀρχὰ μεγάλας ἀρετᾶς,
ὤνασσ' Ἀλάθεια, μὴ πταίσῃς ἐμὰν
σύνθεσιν τραχεῖ ποτὶ ψεύδει.

[34] This date is now attested by *Ox. Pap.* II, p. 88.

[35] Though the "eleventh" was composed before the "tenth," it was placed and numbered after it by the Alexandrian editors, who regarded it as the τόκος mentioned in X 9—an "extra" appended to X as compensation for its lateness. Cp. scholium I b: προσθεὶς ἔτερόν τι ᾠδάριον τὸ ἑξῆς.

[36] Cp. XI 5 (ὑστέρων ἀρχὰ λόγων) and 14 (κελαδήσω).

[37] So Fraccaroli (pp. 297 f., 302), who sees this in the emphatic and repeated allusions to χρόνος. Boeckh. (II 2, pp. 198, 202) believed that Hagesidamus was a grown man when the poem arrived, to be sung at some anniversary. Dornseiff (*Pindar*, p. 89) thinks that only the Sicilian visit intervened between the two odes.

[38] Mezger on v. 12 remarks: "Lokri war eine grosse Handelsstadt, durch deren, von Zaleukos herrührende Gesetze, alle Willkühr im Handel ausgeschlossen und die Creditverhältnisse scharf geregelt waren."

[39] *Il.* XXI 257 ff.: ὡς δ' ὅτ' ἀνὴρ ὀχετηγὸς ἀπὸ κρήνης μελανύδρου
ἂμ φυτὰ καὶ κήπους ὕδατι ῥόον ἡγεμονεύῃ,
χερσὶ μάκελλαν ἔχων, ἀμάρης ἐξ ἔχματα βάλλων·
τοῦ μέν τε προρέοντος ὑπὸ ψηφῖδες ἅπασαι
ὀχλεῦνται· τὸ δέ τ' ὦκα κατειβόμενον κελαρύζει
χώρῳ ἔνι προαλεῖ, φθάνει δέ τε καὶ τὸν ἄγοντα·
ὡς αἰεὶ Ἀχιλῆα κιχήσατο κῦμα ῥόοιο.

[40] Wilamowitz (p. 221) suggests that Pindar sneeringly alludes to the channel made by Heracles when he cleansed Augeas' stable. But all other ancient allusions assert that he diverted a river for the purpose. Hyginus (*fab.* 30) writes: *flumine ammisso totum stercus abluit;* Diodorus (IV xiii 3) and Quintus Smyrnaeus (VI 234) name the Alpheus; Pausanias (V i 10) says τοῦ Μηνίου τὸ ῥεῦμα. The best that can be done to explain ὀχετός as a river is done by Gildersleeve: "The river-bank has yielded, and the doomed city settles into a deep channel of woe."

[41] For βρέχετο πολλᾷ νιφάδι (v. 51) see Lecture IV, note 35.

[42] This may have included the violent happenings that preceded the institution at Olympia: if it did not, we should postulate another book. Farnell (II, p. 82) writes: "Pindar must have derived this account of Herakles' defeat at the hands of the Moliones and his vengeance upon them from some early prose source: it was handled by Pherekudes and Istros (Müller, *F.H.G.* I, p. 81, Pherekudes, fr. 36); it has no resemblance to his epic adventures or the twelve 'labours,' but has the air of realistic history," etc. Wilamowitz (pp. 221, 224) regards the fact that "Heracles is no solitary champion, but leader of an army, which . . . suffered defeat" as evidence that Pindar used a prose authority which rationalized Her-

acles. (It is possible that both the victor's name, Ἀγησίδαμος, and his father's, Ἀρχέστρατος, helped to suggest this form of the narrative.)

As for the Olympian Festival, Wilamowitz suggests that the book dealt with successes won at Olympia by Pheidon of Argos; but see Farnell (II, p. 84). Luebbert holds that Pindar's details had not been published earlier, and that the poet is here attacking the stories (Pausanias V vii) put forth by the Elean priests concerning the origin of the Olympian festival etc. Why he should choose as his vehicle an ode written for the remote Locrians is not explained.

43 *Purg.* IX 16 ff.

44 In a letter to Herder of July, 1772 (about *Götz von Berlichingen*): "Es ist alles nur gedacht."

45 Περὶ ὕψους VII 3: ὅταν . . . ἐγκαταλείπῃ τῇ διανοίᾳ πλεῖον τοῦ λεγομένου τὸ ἀνα θεωρούμενον.

46 Huret, p. 60. "Je crois . . . que, quant au fond, les jeunes sont plus près de l'idéal poétique que les Parnassiens qui traitent encore leurs sujets à la façon des vieux philosophes et des vieux rhéteurs, en présentant les objets directement. Je pense qu'il faut, au contraire, qu'il n'y ait qu'allusion. La contemplation des objets, l'image s'envolant des rêveries suscitées par eux, sont le chant: les Parnassiens, eux, prennent la chose entièrement et la montrent; par là ils manquent de mystère; ils retirent aux esprits cette joie délicieuse de croire qu'ils créent."

Further allusion to "les jeunes"—that is, the *Symbolistes*—will be found in Lecture VIII (pp. 157 ff.).

47 See Cornford's article for a possible allusion in this passage to νοῦς = Hermes and λόγος = Pan.

NOTES TO LECTURE VI

(pp. 117–137)

¹ *Tristia* IV x 49. The words (*Odes* IV ii 11 f.) of Horace, *numeris fertur lege solutis*, allude only to the dithyrambs which he has just mentioned. Dithyrambs could be scanned, but did not show strophic correspondence. Horace no doubt profited by the conversation of the rhetor Heliodorus, *Graecorum longe doctissimus*, who accompanied him on the journey to Brundisium (*Sat.* I v 2 f.), especially if he was the Heliodorus praised by Marius Victorinus, p. 94 k (cited by Orelli-Baiter-Mewes *ad loc.*): . . . *Iuba noster, qui inter metricos auctoritatem primae eruditionis obtinuit, insistens Heliodori vestigiis, qui inter Graecos huiusce artis antistes aut primus aut solus est.* For his studies in the *minutiae* of Pindaric scansion see Keil III, pp. 427 f. We owe sundry fragments to him: 161–167 (177, 178 a).

² *Euripides the Rationalist*, pp. 217–230.

³ P. 240 (preface to *Pyth.* I).

⁴ Pp. 133 f., where he speaks of *Isth.* V (VI). "L' I. V comincia con un'immagine tolta dal propinare: 'Come nel fiorente convivio ...' Questa immagine, su cui tanto il poeta si ferma, non poteva lasciare un'impressione debile, e perciò si capisce come nel mito di Eracle che va a visitare Telamone, l'immagine stessa torni a prendere il centro del quadro, vv. 37 sqq. ... Si può osservare ancora, che questa principale impressione del bere dispone l'immaginativa a reppresentazioni secondarie analoghe, sulle quali si aggira in gran parte la tropica dell'ode. Ci sarà forse chi tratterà queste osservazioni d'oziose, e dirà che ciò che è casuale non ha che fare con l'arte; perchè c'è chi tratta di casuale tutto ciò che non sa spiegare o non deriva da un atto della conscienza o della volontà. A me pare però che il cercare nelle opere d'arte anche quello che si sottrae in certo modo alla nostra elaborazione consciente, ma che non è però meno elaborato per un processo spontaneo—a me pare che il cercar questo, non sia affatto tempo gittato."

⁵ Scholium 23 a (v. 15): ἄριστα ὁ Πίνδαρος τὸ ἐγκώμιον εἰργάσατο· ἐν δὲ τοῖς ἑξῆς σφόδρα ἀκαίρῳ παρεκβάσει ἐχρήσατο. Boeckh (II '2, p. 337): "Interpretis munere si quis rite fungi constituerit vix illi ulla oda tantam, quantam haec, difficultatem obiiciet." Mezger (p. 288): "Die Erklärung des Gedichtes bietet den Auslegern Schwierigkeiten dar, wie kaum ein anderes." Wilamowitz (p. 259): "Pyth. 11 zumal ist eins der dunkelsten seiner Lieder." Gildersleeve, p. 358. Farnell, II, p. 147.

⁶ The inquiry, "What connexion, if any, exists between Pindar's narrative and Aeschylus' *Agamemnon* and *Choephoroe?*" is perhaps less important than has been supposed. If we could prove beyond question that one poet deliberately chose the other's work for imitation, what difference, after all, would such a demonstration make? None whatever to our enjoyment of all three works. If the plays had vanished utterly, we should think and feel concerning the Eleventh Pythian just as we think and feel now. The only result would be interesting and perhaps valuable knowledge of the manner in which one of the two poets used his material. Interesting, because we should welcome further acquaintance with a great man; but that (so far) has nothing to do with literature. Valuable—and here is the sole justification for our original query—because knowledge of Aeschylus' relation to Pindar may benefit us *elsewhere*: we may be justified in attempting to solve an

enigma in (say) the *Septem* by adducing some Pindaric passage. Has it ever been shown that such help is, in fact, available? In *Nem.* X 6, the striking word μονόψαφον reminds us of *Suppl.* 373 and of what we already know concerning the lost plays of the trilogy. We receive a thrill of pleasure, but no information. Certainly Farnell had a right to say (II, p. 318): "it is likely enough that Pindar had seen this Aeschylean trilogy and that in his imagination of Hupermnestra he was influenced by it." But elsewhere (I, p. 229) he actually asserts that Pindar alludes "to her trial for that disobedience and her acquittal"!

Our question becomes, for most scholars: "Which of the two imitated the other?" But that is really two questions: Is there imitation? If so, which is the imitator? Fraccaroli, who answers the second question with "Aeschylus," offers a list (p. 505) of echoes on which he bases his affirmative reply to the first. But of his eleven items only three appear to deserve serious attention:

a) vv. 20 f., Κάσσανδραν πόρευσ' 'Αχέροντος ἀκτὰν παρ' εὔσκιον and *Ag.* 1160 f.:

νῦν δ'ἀμφὶ Κωκυτόν τε κἀχερουσίους
ὄχθους ἔοικα θεσπιῳδήσειν τάχα.

b) v. 30, ὁ δὲ χαμηλὰ πνέων ἄφαντον βρέμει and *Ag.* 1030: νῦν δ' ὑπὸ σκότῳ βρέμει.

c) v. 32, χρόνῳ, v. 36, χρονίῳ σὺν "Αρει, and *Ag.* 46, χρόνῳ, 702, ὑστέρῳ χρόνῳ, 807, χρόνῳ.

Even of these, only the first (perhaps the second also) would strike a reader who was not listening for echoes. I am even less convinced by those which Bowra (see below) adduces in the course of his argument that the ode belongs to 454 B.C., which view commits him to the assertion that Pindar had Aeschylus in mind, not *vice versa*. For instance, that κακολογία, "a small and rather special point," helps to prove Pindar's knowledge of *Agamemnon* will be conceded by few who remember how fond he is of mentioning κακολογία. Fraccaroli (p. 505) uses the same point for the opposite purpose: "Eschilo, e questo è segno che dei due egli è l'imitatore, amplifica ed incalza più di Pindaro il concetto ..." (*Ag.* 456–474). For the general question, as to knowledge of Pindar in the fifth and fourth centuries, see Farnell, II, pp. xiii–xvi: he offers (p. xiii) only one good parallel between our poets, but it is extremely good—*Isth.* VIII "34–35" (40 f. in his own text, 37 f. in Bowra's) and *P.V.* 922–925. He might have added *Ol.* IV 9 and *P.V.* 365: ἷπος, a rare word, is used by Pindar in the same connexion—Typhos and Aetna—as Aeschylus' ἱπούμενος.

Next, supposing the imitation to be nevertheless admitted, we are to decide which poet copied the other. The trilogy was certainly produced in 458, but the date of the ode is disputed. Thrasydaeus won twice at Pytho. Inscriptio a says: γέγραπται ἡ ῷδὴ Θρασυδαίῳ παιδὶ νικήσαντι κη' Πυθιάδα (= 474), καὶ λγ' (= 454) δίαυλον ἢ στάδιον ἄνδρας. For which victory was the ode written? The point was discussed in Alexandrian times, for Inscriptio b says: Θρασυδαίῳ Θηβαίῳ σταδιεῖ· γέγραπται μὲν ἡ ῷδὴ τῷ προκειμένῳ νικήσαντι τὴν λγ' Πυθιάδα διαύλῳ. οὐκ εἰς τὴν τοῦ διαύλου δὲ νίκην γράφει, ἀλλ' εἰς τὴν τοῦ σταδίου.This obscure report must mean:"The ode was written after the second victory, but applies only to the first." It is a bungling result of controversy. I imagine that: first, the ode was recognized as belonging naturally to 474; second, supposed imitation of *Agamemnon* forced the later year upon the critics. Some modern scholars, of whom the most recent is Bowra (*C.Q.*, pp. 129–141) assign our ode to 454; but after studying their arguments I cannot think them nearly so strong as those for 474. Not only do vv. 13 f. imply that Thrasydaeus is still quite young: Pindar says nothing of two victories won by him, which would be inconceivable were the later year correct. In v. 14, no doubt, we read that he brought home a τρίτος στέφανος, but v. 43 shows that his father won at Pytho, and vv. 46 ff. that some other relative won at Olympia (see, further, note 20).

If, then, there was imitation, the imitator was Aeschylus.

[7] For Stesichorus cp. the scholiast on Aesch. Choeph. 733. For Pherecydes cp. the scholiast on v. 17 (25 b): ἰδίως δὲ φησιν ὁ Πίνδαρος Ἀρσινόην εἶναι τὴν Ὀρέστου τροφόν· Φερεκύδης δὲ Λαοδάμειαν λέγων αὐτὴν τὸν ταύτης παῖδά φησιν ἀνῃρῆσθαι ὑπὸ Αἰγίσθου νομιζόμενον Ὀρέστην εἶναι. In connexion with the latter statement note vv. 17 ff., where at first sight Κλυταιμήστρας χειρῶν ὑπὸ κρατερᾶν and ἐκ δόλου δυσπενθέος look tautological. But the second phrase implies "saved him by substituting her own child, a device that broke her heart." The words are (no doubt) brief and obscure if they have to carry so much meaning; but that is often the result when Pindar follows an earlier narrative (cp. note 35 to Lecture IV).

Bowra (Gk. Lyr. P., p. 27) surmises that Pindar invented "Arsinoa" (and Aeschylus "Cilissa") "for the sake of disagreement with Stesichorus," Schroeder (ad loc.) that it was to avoid recalling the death of her son. These suggestions are so weak that they give by contrast much plausibility to the etymology offered on p. 126.

[8] We need not, however, interpret his silence as implying approval; and certainly we have not the least right to think that he applauds matricide because it was commanded by Apollo. Yet Wilamowitz writes (p. 263): "Sie [sc. ὀρθοδίκας ὀμφαλός and ἱερὰ θέμις (vv. 9 f.)] haben die Tat des Orestes gerecht befunden, an der die Menschen sich oft stossen. Was dem Gotte wohlgefällig ist, ist recht, und Recht muss Recht bleiben." Similarly von Leutsch, p. 183. Bowra (C.Q., p. 139) says roundly that "it was Apollo who instigated the deaths of Aegisthus and Clytaemnestra . . . the moral of the myth is that Apollo punishes the presumptuous doer of violence." Pindar does not even hint that Apollo instigated Orestes' act. There exists, indeed, no evidence at all, in literature or in the arts, that Apollo's fiat was heard of before Aeschylus. The scholium on Eur. Or. 268, δὸς τόξα μοι κερουλκά, δῶρα Λοξίου, reports that these words are based on Stesichorus (fr. 40 Bergk), who said that Orestes received a bow and arrow from the god—no doubt (as Bowra remarks, Gk. Lyr. P., p. 132) "to keep off the Furies." Probably this gift and this purpose were transformed, gradually and in anti-Delphian circles (to which of course Pindar was a complete stranger) into the story that Apollo actually initiated the matricide. Schmid (pp. 483 f.) is entirely unjustified in his statement that "Aischylos ist hier Schüler des Stesichoros" etc.

[9] δαμαζομέναν, thus taken, is not so easy as in the other explanation, but not too hard for Pindar; and Bergk need not have substituted δακναζομέναν (particularly in view of the preceding ἔκνιξεν). The arguments for Fennell's view of the passage are strong. First, we banish the tautology of ἑτέρῳ . . . κοῖται; secondly, we get an excellent balance: ἔννυχοι . . . κοῖται corresponds to ἔκνιξεν . . . χόλον, ἑτέρῳ . . . δαμαζομέναν to Ἰφιγένεια . . . πάτρας.

Now, why does Pindar in this short myth stay for an elaborate weighing of reasons, and that without a decision between them? Rauchenstein (Philologus II, pp. 204 f.) sees here only a device for bringing into the light two other evils of the house, but the emphatic πότερον . . . ἤ . . . can hardly mean so little as that. Let us look forward. The next words are (vv. 25 ff.):

> τὸ δὲ νέαις ἀλόχοις
> ἔχθιστον ἀμπλάκιον καλύψαι τ' ἀμάχανον
> ἀλλοτρίαισι γλώσσαις·
> κακολόγοι δὲ πολῖται.

The universal assumption that νέαις ἀλόχοις means Clytaemnestra is beset with difficulties. She was not young at this time, in any version of the legend. Pindar himself mentions the sacrifice of Iphigenia, which occurred before the siege began, when—at any rate according to the most familiar version—she was adolescent. Homer (*Il.* IX 144 ff.) makes Agamemnon say that he has three daughters, any of whom is old enough for marriage in the tenth year of the siege. All this suggests that Clytaemnestra was nearer forty than thirty when she murdered Agamemnon. A second argument is simpler and equally cogent: apart altogether from arithmetic, a νέα ἄλοχος is surely one who has not long been married, and it would not occur to Pindar (or anyone else) to use the phrase of a woman who, on his own showing, has borne a daughter and who at some unstated time after that daughter's death has taken a lover. Thirdly, on the prevalent view, the whole expression reads strangely. νέαις ἀλόχοις ἔχθιστον ἀμπλάκιον should mean "a sin most hateful to young wives": hence Hermann was constrained to translate unnaturally "quod tamquam hostis nocet," and Hecker to suggest αἴσχιστον in place of ἔχθιστον. The irresistible conclusion is that νέαις ἀλόχοις points not to Clytaemnestra but to some others—or other, for the plural of course should not be pressed. In fact, the whole of vv. 22–28 alludes to some discussion of her crime, certainly to popular outcry, possibly to a trial; in this the chaste indignation of a young wife or wives was prominent. Perhaps the incitements of Apollo's oracle, so dominant in Aeschylus (*Choeph.* 269 ff.), were, in Pindar's authority, replaced by the admonitions of Hermione (already Orestes' wife: cp. Apollodorus, *Epit.* VI 14), who overbore him in argument: he excused his mother on the score of Iphigenia, she condemned her because of Aegisthus. In Pindar's authority, I say, for (on any view) this part of the narrative reads like a *résumé* of some fuller account already known to his audience. Such a surmise calls to our mind the *Oresteia** of Stesichorus rather than anything Hesiod is likely to have written, or than anything we read in Homer and Aeschylus.

10 It is hard to believe that, even if Stesichorus made a great deal of her, he made so much that Pindar had that reason only to mention her so often. Those who believe in the later date for this ode will point to *Agamemnon;* but the Cassandra-scene there, for all its magnificence, is an episode; and even if Pindar were definitely following Aeschylus, though he would give her a place, would he for that reason mention her thrice—as often as Agamemnon himself?

---

* For an admirable account of this work see Bowra, *Gk. Lyr. P.*, pp. 125–133. Schroeder adds the numerous passages in the *Odyssey* and Hesiod (in view of frr. 93–100 Rzach). But Homer in none of his accounts says a word of the matricide; as to Hesiod, we cannot tell. (Homer does indeed in one place, *Od.* XI 421 ff., notably refer to Cassandra.) The *Oresteia* was a poem in two books and must have influenced Pindar more strongly than the short accounts in Homer and Hesiod.

After writing this note I observe that Schmid (p. 477) also thinks of possible discussions in Stesichorus of Clytaemnestra's guilt; but he offers no real evidence.

[11] Gildersleeve, giving a list of the persons in the story, actually forgets to include Cassandra: "This [sc. ἴσχει ... φθόνον] is true of all the figures in the piece— Agamemnon, Klytaimnestra, Aigisthos, Orestes." Bornemann, however, writes (*Philologus* LII, p. 45): "Wozu aber die zweimalige Erwähnung der Kassandra, und zwar das erste Mal mit so viel Worten, dass G. Hermann die Richtigkeit der Ueberlieferung bezweifelte?" (His own answer is utterly unconvincing: "Es trägt doch zweifelsohne zur Linderung des Jammers bei, zu wissen, dass selbst bevorzugte Menschenkinder darin verflochten sind; als ein solches wird aber die κόρα Πριάμου bezeichnet...")

[12] So Rauchenstein (*Philol.* XXVII, p. 170) actually proposed to emend, taking ἄφαντος from one MS. and πέλει from his own sense of fitness. For this he was rewarded by Schroeder with "pessime." It should have been "inficete." Intellectually, Rauchenstein was right: he caught Pindar's meaning, but missed his imagination.

[13] Fraccaroli's position is ambiguous. In his version (p. 509) he gives "ma l'uom d'umili sensi oscuro passa"; but in his note (p. 500) he translates by "ma colui chi è in basso stato oscuramente si agita," and remarks later: "ogni sua attività resta ignorata." Tycho Mommsen gives "in Geheimen da haust."

[14] Cp. Lecture III, pp. 67 f.

[15] "The social virtues" (or "noble coöperation") seems a better explanation than "achievements open to all." Though the latter offers an admirable opposition to μέμφομ' αἶσαν τυραννίδων, it makes Iolaus and the Dioscuri (59 ff.) extremely poor examples. Why choose them with such particularity, especially Iolaus, who was not specially noted for achievement in general? But the former explanation fits all three heroes perfectly: Iolaus was famed as the loyal squire of Heracles; and the Dioscuri presented the greatest example in Greek legend of noble coöperation—an example not only celebrated in the Tenth Nemean but pointed at by the language of this very stanza. And this explanation is appropriate enough to μέμφομαι κτὲ.

[16] Unfortunately a *locus vexatus:* see Schroeder's apparatus. I discern no satisfactory meaning in his   τίς ἄκρον ἑλών
ἡσυχᾷ τε νεμόμενος αἰνὰν ὕβριν
ἀπέφυγεν;
The chief *crux* is ἄτᾳ, and I find no tolerable sense in his φθονεροὶ δ' ἀμύνονται|ἄτᾳ. Is it, indeed, possible Greek? The most likely reading appears to be:
... τέταμαι, φθονεροὶ δ' ἀμύνονται.
τᾶν εἴ τις ἄκρον ἑλών
ἡσυχᾷ τε νεμόμενος αἰνὰν ὕβριν
ἀπέφυγεν, μέλανος ἂν ἐσχατιὰν
καλλίονα θανάτου στείχοι, γλυκυτάτᾳ γενεᾷ
εὐώνυμον κτεάνων κρατίσταν χάριν πορών.

[17] The only dissentient is Bornemann (*Philol.* LII), who finds in this ode a *Todtenlied* for the victor's father. He had already found a similar mare's nest in the Seventh Nemean, "emending" right and left to justify himself.

[18] P. 291. He gives a full conspectus (pp. 288-295) of the historical discussion down to 1880, the date of his edition.

[19] P. 506.

[20] Pausanias and his intrigue with Persia have often been suggested, notably by Fraccaroli (pp. 501 ff.) and by Watkiss Lloyd (pp. 406 f.), who identifies Agamem-

non and Cassandra with Pausanias and Xerxes' daughter, and contrives to discern "detailed allusion to Amyclean sanctities" into the bargain. But though the date (474) which I accept for the ode suits Pausanias, he does not fit Pindar's language, which implies established despotism. As for Theban domestic affairs, Rauchenstein's answer (*Philol.* II, pp. 196 f.) is convincing, that the Theban oligarchy, however oppressive, could not naturally be called a τυραννίς. Nor could Sparta, despite her kings, as Perthes supposes, à *propos* of Pausanias. Bowra (*C.Q.*, p. 139), while confining Pindar's meaning to Theban affairs, finds the τυραννίς in the dangerous ascendancy of Athens, which had won Oenophyta in 457. Is this likely? A famous passage in Thucydides (III 37 2) makes Cleon use the word in that application. But whereas the meaning in Thucydides is clear as daylight—τυραννίδα ἔχετε τὴν ἀρχήν—nevertheless αἶσα τυραννίδων, so used, would be grasped by very few. As for Sicily, Bowra (p. 135), opposing the date 474 in favour of 454, says: "If in his denial of tyrannies Pindar refers to his late host in Sicily, it is curious that a man so serious as he was should after this write three odes for Hieron, *Pythian* III, probably in the same year of 474, *Pythian* I in 470 and *Pythian* II, probably in 468." It is important, not only here but in many other passages, to realize that Pindar writes what will please his patron of the moment: *Nemean* VII rather amusingly shows that this did not always pay (see Lecture IV, pp. 83–86).

21 Coppola, p. 116; Rauchenstein, *Philol.* II, p. 209; Wilamowitz, p. 263.

22 So in the *Aratea* of Cicero *claret, ardet*, etc. often mean simply *est*, being applied to stars. Cp. Virg. *Aen.* XI 701, *haud Ligurum extremus, dum fallere fata sinebant*, where Conington remarks: "as if with him to live was to deceive." A more elaborate example occurs in *Aen.* III 641 ff. In Dante, *Purg.* IV 6, "un'anima sovr' altra in noi s'accenda," the verb means, precisely, "exists (—as a soul)."

One or more of the Alexandrian scholars saw the point clearly: preserved in an otherwise dull scholium occur the words ἠχεῖ, οἷον ζῇ.

23 *Pyth.* IV 60, χρησμὸς μελίσσας Δελφίδος, where the scholiasts are rather copious on the theme ὅτι τὰς περὶ τὰ θεῖα διατελούσας καὶ Μελίσσας ἔλεγον. They report that Pindar elsewhere says ταῖς ἱεραῖσι μελίσσαις τέρπεται (fr. 144 = 158), and quote the historian Mnaseas of Patara, who related (*F.H.G.* III, p. 150) that priestesses κατέπαυσαν σαρκοφαγοῦντας τοὺς ἀνθρώπους πεῖσαι τῇ ἀπὸ τῶν δένδρων χρῆσθαι τροφῇ, and that one of them, named Melissa, discovered the use of honey and water as a drink; she called the creatures μέλισσαι after herself and cared greatly for them. Didymus is reported by Lactantius, *Div. Inst.* I 22, to have said in his Ἐξήγησις Πινδαρική: *Melissea Cretensium* [cp. Virg. *Georg.* IV 152] *regem primum diis sacrificasse . . . huius duas fuisse filias, Amaltheam et Melissam, quae Iovem puerum caprino lacte ac melle nutrierint . . . ; Melissam vero a patre primam sacerdotem Matri Magnae constitutam, unde adhuc eiusdem Matris antistites Melissae nuncupantur.* See also Dr. A. B. Cook's article, one of the most interesting citations in which is Josephus, *Arch.* V v 200 f.: Δέβωρα προφῆτις, μέλισσαν δὲ σημαίνει τοὔνομα. A vaguer sanctity surrounds the bee in Hippolytus' address to Artemis (Eur. *Hipp.* 73 ff.): no scythe or sheep may enter her undefiled meadow,

ἀλλ' ἀκήρατον
μέλισσα λειμῶν' ἠρινὴ διέρχεται,

καθαρώτατον γάρ τι ζῷον ἡ μέλισσα, as a scholium there remarks. Cp. Ar. *de Gen. Anim.* 761 a 4: οὐ γὰρ ἔχουσιν οὐθὲν θεῖον, ὥσπερ τὸ γένος τὸ τῶν μελιττῶν. Robert-

Tornow has collected and discussed all the ancient literary evidence on the symbolic and mythological meaning of bees and honey: cp. especially pp. 92 f., 154.

[24] Aesch. *Ag.* 687 f., Soph. *Ajax* 430 ff. Anyone who doubts that Pindar could thus play on words should consider the passages quoted in note 45 below. The idea is in our passage confirmed by the shape of Pindar's phrase (5 f.), where ὀνύμαξεν draws attention to the *ipsissimum verbum.*

[25] Farnell does not solve the difficulty, but remarks (I, p. 318), using Paean IX, that a "sacred marriage" must have been periodically enacted in the Ismenion—"a ritual-drama of which we have other examples in Hellenic cult." As for the invitation to heroines only, not heroes, all he can suggest (II, p. 225) is that, if the κῶμος of Thrasydaeus happened on the day of the sacred marriage,"we may understand why Pindar only invokes the heroines of Thebes, not the heroes, not even his favourites Herakles and Iolaos: the bride Melia would desire female helpers and comrades." Wade-Gery and Bowra escape the difficulty by translating: "Where now he bids assemble together/The folk that inhabits the Princesses' land." But it is hard to believe that ἐπίνομον governs ἡρωΐδων.

[26] Other instances of ταράσσω intransitive are Plato, *Rep.* 564 B, *Hipp. Min.* 373 B. Schroeder, in his commentary, takes the verb as governing φωνάν, understood from the preceding clause; so Liddell and Scott.

[27] The topic imposed on his Muse is, to be sure, bisected by ἤ . . . ἤ . . . , but the "vagrancy" is only between the victor and his father—practically one subject (especially when contrasted with the myth), as Pindar's constant practice and language show.

[28] This led Wilamowitz to his harsh and complicated explanation (*Hier. u. Pind.*, p. 318).

[29] Or, which for our purpose is the same thing, Pindar may well have thought so: from the root seen in ἀραρίσκω.

[30] *Pyth.* X 53 f.

[31] Eustathius, excellent critic as he is, actually says as much: ἀσάφειαν ἐπιτηδεύεται ἐν πολλοῖς (Drachmann III, p. 288, 11): ἡ ἀσάφεια, ἥν ἐπίτηδες πολλὴν ἐπισύρεται . . . (*ibid.*, p. 290, 2 f.); he regards Lycophron as in this respect Pindar's successor.

[32] Most scholars either make ἔπειτα suddenly equivalent to ἐπεί, or prefix an illicit "for" to the correct "afterwards." Two, however, face the word squarely. Bornemann, whose article on *Ol.* VI seems to me perverse, nevertheless translates ἔπειτα simply by "nachher" (p. 595); but he adds no comment. Mr. W. A. Stone (p. 115) writes: "ἔπειτα is not strictly correct, as no new fact is given."

[33] Farnell (II, p. 43) remarks: "The eloquence of the funeral oration of Adrastos in the *Thebais* may have contributed to the later prevalence of the tradition of Adrastos as the ideal orator (cf. Turtaios, fr. 2, 8 [9, 8 Diehl] γλῶσσαν δ' 'Αδρήστου μειλιχόγηρυν, Plat. *Phaedr.*,p. 269 B)." In the Euripidean *Supplices* he delivers set speeches over the Seven.

[34] See Lecture IV, pp. 86 f.

[35] Wilamowitz (p. 308) does worse than ignore it. "Verhehlen wollen wir nicht, dass die beiden Heroinen, die zu nichts weiter da sind, als einem Gotte ein Kind zu gebären und sich seiner schleunigst zu entledigen, und dass der Grossvater, der nach Delphi fährt, um zu erfahren, wer ihm die Tochter verführt hat, und befriedigt nach Hause zurückgeht, als der Gott sich selbst zu der Tat bekannt hat,

ziemlich ebensowenig befriedigende Erfindungen sind wie der Raub des Pelops durch Poseidon." But he goes on: "Aber das verschwindet völlig vor der Darstellung, die hier auf der Höhe von *Pyth.* 9 steht, wenn nicht noch höher." To be sure! "Beauty is its own excuse for being." Fraccaroli (p. 235) chooses for once to be inappropriately facetious: "Evadne pure, che, si vede, non voleva mancare di rispetto agli esempi materni, fece all' amore con Apollo."

36 He might, e.g., have developed the detail mentioned by the scholiasts on v. 29 (48 a): τὴν Εὐάδνην ἐκτεθεῖσαν Αἴπυτος εὑρὼν ἀνέλαβεν—"What have we here? Mercy on's, a barne; very pretty, barne!" etc.

37 Wilamowitz, *Isyllos*, p. 178: "Die doublette macht sich im gedichte selbst nicht gut; der hinweis, dass die tochter mit dem verheimlichen ihres fehltrittes weniger glück hatte als die mutter, wird dem modernen fast anstössig. Pitana hat gar nichts zu tun, als die Evadna zu gebären." The tone of this magisterial note shows how vital it is to appreciate Pindar's symbolism.

38 Gildersleeve (pp. 171 f.) has much of what follows, particularly emphasis on vv. 100 f., and "here there is clearly a recurrent two."

39 This example arises from my interpretation of v. 83 (cp. Lecture V, note 6).

40 In fact, this is perhaps the only ode in which Pindar's symbolism operates by intellect rather than imagination.

41 Though Ortygia was practically a part of Syracuse.

42 Wilamowitz, p. 246, note 3. It is unfortunate that this outbreak should occur in comment on a poem containing the words μαθόντες λάβροι ἄκραντα γαρύετον.

43 Cp. the famous etymology in Aesch., *Ag.* 681 ff., already mentioned in note 24. Pindar has a few other examples: in *Ol.* X 54, ἀλάθειαν ἐτήτυμον is (despite "la vraie vérité," whatever that may be) a bald tautology unless we take it to mean "Truth which does indeed repel oblivion (ἀ-λάθ-εια)"; in *Pyth.* I 68, ἔτυμον λόγον alludes to an etymology of the name Ἀμένας (see Lecture V, note 17); for *Nem.* VII 63, κλέος ἐτήτυμον, see Bury's note. That ἐτυμώτατον in our passage is attached to φέγγος by grammar, matters little or nothing: it suffices that the idea of etymology should be named, as in *Pyth.* I 68 (above).

The doctrine that ἔτυμος and its congeners regularly point to etymology was propounded by Verrall in Appendix II of his *Septem* and elsewhere. It was examined by Headlam (pp. 138, 158), who destroyed many of Verrall's assumptions. His results may be thus summarized: (i) ἔτυμος etc., though they can refer to etymology, by no means always or even normally so refer; (ii) other words, e.g. ὀρθῶς, often refer to it. Though Headlam did good service by disproving fancies of Verrall, he went too far in (i), if the Pindaric examples offered above are sound.

44 After writing the first draft of this long ago, I found that I had been anticipated by Verrall (p. 136): "the fair opportunity for a τοπή offered by his patron's name, ὁ Θηρῶν ... the metaphor of 'chasing success' is Pindaric; see μέριμναν ἀγροτέραν." In Claudian, *De Con. Stil.* III 250, Thero is the name of a huntress-nymph.

45 Ἴαμος and ἴον, *Ol.* VI 56; κερδώ (a certain emendation) and κερδαλέος, *Pyth.* II 78; Ἱέρων and ἱερῶν, fr. 94 (105). See further Stanford, *Ambiguity in Gk. Lit.*, pp. 130 ff.

46 Despite Plut. *Theseus* 33, τὸ γὰρ ἄνω τοὺς Ἀττικοὺς ἀνεκὰς ὀνομάζειν καὶ ἀνέκαθεν τὸ ἄνωθεν, it seems impossible to believe that ἀνεκάς is a synonym of ἄνω. Since ὑψηλόν is predicative, we should then have tautology here; and other passages show that, whereas ἄνω means merely "upwards," ἀνεκάς usually, if not always

signifies "with an upward swing" or "upwards by a twist." The clearest example is Aristophanes, *Daedalus*, fr. 188 (Kock):

ὁ μηχανοποιός, ὁπότε βούλει τὸν τροχὸν
ἱμᾶν (ἐᾶν MS., ἐλᾶν Meineke) ἀνεκάς, λέγε· χαῖρε, φέγγος ἡλίου.

Crates, fr. 10, as cited by Suidas, runs: τὸν αὐχέν' ἐκ γῆς ἀνεκὰς εἰς αὑτοὺς βλέπων. The wording of this, no doubt, is incorrect; but the sense must be "throwing back the neck and looking up at them." No stress can be laid on Pherecrates fr. 169 (Kock), τουτὶ τί ἐστιν ; ὡς ἀνεκὰς τὸ κρίβανον, for ἀνεκὰς τό is Valckenaer's emendation (p. 285) of ἂν ἐκάστῳ τό, and even so the line is obscure. Eupolis fr. 50 (Kock), ἀνεκάς τ' ἐπαίρω καὶ βδελυρὸς σὺ τὸ σκέλος (Suidas), also needs correction. Kock proposes ἀνεκάς γ' ἐπαίρω καὶ βδελυρῶς σοι τὸ σκέλος, which is unconvincing. More satisfactory would be ἀνεκάς γ' ἐπῆρω καὶ βδελυρῶς σὺ τὸ σκέλος—an allusion to the κόρδαξ or the σίκιννις. In any case an upward swing of the leg is indicated. *Vespae* 15 ff. runs:

ἐδόκουν αἰετὸν
καταπτόμενον εἰς τὴν ἀγορὰν μέγαν πάνυ
ἀναρπάσαντα τοῖς ὄνυξιν ἀσπίδα
φέρειν ἐπίχαλκον ἀνεκὰς εἰς τὸν οὐρανόν.

There the simple "upwards" suits well; but, had Aristophanes meant only that, would he not have written ἄνω φέρειν ἐπίχαλκον εἰς κτὲ.?

Together with παλιντράπελον, ἀνεκάς provides sound reason for seeing a wheel in our passage, instead of the more familiar balance (*Il.* VIII 69 ff., XXII 209: cp. Soph. *Ant.* 1158 and Jebb *ad loc.*) which Dissen suggested here. So much was asserted by Jacobs (*ap.* Dissen), Mezger, Fennell, Gildersleeve, Fraccaroli (p. 191), and Jebb (*J.H.S.* III, p. 167). The further step, of recognizing in this wheel-like alternation of joy and sorrow the more impressive picture of "Fortune's Wheel," was taken by Headlam (see next note). Professor D. M. Robinson, independently but later (1934), wrote: "The idea of the Wheel of Fortune I believe to be as old as Pindar, *Ol.* II 23" (note 1 on p. 505 of the article quoted at the close of the next note). I reached the same view (see below) in ignorance of what these two scholars had written.

47 Pindar, by an imaginative process that one is tempted to describe as half-accidental, invented the idea of Fortune's Wheel which ultimately became so familiar and elaborate. But the *full* conception was in antiquity not common. (The rudder and the cornucopia were far more frequent: they have other meanings, of course, than the wheel and do not now concern us.) The earliest subsequent passage of the kind mentions a spherical *stone* (Pacuvius *fr. incert.*, *ap.* Ribbeck): Fortunam insanam esse et caecam et brutam perhibent philosophi, Saxoque instare in globoso praedicant volubili.
Cebes (*Tab.* ll. 101 ff. Jerram) describes τύχη as γυνὴ . . . ἑστηκυῖα ἐπὶ λίθου τινὸς στρογγύλου . . . οὐ μόνον τυφλή, ἀλλὰ καὶ μαινομένη καὶ κωφή. Plutarch (*Fort. Rom.* 4) gives her a σφαῖρα (and a κέρας). Lysippus (Callistratus, *Stat.* 698) made a statue of Καιρός standing on a ball. The stages in the development of "Fortune and her Wheel" appear to be those next enumerated, so far as literature is concerned.

1. Pindar here describes the alternations of joy and sorrow in language plainly suggesting a *wheel*.

2. Herodotus (I 207) uses the *word* κύκλος. Croesus tells Cyrus that κύκλος τῶν ἀνθρωπηΐων ἐστὶ πρηγμάτων· περιφερόμενος δέ, οὐκ ἐᾷ ἀεὶ τοὺς αὐτοὺς εὐτυχέειν.

(That he does not add οὐδὲ ἀτυχέειν is of course due to the point that he wishes to make.) Herodotus was familiar with Pindar's work, as is shown (e.g.) by the famous passage (III 38) about Cambyses, the envoys and νόμος. This notion—simply that there is a wheel in human affairs—became familiar: Aristotle, for instance, quotes it (*Phys.* 223 b 24, *Prob.* 916 a 28) as a well-known remark.

3. Sophocles has three passages:

a) *Trach.* 131 f., quoted in the text: equivalent to the Herodotean passage just mentioned.

b) A papyrus fragment (fr. 575, Pearson II, p. 213) which ends:

πάντ]α γὰρ τροχοῦ δίκην
]. τις κυκλεῖ τύχη

That is the first explicit allusion to the *Wheel of Fortune*.

c) Fr. 871 (*ut sup.* III, p. 70):

ἀλλ' οὑμὸς αἰεὶ πότμος ἐν πυκνῷ θεοῦ
τροχῷ κυκλεῖται καὶ μεταλλάσσει φύσιν·
ὥσπερ σελήνης ὄψις εὐφρόνας δύο
στῆναι δύναιτ' ἄν οὔποτ' ἐν μορφῇ μιᾷ,
ἀλλ' ἐξ ἀδήλου πρῶτον ἔρχεται νέα
πρόσωπα καλλύνουσα καὶ πληρουμένη,
χὥτανπερ αὐτῆς εὐπρεπεστάτη φανῇ,
πάλιν διαρρεῖ κἀπὶ μηδὲν ἔρχεται.

The notion of "God's rapid wheel" is blent with that of the moon's waxing and waning. See Headlam's note in *J.P.* XXX, pp. 291 ff. (quoted by Pearson, *ut sup.*): he cites Hippodamus the Pythagorean (Stob. *Flor.* 98 71), mentions Fortune's Wheel (see preceding note), and concludes that "all these passages derived from older Pythagorean phrasing" (see p. 134, and note 55).

4. The next definite allusion is much later and shows that "the Wheel of Fortune" had now become a stock phrase: Cic. *In Pis.* 10 22, *In quo* [sc. *convivio*] *cum illum saltatorium versaret orbem, ne tum quidem fortunae rotam pertimescebat.*

5. A little later we find for the first time the concept of *Fortune standing on a wheel*, in Ovid, *Ex Ponto* II iii 56: *fieri comitem stantis in orbe deae* (the context proves that the *dea* is Fortune). Tibullus I v 70 is almost as explicit: *versatur celeri Fors levis orbe rotae.*

I can cite no other ancient examples of this complete presentation. For a very full treatment of the idea in the Middle Ages see Professor Patch's work. He omits, no doubt because it does not actually mention Fortuna, a passage from Cedrenus (ed. Par. 142), of the eleventh century, so Herodotean that it is worth quoting in full. οὗτος ὁ Κῦρος αἰχμαλωτεύσας πολλοὺς βασιλεῖς καὶ ἔχων αὐτοὺς ἐν φυλακῇ προσέταξε κατὰ ἑορτὴν τοῖς ὤμοις σύρειν τὸ τετράιππον ἅρμα, ἐν ᾧ αὐτὸς ἐπωχεῖτο. εἷς δὲ ἐκ τῶν βασιλέων ἐπιστρεφόμενος συχνῶς ἑώρα τοὺς τροχοὺς ἀναβαίνοντας. ὃν θεασάμενος ὁ βασιλεὺς καὶ θυμωθεὶς ἤρετο τίνος χάριν πυκνῶς στρεφόμενος οὐκ ἐᾷ τὸ ἅρμα κατ' εὐθεῖαν τρέχειν· ὅσπερ μετὰ φόβου ἀπελογήσατο· τοὺς τροχοὺς ὁρῶν ἀναβαίνοντας καὶ καταβαίνοντας ἐννοῶ τὸ ἄστατον τοῦ βίου, πῶς τὰ κάτω ἄνω γίνεται καὶ τὰ ἄνω κάτω. ὅπερ ἀκούσας ὁ Κῦρος καὶ αἰσθόμενος ἔλυσεν αὐτόν, καὶ τιμήσας φιλοφρόνως ἀνεβίβασεν ἐν τῷ ἅρματι, καὶ ἐλευθερίας ἠξίωσεν οὐ μόνον αὐτὸν ἀλλὰ καὶ τοὺς λοιπούς.

Dr. A. B. Cook (*C.R.*, p. 421 a) says that the Wheel of Fortune was "no metaphor, but an actual cult-utensil, probably a wooden wheel hung up in the temple and consulted as oracular, being made to revolve by means of a rope (hence the rope in Hor. *Od.* 3.10.10)." Cp. his *Zeus* II, p. 57, n. 6.

For a remarkable early mosaic of Fortune's Wheel see Robinson's article, "The Villa of Good Fortune at Olynthos," p. 505. "Near the center of the mosaic . . . is the wheel of good fortune; it has four outer circles and an inner dotted circle, while its spokes form a St. Andrew's cross . . . The interpretation of the wheel as a symbol of good fortune is confirmed by the inscription, ΑΓΑΘΗΤΤΧΗ." Professor Robinson in a letter kindly informs me about the date. "The mosaic with ἀγαθὴ τύχη I should date about 410 B.C., as the figured mosaics in the villa show the influence of the style of Callimachus as well as of the Parthenon and are similar to scenes of vases of Meidias. These mosaics might be as early as 425 and possibly as late as 380, but my own feeling is that they belong to the last quarter or even decade of the fifth century. I can only argue from the coins found in the house and from general analogies." The addition of ἀγαθή might be held to spoil the value of this mosaic for a discussion the very basis of which is Fortune's fickleness. Nevertheless, the symbol chosen—quite irrationally—bears witness to the fact that a wheel was familiar as a presentation of Fortune. See, further, Robinson's *Excavations at Olynthus*, Pt. X, pp. 512 f.

[48] *Trach.* 131 f.:   ἀλλ' ἐπὶ πῆμα καὶ χαρὰ
πᾶσι κυκλοῦσιν, οἷον ἄρκτου στροφάδες κέλευθοι.

[49] Down to the close of the fifth century this sign for *theta* was frequent all over the Greek world: see the tables in Roberts, pp. 382 ff. It occurs repeatedly in the famous inscription enumerating the states which combined to destroy the Medes at Plataea. This was cut—one can almost say—at the very moment when Pindar was composing our ode; and for this pan-Hellenic monument a script would of course be chosen that was most widely familiar. The serpent-base, on which KVΘNIOI and the like may still be seen, rises now in the Hippodrome at Constantinople; it is reproduced in Roberts, p. 259.

[50] That four-spoked wheels were common is proved (if necessary) by the François Vase and by many others, such as the Dipylon vase shown in Baumeister (III, fig. 74). Pindar himself (*Pyth.* II 40) calls Ixion's wheel a τετράκνημος δεσμός. The scholium (73 b) on that passage, which states that among men wheels have six spokes, among gods eight (*Il.* V 7 23), is accordingly inaccurate for Pindar's time, at least with respect to earthly wheels.

[51] Fr. 385 (Nauck). He is least successful, as it happens, with *theta*, then written Θ in Athens: κύκλος τις ὡς τόρνοισιν ἐκμετρούμενος,
οὗτος δ' ἔχει σημεῖον ἐν μέσῳ σαφές.

[52] Purg. XXIII 31 ff.

[53] XVIII 70–114. The form of M is to be understood as a Gothic capital: see the edition of Scartazzini-Vandelli (1932), pp. 775 ff.

[54] To the number belongs *Isth.* VIII 15 f.:
δόλιος γὰρ αἰὼν ἐπ' ἀνδράσι κρέμαται,
ἑλίσσων βίου πόρον.

It is good evidence for Bury's view (see his notes *ad loc.*, on *Nem.* III 8 and on *Isth.* III β 18) that the Greeks connected αἰών with ἄημι: otherwise we must see tautology in αἰών and βίου πόρον. But I cannot accept his idea that "ἐπικρέμαται is chosen with reference to the preceding metaphor of the Tantalean stone." The verb has much the same meaning as in *Ol.* VII 24, and with δόλιος implies that βίος is at the mercy of some tricksy spirit which "bloweth where it listeth," so that human life moves like a tacking ship. "The wind overhead is full of cunning shifts that drive the life of man upon a winding course."

I take this opportunity to express my admiration for Bury's editions of the Nemean and the Isthmian Odes, especially as they are now little esteemed and (so far as appears) never exercised the influence they deserved. Bury combined with an exact knowledge of Greek idiom a delicate sense of poetry—a combination necessary to those who edit Pindar, but rarely displayed. Had his judgment equalled his other merits, he would have been the finest of Pindaric scholars: unhappily, his nimbleness of mind too often lured him into freakishness, as (for example) when on *Isth.* III β 36 he explained ἔχει as the imperfect of χέω. One result is that even those who most admire Bury are usually compelled to reject his novelties of reading or interpretation. Another result is more lamentable: his excesses tend to discredit his entirely sound conception of the manner in which Pindar should be studied.

[55] Professor I. M. Linforth's admirably full and cautious book has convinced me that there was no "Orphic religion," at any rate before 300 B.C. No Orphic "church" existed with distinct adherents, priesthood, a definite ritual, and peculiar doctrine. The word "Orphism" meant nothing more precise (and nothing less momentous) than our phrase "personal religion." A Greek devoted to it was taught by ritual to believe sacred stories which varied from region to region; he received doctrines, a rule of life, and hopes concerning the world to come, which all varied from one centre of worship to another. On p. 173, summing up the evidence earlier than 300 B.C., Linforth writes: "If we must call something Orphism, it must be the entire religion of teletae and mysteries with their magical ritual, the poems of Orpheus and others concerning god and man which were inherent in poems and ritual."

For the Wheel in mystery-religions see (e.g.) Lobeck, pp. 797 ff.; Rohde II, pp. 218 f.; Harrison, pp. 589 ff.

[56] Nevertheless, a few notes may be of some use:

i) In view of Farnell's strangely confused note on vv. 57–60 (backed by mistranslation, I, p. 12) it should be insisted once again that μέν and δέ make the sentence, however surprising, as clear as daylight. First, those souls of the dead which commit sins in the world of the dead are punished here on earth. Secondly, sins committed in our world are punished below. "Earth and Hades are mutual hells," as Gildersleeve puts it. αὐτίκα I take as excluding a view, *prima facie* natural, that sins committed in Hades are punished in Hades, after a sojourn on earth.

ii) That εὐορκία, and no other virtue, is specifically attributed to the blessed (v. 66) suggests some definite allusion, probably to the treachery of Capys and Hippocrates towards Thero, their cousin and benefactor. Cp. the scholium 173g (on v. 95).

iii) Editors have not observed the allusion to Κρόνου τύρσις (v. 70) in Philo *ap.* Euseb., *Praep. Evang.* I 10 37 A: ἐπὶ τούτοις ὁ Κρόνος τεῖχος περιβάλλει τῇ ἑαυτοῦ οἰκήσει, καὶ πόλιν πρώτην κτίζει τὴν ἐπὶ Φοινίκης Βύβλον.

iv) Bergk (II, pp. 707 f.) identifies the Διὸς ὁδός (v. 70) with the λιπαρὰ ὁδός of fr. 10 (30), and both with the Milky Way.

[57] Diog. Laert., *Life of Pythagoras*, VIII 14.

[58] In fr. 26 (Diels), a passage of twelve lines, describing the alternate working of Νεῖκος and Φιλότης upon the four elements:

ἐν δὲ μέρει κρατέουσι περιπλομένοιο κύκλοιο . . .

ταύτῃ δ' αἰὲν ἔασιν ἀκίνητοι κατὰ κύκλον.

[59] See Professor Gilbert Murray's discussion in the Appendix to Harrison's *Prolegomena*, pp. 660 ff. (esp. pp. 668, 670 f.).

[60] Reproduced (Taf. 10) and described (text vol., pp. 47 ff.) by Furtwängler. He says that the wheels are "aufgehängt als Andeutung des Herrenhauses," which is hard to credit. (This Munich picture is by no means the only presentation of wheels in Orphic vase-paintings.)

[61] "Voll recipirt ist die orphische Religion nur in dem engeren Kreise der Gläubigen." E. Meyer II, p. 747.

[62] Dornseiff (*Pindars Stil*, p. 24), discussing Pindar's use of plural for singular, asserts that συνετοί in v. 85 refers to Thero.

[63] *Pyth.* XII 2.

[64] Fr. 105 (119).

[65] Emped. fr. 115 (Diels), especially

τῶν καὶ ἐγὼ νῦν εἰμί, φυγὰς θεόθεν καὶ ἀλήτης,
Νείκεϊ μαινομένῳ πίσυνος.

[66] The explanations of Wilamowitz (p. 494) and Farnell (*ad loc.*) only emphasize the oddity by their feebleness. The former says that Rhea is put in to balance Persephone, the latter that she is mentioned as a way of clearly distinguishing Cronos.

[67] The ancient scholars were at a loss, and Farnell says only that Pindar "could not in delicacy name Hera" and "as he wishes to name a great goddess, Athena occurred most naturally to him; and the cult-facts show that she had far more importance in the religion of Thebes than Hera." But what had Thebes to do with Acragas?

[68] Moreover, Peleus (v. 78) could hardly be thought of without Thetis, or Cadmus (*ibid.*) without his daughters (cp. v. 23).

[69] Boeckh writes (p. 121): "Demaretae causa heroinarum ex ipsius gente fata exponit, tristia primum, mox faustissima."

[70] Diodorus, indeed, says (XI 26) that she herself struck the coins. After their defeat at Himera, the Carthaginians τῆς σωτηρίας παραδόξως τετευχότες ταῦτά τε δώσειν προσεδέξαντο καὶ στέφανον χρυσοῦν τῇ γυναικὶ τοῦ Γέλωνος Δαμαρέτῃ προσωμολόγησαν. αὕτη γὰρ ὑπ' αὐτῶν ἀξιωθεῖσα συνήργησε πλεῖστον εἰς τὴν σύνθεσιν τῆς εἰρήνης, καὶ στεφανωθεῖσα ὑπ' αὐτῶν ἑκατὸν ταλάντοις χρυσίου νόμισμα ἐξέκοψε τὸ κληθὲν ἀπ' ἐκείνης Δαμαρέτειον.

NOTES TO LECTURE VII

(pp. 138-164)

1 See Lecture I, p. 16, and note 45 thereon.

2 Despite what has been said earlier (pp. 30, 35, 91–93), special explanation seems needed here, since gloom enters so markedly into the narratives.

3 Vv. 20 f. διορθῶσαι: Pindar means to "edit" the current version.
In the next lines we already find *chiaroscuro*. On the father's side is glorious birth, Tlepolemus being a son of Heracles the Zeus-begotten; but his mother Astydameia was the daughter of Amyntor, whose life and city (Ormenium in Magnesia) were taken by Heracles (Apollodorus II vii 7, Diodorus IV 37).

4 P. 366, note 2. Boeckh (II 2, p. 174) had remarked that Pindar could not "falsa dicere inter Rhodios de Rhodiorum, quae tum erant, certaminibus."

5 The phrase recurs almost exactly in *Pyth*. III 80, where

εἰ δὲ λόγων συνέμεν κορυφάν, Ἱέρων, ὀρθὰν ἐπίστᾳ

probably means: "If you can understand the truth of that supreme traditional maxim ἐν παρ' ἐσλὸν κτὲ." In *Paean* VIII 3 f., τοιᾷδε κορυφᾷ σάμαινεν λόγων introduces Cassandra's outcry concerning Paris as born for the ruin of Troy: there too it means "momentous utterance,"certainly not "I give you the gist of her lament."

6 I do not mean that the significance of 'Ρόδος for Pindar and his hearers has escaped all modern readers, but that its value for the whole poem has passed unnoticed. The actual "meaning" of 'Ρόδος has often been mentioned. Gildersleeve on v. 62 (αὐξομέναν πεδόθεν) writes: "Allusion to the name 'Ρόδος, the Island of the Rose. Hence also βλάστε (v. 69)." Coppola (p. 161): "Rodi, dunque, appare come un fiore che nasce sulla superficie infinita delle acque." Perrotta (p. 167): "Rhodi che sboccia come un fiore dal mare." Mme. Yourcenar (p. 239): "Rhodon: la rose. L'île consacrée au soleil portait le nom d'une Nymphe et d'une fleur." Wilamowitz (p. 364): "Die Roseninsel." Robinson (p. 62): "Rosy Rhodes." Dr. A. S. Way in his translation writes of "a flower." Dornseiff, in his, gives "keimte" for βλάστε. Mr. Billson gives, in the same place, "An island rose emerging into light": that is exquisite.

7 II 2, p. 177.

8 Boeckh II 2, p. 178. Cp. Fraccaroli, p. 255.

9 The vagueness of the scholiast on v. 74 (173 a) shows that no Alexandrian editor knew of any such calamity: ἐκ τούτου ἐμφαίνει ὅτι ἄνωθεν αὐτῷ περὶ τὸν οἶκον συμφορὰν συνέβη γενέσθαι.

10 In order to make the gradation steeper, Pindar seems to have exaggerated Tlepolemus' offence. The scholiast reports on v. 27 (49 a): οἱ δὲ περὶ Ἀγίαν καὶ Δέρκυλον φασὶν ἀκούσιον τὸν φόνον γενέσθαι. Others, on v. 20 (36), write: . . . ἄκων ἀναιρεῖ· ἐπὶ γὰρ βοῦν βουλόμενος ἀκοντίσαι τὸ σκύταλον ἔρριψε κατὰ τοῦ Λικυμνίου. The scholium on v. 30 (54) is probably mere fancy: τῇ δόξῃ ὁ Πίνδαρος ἔπεται τῶν ἱστορούντων (whom?) διὰ τιμάς τινας καὶ ἀρχὰς (suspiciously vague) τὸν Τληπόλεμον εἰργάσθαι τὸν φόνον· διὰ γὰρ τοῦ χολωθεὶς τὸ τοιοῦτον ὑποφαίνει.

11 ἀτέκμαρτα. Here too, perhaps, the poet exaggerates for his own purpose of *chiaroscuro*. Diodorus (V 56) says that their lapse occurred διὰ τὴν σπουδήν: they wished to anticipate the Athenians, who also had been warned.

12 Farnell I, p. 38: "Pindar in his pleasant wayward fashion reverses the time-order of the events." Illig has some sensible remarks on Pindar's defiance of chronology, e.g., pp. 59 ff.

13 "Loquutionem ductam suspicor ab fructibus pendentibus" (Dissen).

14 A good example of κορυφαί as used to suggest a flowering plant is *Ol.* I 13: δρέπων μὲν κορυφὰς ἀρετᾶν ἄπο πασᾶν.

15 πίπτω is of course often used as the passive of βάλλω in compounds.

16 Cp. Dante, *Purg.* XVI 113 f.:   pon mente alla spiga,
ch'ogn'erba si conosce per lo seme.

In his essay on "Compensation" Emerson writes: "Cause and effect, means and ends, seed and fruit, cannot be severed; for the effect already blooms in the cause, the end pre-exists in the means, the fruit in the seed."

17 σκληρότερον καὶ διθυραμβωδῶς εἶπε.

18 The scholiast on v. 48 (93 a) paraphrases by τὸν ἐπέραστον τῆς παρθενίας ὑπολύοι δεσμὸν τῷ ἥρωϊ Πηλεῖ.

19 Bury (*Isthmians*, p. 33) emphasizes this: "Pindar has made *deliverance* the note of this epinician hymn." See also his note on diction (pp. 135 f.).

20 Here only in the work of Pindar and of Aeschylus do we find quite certain "imitation" (see Lecture VI, note 6). The likeness of vv. 36 ff. and *P.V.* 922–925 cannot be accidental.

21 Her speech has raised other questions besides χαλινὸν παρθενίας (see above). νεικέων πέταλα (v. 47) can no longer, after Farnell's discussion, be explained by the Sicilian πεταλισμός. Three considerations will help us. First, garlands of victory are in the poet's mind, and similarity of sound could suggest garlands not of νείκη but of νίκη, though Themis no doubt thinks here of the quarrel itself more than of success therein. Secondly, Pindar somewhere may (fr. dub. 339 = 326) have called fountains Ὠκεανοῦ τὰ πέταλα. Thirdly, Bacchylides (V 186) writes that Pherenicus by his victory brings to Hiero εὐδαιμονίας πέταλον, which means, as Jebb remarks *ad loc.*, that "victory is the leaf which εὐδαιμονία puts forth." Taken together, these passages suggest that πέταλον was felt to mean not only an actual leaf but something that πετάννυται—an "unfolding" or "development." Thus Ὠκεανοῦ πέταλα would be far less harsh, not precisely implying that Ocean is a tree, but meaning "extensions of Ocean." We conclude, then, that νεικέων πέταλα describes a quarrel that will or may spread, and that the phrase is helped by the epinician associations of πέταλα.

δίς has caused needless perplexity. "Let us not have two quarrels. The dispute between Zeus and Poseidon is settled by giving Thetis to a mortal. Let us have no further dispute as to who that mortal shall be: let us fix at once on Peleus." That explains also the seeming tautology of εὐθύς and αὐτίκα. To avoid it by understanding εὐθύς as governing Χείρωνος is, indeed, consonant with good Greek.* Still, the sense is in this context clumsy, after ἐς ἄφθιτον ἄντρον, and there seems no reason to be so emphatic about Chiron. We should, then, take εὐθύς as "without more ado."

22 Aesch. *Ag.* 32, τὰ δεσποτῶν γὰρ εὖ πεσόντα θήσομαι, quoted by Farnell, will not serve. Had Aeschylus chosen to say τοὺς δεσπότας γὰρ εὖ πεσόντας ᾐσθόμην, omitting the next line, τρὶς ἓξ βαλούσης κτὲ., the parallel would have been sound.

---

* Hermann altered it to εὐθύ. That would be necessary in Attic; but if Homer says ἰθὺς Διομήδεος, why should Pindar not say εὐθὺς Χείρωνος?

[23] See Farnell's admirable note (II, pp. 198 f.) on the reading and meaning of these lines and the next. He inclines, however, to believe that "the metaphor is drawn from ball-play, tossing up and dropping balls."

[24] I ix 23 f.:   nullus Amor cuiquam faciles ita praebuit alas
                ut non alterna presserit ille manu.
On this Postgate quotes *Romeo and Juliet*, II ii 177 ff.

[25] A hint of this idea, that what soars must fall, is heard now in the proem—heard now, for ἔσφαλεν (v. 15) is too natural in that context to strike our attention at the moment. So, too, the Ship of Insolence is sunk by the Daughter of Justice (vv. 10 ff.). That great name, Justice, may arouse misgiving. Is Pindar's last ode, then, coloured by the thought of God as a whimsical owner of men, idly playing with them as some child with his bird; and does it nevertheless proclaim His just government of the Universe? Such contradictions are too deep for Pindar, as for others, to solve. We may reflect, if we choose, that the man who wrote
            As flies to wanton boys, are we to the gods;
            They kill us for their sport,
wrote in the same play: "The gods are just." Or are we to construct a formal reconciliation: the moment's happiness in sunshine is all that even divine benevolence can bestow on so frail and momentary a being as Man? Pindar says no word in resolution of the enigma.

[26] In v. 40b I retain, instead of Bury's οἴνας (accepted by Bowra), Boeckh's ᾄσσει, offered *metri gratia* for the MS. ἀίσσει. Wilamowitz (p. 408, n. 1) finds ἀίσσει "undenkbar" when used of a sapling; but, apart from its great symbolic value (a feature of which he perceives nothing in Pindar), he might have remembered *Iliad* XVIII 55 f., and *Georgics* II 363 f.

[27] Farnell (II p. 304), with beautiful adroitness, translates it "rulings," but the idea of kingship should be emphasized more; yet Sandys' "rule" is too definite. Pindar is intentionally vague: he hints that Athens and Sparta were subject to Aeacus, but of course cannot openly put forth an idea so utterly at variance with legend and probability. Perhaps it is best to translate the whole sentence: "were fain to bring each his willing homage."

[28] L. V. Schmidt (pp. 436, 438) has shown that Pindar was much concerned about Deinis' future, warning him against the wrong ἔρωτες (vv. 3 ff.) and in the penultimate stanza urging him to guard against "evil communications" by association with righteous poets. This concern may partly account for the iridescence of the latter passage: χλωραῖς, used primarily of the dew, suggests youth also, and ᾄσσει reminds us of those "glorious feet" (v. 47) which gained victory in the *diaulos* at Nemea.

[29] L. V. Schmidt (pp. 440 ff.) has anticipated most of this paragraph.
    The Sapling gives imaginative, poetical, unity to this ode. Unity of thought is provided by a clear moral connexion between the three parts, which may be called after Aeacus, Odysseus, and Deinis.

[30] See Lecture VI, pp. 130-137.

[31] The verbs used of him (vv. 37 ff.) are in the past tense.

[32] Cp., e.g., Dissen *ap.* Boeckh, p. 498; Sandys, p. 453.

[33] Perrotta (p. 230): "Questo è cattivo gusto che nulla può giustificare, tanto è barocca l'immagine."
    Long before Heywood, Athenaeus (37 b) tells a racy story of a house that gained

the name τριήρης from just such another frolic—a house, moreover, situated in this same city of Acragas.

34 Paton (pp. 180, 261) explains this by the custom of a modern Greek musician in a circle of dancers, who sticks on his face the silver coins given them by onlookers.

35 P. 655.

36 P. 311.

37 P. 270; see also p. 272.

38 Fr. 109 (124). See note 62 to Lecture IV.

39 See (e.g.) Dissen *ap.* Boeckh, p. 493; and Fennell *ad loc.* Wilamowitz (p. 312) accepts the old idea that Pindar is aiming at "Simonides and his famous φιλοκέρδεια," apparently without considering how obviously such a gibe recoils on Pindar himself. He then goes off (led by his unfortunate insistence on Pindar's career instead of his poetry) into a long disquisition upon Simonides, Hiero, and poor Bacchylides.

40 *Pyth.* VI 49: σοφίαν ἐν μυχοῖσι Πιερίδων.

41 V. 38. The only editor, apparently, to find trouble here was Erasmus Schmid, who emended with κομίζων, not attractively.

42 Frr. 136, 137 (Kaibel): in the second passage someone proposes to buy a calf δέκα νόμων. Pollux (IV 79 f.) says that νοῦμμος was in use among the Dorians of Italy and Sicily.

43 Fr. 162 (Kaibel). Sophron, like Epicharmus, wrote in Syracuse, but "flourished" later, in the second half of the fifth century.

44 Of the forty-five odes, fourteen have now been discussed with respect to symbolism; one has been dealt with by Fraccaroli (see Lecture VI, p. 118); two, the Second Pythian and the Fifth Isthmian, will be treated in Appendices A and B. As for the remaining twenty-eight:

i) I regard not only *Ol.* V but also *Isth.* III and IV as spurious (see Lecture VIII, pp. 171–175).

ii) *Ol.* IV and XI, *Pyth.* VII and XII, *Nem.* II are (with the possible exception of *Pyth.* XII) too slight, as well as too short, to "carry" symbolism. Pindar painted frescoes, not miniatures.

iii) Three important odes may be said actually to exclude symbolism, each for a different reason. The Tenth Pythian is Pindar's earliest extant work, composed when he was but twenty, and clearly had not yet conceived this method; for an opportunity faced him which he would have seized a few years later: the noble who commissioned this ode was named Thorax ("Breastplate"). The Thirteenth Olympian was written against the grain for a vulgarian whom Pindar regarded with scarcely half-concealed distaste (see Lecture I, pp. 18–21). In the Sixth Nemean he was hampered by instructions to use a family chronicle* composed by some relative or relatives of the victor (v. 53); and describes himself, almost in so many words (v. 57), as, like Issachar, a strong ass couching down between two burdens—his own notion of writing, I take it, and the *dossier* which has been thrust into his hands.

iv) Three odes—*Nem.* IV, IX, and XI,—though long and elaborate enough to

* Thus only can I explain such lumps of padding as (προπάτορος) ὁμαιμίου (v. 16), οἵ τε πόνων ἐγεύσαντο (v. 24), and ἀγώνων, τοὺς ἐνέποισιν ἱερούς (v. 59): these are condensations of the kind described in note 35 to Lecture IV. Notice also ἴδια ναυστολέοντες ἐπικώμια (vv. 31 f.).

admit fully the symbolic technique, seem to contain no trace of it. I cannot offer a definite reason for its absence from two of them, nor is that disconcerting: why should Pindar always address himself to his task in the same mood and with the same intensity of imagination? In *Nem.* IV the normal symbol is replaced by the Aeacid Dispersion as analogous to Pindar's "digressions" (cp. Lecture VIII, pp. 180 f.).

v) Fourteen odes remain. In all I perceive symbolism, but slight and sometimes disputable. It seemed wise, therefore, not to swell the lectures or notes with discussion of these.

[45] Baudouin, p. 203.

[46] Barre (p. 33) writes concerning Chateaubriand's *René:* "Le héros de cette confession lyrique connaît le tourment de l'infini: 'Je cherche ailleurs, s'écrie-t-il, un bien inconnu dont l'instinct me poursuit. Est-ce ma faute si je trouve partout des bornes, si tout ce qui est fini n'a pour moi aucune valeur?' Et cette exclamation pourrait servir d'épigraphe à tous les poèmes du symbolisme."

[47] A prominent *symboliste*, Vielé-Griffin, asserted that "le travail du poète demeurerait d'auto-psychologie intuitive" (Barre, p. 361).

[48] Much interesting material will be found in Professor D. M. Robinson's *Pindar: A Poet of Eternal Ideas.* As will be seen, I find myself compelled to differ from him on the present topic as strongly as in Lecture III, on Pindar's ideas. But that, of course, is not to say that I fail to admire his immense reading and his fine gusto for literature.

[49] Is one of his finest lyrics, *A un vincitore nel pallone*, Pindaric? The distinguished critic de Sanctis (quoted by Professor Bickersteth in his edition of Leopardi, p. 402) compares it with Pindar's work; but, I think, on the whole mistakenly. The chief thoughts and emotions are alien to Pindar, who would never have dreamed of extolling athletic ardour because it leads to something that transcends success in the Games. Contrast the remarks, and the passages adduced, on pp. 64, 66 f., 194–196 with Leopardi's implication (vv. 27 ff.) that athletics may not unreasonably be considered trivial at first sight. The only possible kinship is in verbal style. Now, Leopardi here, as always, writes nobly; but is the nobility Pindaric, rather than (let us say) akin to Hardy's? Most readers will find it hard to decide, because part of the subject-matter—success in athletics and the battle of Marathon—irresistibly recalls the Greek odes. My own feeling is that only in two brief passages do we hear the real Pindaric voice: vv. 5 f.:

> S'alla veloce
> Piena degli anni il tuo valor contrasti
> La spoglia di tuo nome,

and vv. 22 ff.:
> Tal che le greche insegne e il greco acciaro
> Guidò de'Medi fuggitivi e stanchi
> Nelle pallide torme; onde sonaro
> Di sconsolato grido
> L'alto sen dell'Eufrate e il servo lido.

[50] Dornseiff, *Pindars Stil*, p. 74. "Pindar auf . . . den Klopstock-Stil hinstrebt."

[51] I, p. 8.

[52] Cp. Lecture I, p. 8, and Lecture V, p. 94 (with note).

[53] See Egger, I, pp. 346 ff., on Pindar in France during the sixteenth century, and especially on Ronsard's *Hercule Chrétien* (pp. 354 f.).

[54] *Odes*, I iv, strophe 2; iii, epode 2. Ronsard repeatedly implies that he is a French Pindar, and in Odes II ii writes:

> Dez mon enfance
> Le premier de France
> I'ay pindarizé.

Rabelais, in 1533, was the first to use the word "pindariser," in his description of the monstrous verbal affectation displayed by "l'escholier Limosin" (II 6).

[55] VII, p. 235.

[56] *The Muse*, stanza 1.

NOTES TO LECTURE VIII

(pp. 165–186)

1 *Ol.* I 7 ff. Cp. *Ol.* III 6 ff., *Nem.* I 4 ff.

2 *Nem.* IV 35: ἴυγγι δ' ἕλκομαι ἦτορ νεομηνίᾳ θιγέμεν. Cp. *Pyth.* IV 213 ff.

3 *Ol.* III 38 ff. Cp. the Homeric εἶπε πρὸς ὃν μεγαλήτορα θυμόν, *Il.* XI 403, etc., and, e.g., *Ol.* II 89, *Nem.* III 26. Other apparently similar words—μῆτις φρήν, νόος—are not so used, but mean the *matrix* whereon the inspiring cause works. That is well put in the words translated above, ὕμνος ἀμφιβάλλεται σοφῶν μητίεσσι: the song besets the poet's mind, demanding expression. φυά, when used in this connexion, is "genius"—a fine potentiality, a splendid equipment of μῆτις, φρήν, or νόος.

4 This passage sounds like a prophecy of that modern discovery the unconscious, and of the symbolic manner practised by Mallarmé and his school (cp. Lecture VII, pp. 157 f.).

5 Dr. K. Freeman (pp. 149 ff.) offers the excellent suggestion that Pindar reacts here to the criticisms aimed by Xenophanes at unedifying elements in Homer and Hesiod, thus anticipating the demands made upon poetry in Plato's *Republic*. Cp. Schmid, p. 587.

6 Cp. Lecture IV, p. 80 and note 35 thereon.

7 *Ol.* I 27 ff.: ἦ θαυματὰ πολλά, καί πού τι καὶ βροτῶν
    φάτιν ὑπὲρ τὸν ἀλαθῆ λόγον
    δεδαιδαλμένοι ψεύδεσι ποικίλοις ἐξαπατῶντι μῦθοι.
Here λόγος is the scientific, μῦθος the artistic, word for "story."

8 *Nem.* VII 22 ff. For "lies" in Homer and others cp. Sikes, pp. 4–18. Hesychius reports the verb ὁμηρίδδειν in the sense ψεύδεσθαι. Cp. Ar. *Poetic* 1460 a 21 f.: δεδίδαχεν δὲ μάλιστα Ὅμηρος καὶ τοὺς ἄλλους ψευδῆ λέγειν ὡς δεῖ.

9 Schadewaldt (p. 311) remarks, though far too sweepingly: " 'Wirklich' und 'wahr' sind für Pindar ausschliesslich ethische Begriffe." The celebrated phrase γενναῖον ψεῦδος does not actually occur in Plato, but γενναῖόν τι ἐν ψευδομένους (*Rep.* III 414 B) implies it. For Aeschylus, cp. note 35 on Lecture III.

10 *Nem.* IV 33 f.: τὰ μακρὰ δ' ἐξενέπειν ἐρύκει με τεθμὸς
    ὧραί τ' ἐπειγόμεναι.
See *Ol.* VII 88, *Isth.* VI 20.

11 *Isth.* I 60 ff.: πάντα δ' ἐξειπεῖν, ὅσ' ἀγώνιος Ἑρμᾶς
    Ἡροδότῳ πέπορεν
    ἵπποις, ἀφαιρεῖται βραχὺ μέτρον ἔχων
    ὕμνος.

12 *Pyth.* IV 247: ὥρα γὰρ συνάπτει. See below.

13 *Pyth.* I 82: ἐν βραχεῖ. See below.

14 *Pyth.* IX 77: βαιά. See below.

15 *Pyth.* I 28 f., IX 78, *Isth.* I 63.

16 Certainly it is not the triadic system, which was Stesichorus' invention. Hardly more probable is Westphal's idea (pp. 82 ff.) that the τεθμός was the form of Terpander's νόμος; cp. Smyth, p. lxv. Croiset (pp. 156 f.) talks of Corinna, etc., and compares the "ateliers des peintres et sculpteurs." He appears to understand τεθμός as the current lyric technique; but surely it was something new.

17 *Ol.* II 83 ff.

[18] *Pyth.* I 81 ff.:   καιρὸν εἰ φθέγξαιο, πολλῶν πείρατα συντανύσαις
ἐν βραχεῖ, μείων ἕπεται μῶμος ἀνθρώ-
πων, ἀπὸ γὰρ κόρος ἀμβλύνει
αἰανὴς ταχείας ἐλπίδας.

For the meaning of καιρός see note 20 below.

[19] *Pyth.* IV 247 f.:   μακρά μοι νεῖσθαι κατ' ἀμαξιτόν· ὥρα
γὰρ συνάπτει· καί τινα
οἶμον ἴσαμι βραχύν.

[20] *Pyth.* IX 76 ff.:   ἀρεταὶ δ' αἰεὶ μεγάλαι πολύμυθοι·
βαιὰ δ' ἐν μακροῖσι ποικίλλειν
ἀκοὰ σοφοῖς· ὁ δὲ καιρὸς ὁμοίως
παντὸς ἔχει κορυφάν.

The last sentence is difficult, and such versions as "all things alike have for their crown the fitting season" (Sandys) are surely vaguer than Pindar would allow himself to become in such a place. Help is found in the preceding words. καιρός is here "the critical moment," as in *Isth.* II 22 and *Pyth.* I 81 (see note 18 above). It corresponds to βαιά, the brief occurrence selected for treatment. Pindar's way is to seize on the critical moment, the climax in a legend: cp. *Nem.* I 18 f., πολλῶν ἐπέβαν καιρόν. Next, ἔχει κορυφάν is, literally, "involves consummation"—that is, "brings out the dominating interest"—κορυφά being used as in *Pyth.* III 80 and *Paean* VIII 3 f. (see Lecture VI, note 5). Thus ἔχει κορυφάν corresponds to ποικίλλειν, which implies "bring out all the hues of the culminating incident." παντός means "the whole (original and unabbreviated) story," answering ἐν μακροῖσι. ὁμοίως should be attached not to παντός but to ἔχει, "equally well": that is (by the favourite litotes), "better than" the Stesichorean way.

[21] X i 62: *epici carminis onera lyra sustinentem.*

[22] Schmid repeatedly (pp. 456, 483, 485 f., 598) makes the baseless assertion that Pindar derived his method of narrative from Stesichorus. Apart from the evidence I find in Pindar, the fragments of Stesichorus, so far as they go, contradict this; we have, also, Quintilian's testimony (quoted by Schmid), X i 62: *videtur aemulari proximus Homerum potuisse, sed redundat atque effunditur, quod ut est reprehendendum ita copiae vitium est,* which description is utterly unsuited to Pindar.

[23] By "dramatic" I of course mean, among other things, that the persons speak "in character." Wilamowitz (p. 459) strangely remarks: "Reden, die er gern einführt, sind durchaus nicht aus der Seele des Redenden gesprochen. An Ol. 1, 6, P. 4, 9, N. 10 genügt es zu erinnern." Pelops' prayer in *Ol.* I comes from "the speaker's soul," if ever speech did. In *Ol.* VI, no doubt he refers to the brief remark (16 f.) of Adrastus, which is taken from the *Thebais,* just as in a complimentary speech one might borrow a eulogistic line from Shakespeare; Wilamowitz surely cannot mean the report of Aepytus (49 ff.) or Apollo's address to Iamus (62 f.), which are quite in character. In *Pyth.* IV, Medea's speech does not (it is true) come very markedly "from her soul": she is giving a useful narrative; but all the others are splendidly dramatic. In *Pyth.* IX, the speeches of Apollo (30 ff.) and of Chiron (39 ff.), whatever their relation to the *Eoeae* (cp. Lecture IV, note 35), are mostly dramatic, being indeed similar to the "high comedy" of Menander and Marivaux; but Chiron's passes over into quasi-narrative. As for *Nem.* X, how can anyone mistake the appropriateness, sincerity, and power of the words that fall from Polydeuces and Zeus?

[24] Athenaeus (VIII 347 E) writes: . . . τὸ τοῦ καλοῦ καὶ λαμπροῦ Αἰσχύλου, ὃς τὰς αὐτοῦ τραγῳδίας τεμάχη εἶναι ἔλεγεν τῶν Ὁμήρου μεγάλων δείπνων. The current translation, "*slices* from the great banquets . . . ," is misleading, and unfair to Aeschylus. Euripides in the *Frogs* did his work adroitly: he has apparently enabled some of us to believe that the creator of tragedy did not know what he had created. "Slices from Homer," like the more famous phrase "a slice of life" coined by a less notable dramatist,* would abolish the very idea of dramatic method. Every playwright who deserves the name, whatever his epoch, school, or degree of talent, takes a portion of real life, or a legend or an event imagined by himself, and (instead of flinging it without more ado upon the stage) proceeds to give it structure—relevance of every item, interdependence of parts, rise and fall of interest, and so forth. Had Aristotle never written, that should have been obvious. Further, if Aeschylus had meant "slices" he would have said τόμοι, not τεμάχη. τέμαχος, which only in late Greek appears as a synonym of τόμος, meant a slice (of fish) cut off and fried as a separate meal: the frying corresponds to the dramatic treatment of the original story. Aeschylus uttered an epigram, not a stupidity.

[25] This does not contradict what has been said earlier (Lecture I, p. 10) against the assertion of Eustathius and Farnell, that Pindar, when a student in Athens, was influenced by Aeschylus.

[26] In the circumstances, Pindar must have known at least some of Epicharmus' work. But the actual evidence seems limited to the following items.

i) Fr. 151 (168), on Heracles' gigantic dinner, recalls Epicharmus fr. 21 (Kaibel):

πρᾶτον μὲν αἴ κ' ἔσθοντ' ἴδοις νιν, ἀποθάνοις.

βρέμει μὲν ὁ φάρυγξ ἔνδοθ', ἀραβεῖ δ' ἁ γνάθος,

ψοφεῖ δ' ὁ γόμφιος, τέτριγε δ' ὁ κυνόδων,

σίζει δὲ ταῖς ῥίνεσσι, κινεῖ δ' οὔατα.

ii) Fr. 295 (283). We have not Pindar's words: but Boethus on Plato, *Rep.* II 378 D, says: παρὰ Πινδάρῳ . . . ὑπὸ Ἡφαίστου δεσμεύεται [*sc.* ἡ Ἥρα] ἐν τῷ ὑπ' αὐτοῦ κατασκευασθέντι θρόνῳ. Cp. my *Gk. Com.*, pp. 101 f.

iii) In *Pyth.* VIII 1 ff., Ἡσυχία is deified. So in Epicharmus fr. 101 (Kaibel) Farnell (II, p. 192) is therefore mistaken in saying that Pindar is the first to personify her.

iv) I believe (Lecture VII, p. 156) that Pindar in *Isth.* II uses νόμος with the meaning "coin." Epicharmus (frr. 136, 137 Kaibel) uses it thus.

[27] *Nem.* VI 53 f. might seem to contradict this:

καὶ ταῦτα μὲν παλαιότεροι

ὁδὸν ἀμαξιτὸν εὗρον.

But I take the allusion as pointing to that family chronicle which Pindar was instructed to use for his ode: see note 44 to Lecture VII.

Nothing to the purpose is known about Simonides' epinicians. But what of Bacchylides XVII? That dithyramb, concerning the youthful Theseus' exploits on his way to Athens from Troezen and the uneasiness aroused by his approach, is a lyric dialogue between Aegeus, king of Athens, and one of his subjects, whom it

---

* The *Larousse Universel* attributes the phrase to Jean Jullien, one of the Théâtre-Libre dramatists, who, in 1892, writing of realist plays and novels, remarked (*Le Théâtre vivant*, p. 13): "Ce n'est donc qu'une tranche de la vie que nous pouvons mettre en scène."

is natural (but, for all we know, quite wrong) to regard as leader of a chorus. The style is feeble, but the subject-matter exactly what might have been given by Aeschylus in a trochaic dialogue like that between Atossa and the *coryphaeus* of the *Persae*. Such work at once recalls Aristotle's statement (*Poetic* 1449 a 10 f.) that tragedy originated ἀπὸ τῶν ἐξαρχόντων τὸν διθύραμβον. Nevertheless, this poem has no great interest for the historian of literature. Written probably "about 476"* and therefore in days when Attic tragedy, if not mature,† was established as a literary form, it cannot have figured among the works that helped to engender tragedy. Nor has it any connexion with Pindar's "tragic" method of writing myths. For it is not truly dramatic. We cannot even say that the singers "acted" Aegeus and the citizen: they may have sung the parts as do modern performers in Mendelssohn's *Elijah*, for example. Its only dramatic feature is the dialogue form: it shows neither collision of characters nor plot-development.‡ Pickard-Cambridge (p. 44), who is still more doubtful about the method of performance, inclines to "suppose that we may have here an experimental anticipation or adoption by Bacchylides of that introduction of solo parts into the dithyramb, which was taken up by the n ewer school, some of whom he must have overlapped in time."

28 *Pyth.* X 53 f.:   ἐγκωμίων γὰρ ἄωτος ὕμνων
                    ἐπ' ἄλλοτ' ἄλλον ὥτε μέλισσα θύνει λόγον.

29 *Nem.* VII 77 ff. See Lecture V, pp. 107 f.

30 *Nem.* III 76 ff.:   ἐγὼ τόδε τοι
         πέμπω μεμειγμένον μέλι λευκῷ
         σὺν γάλακτι, κιρναμένα δ' ἔερσ ἀμφέπει,
         πόμ' ἀοίδιμον.

All commentators understand this as "honey mingled with white milk, and the foam of its blending mantleth upon it." Whether they have experimented with these ingredients and (if so) how much foam they produced, is not recorded; none accrued for me on a day of early summer in Canada. Virgil, indeed, writes of *spumantia mella* (*Georg.* IV 140 f.); but he is thinking of the fermentation that precedes and accompanies the clearing of honey for use (cp. Columella IX xv 13). In any case, ἔερσα' means, not "foam," but "dew," and thence "water" (cp. *Nem.* VII 79). Moreover, κιρναμένα ἀμφέπει is better taken as "sheds itself through the blending" than as "frothing on the surface," since froth is not mixed with the liquor from which it rises. There are three ingredients, not two.

31 *Pyth.* IV 248: πολλοῖσι δ' ἄγημαι σοφίας ἑτέροις.

32 Suidas mentions one Πίνδαρος Σκοπελίνου Θηβαῖος, καὶ αὐτὸς λυρικός, ἀνεψιὸς τοῦ προτέρου—i.e., of the great Pindar. Nothing more is known of him. Did he perhaps write *Isth.* III and IV? In any case, he was not a "subsequent lyrist."

---

* Bowra, *Gk. Lyr. P.*, p. 335. He gives no reason for naming that year, nor is there any evidence. Schmid, who offers (p. 529, note 1) this year 476 for XVI on grounds attractive but not certain, makes no suggestion for our poem. Still, as Bacchylides' *floruit* is set by Eusebius at 467, he can hardly have been writing for Athens much earlier than 476.

† Jebb's word (p. 233). But he suggests no date for XVII, and may have thought it later than 476.

‡ Pohlenz is mistaken, therefore, when he says (p. 3): "Rein 'dramatisch' ist der Aufbau dieses Gedichtes." He rightly adds (p. 4): "Bakchylides hat erst im fünften Jahrhundert gedichtet, aber seine Form schwerlich aus der damals schon ganz anders gestalteten Tragödie entwickelt. Jedenfalls müssen wir uns Thespis' Tragodia nach dieser Dichtung vorstellen."

[33] The Inscriptio says: αὕτη ἡ ᾠδὴ ἐν μὲν τοῖς ἐδαφίοις οὐκ ἦν, ἐν δὲ τοῖς Διδύμου ὑπομνήμασιν ἐλέγετο Πινδάρου.

[34] The passage in single inverted commas is a résumé of Jurenka, Wien. Stud. XVII, pp. 1–20. He less plausibly suggests that the poet was one of the κόρακες in Ol. II 87. Von Leutsch, the first modern to impugn Ol. V (Philol. I), maintained (pp. 126 f.) that the author was a Sicilian, and Fraccaroli (p. 230) that he was "un ammiratore devoto e conscienzioso di Pindaro."

[35] The Inscriptio remarks: πρόσκειται δὲ τῇ ᾠδῇ ἵπποις διὰ τὸ μὴ δηλοῦν τὸν Πίνδαρον τὸ τοῦ ἀγωνίσματος εἶδος, πότερον κέλητι ἢ τεθρίππῳ· μόνον δὲ ἱπποδρομίᾳ λέγει (III 13) ἐστεφανῶσθαι. Modern scholars agree that it was a chariot-race: see especially Bury on III 13.

[36] This account, first put forward by C. Bulle, has been generally accepted.

[37] Schnitzer, Interpolation im Pindar, thought that III was written by a later poet or "grammarian" to replace a lost genuine opening of IV. (I have been unable to consult this work, but it is discussed at length by Bulle.)

[38] IV 52: χρὴ δὲ πᾶν ἔρδοντ' ἀμαυρῶσαι τὸν ἐχθρόν.

[39] Villemain, pp. 14–34. Egger (II, pp. 227 f.) strangely endorses this judgment.

[40] Wilamowitz (p. 341): "Hier (in III) wird auch sehr dringender eingeschärft, dass das Glück Dauer nur hat ὀπιζομένων... Dem Melissos mochte der Kamm schwellen: Pindar hielt es nun geraten, ihm einen anderen Rat zu erteilen als χρὴ δὲ πᾶν ἔρδοντ' ἀμαυρῶσαι τὸν ἐχθρόν." Farnell (I, p. 259): "Nowhere else in his moralizing does Pindar sink to this level." Plutarch (Quomodo adulesc. 21 A) objects to the maxim and refutes it with Pindar's own words, τὸ γὰρ δίκαν γλυκὺ πικρότατα μένει τελευτά (Isth. VII 47 f.).

[41] Schol. 83 b (v. 53): τὸ ὑπεράγαν εὐσωματεῖν καὶ ἀνδρεῖον εἶναι βλάβην ὑπαινίττεται, ὅτι δὴ ὁ Ὠρίων τοιοῦτος ὢν τῶν ὑπὲρ ἑαυτὸν ἐπεθύμησε καὶ τὴν Ἄρτεμιν ἐπεχείρει βιάζεσθαι.

[42] He says also that Heracles was small only in comparison with the gigantic Antaeus. This evasion, surprisingly accepted by Fraccaroli (p. 675, note 2) and Wilamowitz (p. 340), is easily refuted by Farnell ad loc., whose own tentative suggestions are useless, and who is clearly staggered (I, p. 260) by what is nothing more than a strange joke.

[43] Nem. III 44: ἄθυρε μεγάλα ἔργα.

[44] Even the scholiast at length revolts: σκληροτέρᾳ κέχρηται μεταφορᾷ· ἐχρῆν γὰρ εἰπεῖν ψαύουσα κτἑ. He prefers Il. I 317.

[45] The scholiast again tries to patch things up, by asserting that παῖδες θεῶν is equivalent to θεοί—ὡς καὶ παῖδες Ἑλλήνων οἱ Ἕλληνες (III. 19). That is no parallel. The sons of Greeks are Greeks; but παῖδες θεῶν would certainly not mean "gods" to a normal Hellene. Christ does not help matters by quoting St. Matthew's τὸν υἱὸν τοῦ ἀνθρώπου, which is a Hebraism.

[46] We must not be led to deny this by the presence here of an Ajax-passage that recalls Nem. VII 25 ff. and VIII 23 ff. In Nem. VII, Ajax' end is used to prove nothing more fundamental than human stupidity; in Nem. VIII, nothing more fundamental than the power of lies and cunning. But here it becomes evidence for doctrine about the dealings of Heaven with mankind. Not only is this thought more basic than the other two: Pindar (so far as appears elsewhere) was prevented from forming it by his strong, however confused, notions about the efficacy of φυά, effort and God's grace (cp. Lecture III, pp. 49–52). Our poet clearly sees and

clearly states a fact of which Pindar, at the best, was but dimly conscious. Ajax, we can see, troubled Pindar sorely; but there is nothing to suggest that he ever attempted to relate Ajax to his ideas of human life and endeavour.

47 Some have called it a myth, but it is much too brief. Farnell (II, p. 351) writes as if it were a narrative: "This passage . . . is a brilliant example of his epic-lyric style." What it is to have an established reputation! Had not this poem been attached to a great name, Farnell and everyone else would have seen that the passage is, for lyric, quite unremarkable.

48 See the scholia and Farnell's admirable note.

49 My list of parallels omits *Isth.* IV 1 and *Isth.* VI 22, because of Bacchylides. Consider these three passages:

Pindar writes (*Isth.* VI 22):

μυρίαι δ' ἔργων καλῶν τέ-
τμανθ' ἑκατόμπεδοι ἐν σχερῷ κέλευθοι.

The Anonymous (*Isth.* IV 1 ff.):

ἔστι μοι θεῶν ἔκατι μυρία παντᾷ κέλευθος . . .
ὑμετέρας ἀρετὰς ὕμνῳ διώκειν.

Bacchylides (V 31 ff.):

τὼς νῦν καὶ ἐμοὶ μυρία παντᾷ κέλευθος
ὑμετέραν ἀρετὰν
ὑμνεῖν.

As parallel passages go, the second is rather close to the first. But its similarity to the third is far greater. It is indeed impossible to believe that the identity of phrase, μυρία παντᾷ κέλευθος, and an almost identical sequel, point to anything less than conscious borrowing. Either the Anonymous copied Bacchylides, or *vice versa*: so much is certain.

Can we discover, then, which was the original, which the copy? Jebb (p. 273) says that the Isthmian was "composed perhaps in 478, and in any case before this ode of Bacchylides." He concludes: "This is the only instance in which a verbal parallelism between a passage of Bacchylides and an earlier passage of Pindar suffices to prove imitation on the part of the younger poet." Jebb's caution equalled his scholarship; but for once he seems to have been hasty, perhaps because he never thought of doubting the Isthmian's genuineness. For we cannot argue from dates here. Bacchylides' ode celebrates Hiero's victory of 476 B.C., and was almost certainly written in that year; but the Isthmian cannot be dated precisely. Our sole indication is 16 ff., where we learn that four kinsmen of the victor Melissus fell in battle on the same day. Probably this was at Plataea (479 B.C.); and νῦν αὖ (v. 19) strongly suggests that the ode was written a considerable time— quite possibly a dozen years—later. There is no real ground, then, for placing the Isthmian before the poem of Bacchylides. (Wilamowitz, indeed, p. 341, confidently dates it after 474 B.C., though for reasons which I cannot accept.)

A quite different consideration, however, appears to settle the matter. Dates apart, Bacchylides might have copied the Isthmian phrase—once: are we to believe that he did so thrice? To V 31 ff. we must add VIII 47 f.:

στείχει δι' εὐρείας κελεύθου
μυρία παντᾷ φάτις
σᾶς γενεᾶς λιπαρο-
ζώνων θυγάτρων . . .

and XVIII 1 f.: πάρεστι μυρία κέλευθος
ἀμβροσίων μελέων,
ὃς ἂν παρὰ Πιερίδων λά-
χῃσι δῶρα Μουσᾶν . . .

Surely such fond repetition means that the phrase μυρία παντᾷ κέλευθος is Bacchylides' own. We are to infer that the borrower was not Bacchylides but the Anonymous. The latter, therefore, was not copying Pindar.

My reason for discussing the relation between Bacchylides and the Anonymous, despite certain remarks in note 6 to Lecture VI, is this. Pindar was in general a haughty soul, and in particular disdained Bacchylides. If, then, the Anonymous imitated Bacchylides, we are confirmed in the belief that the Anonymous must not be identified with Pindar.

[50] θαυμαστὸς ὕμνος. Cp. v. 29, τοιάδε τῶν τότ᾽ ἐόντων φύλλ᾽ ἀοιδᾶν.

[51] *Odes* IV ii 1 ff.: *Pindarum quisquis* . . .

[52] The discussions of the friction between Pindar and his Cean rivals are usefully summarized by Schmid, p. 513, note 2. See also Jebb's Introduction, pp. 13–24.

[53] Fr. 49 (Diehl):   ἐξελέγχει
ὁ νέος οἶνος οὔπω τὸ πέρυσι δῶρον ἀμπέλου· μῦθος
κενεόφρων κούρων ὅδε.

[54] Determined efforts have been made to elude the termination of γαρύετον. Some, including Friederichs (pp. 10 f.) and Mezger (*ad loc.*), found the hardihood to maintain that the dual can be used instead of the plural. The evidence which they can adduce is of course scanty in the extreme*: see Allen and Sikes on *H. Hymn to Apollo*, v. 456. For γαρύετων, heartily approved by Schroeder, see Jebb, p. 17, n. 1, and Farnell's comments. To them it should be added that the alleged contemptuous imperative ("Let them cry! What does it matter?") is very doubtful idiom. In Aesch. *P.V.* 935 (ὁ δ᾽ οὖν ποιείτω), Soph. *Ajax* 961 (οἱ δ᾽ οὖν γελώντων), and Ar. *Ach.* 181 (οἱ δ᾽ οὖν βοώντων), δ᾽ οὖν makes a vast difference.

[55] Farnell on *Nem.* III 40 ff. Sandys writes (p. 105) that "the contrast between natural genius and imitative accomplishment is common in Pindar." See Lecture III, note 28.

[56] Cp. Gaspar, pp. 116 ff.; Farnell II, p. 263.

[57] καίπερ ἔχει βαθεῖα ποντιὰς ἅλμα μέσσον is difficult. Three explanations are possible. (i) Pindar wrestles with a sea of detraction (cp. Ar. *Clouds* 1047, εὐθὺς γάρ σ᾽ ἔχω μέσον λαβὼν ἄφυκτον). The mixture of metaphors, as in "take arms against a sea of troubles," will distress few. But is not σέ indispensable to this view? And can we accept the grotesque picture of a man so buoyant as to be only half-submerged? (ii) We may follow certain scholia and explain: "although the sea intervening keeps you away from Aegina, yet must you make head, etc." μέσσον can be taken adverbially, and the sense is good. But ἔχει, unsupported by any accusative, will scarcely suffice for "restrains." (iii) The best is: "though the sea holds (i.e., fills) the space intervening (between you and Aegina) yet do not yield . . ." ἀντίτεινε will then have, in addition to the primary meaning, a subsidiary hint of "press across the sea."

[58] I do not recall any passage, as early as this, in which γνώμη means "maxim." At this date the word would be ὑποθήκη, as in the collection of *dicta* called Χείρωνος

---

* The usage is, however, frequent in late Greek epic: cp., e.g., pseudo-Oppian *Cyneg.* I 145.

ὑποθῆκαι. The clear evidence for that name is late: cp. Kinkel, pp. 148 f.; but Cratinus fr. 235 (Kock) makes it reasonably certain for the fifth century.

[59] Vv. 14 ff., 78 f., 89 f. The first passage seems to mean that Pindar, in compliment to the family, used for this ode a tune which the lad's father had employed once or many times.

[60] ἔκφερεν I take to imply process and effort—"saw it through." Wilamowitz (p. 175) understands it as "revealed"; so a scholium: ὑπεδείκνυε τὸ πεπρωμένον. That is unlikely.

[61] Just as Hippolyta, with a specific grudge, caused Acastus to hate Peleus, so the ἄλλος ἀνήρ, with a specific grudge, set a group of Aeginetans against Pindar. This latter grudge I understand to be based on his "digressions": see below.

[62] Plato, Rep. I 331 A; Goethe, Letter to Herder (mid-July, 1772). Of many passages I cite the first two that come to mind. For Goethe see Trevelyan, with Robinson's searching review.

[63] Athen. I 3 a: τὰ Πινδάρου ὁ κωμῳδιοποιὸς Εὔπολίς φησιν ἤδη κατασεσιγασμένα ὑπὸ τῆς τῶν πολλῶν ἀφιλοκαλίας.

[64] Eckermann (Jan. 18th, 1825): "Lord Byron ist nur gross, wenn er dichtet: sobald er reflectirt, ist er ein Kind."

[65] Ajax 520 f.

[66] Nem. V 51 f.:   ἀνὰ δ' ἱστία τεῖνον
                προς ζυγὸν καρχασίου.

[67] Od. IV 277 ff.:   τρὶς δὲ περιστείξας κοῖλον λόχον ἀμφαφόωσα,
                ἐκ δ' ὀνομακλήδην Δαναῶν ὀνόμαζες ἀρίστους,
                πάντων Ἀργείων φωνὴν ἴσκουσ' ἀλόχοισιν.

BIBLIOGRAPHY
OF MODERN WORKS QUOTED IN THE NOTES

BIBLIOGRAPHY
OF MODERN WORKS QUOTED IN THE NOTES

ALLEN, T. W., and E. E. SIKES. The Homeric Hymns. London. 1904.

ARNOLD, MATTHEW. Essays in Criticism: First Series. London. 1925.

BACON, J. R. The Voyage of the Argonauts. Boston. N.D.

BARRE, A. Le Symbolisme. Paris. 1911.

BAUDOUIN, C. Contemporary Studies. (Trans. E. and C. Paul.) London. 1924.

BAUMEISTER, A. Denkmäler des klassischen Altertums. Munich. 1889.

BERGK, T. Kleine philologische Schriften. Halle. 1884–1886.

BILLSON, C. J. Pindar's Odes of Victory. Text, with introductions and translation into English verse. Oxford. 1928–1930.

BOECKH, A. Pindari Opera. Leipzig. 1811–1821.

BORNEMANN, L. Pindar's siebente nemeische Ode ein Siegertodtenlied. Philologus XLV, pp. 597 ff.

———. Pindar's sechste olympische Ode. Philologus XLVII, pp. 589 ff.

———. Pindar's elfte pythische Ode ein Sieger- und Todtenlied. Philologus LII, pp. 38 ff.

BOWRA, C. M. Pindari Carmina. Oxford. 1935.

———. Pindar, *Pythian* XI. Classical Quarterly XXX, pp. 129 ff.

———. Greek Lyric Poetry. Oxford. 1936.

See also WADE-GERY.

BRADLEY, A. C. Oxford Lectures on Poetry. Oxford. 1934.

BULLE, C. Pindars dritter (und vierter) isthmischer Siegesgesang. Bremen. 1869.

BURY, J. B. The Nemean Odes of Pindar. London. 1890.

———. The Isthmian Odes of Pindar. London. 1892.

CERRATO, L. Le Odi di Pindaro. Sestri Ponente. 1918.

CHRIST, W. Pindari Carmina. Leipzig. 1896.

COLERIDGE, S. T. Biographia Literaria. Oxford. 1907.

———. Anima Poetae. London. 1895.

COMPARETTI, D. Die Strafe des Tantalos nach Pindar. Philologus XXXII, pp. 227 ff.

CONWAY, R. S. On the Interweaving of Words with Pairs of Parallel Phrases. Classical Review XIV, pp. 357 ff.

Cook, A. B. The Bee in Greek Mythology. Journal of Hellenic Studies XV, pp. 1 ff.

———. Zeus, Jupiter and the Oak. Classical Review XVII, pp. 174 ff., etc.

———. Zeus. Cambridge. 1914–1940.

Cookesley, W. G. Pindari carmina. Eton. 1853.

Coppola, G. Introduzione a Pindaro. Rome. 1931.

Cornford, F. M. Hermes-νοῦς and Pan-λόγος in Pindar Ol. II. Classical Review XXVI, pp. 180 f.

Cowley, A. Works. Ed. A. R. Waller. Cambridge. 1905, 1906.

Croiset, A. La Poésie de Pindare. Paris. 1880.

Dante. Le opere. Ed. E. Moore and P. Toynbee. Oxford. 1924.

Diehl, E. Anthologia Lyrica Graeca. Leipzig. 1925–1936.

Diels, H. Die Fragmente der Vorsokratiker. Vol. I. Leipzig. 1922.

Dissen, L. Pindari Carmina. Gotha and Erfurt. 1830.

Donaldson, I. W. Pindar's Epinician or Triumphal Odes. London. 1841.

Dornseiff, F. Pindars Stil. Berlin. 1921.

———. Pindar übersetzt und erläutert. Leipzig. 1921.

Drachmann, A. B. Scholia vetera in Pindari Carmina. Leipzig. 1903, 1910, 1927.

———. Review of Schadewaldt (q.v.), Deutsche Literaturzeitung, 1929, 1092 ff.

Eckermann, J. P. Gespräche mit Goethe. Leipzig. 1885.

Egger, E. L'Hellénisme en France. Paris. 1869.

Eliot, T. S. The Use of Poetry and the Use of Criticism. London. 1933.

English, B. R. The Problem of Freedom in Greece. Toronto. 1938.

Farnell, L. R. The Works of Pindar. London. 1930–1932.

———. The Cults of the Greek States. Oxford. 1896–1909.

Feine, P. De Aristarcho Pindari interprete. Leipzig. 1883.

Fennell, C. M. Pindar: The Olympian and Pythian Odes. Cambridge. 1893.

———. Pindar: The Nemean and Isthmian Odes. Cambridge. 1883.

Forman, M. B. The Letters of John Keats. Oxford. 1935.

Fraccaroli, G. Le Odi di Pindaro dichiarotte e tradotte. Verona. 1894.

Frazer, Sir J. G. Apollodorus: *The Library*. London. 1921.

Freeman, E. A. A History of Sicily from the Earliest Times. Oxford. 1891–1894.

FREEMAN, K. Pindar—The Function and Technique of Poetry. Greece and Rome VIII, No. 24, pp. 144 ff.

FRIEDERICHS, K. Pindarische Studien. Berlin. 1863.

FRIESE, E. Pindarica. Berlin. 1872.

FURTWÄNGLER, A. and R. K. Griechische Vasenmalerei (Erste Serie). Munich, 1904–1932.

GASPAR, C. Essai de Chronologie pindarique. Brussels. 1900.

GELZER, H. Sextus Iulius Africanus und die byzantinische Chronographie. Leipzig. 1880–1885.

GILDERSLEEVE, B. L. Pindar, The Olympian and Pythian Odes. London. 1907.

GRENFELL, B. P., and A. S. HUNT. Oxyrhynchus Papyri. London. Part II, 1899; VII, 1908.

GUNDERT, H. Pindar und sein Dichterberuf. Frankfort. 1935.

HARRISON, J. E. Prolegomena to the Study of Greek Religion. Cambridge. 1903.

HEADLAM, W. On Editing Aeschylus. London. 1891.

———. A Book of Greek Verse. Cambridge. 1907.

———. Emendations and Explanations. Journal of Philology XXX, pp. 290 ff.

HEIMSOETH, F. Erklärungen zu Pindar. Rheinisches Museum, N.F. 5, pp. 1 ff.

———. Addenda et Corrigenda in Commentariis Pindari. Bonn. 1840.

HERMANN, G. Opuscula. Leipzig. 1827–1877.

HEYNE, C. G. Pindari Carmina et Fragmenta. Oxford, 1807.

HIGHET, G. See under JAEGER.

HÖLDERLIN, J. C. F. Sämtliche Werke. Berlin. 1922.

HORN, E. De Aristarchi studiis Pindaricis. Greifswald. 1883.

HUMBOLDT, W. VON. Gesammelte Werke, Vol. VIII. Berlin. 1909.

HUNT, A. S. See under GRENFELL.

HURET, J. Enquête sur l'Evolution littéraire. Paris. 1891.

ILLIG, L. Zur Form der pindarischen Erzählung. Berlin. 1932.

JACOBY, F. Die Fragmente der griechischen Historiker. Berlin. 1923–1930.

JAEGER, W. Paideia. Berlin and Leipzig. 1934. English translation of ed. 2 by G. Highet. Oxford. 1939.

JEBB, SIR R. C. Bacchylides. Cambridge. 1905.

———. Translations into Greek and Latin Verse. Cambridge. 1873.

———. The *Oedipus Coloneus* of Sophocles. Cambridge. 1907.

278 BIBLIOGRAPHY

JEBB, SIR R. C. Article "Pindar" in Encyc. Brit. (ed. 14).

――――. Pindar. Journal of Hellenic Studies III, pp. 144 ff. (Reprinted *in* Essays and Addresses, Cambridge, 1907.)

JURENKA, H. Zur Kritik und Erklärung der sechsten olympischen Ode des Pindar. Zeitschr. f. d. österr. Gym., 1893, pp. 1057 ff.

――――. Pindars erste und dritte olympische Ode. Vienna. 1894.

――――. Psaumidea. Wiener Studien XVII, pp. 1 ff.

――――. Pindars Diagoras-Lied und seine Erklärer. *Ibid.*, pp. 180 ff.

――――. Analecta Pindarica. *Ibid.*, pp. 196 ff., XIX, pp. 71 ff.

KAIBEL, G. Comicorum Graecorum Fragmenta. I i. Berlin. 1899.

KARST, J. Eusebius Werke. Fünfter Band: Die Chronik. Leipzig. 1911.

KEATS, J. Letters. Ed. M. B. Forman. Oxford. 1935.

KEIL, H. Grammatici Latini. Leipzig. 1855–1880.

KINKEL, G. Epicorum Graecorum Fragmenta. Vol. I. Leipzig. 1877.

KLOPSTOCK, F. G. Oden. Quedlinburg edition. Stuttgart. 1889.

KOLF, M. C. VAN DER. Quaeritur quomodo Pindarus fabulas tractaverit quidque in eis mutarit. Rotterdam. 1923.

KOSTER, W. J. W. Traité de Métrique grecque. Leyden. 1936.

LANDOR, W. S. Complete Works. Ed. T. E. Welby. London. 1927.

LEUTSCH, E. VON. Pindaros. Philologische Anzeiger VII, pp. 15 ff.

――――. Ist die fünfte olympische Ode von Pindar? Philologus I, pp. 116 ff.

LINFORTH, I. M. The Arts of Orpheus. Berkeley and Los Angeles. 1941.

LIVINGSTONE, SIR R. W. The Greek Genius and Its Meaning to Us. Oxford, 1924.

LLOYD, W. On the Eleventh of Pindar's Pythian Odes. Classical Museum VII, pp. 394 ff.

LOBECK, C. A. Aglaophamus. Königsberg. 1829.

LUEBBERT, E. De Pindari Carmine Olympico Decimo. Kiel. 1881.

MAHAFFY, J. P. A History of Classical Greek Literature. Vol. I, The Poets. London. 1883.

MANCUSO, V. La Lirica greca in Sicilia e nella Magná Grecia. Parte I. Pisa. 1912.

MEINEL, G. Beiträge zur Erklärung Pindars. Kempsten. 1890.

MEZGER, F. Pindars Siegeslieder. Leipzig. 1880.

MEYER, E. Geschichte des Alterthums. Stuttgart. 1884–1901.

MOMMSEN, T. Pindari Carmina. Berlin. 1864.

MOMMSEN, T. Des Pindaros Werke in die Versmasse des Originals uebersetzt. Leipzig. 1852.

MURRAY, G. G. A. A History of Ancient Greek Literature. London. 1898.

——. Appendix to Harrison's Prolegomena (q.v.).

MYERS, E. The Extant Odes of Pindar (trans.). London. 1874.

——. Virgil (*in* Essays Classical). London. 1904.

NEIL, R. A. The *Knights* of Aristophanes. Cambridge. 1901.

NORWOOD, G. Greek Tragedy. London. 1928.

——. Greek Comedy. London. 1931.

——. Pindarica, Classical Quarterly IX, pp. 1 ff.; *Ol.* VI, 82–88, Classical Philology XXXVI, pp. 394 ff.; *Pyth.* II, 72 ff., American Journal of Philology LXII, pp. 340 ff.; *Isth.* I, 67 f., *id.* LXIII, pp. 460 f.; *Nem.* VII, 31–35, *id.* LXIV, pp. 325 f.

PATCH, H. R. The Goddess Fortuna in Mediaeval Literature. Cambridge, Mass. 1927.

PATER, W. H. Greek Studies. London. 1922.

——. Plato and Platonism. London. 1920.

PATON, W. R. Classical Review II, p. 180.

PEARSON, A. C. The Fragments of Sophocles. Cambridge. 1917.

PERROTTA, G. Saffo e Pindaro. Bari. 1935.

PERTHES, DR. Beiträge zur Erklärung Pindars (3. isthmische und 11. pythische Ode). Treptow. 1871.

PICKARD-CAMBRIDGE, A. W. Dithyramb Tragedy and Comedy. Oxford. 1927.

POHLENZ, M. Die griechische Tragödie. Leipzig and Berlin. 1930.

PUECH, A. Pindare. Paris. 1922–1923.

RAUCHENSTEIN, R. Zur Einleitung in Pindar's Siegeslieder. Aarau. 1843.

——. Commentationum Pindaricarum Particulae. Prima: Aarau, 1844; altera: Aarau, 1845.

——. Ueber die Tendenz und die Zeit der elften pythischen Ode Pindars. Philologus II, pp. 193 ff.

——. Zu Pindaros. Philologus XXVII, pp. 168 ff., 332 ff.

ROBERT-TORNOW, W. De Apium Mellisque apud Veteres Significatione et Symbolica et Mythologica. Berlin. 1893.

ROBERTS, E. S. Introduction to Greek Epigraphy. Cambridge. 1887–1905.

ROBERTS, W. R. Dionysius of Halicarnassus on Literary Composition. London. 1910.

ROBERTSON, D. S. Review of Schadewaldt (q.v.). Classical Review XLIV, pp. 40 f.

ROBINSON, D. M. The Villa of Good Fortune at Olynthos. American Journal of Archaeology, Ser. 2, Vol. XXXVIII, pp. 501 ff.

——. Pindar: A Poet of Eternal Ideas. Baltimore. 1936.

——. Excavations at Olynthos. X. Baltimore. 1941.

——. Review of Trevelyan (q.v.), Classical Weekly XXXVI, No. 7, pp. 76 ff.

ROHDE, E. Psyche. Tübingen. 1907.

ROMAGNOLI, E. Pindaro. Le Odi e i Frammenti. Bologna. 1927.

ROSE, H. J. The Ancient Grief. (*In* Greek Poetry and Life.) Oxford. 1936.

——. Mythological Scraps. Classical Quarterly XXIV, pp. 107 f.

——. The Grief of Persephone. Harvard Theological Review XXXVI, No. 3, pp. 247 ff.

RZACH, A. Hesiodi Carmina. Leipzig. 1902.

SANDYS, SIR J. E. The Odes of Pindar. London. 1924.

——. A History of Classical Scholarship, I. Cambridge. 1921.

SCHADEWALDT, W. Der Aufbau des pindarischen Epinikion. Halle. 1928.

SCHMID, E. Pindar. Wittenberg. 1616.

SCHMID, W. Geschichte der griechischen Litteratur. (Vol. VII 1 1 of Müller's Handbuch der klassischen Altertumswissenschaft.) Munich. 1912.

SCHMIDT, J. H. H. Die Kunstformen der griechischen Poesie. Leipzig. 1868–1872.

SCHMIDT, L. V. Pindar's Leben und Dichtung. Bonn. 1862.

SCHNEIDER, J. G. Versuch über Pindars Leben und Schriften. Strassburg. 1774.

SCHNITZER, C. F. Interpolation im Pindar. Ellwangen. 1868.

SCHODER, R. V. The Artistry of the First Pythian Ode. Classical Journal XXXVIII, No. 7. pp. 401 ff.

SCHROEDER, O. Pindari Carmina. Ed. maior. Leipzig. 1923.

——. Pindars Pythien. Leipzig and Berlin. 1922.

——. Nomenclator metricus. Heidelberg. 1929.

SIKES, E. E. The Greek View of Poetry. London. 1931.
See also ALLEN.

SITTL, K. Archäologie der Kunst. (Vol. VI of Müller's Handbuch der klassischen Altertumswissenschaft.) Munich. 1895.

SMYTH, H. W. Greek Melic Poets. London. 1906.

STAEHLIN, F. Der Dioskurenmythus in Pindars 10. nemeischer Ode. Philologus LXII, pp. 182 ff.

STANFORD, W. B. Greek Metaphor. Oxford. 1936.

———. Ambiguity in Greek Literature. Oxford. 1939.

STONE, W. A. Three Notes on Pindar. Classical Review XLIII, pp. 115 f.

SYMONDS, J. A. Studies of the Greek Poets. London. 1893.

THOMSON, G. Greek Lyric Metre. Cambridge. 1929.

TREVELYAN, H. Goethe and the Greeks. Cambridge. 1941. See also ROBINSON.

TREZZA, G. Pindaro e il Lirismo greco. (*In* Nuovi Studi Critici, pp. 9 ff.). Verona. 1881.

TURNER, D. W. The Odes of Pindar (trans.). London. 1915.

TYRRELL, R. Y. (?) Pindar's Odes of Victory. Quarterly Review CLXII, pp. 156 ff.

UNTERSTEINER, M. Pindaro. Milan. N.D.

USENER, H. Götternamen. Bonn. 1929.

VALCKENAER, L. C. Diatribe in Euripidis perditorum Dramatum Reliquias. Leyden. 1822.

VERRALL, A. W. On a Chorus of the *Choephoroe*. Journal of Philology IX, pp. 114 ff.

———. Aeschylus, *Seven against Thebes*. London. 1887.

———. Euripides the Rationalist. Cambridge. 1895.

———. Aeschylus, *Eumenides*. London. 1908.

VILLEMAIN, M. Essai sur le Génie de Pindare. Paris. 1859.

WADE-GERY, H. T., and C. M. BOWRA. Pindar: Pythian Odes Translated. London. 1928.

WAY, A. S. Odes of Pindar in English Verse. London. 1922.

WESTPHAL, R. Prolegomena zu Aeschylus Tragödien. Leipzig. 1869.

WILAMOWITZ-MOELLENDORFF, U. VON. Pindaros. Berlin. 1922.

———. Isyllos von Epidauros (Philol. Untersuch. 9). Berlin. 1886.

———. Die Textgeschichte der griechischen Lyriker. Berlin. 1900.

———. Hieron und Pindaros (Sitzber. d. Akad. d. Wiss.). Berlin. 1901.

———. Einleitung in die griechische Tragödie. Berlin. 1907.

———. Sappho und Simonides. Berlin. 1913.

YOURCENAR, M. Pindare. Paris. 1932.

INDEX

INDEX

Olympian festival, 67, 113, 166, 244; games, 27 ff.; "origins of the Olympian festival," 114

Olympus, 120

Ὁμηρίδδειν, 264

Omphalos, 73

Opus (city), 17; (hero), 87

Opuscula, Hermann's, 105

Orchomenus, 11, 16, 100

"Ordinance" (τεθμός), 168 f.

Oresteia, of Aeschylus, 220, *see also* Aeschylus; of Stesichorus, 248

Orestes, 120, 123, 170, 247

Orestes-myth in *Pyth*. XI, 120–126

Orion, 34, 173

Ormenium, 258

Oropus, 127, 128

Orpheus, 41, 135

Orphic religion, 134, 228, 256, 257; vase-paintings, 257; verses, 135; wheel, 137

Ortygia, 129, 252

Ovid, 3, 117; *Ex Ponto* II iii 56: p. 254; *Met*. VI 113: p. 218

Oxyrhynchus, 16, 22, 23, 75